Human Development

Dimensions and Strategies

Human Development

Dimensions and Strategies

Edited by

Himanshu Sekhar Rout
Prasant Kumar Panda

New Century Publications
New Delhi, India

NEW CENTURY PUBLICATIONS
4800/24, Bharat Ram Road,
Ansari Road, Daryaganj,
New Delhi -110 002 (India)

Tel.: 011 – 2324 7798, 4358 7398, 6539 6605
Fax: 011 – 4101 7798
E-mail: indiatax@vsnl.com
www.newcenturypublications.com

Editorial office:
34, Gujranwala Town, Part-2,
Delhi - 110 009

Tel.: 27247805, 27464774

Copyright © 2009 by the editors

All rights reserved. No part of this book may be reproduced, stored in a retrieval system, or transmitted in any form or by any means, mechanical, photocopying, recording, or otherwise without the prior written permission of the publisher.

First Published – **2009**

ISBN: 978-81-7708-198-5

Published by New Century Publications and printed at Salasar Imaging Systems, New Delhi

Designs: Patch Creative Unit, New Delhi

PRINTED IN INDIA

ACKNOWLEDGMENTS

This book has emerged from the research papers contributed by economists and academicians from different parts of the country and abroad. We express our deep sense of gratitude to all paper contributors who accepted our request and put hard work in preparing and sending the papers at short notice. Our sincere thanks are especially due to Professor Prasanta K. Pattnaik who, in spite of his busy academic schedule and appointments, accepted our request and contributed to the volume, and provided immense encouragement.

We would also like to extend our sincere thanks to Mr. Sandeep Sury of New Century Publications, for accepting our proposal to publish this volume and extending his active cooperation at each stage to bring the volume in its present form.

Thanks are also due to our family members, teachers and colleagues who motivated and inspired us to undertake this work.

Himanshu Sekhar Rout
Prasant Kumar Panda

THE BOOK

Human development is a relative concept and it needs to be understood from an interdisciplinary perspective. It includes widening of choices, expansion of freedom and fulfilment of human rights. The human development index (HDI) in the UNDP's Human Development Report (HDR) considers literacy rate, life expectancy at birth along with GDP per head for the purpose. It is important to understand an appropriate methodology for measuring human development and its linkage with economic development.

This book addresses specific problems and issues pertaining to human development. The main themes which the book covers include theoretical issues in human development, measurement, determinants and various dimensions and strategies for sustainable human development.

THE EDITORS

Himanshu Sekhar Rout and Prasant Kumar Panda are with the Post-graduate Department of Economics, Dr. SRK Government Arts College (Pondicherry University), Yanam, India.

PREFACE

Human development is a relative concept and it needs to be understood from an interdisciplinary perspective. Thanks to the United Nations Development Program (UNDP) for bringing out its first human development report (HDR) in 1990 under the guidance of an eminent economist Mahbub ul Haq and undertaking the task of devising human development index (HDI). Since then different countries have tried to bring out similar reports for their countries. But the concept - approach to human development and the selection of measures for HDI have not completely resolved and attract the attention of researchers and policy makers. Again gross national product (GNP) can not alone address the issues of Human development. It is understood as growth (economic) plus. The narrow meaning of development as economic performance / expansion alone has been extended though it is important. Today, it includes widening of choices, expansion of freedom and fulfilment of human rights. GNP alone can not be considered as a satisfactory measure of human welfare. The HDI in the UNDP's HDR considers literacy rate, life expectancy at birth along with GDP per head for the purpose. These indicators have become yardsticks for subsequent reports and different Governments, with minor modifications, for measuring human development. Critics have said that not only are the weights of these three components arbitrary, but also what is excluded, and what is included. It is important to understand an appropriate methodology for measuring Human Development and its linkage with Economic Development. In this perspective an edited volume covering the theoretical and measurement issues, various dimensions and strategies of human development is highly imperative.

Though the technological breakthroughs of the 20th century are used to empower people, allowing them to harness technology to expand the choices in their daily lives, but there are significant challenges still ahead and are the matters of concern in addressing human development issues. Despite considerable efforts in advocacy, creation of awareness, different strategies and programs, gender discrimination remains pervasive in many dimensions of life-worldwide. Gender gaps are widespread in access to and control of resources, in economic opportunities, in power, and political voice. Women are still exploited, discriminated, and subject to harassment and violence. Without emphasizing gender parity human developmental programs may result in sectional development and, not of masses. The plan of complete eradication of poverty and hunger still remains in slogan than being achieved. Similarly neither the provisions of education and health care services are adequate to meet their demand, nor are they designed to work effectively for the weaker section and poor. Interregional conflicts and issues in and between countries are emerging threats to peace and economic advancement. Fighting terror and HIV is a matter of great concern for the world today. Environmental degradation and issue of global warming pose new challenge. In this backdrop creating an environment for advancing human development and making people to lead lives that they like, is a real challenge for countries. The present volume is an initiative to partially address these diversified issues and draw the attention of the policy makers and planners.

This volume has emerged from the research papers contributed by research scientists and academicians from different parts of the country and abroad, selecting specific problems and issues pertaining to human development. The main themes which the volume covers are theoretical issues in human development, measurement, determinants and various dimensions and strategies for Sustainable human development.

We hope that the volume will provide some inputs and help to the academicians, researchers, policy makers, and government.

Yanam

Himanshu Sekhar Rout
Prasant Kumar Panda

CONTRIBUTORS

BENSAHEL, LILIANE — Professor, Université de Grenoble, UPMF, CREPPEM, France

CHAKRABORTY, DEBASHIS — Assistant Professor, Indian Institute of Foreign Trade (IIFT), New Delhi, India

CHATTERJEE, BANI — Professor in Economics, Department of HSS, Indian Institute of Technology (IIT), Kharagpur, India

CHATTERJI, MANAS — Professor, School of Management, Binghamton University, Binghamton, New York

COISSARD, STEVEN — Professor, Université de Grenoble, CREPPEM et IDRAC, école de commerce, Lyon, France

DUTTA, SUMANASH — Professor and Head, Department of Economics, Assam University, Silchar, Assam, India

KENCHAIGOL, S. D. — Centre for Multi-Disciplinary Development Research (CMDR), Dharwad, Karnataka, India

LAZRAK, ASMA BEN — Université de Grenoble, UPMF, CREPPEM, France

MAHAPATRA, MIHIR K.	Assistant Professor, Goa Institute of Management, Ribandar, Goa, India
MISHRA, ASWANI K.	Indian Institute of Management Ahmedabad (IIM- A), Ahmedabad, India
MISHRA, SRIJIT	Associate Professor, Indira Gandhi Institute of Development Research (IGIDR), Mumbai, India
MISHRA, S. K.	Professor in Economics, Department of Economics, School of Economics, Management and Information Sciences, North–Eastern Hill University, Shillong, Meghalaya, India
MISHRA, TAPAS	International Institute for Applied Systems Analysis (IIASA) Schlossplatz, Laxenburg, Austria
MOHANTY, AMAR K.	Department of HSS Indian Institute of Technology (IIT), Kharagpur, India
MUKHERJEE, S.	Senior Manager, Water Resources and Policy, WWF-India, Secretariat, New Delhi, India

NATHAN, HIPPU S. K.	Indira Gandhi Institute of Development Research (IGIDR), Mumbai, India
NAYAK, N. C.	Associate Professor in Economics, Department of HSS Indian Institute of Technology IIT), Kharagpur, India
NAYAK, PURUSOTTAM	Professor and Head, Department of Economics, School of Economics, Management and Information Sciences, North –Eastern Hill University, Shillong, Meghalaya, India
PANDA, PRASANT K.	P.G. Department of Economics, Dr. SRK Government Arts College, Yanam, India.
PARHI, MAMATA	BETA-Theme, Universit'e Louis Pasteur, Strasbourg 1 61, Avenue de la For^et Noire, F-67065 Strasbourg Cedex, France
PATRA, BISWABAS	Nabakrushna Choudhury Centre for Development Studies, Chandra Sekhar Pur, Bhubaneswar, Orissa, India
PATTANAIK, PRASANT K.	Emirates Professor In Economics Department of Economics, University of California, Riverside, CA 92521, U.S.A.

RAJESH RAJA S. N.	Centre for Multi-Disciplinary Development Research (CMDR), Dharwad, Karnataka, India
ROUT, HIMANSHU S.	PG Department Of Economics, Dr. SRK Government Arts College, Yanam, India
SENGUPTA, KEYA	Professor in Economics, Department of Economics Assam University Silchar, Assam, India
SUJITHKUMAR, P. S.	Department of Economics, Bharathidasan Government College For Women, Puducherry, India

CONTENTS

The Book	vii
The Editors	viii
Preface	ix
Contributors	xi

1. Introduction and Overview — 1
Himanshu Sekhar Rout and Prasant Kumar Panda

2. A Note on Some Aggregation Problems in the Functioning Approach to Individual Well-Being — 40
Prasanta K. Pattanaik

3. On Measuring Group Differential: Some Further Results — 54
Hippu Salk Kristle Nathan
Srijit Mishra

4. Status and Trend of Human Development in North East Region of India — 62
Purusottam Nayak

5. A Note on Human Development Indices with Income Equalities — 87
S K Mishra

6. Regional Planning, National Development and Conflict Resolution — 101
Manas Chatterji

7. Age-structured Human Capital Dynamics and Economic Growth: A Note on Interdependence, Coordination and Welfare — 129
Tapas Mishra and Mamata Parhi

8. **Human Development in India: Issues and Challenges** — 184
Mihir K. Mahapatra and Rajesh Raj S. N.

9. **The Perspectives of Economic Growth and Social Insecurity on Human Development for Lagging States in India** — 211
Aswini Kumar Mishra and Biswabas Patra

10. **Environment, Human Development and Economic Growth of Indian States after Liberalisation** — 232
Sacchidananda Mukherjee and Debashis Chakraborty

11. **Gender and Human Development** — 281
Liliane Bensahel, Steven Coissard and Asma Ben Lazrak

12. **Recasting Human Development Indices: A Look into the State of Gender Empowerment in Karnataka** — 300
Sanjeev D Kenchaigol

13. **Human Development in Orissa: An Inter-District Analysis from the Perspective of Infrastructure** — 327
Amar Kumar Mohanty, Narayan C Nayak and Bani Chatterjee

14. **Human Development, Economic Development and Income Earning Capacities of the Common Man: The Case of North East India** — 355
Keya Sengupta

15. Disparities in Human Development and Economic Development: The Case of Assam 374
Sumanash Dutta

16. Livelihood Diversification: Pathway Out of Rural Poverty 386
P.S. Sujithkumar

Index 397

1

Introduction and Overview

Himanshu Sekhar Rout[1]
Prasant Kumar Panda[2]

A. INTRODUCTION

In recent days, Human development (hereafter HD) has become a popular phrase among media, politicians, researchers, academics, government, and non-government organizations (NGOs) around the globe. With the introduction of the concept of HD in 1990 and the publication of the annual series of *Human Development Report* (HDR) of United Nations Development Program (UNDP), the development perspective underwent a fundamental change. The narrow meaning of development as economic performance / expansion alone has been extended though it is important. Today, it includes widening of choices, expansion of freedom and fulfillment of human rights. HD has added human face in the methods of measuring development. Actual development includes improvements in the lives of human being – in their income, health, education, security, freedom, choices, human rights, and many other factors. Many eminent scholars were

---

[1] P.G. Department of Economics, Dr. SRK Government Arts College (Pondicherry University), Yanam, India, E-mail: hsrout1970@gmail.com
[2] P.G. Department of Economics, Dr. SRK Government Arts College (Pondicherry University), Yanam, India, E-mail: pkp.pondyedu@gmail.com

behind the public popularity of HDR. Among them, the Pakistani economist Mahbub ul Haq, the principal architect and advocate of the Report; Amartya Sen, the Noble laureate; Martha C. Nussabaum, Sudhir Anand; Sakiko Fukuda-Parr are prominent.

I. DEFINING HD

HD refers to the expansion of people's choices by enhancing their capabilities[3] and functionings[4]. Its goal is to create an enabling environment in which people's capabilities can be enhanced and their range of choices expanded. 'The enhancement of capabilities requires changing technologies, institutions and social values so that the creativity within human beings can be unlocked. This, in turn, results in economic growth, but growth of gross domestic product (GDP) is not the same thing as an expansion of capabilities. The two are, of course, linked but they are not identical' (Griffin and Knight, 1990).

HD is "*of* the people, *for* the people and *by* the people – '*of* the people' referring to human capital formation and human resources development through nutrition, health and education; '*for* the people' stressing the need for the benefits of economic growth to be translated into people's lives; and '*by* the people' meaning that people must be able to influence a process that affects their lives" (Jahan, 2005).

HD means human flourishing in its fullest sense – in matters of public and private, economic and social and political and spiritual. This is wider than some definitions of well-being that relate only to material deprivations or to aspects of well-being that can be publicly provided (Alkire, 2002)[5]. Alkire (2002)

---

[3] The powers or abilities to generate an outcome(s).
[4] A functioning is an achievement of a person: what s/he manages to do or to be, and any such functioning reflects, as it were, a part of the state of that person (Sen, 2005).
[5] This is the sense of well-being employed by Sen (1987) but is distinct from, for example, the concept of well-being by Qizilbash (1997a, b).

use this definition because the pursuit of narrow goals affects wider aspects of well-being. This definition is also narrower than human-centered development as a whole because it relates only to well-being considered person by person (evaluative). For HD consists, as Amartya Sen would argue, of other things besides well-being achievement for any particular person at time t; it also considers their agency aspects – what they are able to do about the causes they follow, such as space exploration or saving the seals. In addition, it consists of nonindividualist aspects of social living that are of utmost importance (Alkire, 2002)

According to UNDP, "HD is a development paradigm that is about much more than the rise or fall of national income. It is about creating an environment in which people can develop their full potential and lead productive, creative lives in accord with their needs and interests. People are the real wealth of nations. Development is thus about expanding the choices people have to lead lives that they value. And it is thus about much more than economic growth, which is only a means —if a very important one —of enlarging people's choices" (available at http://hdr.undp.org/en/humandev). HD as 'an approach to overall development which put the well-being of people first, which regards human beings simultaneously as the both means and the ends of social and economic policy. It is not, of course, a formula that can be applied mechanically, but it does contain ingredients which distinguish it from commodity-centered approaches to development' (Griffin, 2006).

HD is assumed to have two sides. One is the formation of human capabilities – such as improved health, knowledge, and skill. The other is the people make use of their acquired capabilities – for employment, productive activities, political affairs or leisure. A society needs to build up human capabilities as well as ensure equitable access to human opportunities. Considerable human frustration results if the scales of HD do not finely balance the two sides (Haq, 1995).

The HD paradigm is based on the following fairly broad agreements: (i) development must put people at the center of its concern; (ii) the purpose of development is to enlarge all human choices, not just income; (iii) the HD paradigm is concerned both with building of human capabilities (through investment in people) and with using those human capabilities fully (through an enabling framework for growth and employment); (iv) HD has four essential pillars: equality, sustainability, productivity, and empowerment. It regards economic growth as essential but emphasizes the need to pay attention to its quality and distribution, analyses at length its link with human lives and questions its long-term sustainability; and (v) the HD paradigm defines the ends of HD and analyses sensible options for achieving them (Haq, 1995).

II. DEVELOPMENT OF THE CONCEPT OF HD

HD is not a new concept. The full development of human beings as the end of our all the activities was recurring theme in the writings of most philosophers from the ancient Greeks to David Hume, Immanuel Kant, and John Stuart Mill, and of such political economists as Adam Smith, Karl Marx, Alfred Marshall, John Maynard Keynes and Mahbub ul Haq (Streeten, 2005). Promotion of "Human Good" dates back to at least Aristotle (384-322 B.C.). Immanuel Kant (1724-1804) continued the tradition of treating human beings as the real end of all activities. Adam Smith (1723-1790) showed his concern that economic development should enable a person to mix freely with others without being "ashamed to appear in publick", he was expressing a concept of poverty that went beyond counting calories – a concept that integrated the poor in to the mainstream of the community. A similar strain was reflected in the writings of the other founders of modern economic thought, including Robert Malthus, Karl Marx, and John Stuart Mill (Haq, 1995)

"Throwing light on the intellectual origins and to evaluate the innovative contributions to the area of development, Desai (1991, p.353) said the concept of HD derives from the twin stands of the inequality / poverty literature and the noneconomists concern that income be not the sole criterion of development. The first stand points to the interpersonal distribution – the structure – of income as a corrective to the level and growth of per capita income. The second stand is the value achievements that do not show up at all, or not immediately, in higher measured income or growth figures by the people: better nutrition and health services, greater access to knowledge, more secure livelihoods, better working conditions, security against crime and physical violence, satisfying leisure hours, and a sense of participating in the economic, cultural and political activities of their communities".

T. W. Schultz introduced the concept of 'human capital' to capture the idea that expenditure on such things as education and training, health and nutrition, family planning and child care, agricultural research and extension were similar for investments in physical capital in that they raised the productivity of labour and contributed to economic growth (Griffin, 2006). Amartya Sen took the analysis a step further, arguing that the objective of development should be reconceptualized as the enhancement of human capabilities. Human capital concentrates on the agency of human beings – through skill and knowledge as well as efforts – in augmenting production possibilities where as human capabilities focuses on the ability of human beings to lead lives they have reason to value and to enhance the substantive choices they have. The two perspective cannot but be related since both are concerned with the role of human beings, and in particular with the actual abilities that they achieve and acquire (Sen, 1997).

In 1988 a committee of the United Nations brought these two stands of thought together and produced a report in which a human capabilities approach was advocated. The ideas contained in the report were picked up by the UNDP and under the brilliant leadership of Mahbub ul Haq, UNDP promoted HD as an alternative to the conventional approaches offered by World Bank, the International Monetary Fund and mainstream development agencies. Beginning in 1990, UNDP published an annual *Human development Report* and few years later, member countries were encouraged to publish each year a nation HD report. Both the national and international reports contain a wealth of statistical information on many dimensions of HD as well as analysis of specific topics. In 2000 the HD approach was further institutionalized by the creation of the *Journal of Human Development* (Griffin, 2006).

III. THE SCOPE OF HD
Wider than mere education and health

HD is the all round development of human beings. It is related with all walks of life. It is multi-dimensional and multi-disciplinary, i.e., embraces all disciplines. It is certainly wider than mere education and health and the capabilities for them. Its scope is widened to the eradication of poverty, development of education, health, economic growth, human rights, gender equality, political freedom, people's participation, cultural liberty, human security, environment, climate change, and many more. The scope of HD can also be judged from the 18 years "intellectual journey" of UNDP's dynamic annual series HDR which takes the recent big issues[6] in its different incarnations.

---

[6] **HDR 1990** – Concept and Measurement; **HDR 1991** – Financing Human Development; **HDR 1992** - International Dimensions of Human Development; **HDR 1993** - People's Participation; **HDR 1994** – Human Security; **HDR 1995** - The Evolution for gender Equality; **HDR 1996** - Growth for Human Development; **HDR 1997** - Human Development to eradicate poverty; **HDR 1998** - Changing today's Consumption Patterns – for tomorrow's Human Development; **HDR 1999** - Globalization with a Human Face; **HDR 2000** - Human Rights and Human Development—for Freedom and Solidarity; **HDR 2001** - Making new Technologies Work for Human Development; **HDR 2002** - Deepening Democracy in a Fragmented World; **HDR 2003** - Millennium Development Goals: A Compact among Nations to End Human Poverty; **HDR 2004** - Cultural Liberty in today's Diverse world; **HDR 2005** - International Cooperation at a Crossroads: Aid, Trade and Security in an Unequal World; **HDR 2006** - Beyond Scarcity: Power, Poverty and the Global Water Crisis;

Economic growth and HD

Economic growth (or development) is a subset of HD. The latter embraces the enlargement of all human choices – economic, social, cultural, political and many others – where as the former relates to income only. It might well be argued that the expansion of income can enlarge all other choices as well. But that is not necessarily so, for a variety of reasons. Many human choices (knowledge, health, clean physical environment, political freedom, pleasure of life et cetera) are not exclusively, or largely dependent on income. Moreover, rejecting an automatic link between income expansions and flourishing human lives is not rejecting growth itself. Economic growth is essential in poor societies for reducing or eliminating poverty. But the quality of this growth is just as important as its quantity. Conscious and deliberate public policy is needed to translate economic growth into people's lives (Haq, 1995).

Technology and HD

People all over the world have high hopes that new technologies will lead to healthier lives, greater social freedoms, increased knowledge and more productive livelihoods. There is a great rush to be part of the network age—the combined result of the technological revolutions and globalization that are integrating markets and linking people across all kinds of traditional boundaries. Technologies – cellular phone, internet, meteorological advancement, Telemedicine, improvement in pharmaceutical drugs, satellite education and many more – enhance human capabilities. Throughout history, technology has been a powerful tool for HD and poverty reduction. The 20th century's unprecedented gains in advancing HD and eradicating poverty came largely from technological breakthroughs. Technology is used to empower people, allowing them to harness technology to expand the choices in their daily lives (UNDP, 2001).

---

and **HDR 2007/2008** - Fighting Climate Change: Human Solidarity in a Divided World.

Culture and HD

If the world is to reach the Millennium Development Goals and ultimately eradicate poverty, it must first successfully confront the challenge of how to build inclusive, culturally diverse societies. Not just because doing so successfully is a precondition for countries to focus properly on other priorities of economic growth, health and education for all citizens. But because allowing people full cultural expression is an important development end in itself.

Economic sustainability and HD

Anand and Sen (2000) attempted to integrate the concern for HD *in the present with that in the future*. In arguing for sustainable HD, it appeals to the notion of ethical "universalism" – an elementary demand for impartiality of claims – applied within and between generations. Economic sustainability is often seen as a matter of intergenerational equity, but the specification of what is to be sustained is not always straightforward. They also explored the relationship between distributional equity, sustainable development, optimal growth, and pure time preference.

Globalization and HD

Economic globalization leads to greater transparency and economic freedom, society avails of opportunities to achieve a higher standard of living. This is a promising aspect of globalization. The relation between economic globalization and HD is mediated by economic freedom and corruption. Findings suggest that economic globalization affects economic freedom positively and corruption negatively. In turn, economic freedom has a positive effect and corruption has a negative effect on HD. All relations are in the hypothesized directions and significant (Akhter, 2004).

Human Rights and HD

"Human rights" and "HD" are different concepts. Human rights are legal norms, whereas HD is a dynamic process. Human rights and HD may have common objectives; although usually these are defined more clearly by human rights because they specify specific components (e.g. the right to work includes decent work conditions, free choice, non-discrimination, etc.). Also, the scope of HD evolves rapidly with social and technological changes, whereas creating human rights is a slow process. Therefore, the scope of HD is likely to be larger than the scope of human rights (Tomas, 2005).

IV. MEANS AND ENDS DEBATE

Human beings are the agents, beneficiaries, and adjudicators of progress, but they also happen to be – directly or indirectly – the primary means of all productions. This dual role of human beings provides rich ground for confusion of ends and means in planning and policy making (Sen, 1989).

Human beings are both ends (*humanitarians*[7]) in themselves and means (*human resources developers*[8]) of production (Streeten, 1994). Paul Streeten (1994) has explained six reasons why we should promote HD and poverty eradication. First, and above all, it is an end itself. Second, it is a means to higher productivity. A well-nourished, healthy, educated, skilled, alert labor force is the most important productive asset. Third, it reduces human reproductivity, by lowering the desired family size. This is generally regarded as desirable. Fourth, HD is good for the physical environment. The poor are both a cause (though not as large a cause as the rich) and the main victim of environmental degradation. Deforestation, desertification, and soil erosion are reduced with poverty reduction. Fifth, reduced poverty contributes to a healthy civil society, democracy, and greater social stability. China has witnessed a rapid reduction in poverty, while maintaining an autocracy, but the call for freedom cannot be

---

[7] The *humanitarians* are those who stress human beings as the end.
[8] The *Human-resource developers* are those who stress human being as the means or productivity aspect, with a strong emphasis on income and production (an extreme form of whom are the human capitalists who adopt the human capital approach).

suppressed for long. Sixth, it has political appeal, for it may reduce civil disturbances and increase political stability.

Theories of human capital formation or human resources development treat human beings as a means to economic growth. But the end-means relationship is reversed in the HD framework, in which development is about people's well-being and the expansion of their capabilities and functionings. Expansion of material output is treated as a means and not an end. This approach is defining well-being as the purpose of development and treating economic growth as a means. The ends-means relationship has been developed in new concepts and measures, and in articulating policy priorities (Fukuda-Parr, 2005). This end-means relationship is valid, if HD is the ultimate. If, it is the end then it has no further improvement. But HD has always potentialities to develop further.

V. DIMENSIONS OF HD

Plethora of literatures (Andrews and Withey, 1976; Finnis, Boyle and Grisez, 1987; Grisez, Boyle, and Finnis, 1987; Lasswell, 1992; Ramsay, 1992; Doyal and Gough, 1993; Rawls, 1993; Max-Neef, 1993; Allardt, 1993; Schwartz, 1994; Galtung, 1994; Cummins, 1996; Cummins, 1996; Qizilbash, 1996a, b; Nussabaum, 2000; Narayan et al., 2000; Diener and Biwas, 2000) are available in the dimensions of HD (see Table 1) with disagreements which can broadly be put into 'two approaches: some aim to identify the *constitutive elements* of a good or flourishing life, while others are concerned primarily with the *necessary requirements* of such life. Those looking at the constitutive requirements of a good life place less emphasis on material aspects, where those exploring the necessary requirements for such a life tend to emphasize material aspects more. For example, Finnis, Boyle and Grisez (1987) and Nussabaum (2000) are quite thin on material aspects, but emphasize nonmaterial aspects such as friendship and emotions, which are given little or no emphasis by others. Environmental issues appear explicitly in Nussabaum (2000) while they are neglected or discussed briefly by others. Martha C. Nussabaum is the only author to record 'respect for other species' as a significant dimension (Ranis, Stewart and Samman, 2006).

Dimensions of HD are *nonhierarchical, irreducible, incommensurable* and, hence, *basic kinds of human ends*. Dimensions do not derive from nor divide up an idea about what the good life is, but rather are values or "reasons for action" which people from different language groups and neighborhoods could recognize based on practical reason – that is, on their own experience of figuring out what they are going to do, or on their observation of other people's experience (Alkire, 2002). Alkire (2002) considered the Finnis' foundational account of basic reasons for action (see Box 1) as the "dimensions of HD".

HD is defined as the enlargement of the range of choices. Some basic-needs interpretations have run in terms of commodity bundles or specific needs satisfactions (Streeten, 1994). In their book *'First Things First'* (Streeten et al., 1981 as cited in Streeten, 1994), Streeten, Burki, Haq, Hicks, and Stewart (1981) said "First, and most important, the basic needs concept is a reminder that the objective of the development effort is to provide all human beings with the *opportunity* for a full life. In the past two decades, those concerned with development have sometimes got lost in the intricacies of means . . . and lost sight of the end. They came near to being guilty, to borrow a term from Marx, of 'commodity fetishism'." "Opportunity" is near in meaning to Sen's (1984, 1985, 1987 as cited in Streeten, 1994) "capability" (see also Dreze and Sen, 1989 as cited in Streeten, 1994). Amartya Sen goes beyond the analysis of commodities in terms of their characteristics, which consumers' value, and analyzes the characteristics of the consumers; whether they have the capability to make use of commodities. Streeten, Burki, Haq, Hicks, and Stewart (1981) tried hard to get away from "the detached objects people happen to possess" and to emphasize the end: the opportunity for people to live full lives (Streeten, 1994).

The Philosopher John Rawls defined deprivation in terms of the availability of "primary goods" or "things it is supposed a rational man wants what ever else he wants" (Rawls, 1971 as quoted in Griffin and Knight, 1990) and the International Organization (ILO) attempted to translate the concept into operational terms with its advocacy of "basic needs" (ILO, 1976 as quoted in Griffin and Knight, 1990). Basic needs, however, remains a good-oriented view of development, where as what is wanted is a view that puts people first. This is the great merit of human capability approach pioneered by Amartya Sen. The connection between goods and capabilities can readily be illustrated. A bicycle, for instance, is a good; by providing transport, it gives a person the capability of moving from one place to another. It is the concept of capabilities that comes closest to our notion of development (Griffin and Knight, 1990). Primary goods are the means to freedom, where as capabilities are the expressions of freedom themselves. The motivation underlying the Rawlsian theory and the capability approach are similar, but the accountings are different (Sen, 1989).

As stated above, HD is multidimensional. But valuing the human well-beings, the HDRs count three important dimensions only: longevity, knowledge and income. 'Extensive literature in development economics concerned with valuing the quality of life, the fulfillment of basic needs and related matters have been typically comprehensively ignored in the theory of welfare economics, which has tended to treat the contribution of capability approach as essentially *ad hoc* suggestions' (Sen, 1989).

VI. HD STRATEGIES

There is more than one path to HD, and hence the need to consider alternative strategies, but any successful strategy will have to pay careful attention to the structure of incentives that guides economic activity, the allocation of public expenditure and the institutional arrangements that determine the distribution of wealth and income and the vulnerability of various sections of the population to events which can threaten their livelihood and perhaps even their life (Griffin and McKinley, 1992).

BOX 1
FINNIS: BASIC REASONS FOR ACTION

Life itself – its maintenance and transmission – health, and safety

Knowledge and aesthetic experience – "Human persons can know reality and appreciate beauty and whatever intensely engages their capacities to know and to feel"

Some degree of excellence in *Work and Play* – "Human persons can transform the natural world by using realities, beginning with their own bodily selves, to express meanings and serve purposes. Such meaning-giving and value creation can be realized in diverse degrees"

Friendship – "Various forms of harmony between and among individuals and groups of persons – living at peace with others, neighbourliness, friendship"

Self-integration – "Within individuals and their personal lives, similar goods can be realized. For feelings can conflict among themselves and be at odds with one's judgments and choices. The harmony opposed to such inner disturbance is inner peace"

Self-expression or Practical Reasonableness – "One's choices can conflict with one's judgments and one's behavior can fail to express one's inner self. The corresponding good is harmony among one's judgments, choices, and performances – peace of conscience and consistency between one's self and its expression"

Religion – "Most persons experience tension with the wider reaches of reality. Attempts to gain or improve harmony with some more-than-human sources of meaning and value take many forms, depending on people's world views. Thus, another category. . .is *Peace with God, or the gods, or some nontheistic but more-than-human source of meaning and value*"

Source: Grisez, Boyle, and Finnis (1987) as cited in Alkire (2002)

TABLE 1: DIMENSIONS OF HD

Grisez et al. (1987)	Nussbaum (2000)	Max-Neef (1993)	Narayan et al. (2000)	Schwartz (1994)	Cummins (1996)	Ramsay (1992)	Doyal & Gough (1993)
Basic Human Values	Central Human Capabilities	Axiological Categories	Dimensions of well-being	Human values	Domains of life satisfaction	Human needs	Intermediate needs
Life: Knowledge and appreciation of beauty; Some degree of excellence in work and play; Friendship: Self-integration; Coherent self-determination; Religion, or harmony with some greater than- human source of meaning and value	Life; Bodily health; Bodily integrity; Senses, thought, Imagination; Emotions; Practical reason; Affiliation; Other species; Play; Control over one's Environment	Subsistence; Protection; Affection; Understanding; Participation; Leisure; Creation; Identity; Freedom	Material well-being; Bodily; well-being Social well-being; Security; Freedom of choice and action; Psychological well-being	Power; Achievement; Hedonism; Stimulation; Self-direction; Universalism; Benevolence; Tradition; Conformity; Security	Material well-being Health Productivity Intimacy/ friendship Safety Community Emotional well-being	Physical survival; Sexual needs; Security; Love and Relatedness; Esteem and Identity; Self-realization	Nutritional food/water; Protective Housing; Work; Physical Environment; Health care; Security in Childhood; Significant primary relationships; Physical security; Economic Security; Safe birth control/ childbearing, Basic education

Continued...

Introduction and Overview

Rawls (1993) Political liberalism	Qizilbash (1996a,b) Prudential values for development	Allardt (1993) Comparative Scandanavian welfare study	Andrews and Withey (1976) Concern clusters	Lasswell (1992) Human values	Diener and Biswas (2000) 12 life domains	Galtung (1994) HR in another key
The basic liberties; Freedom of movement, freedom of association and freedom of occupational choice against a background of diverse opportunities; Powers and prerogatives of office and positions of responsibility in political	Health/nutrition/ sanitation/rest/ shelter/security; Literacy/basic intellectual and physical capacities; Self-respect and Aspiration; Positive freedom, autonomy or self determination; Negative freedom or liberty . enjoyment; Enjoyment; Understanding or knowledge; Significant relations with	*Having:* Economic resources, Housing, Employment, Working Conditions, Health Education; *Loving:* Attachments/ contacts with local community, family and kin, friends, associations, work-mates; *Being*: Self determination, Political Activities, Leisure-time	Media; Societal Standards; Weather; Government; Safety; Community; House; Money; Job; Services; Recreation facilities; Traditions; Marriage; Children; Family relations; Treatment; Imagination; Acceptance; Self-adjustment; Virtues; Accomplishment;	Skill Affection Respect Rectitude Power Enlightenment Wealth Well-being	Morality; Food Family; Friendship; Material Resources; Intelligence; Romantic Relationship; Physical Appearance; Self; Income; Housing; Social life	1. *Survival needs: to avoid violence* Individual and collective 2. *Well-being needs: to avoid misery* Nutrition, water, air, movement, excretion, sleep, sex. protection against climate, against diseases, against heavy degrading boring work, self-expression, dialogue, education 3. *Identity needs: to avoid alienation* Creativity, praxis, work, self-actuation, realizing potentials, well-being, happiness, joy being active subject, not passive client/object, challenge and new experiences, affection, love, sex; friends, offspring, spouse, roots, belongingness,

and economic institutions; Income and Wealth; The social bases of self-respect	others and some participation in social life; Accomplishment (sort that gives life point/weight)	activities, Opportunities to enjoy nature, Meaningful work	Friends; Religion; Health; Own education; Beneficence; Independence; Mobility; Beauty networks, support, esteem, understanding social forces, social transparency, partnership with nature, a sense of purpose, of meaning, closeness to the transcendental, transpersonal 4. *Freedom needs: choice* In receiving/expressing information and opinion, of people/ places to visit and be visited in, consciousness formation, in mobilization, confrontation, occupation, job, spouse, goods/services, way of life

Source: Allardt in Nussbaum and Sen (1993) as cited in Alkire (2002)

Collective agencies of social action
　　HD strategies initially (in 1990s) emphasized education and health, paid less attention to political and social freedoms, and laid emphasis on individual rather than on collective agency. But it shifted its emphasis in the era of rapid globalization to capabilities to participate, and collective agencies of social action have become more important. Against economic entrepreneurship that drives markets; social entrepreneurship is expected to drive policy debates on issues that matter for people's well being - for HD (Fukuda-Parr, 2005). Acceleration of human investment and improvement in global economic environment can make a significant contribution to supporting HD strategies of developing countries.

Efficient and full utilization of human potentials
　　Human potentials will be wasted unless it is developed - and used. Economic development should create a suitable environment for the use of human talents. It should match the human dexterity the society needs with the human skills that are cultivated. But national production must also expand to make good use of human potential (UNDP, 1990).

Change in priorities for resources allocation
　　The major allocations of funds of every government are made to the 'production' ministries (industry, agriculture and commerce) and 'law and order' ministries (home and defense). It has no *significant* contribution to the enhancement of human capabilities and well-being in spite of increased economic growth. Moreover, the scanty budgetary allocation to the 'social services' ministries (education, health, labour, women welfare) are not sufficient for the recurring expenditure. Really, it does not produce / enhance the human capital formation which in turn may enhance the human capabilities. Therefore, the strategy is here to shift the priorities of allocation of resources by the government from 'production' and 'law and order' ministries to 'social services'

ministry and more importantly, efficient management and use of the allocation for the enhancement of human capabilities.

People Centered Strategies[9]

HD is the end or objective of development. It is a way to fulfill the potential of people by enlarging their capabilities, and this necessarily implies empowerment of people, enabling them to participate actively in their own development. HD is also a means since it enhances the skills, knowledge, productivity and inventiveness of people through a process of human capital formation broadly conceived. HD is, thus, a *people centered strategy*, not a *goods centered or production centered strategy* of development (Griffin and McKinley, 1992).

Incentives for HD

Human resources are the most valuable asset to be utilized carefully and sensibly. An appropriate incentive system can fully exploit the full potentialities of the human resources in order to enhance the capabilities to reduce poverty, inequality of income, gender equity et cetera. The set of relative prices also encourage the growth of stock of human resources.

Clean Society

Here, 'clean society', we mean, 'clean environment' and 'clean government'. A clean society is the basic and fundamental requirement for HD. Uninterrupted environmental degradation including climate change contracts the development of human beings. In HDR 2007/2008 the important issue highlighted is *'Fighting Climate Change'*. Converting the basic strategy of growth from 'trickle down' to 'direct tackle' is necessary for 'clean government'. Now corruptions become the normal life, which contracts the capabilities instead of expansion. Therefore, 'clean society' may be the need of the hour for HD.

---

[9] The empowerment of local people to identify their own priorities and to implement programs and projects of direct benefit to them. This strengthening of civil society need not imply a smaller role for government. HD is not politically neutral; it is not a technocratic solution to development problems; it requires broadly based popular support (Griffin and McKinley, 1992).

Shifting of importance from foreign aid to conventional alternatives

HD strategies are likely to be less intensive in the use of foreign aid than more conventional alternatives. The reason for this is that HD strategies require less imported capital equipment than alternative strategies and in general have lower demands for foreign exchange. Given that foreign finance is likely to be less readily available in future than in the past, this characteristic of HD is to be welcomed (Griffin and McKinley, 1992).

Inclusive growth

The link between economic growth and HD is not automatic. Economic growth can improve HD through expansion of human capabilities. For this, the commodity base of the country must be broadened. Deliberate, honest and effective public actions can enable the people to participate in, and benefit from the process of development. This can ultimately improve HD via enhancement of human capabilities.

Freedom: the vital component

Freedom is the most vital component of HD strategies. People must be free to actively participate in economic and political life – setting developmental priorities, formulating policies, implementing projects and choosing the form of government to influence their cultural environment. Such freedom ensures that social goals do not become mechanical devices in the hands of paternalistic governments. If HD is the outer shell, freedom is its priceless pearl! (UNDP, 1990).

Integral HD Strategies

People employ a variety of strategies to realize their desired outcomes. The Integral Human Development (IHD) conceptual framework uses six categories of strategies: *Asset*[10]

---

[10] Here, assets are the resources people draw upon to make their strategies work. The IHD conceptual framework identifies six asset categories: *Human and Spiritual Assets*: education, wisdom, health, religious faith; *Social Assets*: family, friends, and groups that form our support networks; *Political Assets*: the power people possess to advocate for change and claim rights; *Physical Assets*: homes, clothes, equipment, tools; *Financial Assets*: cash and income, or things like livestock that can be sold for cash; *Natural Assets*: resources like soil, water, plants, trees, animals and air.

Maximization; Asset Diversification; Empowerment; Asset Recovery; Coping and Survival Mechanisms; and Risk Reduction.

An IHD analysis helps us to identify and strengthen successful strategies while reducing reliance on strategies that might have short-term benefits but are unsustainable over the long term. It also helps us to broaden the range of available strategies that people can use. Successful IHD strategies sustain and increase assets over time, whereas unsuccessful ones lead to asset loss (CRS, 2007).

HDR 1990 challenged some of the conventional wisdom, exploded some of the old myths and reached some important policy conclusions that would have significant implications for development strategies (Haq, 1995).

1. It is wrong to suggest that development process has failed in most developing countries in the past three decades. Judged by real indicators of HD, it has succeeded spectacularly.
2. It is wrong to suggest that economic growth is unnecessary for HD. No sustained improvement in human well-being is possible without growth. But it also wrong to suggest that high economic growth rates will automatically translate into higher levels of HDs.
3. It is conceptually and practically wrong to regard poverty alleviation as a global distinct from HD. Most poverty can be explained by inadequate access to income, assets, credits, social services and job opportunities. The only long term remedy is to invest in poor people, particularly in their education and training, and to bring them back into the mainstream of development.
4. It is wrong to suggest that developing countries lack enough resources to address their HD goals. In reality, considerable potential exists for restructuring present priorities in their national budgets and in foreign assistance allocation.
5. It is wrong to pretend that markets alone can deliver balanced patterns of economic growth and HD. Instead, there must be judicious mix of market efficiency and social compassion.

VII. MEASURING HUMAN WELL BEING: HUMAN DEVELOPMENT INDEX (HDI)

There has been considerable dissatisfaction with gross national product (GNP) as a measure of human welfare. This prompted a long search for a more comprehensive measure of development that could capture all, or many more, of the choices people make – a measure that would serve as a better yardstick of the socioeconomic progress of nations. The search for a new composite index of socio economic progress began in earnest in preparing the *Human Development Report* under the sponsorship of UNDP in 1989. Several principles guided this search. First, the new HDI would measure the basic concept of HD to enlarge people's choice. Second, the new index would include only a limited number of variables to keep it simple and manageable. Third, a composite index would be constructed rather than a plethora of separate indices. Fourth, the HDI would cover both social and economic choice. Fifth, keep the coverage and methodology of HDI quite flexible – subject to gradual refinements as analytical critics emerged and better data became available. Sixth, persuade and put pressure on the policy-makers to invest adequate amounts in producing relevant data and to encourage international institutions to prepare comparable statistical data system (Haq, 1995).

As stated above, the first HDR of UNDP was published in 1990 under the brilliant leadership of Mahbub ul Haq. The most eye-catching and head-line contribution of it was the HDI. It comprises (1) the logarithm of GDP per head, calculated at the real purchasing power, not at exchange rates, up to the international poverty line; (in subsequent reports this was modified in various ways); (2) literacy rate (and since the 1991 Report, mean year of schooling); and (3) life expectancy at birth. These disparate items are brought to a common denominator by counting the distance between the best and worst performers and thereby achieving a ranking of countries. Critics have said that not only are the weights of the three components arbitrary, but also what is excluded, and what is included (Streeten, 2005).

(Dis)Satisfactions over and Limitations of HDI

HDRs of UNDP are a challenge to the traditional conception and measures of economic development which are based on income and employment levels as well as on economic growth rates reflected in the GNP. UNDP's "HD" is much more comprehensive as it considers the traditional measures insufficient for determination of HD of all societies (Holbik, 1992). Immediately after the publication of HDR, several discontents also emerged: recognition of "basic needs", various indicators of "Physical Quality of Life Index", focusing in the disparities in "living conditions", focus on "the state of the world children", concerned over "hunger, morbidity and mortality, rather than only with income poverty", voicing the need for social justice in the distribution of opportunities that people have, and questioning the radical shift from "commodities to capabilities" (Sen, 2005).

MacGillivray (1991) showed his dissatisfaction and questioned composition and usefulness of composite development indicator, i.e., HDI (published by the UNDP's in 1990 in its HDR 1990). On the basis of the results of the statistical analysis the following conclusions have emerged: (a) the composition of the index is flawed as it is significantly and positively correlated with each of its component variables individually; (b) as a consequence, assessing inter country development levels on any one of these variables yields similar results to those that the index itself yields, and more profoundly; (c) with the exception of a minority of country group, the index largely provides us with little more information regarding inter country development levels than the more traditional indicator, GNP per capita, alone provides. Conclusion (b) and (c) lead to the assessment that the UNDP,s index is yet another redundant composite inter country development indicator (MacGillivray, 1991). But the very next page of this article, Michael Hopkins stated that measuring development of countries with the aid of HDI gives a significantly different ordering to one based on GNP per capita. This point is not disputed, although success on the index is not a necessary and sufficient condition for success in terms of rapid economic growth, as is shown by Sri Lanka. Nevertheless, the report is welcome for its attention to HD issues, for its useful statistical annex, and for its observation that the poverty of the people of the developing world has been no barrier to the affluence of their armies (Hopkins, 1991). 'Although HDI fails to include any ecological considerations, it has broadened the discussion surrounding the evaluation of development. Unfortunately, over the years, the HDRs seem to have become stagnant, repeating the same rhetoric without necessarily increasing the HDI's utility' (Sagar and Najam, 1998). Sagar and Najam (1998) evaluated how well these reports have lived up to their own conceptual mandates and assess the ability of the HDI to further the development debate. They found that the reports have lost touch with their original vision and the index fails to capture the essence of the world it seeks to portray. In addition, the index focuses almost exclusively on national performance and ranking, but does not pay much attention to development from a global perspective.

There has been a tendency to imprison HD strategies and ideas within the HDI. Ironically, the success of HDI has only served to reinforce the narrow interpretation of HD (Fukuda-Parr, 2005). HDI is a subset of HD literature. But it is also obvious for the public to imprison HD strategies and ideas within HDI because of the following reasons.

1. In 1955 the Noble prize winning West Indian economist Arthur Lewis defines the purpose of development as widening "the range of human choice", exactly as the *Human Development Reports* since 1990 have done (Streeten, 2005).
2. Major portion of the UNDP's annual series *Human Development Reports* are on the calculation, comparison and tables of HDI.

3. Individual country and state level *Human Development Reports* prepared by the respective national and state governments are actually (in the sense Fukuda-Parr, 2005 discussed) not *Human Development Reports* but *Human Development Index Reports*.

The major limitations of HDI are as follows.

First, Human well-being and freedom are influenced by great variety of factors – social, economical, political, legal, epidemiological and others – but HDI is based on the three heroic factors – basic education, life expectancy and income per head – while totally neglects others (Sen, 2005).

Second, HDI is calculated by assigning equal and constant weightage to each of the three factors, which is an oversimplification as the ingredients of each factor are different from each other (Sen, 2005).

Third, the item HDI in the HDRs of UNDP that has caught the public's eye and caused most controversy is perhaps analytically the weakest. It is clear that the concept of HD is much deeper and richer than what can be caught in *any* index or set of indicators. This is also true of other indicators. But, it might be asked, why try to catch a vector in a single number? (Streeten, 1994).

Fourth, Achievement of higher HD indices (HDI's), which are superior to higher levels of GNP, depends also on new/changed political strategies including modified power structures and encouragement of democratic freedoms. HD puts people at the center of development and emphasizes that "we are a global, not just economically interdependent, community." This requires establishment of a new human order permitting all issues to be considered from a human perspective. The criterion of HD is not how much a nation produces, but how its people are faring (Holbik, 1992).

Fifth, the exclusion of the reference to political freedom and participation always hunts the concept of HDI (Fukuda-Parr, 2005).

Sixth, the implicit trade-off between life expectancy and income is a problem with HDI. For a country with an income per head less than the world average ($5,711 per year at 1993 purchasing power parity, which is about the income per head of Costa Rica), an increase of annual GDP per head of $99 will exactly compensate for one year less of life expectancy so as to keep the HDI constant (Ravallion, 1997 as quoted in Streeten, 2005).

When the HDI caught by the turbulent water, Haq (1995) wrote "in economic science, nothing is ever new, and nothing is permanent. Ideas emerge, flourish, wither and die, to be born again a few decades later. Such is the case for ideas about HD". He also told to the world "here we have a broad framework; if you want something else to be included here, which may deserve a table in the *Human Development Report* (and with some luck, may even be considered for inclusion in one of the aggregate indicators we use), tell us *what*, and explain *why* it must figure in this accounting. We *will* listen" (Sen, 2005).

B. OVERVIEW OF THE VOLUME

The Present Volume is an attempt to put scholarly articles together on important issues of HD. The papers here highlight on major dimensions of Human development and different strategies for the same. All the contributors have been selected for their direct knowledge and recent experience of working on issues pertaining to HD and for their ability in exploring into the various aspects of HD, dimensions and strategies, necessary ways, means and policy changes inherent for sustainable HD.

"**A Note on Some Aggregation Problems in the Functioning Approach to Individual Well-Being**", an important contribution to the volume by Prasanta K. Pattanaik highlights a specific issue, namely, the problem of aggregation over different dimensions of an individual's well-being, which arises in the functioning and capability approach and which has considerable importance for certain applications of the approach in practice. He also discusses on some basic features of the functioning and capability approach, different purposes which the approach may be expected to serve the importance of aggregation over functionings for some of these purposes and the problems that the approach faces in overall well-being comparisons. He concludes, while such aggregation may not be essential for all purposes, in the absence of such aggregation the functioning and capability approach is likely to be of limited use in many important contexts.

The paper entitled **"On Measuring Group Differential: Some Further Results"** by Hippu Salk Kristle Nathan and Srijit Mishra discusses measures of group differentials for failure indicators. It identifies the limitations of the measures in the literature and proposes an alternative which satisfies the axioms of level sensitivity and normalization. It also does away with the subjectivity associated in the choice of parameters in some existing measures. Empirical illustration with infant mortality rate data for selected Indian states has also been provided in the paper which shows the advantages of the proposed alternative. The authors state that these measures can also be used to evaluate success in some of the Millennium Development Goals.

In his paper **"Status and Trend of Human Development in North East Region of India"**, Purusottam Nayak examines the status of human development across different states in northeast India and its trend over a period of two decades. The study reveals that the region has not been able to keep pace with the country as a whole in terms of growth of per capita income and reduction of poverty. Rural-urban disparity, gender disparity and uneven human development across the states in the region are quite significant. The disturbing trend of increasing gender disparity in Nagaland and escalating rural-urban gap, particularly in the states of Assam and Meghalaya, is a matter of concern.

"A Note on Human Development Indices with Income Equalities" by S K Mishra provides an analysis on the inclusion of income equality, as one among the other indices like health attainment, educational attainment and income attainment for obtaining human development index (HDI) and different methodological alternatives of assigning relative weight to these indices .The paper obtains HDI by all these methods, compares them and supports the use of egalitarian weighting method for constructing human development index .

The paper entitled "**Regional Planning, National Development and Conflict Resolution**" by M. Chatterji tries to show how inter-regional cooperation will help in resolving conflict and lead to increased benefits for the interested regions and the nation as a whole, from a broad perspective of peace and human development. The paper cites examples in the field of environmental conflict in India and the problem of sharing of river water and shows the way to deal with the same. The author argues that these conflicts are often overemphasized and used against the concept and implementation of regional plans, but enough is not said about how these conflicts can be resolved through inter-regional cooperation and at the same time the potentialities of development of respective regions can be maximized. The author foregrounds the scope of applying conflict resolution researches in regional planning in India emphasizing the need of objective scientific studies to explore the benefits of cooperation.

In their paper entitled "**Age-Structured Human Capital Dynamics and Economic Growth: A Note on Interdependence, Coordination and Welfare**", Tapas Mishra and Mamata Parhi critically review the role of age-structured human capital in economic growth in the space-time domain and suggest (i) a theoretical framework for modeling growth interdependence across countries due to cross-country human capital accumulation and (ii) construct an empirical test for dynamic spatial growth correlations. For empirical illustration they have examined the case of four geographically clustered set of countries and found that cooperation in human capital accumulation policy across countries is welfare improving and that a dynamic correlation among countries growth processes exists, which occur due to human capital accumulation differentials among them.

The paper entitled **"Human Development in India: Issues and Challenges"** by Mihir K. Mahapatra and Rajesh Raj S.N examines the level of human development in India vis-à-vis the neighboring countries with different levels of development. The paper also looks at examining the variation in human development across selected Indian states. In order to identify the determining factors of Human Development, the paper has focused on healthcare scenario both in the country and major states. The study finds persistence of wide disparity in human development across the states especially BIMARU states vis-à-vis some of the middle income and developed states. This is primarily on account of inadequate effort made to improve accessibility to health infrastructure, safe drinking water and sanitation. It is also argued that in the absence of adequate effort to improve health care scenario, progress in human development does not seem to be feasible as it can have adverse impact on education and level of poverty.

In their paper **"The Perspectives of Economic Growth and Social Insecurity on Human Development for Lagging States in India"**, Aswini Kumar Mishra and Biswabas Patra analyze the two major placards of human development namely, the growth-mediated and support-led strategies- aiming at promoting economic growth in order to improve public and private incomes and envisaging at wide-ranging public support in areas such as education, health care, employment provision, assets redistribution, social assistance respectively across the major states in India .They find that the state of human development is low for economically less developed and for those states where public provisioning of social security that is measured in terms of levels of social security expenditure, is low.

Economic growth does not necessarily ensure environmental sustainability for a country. The relationship between the two is far more complicated for developing countries like India, given the dependence of a large section of the population on natural resources for livelihood. Under this backdrop, the paper entitled **"Environment, Human Development and Economic Growth of Indian States after Liberalization"** by Sacchidananda Mukherjee and Debashis Chakraborty attempts to analyze the relationships among Environmental Quality (EQ), Human Development (HD) and Economic Growth (EG) for 14 major Indian States during post liberalisation period (1991-2004). Considering 63 environmental indicators, an overall index of EQ is calculated by using the HDI methodology. The EQ ranks of the States exhibit variation over time, implying that environment has both spatial and temporal dimensions. The HDI rankings of the States for the two periods are constructed by the HDI technique following the National Human Development Report 2001 methodology. The authors attempt to test for the Environmental Kuznets Curve hypothesis through multivariate OLS regression models, which indicate presence of non-linear relationship between several individual environmental groups and per capita net state domestic product (PCNSDP). The relationship between EQ and economic growth however does not become clear from the current study. The regression results involving individual environment groups and HDI score indicate a slanting N-shaped relationship. The paper concludes that individual States should adopt environmental management practices based on their local (at the most disaggregated level) environmental information. Moreover, since environmental sustainability and human well-being are complementary to each other, individual States should attempt to translate the economic growth to human well-being.

The paper entitled **"Gender and Human Development"** by Liliane Bensahel, Steven Coissard and Asma Lazrak aims at demonstrating the importance of an approach of the human development in terms of reducing gender disparities. The gender approach, by the study of the situations, the roles and the social functions of the man and the woman, the relations between these two poles with for ambition to be in closer of the human being and to allow it to position in best in our world, can be vital. The authors argue that it is not a question of establishing a feminine power on the male, it is a question of recognizing both to allow the birth of the fruit, the opening of the other glances. The increase of the poverty in the world and the ecological imbalance led the economists to question the relation between the development and the growth. The new surrounding areas of the wealth are born and the women have certain role to be played.

The paper **"Recasting Human Development Indices: A Look into the State of Gender Empowerment in Karnataka"** by Sanjeev D Kenchaigol analyses the status of women in Karnataka from the perspective of human and gender development. The paper follows the methodology of UNDP human development report 1995 and the methodology of Karnataka human development report 2005 respectively for computation of gender empowerment measure (GEM) index and the computation of earned income index for the different districts of Karnataka, with necessary modifications in variable selection and computation to reflect the micro level situations. The paper reveals persistent gender bias in important human capabilities in different districts of Karnataka and the gender empowerment does not necessarily relate to level of economic development and human development in different districts of the state. The author states that the persisting gender disparities in human development and gender empowerment create a context for the micro-level research for further understanding of the nature and trends in gender inequalities and the status of women's empowerment.

The paper entitled "**Human Development in Orissa: An Inter-District Analysis from the Perspective of Infrastructure**" by Amar Kumar Mohanty, Narayan C. Nayak and Bani Chatterjee examines the state of human development in Orissa taking districts as the units of analysis. Following the criteria as developed by UNDP, the study finds that human development is abysmally low in most of the districts. In the entire state, no district has yet attained high human development. Besides, although relative disparities amongst the districts are recorded unchanged over study periods i.e. 1993-94, 1997-98 and 2003-04, there still persist severe inequalities in human development across districts in any single period. Further the paper links the attainment of Human development with the availability of quality infrastructure. The study finds that the composite index of infrastructure as estimated using principal component analysis tend to get skewed towards a few advanced districts primarily located in the coastal region of the state. The districts which record poor infrastructure base are the ones that register low human development, barring exceptions. The districts dominated by tribal population are the ones which fare very badly in human development front and they lag far behind in terms of availability of infrastructure. The authors opine, for improving human development for the entire state, while all the districts may need attention, the states dominated by tribal population may deserve special attention.

The paper entitled "**Human Development, Economic Development and Income Earning Capacities of the Common Man: the Case of North East India**" by Keya Sengupta discusses how various policy issues are important, in the context of the north eastern region of India, in turning high level of economic development into higher human development. The paper tries to establish an inter linkage between human development, economic development and income earning capacities of the common man. The paper reveals that work participation rate (WPR) which may be used as a proxy for the economic development of the respective place is extremely low in most of the districts of the region. Only the districts having the state capital fares marginally better. No direct relationship between WPR and human development can be discerned, though this is not to deny that influence of WPR can be observed only after a time lag. The paper also shows that there is a high degree of correlation between income poverty and human development.

In his paper entitled **"Human Development and Economic Development: the Case of Assam"**, Sumanash Dutta seeks to identify poorer regions in terms of some selected indicators in the state Assam. The paper evaluates the district-level disparities in human development and economic development in Assam. The Human Development Index(HDI) values and HDI rank of the Districts as shown in Assam Human Development Report-2003, the calculated Composite Development Score (CDS, the Dimension Index of Development (DID) and the DID rank of the Districts are considered to highlight disparity among different districts of Assam in economic and Human Development. It is observed that the disparities of economic development are much higher among the Districts of Assam in comparison to human development, as is evident from the values of C.V (HDI) and C.V (DID).The author states that the regional disparities of economic development are glaring and there is a need to address the problem through purposive planning and compassionate outlook.

The paper entitled **"Livelihood Diversification: Pathway Out of Rural Poverty"** by P.S. Sujithkumar analyses the occupational diversification in rural India over the last two decades and the kind of diversification required to reduce poverty. There has been a considerable occupational diversification that happened during this two decades and the diversification is much prominent in the reform period. The paper also points out some policy areas where government steps are necessary for accelerating the process of diversification. It is argued in the paper that the process of diversification should turn the tiny and marginal farmers to 'part-time' agriculturists, to bring down rural poverty.

The papers in the volume widely discuss on issues of measurement, different dimensions and strategies of human development and empirically examine the state of human development in different states. This volume will be in some help in understanding the concepts, theories and developments in Human development and bringing out certain issues which need to be further explored with a broad perspective of sustainable human development.

REFERENCES

Akhter, Syed H. (2004): Is Globalization What it's cracked up to be? Economic Freedom, Corruption, and Human Development, *Journal of World Business*, 39(3): 283-295.

Allardt, E. (1993): Having, Loving Being: An Alternative to the Swedish Model of Welfare Research, In M. Nussbaum, and A. Sen (Eds.), *The Quality of Life*, Clarendon Press, Oxford, pp. 88–94.

Alkire, Sabina (2002): Dimensions of Human Development, *World Development*, 30(2): 181-205.

Anand, Sudhir and Sen, Amartya (2000): Human Development and Economic Sustainability, *World Development*, 28(12): 2029-2049.

Andrews, F. M. and Withey, S. B. (1976): *Social indicators of well-being: Americans' Perceptions of Life Quality*, Plenum Press, New York.

Catholic Relief Services (CRS) (2007): *Education and the CRS Integral Human Development Framework: Building Assets and Transforming Structures and Systems around the World*, CRS Education Technical Advisors, Program Quality and Support Department, A CRS Internal Working Paper, http://crs.org/publications/showpdf.cfm?pdf_id=19, accessed on the 24th August 2008.

Cummins, R. A. (1996): Domains of Life Satisfaction: an Attempt to Order Chaos, *Social Indicators Research*, 38 (3): 303-328.

Desai, Meghnad (1991): Human Development: Concepts and Measurement, *European Economic Review*, 35 (2-3): 350-357.

Diener, E. and Biswas-Diener, R. (2000): *New Directions in Subjective Well-Being Research: The Cutting Edge*, Mimeo, University of Illinois.

Doyal, L. and Gough, I. (1993): Need Satisfaction as a Measure of Human Welfare, In W. Blass and J. Foster (Eds.), *Mixed Economies in Europe*, Edward Elgar, London.

Dreze, Jean and Sen, Amartya (1989): *Hunger and Public Action*, Clarendon, Oxford.

Finnis, J., Boyle, J. M., and Grisez, G. (1987): *Nuclear Deterrence, Morality and Realism*, Clarendon Press, Oxford.

Fukuda-Parr, Sakiko (2005): Rescuing the Human Development Concept from the HDI: Reflections on a New Agenda, In Sakiko Fukuda-Parr and A. K. Siva Kumar (Eds) *Readings in Human Development*, Oxford University Press, New Delhi, pp.117-124.

Galtung, J. (1994): *Human Rights in another Key*, Polity Press, Cambridge.

Griffin, Keith B. (2006): A Witness of Two Revolutions, In James K. Boyce, Stephen Cullenberg, Prasanta K. Pattanaik, and Robert Pollin (Eds.), *Human Development in the Era of Globalization: Essays in Honor of Keith B. Griffin*, Edward Elgar, Cheltenham, UK, pp. 15-27. The original version was presented as the Humanist Achievement Lecture at the University of California, Riverside in January 2003.

Griffin, Keith B. and Knight, John (1990): Human Development: the Case for Renewed Emphasis, In Keith B. Griffin and John Knight (Eds), *Human Development and the International Development Strategies for the 1990s*, Macmillan in association with United Nations, London, pp. 9-40.

Griffin, Keith B. and McKinley, Terry (1992): *Towards a Human Development Strategy*, Occasional Paper 6, UNDP, available at http://hdr.undp.org/en/reports/global/hdr1992/papers/keith_griffin_terry_mckinley.pdf, accessed on the 20th August 2008.

Grisez, G., Boyle, J., and Finnis, J. (1987): Practical Principles, Moral Truth and Ultimate ends, *American Journal of Jurisprudence*, 32: 99-151.

Haq, Mahbub ul (1995): *Reflections on Human Development*, Oxford University Press, New York.

Holbik, Karel (1992): Measuring Human Development, *American Journal of Economics and Sociology*, 51 (4): 493-494.

Hopkins, Michael (1991): Human Development Revisited: A New UNDP Report, *World Development*, 19(10): 1469-1473.

ILO (1976): *Employment, Growth and Basic Needs: A One Word Problem*, Geneva,

Jahan, Selim (2005): Evolution of the Human Development Index, In Sakiko Fukuda-Parr and A.K. Shiva Kumar (Eds.) *Readings in Human Development*, Oxford University, New Delhi, pp.152-163.

Lasswell, H. D. (1992): *Jurisprudence for a Free Society: Studies in Law, Science and Policy*, New Haven Press, New Haven.

MacGillivray, Mark (1991): The Human Development Index: Yet another Redundant Composite Development Indicator, *World Development*, 19(10): 1461-1468.

Max-Neef, M. (1993): *Human Scale Development: Conception, Application and Further Reflection*, Apex Press, London.

Mishra, Srijit (2007): On Measuring Group-Differentials Displayed by Socio-economic Indicators: an Extension, *Applied Economics Letters*, 99999 (1): 1-4, http://www.informaworld.com/10.1080/13504850600972238, (accessed 28 September 2007). IGIDR working paper version of this paper is available at http://www.igidr.ac.in/pdf/publication/WP-2006-005.pdf.

Mishra, U. S. and Subramanian, S. (2006): On Measuring Group-Differentials Displayed by Socio-economic Indicators, *Applied Economics Letters*, 13 (8): 519-521.

Narayan, D., Chambers, R., Shah, M. K., and Petesch, P. (2000): *Voice of the Poor: crying Out for Change*, Oxford University Press for World Bank, New York.

Nussabaum, M. C. (2000): *Women and Human Development: The Capabilities Approach*, Cambridge University Press, Cambridge.

Nussabaum, M. C. and Sen, A. (Eds.) (1993): *The Quality of Life*, Clarendon Press, Oxford.

Qizilbash, M. (1997a): Needs, Incommensurability and Well-being, *Review of Political Economy*, 9(3): 261–276.

Qizilbash, M. (1997b): Pluralism and Well-being Indices, *World Development*, 25(12): 2009–2026.

Ramsay, M. (1992): *Human Needs and the Market*, Avebury, Aldershot.

Rawls, John (1971): *A Theory of Justice*, Harvard University Press, Cambridge, p.92.

Rawls, J. (1993): *Political Liberalism*, Columbia University Press, New York.

Ranis, G., Stewart, F. and Samman, E. (2006): Human Development: Beyond the Human Development Index, *Journal of Human Development*, 7 (3): 323 – 358.

Ravallion, Martin (1997): Good and bad Growth: The Human Development Reports, *World Development*, 25(5): 631-638.

Sagar, A. D. and Najam, A. (1998): The Human Development Index: A Critical Review, *Ecological Economics*, 25(3): 249-264.

Schwartz, S. H. (1994): Are the Universal Aspects in the Structure and Contents of Human Values? *Journal of Social Issues*, 50 (4): 19-45.

Sen, Amartya (1984): *Resources, Values and Development*, Blackwell, Oxford.

Sen, Amartya (1985): *Commodities and Capabilities*, North-Holland, Amsterdam.

Sen, Amartya (1987): The Standard of Living, In G. Hawthorne et al. (Eds.), *Tanner Lectures on Human Values*, Cambridge University Press, Cambridge.

Sen, Amartya (1989): Development as Capability Expansion, Journal of Development Planning, 19: 41-58; Reprinted in Keith B. Griffin and John Knight (Eds) (1990), *Human Development and the International Development Strategies for the 1990s*, Macmillan in association with United Nations, London, pp. 41-58; and in Sakiko Fukuda-Parr and A. K. Siva Kumar (Eds.) (2005): *Readings in Human Development*, Oxford University Press, New Delhi, pp.03-16.

Sen, Amartya (1997): Human Capital and Human Capabilities, *World Development*, 25(12): 1959-61.

Sen, Amartya (2005): Foreword, In Sakiko Fukuda-Parr and A. K. Siva Kumar (Eds.) *Readings in Human Development*, Oxford University Press, New Delhi, p.viii-ix.

Streeten, P., Burki, J. S., Haq, M., Hicks, N., and Stewart, Frances (1981): *First Things First: Meeting Basic Human Needs in Developing Countries*, Oxford University Press, New York.

Streeten, Paul (1994): Human Development: Means and Ends, *American Economic Review*, 84 (2): 232-237.

Streeten, Paul (2005): Shifting Fashions in Development Dialogue, In Sakiko Fukuda-Parr and A.K. Shiva Kumar (Eds.) *Readings in Human Development*, Oxford University, New Delhi, pp.92-105. Article originally published in 2003, *International Journal of Applied Economics and Econometrics* 11 (1).

Tomas, Amparo (2005): *A Human Rights Approach to Development*, available at http://www.unifem.org.in/PDF/RBA%20Primer%20.pdf, accessed on the 24th August 2008.

United Nations Development Program (2001): *Human Development Report 2001*, Oxford University Press, New York.

UNDP (1990): *Human Development Report 1990*, Oxford University Press, New York.

2

A Note on Some Aggregation Problems in the Functioning Approach to Individual Well-Being

Prasanta K. Pattanaik[1]

I. INTRODUCTION

An analysis of the ethical basis of public policy has to face, right at the outset, the issue of how one should conceive the well-being of an individual. Further, in practical applications of such analysis to the choice of public policies, one also has to face the problem of how to measure, at least ordinally, the well-being of an individual. Nearly two decades ago, Amartya Sen and Martha Nussbaum initiated their functioning and capability approach with a notion of personal well-being very different from the notion familiar in traditional welfare economics [for some foundational expositions of the approach, see Sen (1985, 1987) and Nussbaum (1988, 2000)]. The contributions of Sen and Nussbaum have inspired a large volume of literature. A review and assessment of this literature is far beyond the scope of this note. The main purpose of this note is to highlight a specific issue, namely, the problem of aggregation over different dimensions of an individual's well-being, which arises in this approach and which has considerable importance for certain applications of the approach in practice. Throughout this note, I shall be

---

[1] Department of Economics, University of California, Riverside, CA 92521, U.S.A., E-mail: prasanta.pattanaik@ucr.edu

concerned with the well-being of single individuals; I do not consider issues relating to the well-being of groups of individuals. The plan of the paper is as follows. In Section II, I briefly outline some problems with the conventional conception of well-being in welfare economics, which have often motivated the search for alternative conceptions. In this section, I also outline some basic features of the functioning and capability approach. In Section III, I distinguish several different purposes, which the functioning and capability approach may be expected to serve, and emphasize the importance of aggregation over functionings for some of these purposes. In Section IV, I discuss the problems that the approach faces in overall well-being comparisons. I conclude in Section V.

II. TWO ALTERNATIVE CONCEPTIONS OF HUMAN WELL-BEING

In conventional welfare economics, the well-being of an individual is conceived as her utility interpreted as desire fulfillment or preference satisfaction. In practical applications of welfare analysis, the value of a person's consumption bundle is often taken to be the index of her utility[2], though standard economic theory tells us that, even when a person's well-being is identified with her utility and the person is assumed to be a utility maximizer, a change in the value of the consumption bundle of a person, calculated at constant prices, may be a poor indicator of the change in the individual's well-being. Consider a given consumer. Let p^0, x^0, and u^0 be the vector of market prices, the (price-taking) consumer's consumption bundle, and the consumer's utility level,

---

[2] It may be worth clarifying here a point which is analytically obvious but is sometimes overlooked: if a change in the value of a given person's consumption bundle at constant prices is to serve as any indicator of the change in the utility of the person, the consumption bundle needs to include the leisure consumed by the person unless the amount of leisure is assumed to be fixed or the amount of leisure does not matter for the person's utility.

respectively, for year 0. Similarly, we have p^1, x^1, and u^1 for year 1. Then all that we know from standard economic theory is that, if $p^1.x^1 > p^1.x^0$, then $u^1 > u^0$, and, if $p^0.x^0 > p^0.x^1$, then $u^0 > u^1$. If, however, either $p^1.x^1 < p^1.x^0$ or $p^0.x^0 < p^0.x^1$, then that, by itself, does not tell us anything about the comparison of u^0 and u^1 (this inability to compare u^0 and u^1 remains even when x^0 and x^1 are assumed to be 'close' to each other[3]). Of course, even the very limited conclusion that if $[p^1.x^1 > p^1.x^0$, then $u^1 > u^0$; and, if $p^0.x^0 > p^0.x^1$, then $u^0 > u^1]$ does not necessarily hold if there are non-marketed commodities (e.g., clean air, absence of crime, etc.) which affect the individual's utility but which do not figure in the calculation of the value of the consumer's consumption bundle.

These are familiar problems with using the value of the consumption bundle at a fixed set of prices as a measure of a person's well-being[4]. They point to reasons why changes in the value of a person's consumption bundle may not be a good indicator of a change in her well-being, even when one does not question the assumption that the utility achieved by an individual constitutes her well-being.

The functioning and capability approach of Sen and Nussbaum, however, questions the foundational assumption in much of welfare economics that identifies a person's well-being with her utility (interpreted as desire fulfillment or preference satisfaction). The approach starts by distinguishing between what people value and what they desire. It claims that what people desire may diverge significantly from what they value, and argues that the well-being of people should be assessed on the basis of what they value rather than what they desire.

---

[3] Cf. Dutta, Pattanaik, and Russell (2003).
[4] There is very little in standard economic theory that enables us to make interpersonal comparisons of utilities on the basis of the values of different persons' consumption bundles at a fixed set of prices.

The distinction between the act of valuation and the act of desiring provides the philosophical basis of the functioning and capability approach. In Sen's (1987, p.29) terminology, functionings are the "doings" and "beings" that people value and a person's capability set is the set of all alternative functioning bundles available to her. Being well nourished, being protected from the elements, being healthy, taking part in the life of the community, and not being ashamed of one's status in the society are some of the examples of functionings that often figure in the literature. A person's well-being, it is claimed, is determined by the capability set, which reflects her freedom to choose a functioning bundle, and the specific functioning bundle belonging to the capability set that she actually achieves. Though the capability set is an important element in the assessment of a person's well-being in the functioning and capability approach, to simplify my exposition in this note I shall concentrate on the person's achieved functioning bundle alone and ignore the capability set. The introduction of the capability set as a determinant of well-being does not change much the conceptual structure of the problem of aggregation over the different dimensions of well-being, on which I focus here, though it does add an extra item to the list of such dimensions.

III. TYPES OF COMPARISON AND THE NEED FOR AGGREGATION

In the context of the multidimensional conception of well-being in the functioning approach, one can think of various different types of comparisons[5] of situations involving individuals and their achievements in terms of functionings;

---

[5] Here I have in mind only ordinal comparisons. If one likes, one may also require the comparisons to be cardinal.

each of these types of comparison can be useful, depending on one's purpose. Consider the following:

(i) *Person-specific one-dimensional comparisons*: comparison of alternative situations on the basis of a given person's achievements in terms of a single functionings, taken one at a time;

(ii) *Person-specific overall comparisons*: comparison of different situations on the basis of a given person's overall well-being, taking into account all functionings;

(iii) *Interpersonal one-dimensional comparisons*: comparison of different persons' achievements in terms of single functionings, taken one at a time;

(iv) *Interpersonal overall comparisons*: comparison of different persons' overall well-being levels, taking into account all functionings.

Of course, one may be simultaneously interested in more than one of these comparison types. Consider first one-dimensional comparisons. By definition, such comparisons do not require us to find any measure of anybody's overall well-being from functioning bundles. Yet the information yielded can be very useful for many purposes. We are not always necessarily interested in comparisons of overall achievements in terms of all functionings. We may simply want to know whether the health of a person (or a group) has improved over time or whether one person's (or one group's) achievement in terms of health is greater than that of another person (or, group)[6]. One may carry out such comparisons for each of several functionings separately and gain considerable insight without necessarily going into any overall comparison with respect to all functioning either for a given individual or across individuals. As Sen (1987, p. 33) observes

---

[6] Typically, for policy purposes, one is interested in groups rather than individuals, but I confine myself to individuals only, so as to avoid the extra complications involved in aggregating over the members of a group.

"The passion for aggregation makes good sense in many contexts, but it can be futile or pointless in others. ... When we hear of variety, we need not invariably reach for our aggregator".

Nevertheless, it is also important to recognize the need for overall well-being comparisons. In choosing one of several alternative public policies, it is often necessary to make overall comparisons of achievements in terms of all functionings taken together. Public policies often affect simultaneously a person's achievements in terms of several functionings. The establishment of a steel factory in an area may reduce hunger and malnourishment in the area by increasing employment opportunities, but this may be accompanied by new diseases in the area if pollution increases drastically because of the steel factory. In such cases, to decide whether to establish the steel factory, we need overall well-being comparisons between the situation before the establishment of the factory and the situation after its establishment. Similarly, in deciding whether to allocate more resources to individual j or individual k, when j has less of some functionings than k and k has less of some other functionings than j, the public authorities may like to know the overall ranking of the two individuals taking into account all functionings. While comparisons of achievements based on single functioning can be very useful for many purposes, the same is also true of comparisons of overall achievements in terms of all functionings taken together.

Nor is the need for aggregation confined to aggregation over different functionings as they are conceived in the literature. Some functionings are themselves multi-dimensional. Consider the functioning of being educated. There are different aspects of being educated. At a very basic level, one can, for example, distinguish between literacy and numeracy. At a somewhat higher level, is one better educated when one has a good training in information technology but very little familiarity with literature and history, or, is one better educated when one has somewhat less training in information technology but greater familiarity with literature and history? Similarly, consider another abstract functioning, namely, the functioning of being protected from the elements. Am I better protected from the elements when I live in a house that protects me reasonably from the heat and cold outside but suffers from continuous dampness rising from the ground or am I better protected in a house that does not suffer from dampness but leaves me exposed to excessive heat during the summer? On closer examination, many of the functionings seem to involve multi-dimensionality. The problems arising from such multidimensionality of a functioning are often described as difficulties of measuring the functioning. But the difficulties that arise in measuring an individual's achievement in terms of a functioning, such as being educated or being healthy are often due to the fact that the functioning under consideration is multidimensional and these different dimensions need to be aggregated to have even an ordinal measure of an individual's achievement in terms of the functioning. Conceptually, the issue of aggregating the different dimensions of a single functioning is not much different from the issue of aggregating over different functionings. From a practical point of view, however, when both these types of aggregation are taken into account, the need for aggregation would seem to be more extensive than it may appear at first sight.

IV. AGGREGATION OVER FUNCTIONINGS

As I have just noted, aggregation over different dimensions of a single functioning is, at least conceptually, analogous to the problem of aggregation over the functionings themselves. For the sake of simplicity, I shall, therefore, abstract from the former aggregation problem and concentrate only on the issue of aggregating over functionings so as to arrive at an overall ranking of achieved functioning bundles (I continue to ignore the freedom aspect of the functioning and capability approach). How do we compare an individual's overall achievements in terms of all functionings in two different situations, and, further, how do we compare one individual's overall achievement in terms of all functionings with the corresponding achievement of another person? It may be worth noting that some of the issues that arise here have their counterparts in other approaches to human well-being where well-being is thought of in a multi-dimensional fashion. Thus, John Stuart Mill (1863, Chapter II) faced somewhat similar problems when he admitted into the utilitarian framework the notion of different types of pleasure that may have different 'desirability' or 'value' in assessing the happiness of a person.[7]

If one is to aggregate a person's achievements of different functionings, then an appeal to values is inevitable; such values will be reflected in whatever aggregation rule we may decide to use. The problem of identifying these values is often posed as the problem of determining a fixed set of relative weights for the different functionings. The assumption of a fixed set of weights for different functionings, which can be used to evaluate all functioning bundles, is, however, problematic. It implies that the marginal rate of substitution between any two functionings remains the same irrespective of the point in the functioning space where one considers these marginal rates of substitution (in a two-dimensional functioning space, this gives us straight line and parallel iso-well-being curves). This is clearly implausible.

Which values should constitute the basis of overall well-being comparisons? Consider first the relatively simpler problem of comparing a given person's overall well-being

---

[7] Mill's (1863, Chapter II, paragraphs 4, 5, 6, 7, and 8) well-known discussion of whether, in assessing happiness, one should use the weights that the fool or the pig attaches to different types of pleasure or whether one should use the weights of Socrates, reflects his struggle with these problem.

levels corresponding two different functioning bundles. One can take two alternative routes here. First one can use the values of the person whose well-being is under consideration; Sen (1987, p. 30) calls this procedure 'self-evaluation'. Alternatively, one can use the norms widely prevailing in the society; Sen calls this 'standard evaluation'.

Self-evaluation, which embodies the principle of respecting an individual's values in the assessment of her own well-being in alternative situations, is immune to charges of paternalism and has its own attractions. One can, however, rise against self-evaluation objections, which are similar to certain objections often raised in the functioning approach against the interpretation of a person's well-being as the fulfillment of her desires. It has been argued that individuals often adapt their desires to their circumstances. Thus, women who have been repressed by law or social conventions for a long time may learn not to desire certain things so as to avoid predictable disappointments that come from having those desires. It is claimed that, in such cases it will be unreasonable to identify a person's well-being with the fulfillment of her self-censored desires. A similar problem can arise in the case of values too. Not only do people often adapt their desires to avoid disappointment, but they also often adapt their own values to conform to social conventions and customs. The values of a person may also be based on inadequate information and experience. Women who have been traditionally deprived of education and have never enjoyed the opportunity to participate in the life of the community may not attach much value to either education or participation in the public life of the community[8]. Self-evaluation may be questionable in such cases.

---

[8] John Stuart Mill (1863, Chapter II, paragraphs 6, 7 and 8) was concerned with the counterpart of this problem in the context of pleasure: he would not attach much weight to the opinion of a person regarding the relative

The overall evaluation of functioning bundles for a given person by the norms and values prevailing in the society can also be problematic in the absence of consensus in the society. In the absence of such consensus, one can, of course, choose to go by the values subscribed to by most people in the society, but doing so involves the obvious problem of ignoring the values of minorities in the evaluation of their own wellbeing. In fact, there seems to be some intuitive tension between the principle of standard evaluation interpreted as evaluation of a person's well-being by the values subscribed to by most people in the society and the spirit underlying the emphasis, in the literature on functionings and capability, on freedom as the opportunity to choose. A person's freedom, viewed as her opportunity to choose from among alternative functioning bundles, is intrinsically valuable presumably because it allows the individual to pursue her own objectives in life. The idea of such intrinsic value of freedom, however, does not fit very well in an evaluative exercise where a given individual's well-being levels corresponding to different functioning bundles are compared on the basis of the general norms prevailing in the society even when the values and norms of the individual himself differ significantly from the generally prevailing norms.

The case of interpersonal overall comparisons of functioning bundles is fraught with even more difficulties than the case of overall comparisons of functioning bundles for a fixed individual. The concept of self-evaluation is not meaningful when we want to compare individual j' well-being from functioning bundle x with individual k's well-being from functioning bundle y. It is possible that, in terms of j's values, j's well-being from x is higher than j's well-being from y, and, in terms of k's values, k's well-being from functioning bundle y is higher than k's well-being from functioning bundle x. In

---

desirability or value of two different types of pleasure if the person concerned had not experienced both the types of pleasure.

any case, there are difficulties even with the criterion that, for all individuals j and k and for all functioning bundles x and y, if, in terms of the values of j, x offers a higher level of well-being to j than y, and, in terms of the values of k, x offers a higher level of well-being to k than y, then j's well-being from x is higher than k's well-being from y. It is easy to see that, if there are at least three individuals and at least three functioning bundles a, b, and c, and if one uses the criterion just mentioned, then, depending on the values of the three individuals, one may end up by saying that 1's well-being from x is higher than 2's well-being from y, 2's well-being from y is higher than 3's well-being from z, and 3's well-being from z is higher than 1's well-being from x. One possibility is to appeal to the norms and values generally prevailing in the society for the purpose of comparing j's well-being from functioning bundle x with k's well-being from functioning bundle y, but, of course, in that case, we may ignore completely the values of both j and k if j and k happen to have values different from the values shared by most people in the society.

Sen (1987, pp. 29-30) suggests a highly plausible 'dominance criterion' for interpersonal overall comparisons of achievements in terms of functionings. He suggests that, if x is a bigger functioning bundle than y in the sense that x has at least as much of every functioning and strictly more of some functionings as compared to y, then the well-being of any person who has x is higher than the well-being of any person who has y. While Sen's dominance criterion seems to be a very desirable and weak restriction on interpersonal overall well-being comparisons, Pattanaik and Xu (2007) show that, in the presence of a mild continuity property, Sen's dominance criterion runs into a conflict with another very desirable criterion, which Pattanaik and Xu (2007) call 'minimal relativism'.[9] Minimal relativism embodies the idea that people's personal values and/ or their social and cultural backgrounds should play some role somewhere in person-specific overall comparisons of functioning bundles. More precisely, minimal relativism requires that there should be at least two individuals, j and k and at least two functioning bundles x and y such that j's well-being corresponding to x is judged to be higher than j's well-being corresponding to y and k's well-being corresponding to y is judged to be higher than k's well-being corresponding to x. In some ways, this tension between two highly appealing properties is indicative of the pitfalls that beset overall well-being comparisons in the functioning approach.

V. CONCLUDING REMARKS

The functioning and capability approach to human well-being is one of the most interesting and promising recent developments in welfare economics. There are, however, many analytical issues in this approach that need much further exploration. In this note, I have sought to highlight one of these issues, namely the problem of aggregation over functionings and also over different dimensions of some complex multi-dimensional functionings. While such aggregation may not be essential for all purposes, in the absence of such aggregation the functioning and capability approach is likely to be of limited use in many important contexts.

REFERENCES

Dutta, I., Pattanaik, P. K. and Russell, R. R. (2003): On Measuring Changes in Welfare when Changes in Consumption Bundles are Small, *Economics Bulletin*, 4 (27): 1-9.

---

[9] See also Pattanaik and Xu (2008) for a generalization of this result.

Mill, J.S. (1863): *Utilitarianism*; reprinted in Mary Warnock (ed.), *'Utilitarianism'*, *'On Liberty'*, *'Essays on Bentham'* together with selected writings of Jeremy Bentham and John Austin (New York: Meridian, an imprint of New American Library, a division of Penguin Books USA Inc, 1962).

Nussbaum, M. (1988): Nature, Function and Capability: Aristotle on Political Distribution", *Oxford Studies in Ancient Philosophy*, Supplementary volume I, 145-184.

Nussbaum, M. (2000): *Women and Human Development*, Cambridge University Press, Cambridge.

Pattanaik, P. K. (2006): On Comparing Functioning Bundles and Capability sets, In J. K. Boyce, S. Cullenberg, P. K. Pattanaik, and R. Pollin (eds.), *Human Development in the Era of Globalization: Essays in Honor of Keith B. Griffin*. Edward Elgar, Cheltenham.

Pattanaik, P. K. and Xu, Yongsheng (2007): Minimal Relativism, Dominance, and Standard of Living Comparisons Based on Functionings, *Oxford Economic Papers*, 59 (2): 354-374.

Pattanaik, P. K. and Xu, Yongsheng (2007): Conceptions of Rights and Freedom in Welfare Economics: A Re-examination, forthcoming in P. Dumouchel and R. Gotoh (eds.), *Against Injustice: Ethics, Economics and the Law*, to be published by Cambridge University Press, Cambridge.

Pattanaik, P. K. and Xu, Yongsheng (2008): *The Dominance Principle in Multi-Attribute Decision-Making*, mimeograph.

Sen, A. (1985): *Commodities and Capabilities*, North-Holland, Amsterdam.

Sen, A. (1987): *The Standard of Living*, Cambridge University Press, Cambridge.

3

On Measuring Group Differential: Some Further Results[1]

Hippu Salk Kristle Nathan[2]
Srijit Mishra[3]

I. INTRODUCTION

Group differential is an important class of measures to know the gap with regard to failure (or attainment) indicators between two groups.[4] Conventionally, this has been expressed by simple difference or simple ratio. To be the basis for comparison, these measures should have certain properties In line with the transfer-sensitivity property of poverty indices

---

[1] The second author's discussions with student in the class on Contemporary Issues in Human Development and Policy (January-May 2008) at the Indira Gandhi Institute of Development Research (IGIDR), Mumbai were helpful.
[2] Indira Gandhi Institute of Development Research (IGIDR), Mumbai, India, Email: hnathan@igidr.ac.in
[3] Indira Gandhi Institute of Development Research (IGIDR), Mumbai, India, Email: srijit@igidr.ac.in
[4] There are genuine failure indicators like Infant Mortality Rate (IMR), Maternal Mortality Rate (MMR), and Death Rate. There are genuine attainment indicators like literacy rate and income. An attainment indicator can be converted as failure by taking its inverse, like when literacy rate is replaced with illiteracy rate, or in case of income, a maximum may be posited and the actual observations subtracted from this to obtain an indicator of failure. However, axioms of level sensitivity should be different for attainment indicators. This forms a larger exercise which is being currently carried out by the authors.

(Kakwani, 1993; and Sen, 1976), Mishra and Subramanian (2006) have introduced two axioms on level sensitivity, difference-based level sensitivity (DBLS) and ratio-based level sensitivity (RBLS). These axioms indicate that for a failure (attainment) indicator a given hiatus between two groups should acquire a greater salience the lower (higher) the level at which the hiatus arises. It subscribes to a value judgment that a decrease in failure should be accompanied by a decrease in gap (difference or ratio between sub-groups). In other words, the same gap at lower levels of failure is to be considered worse off. They discuss three existing and a fourth new measure of group differential, which were later refined by Mishra (2008), who also added the axiom of normalization. At a basic level, it means that the group differential measure lies between zero and unity. However, at a fundamental level it should also mean that zero indicates no differential between the two sub-groups whereas unity indicates maximum differential between the two sub-groups. The suggested new measure in the above-mentioned two papers gave a positive non-zero value when there were no differences between sub-groups – a failure of the normalization axiom at a fundamental level. Further, the comparison between two situations under this measure also happened to be dependent on the choice of some parameters. This paper suggests a measure that tries to address these. Empirical illustration has been provided with the same set of infant mortality rate data, as has been used by Mishra (2008).

II. AXIOMATIC CHARACTERIZATION OF GROUP DIFFERENTIAL

Consider a socio economic failure indicator, $I_{js}\varepsilon[0,1]$; 0=no failure and 1=complete failure for j^{th} group ($j=a,b$), under situation s ($s=A,B$). Without loss of generality, given a situation s let group b be considered to be at lower failure level than a, $I_{as}>I_{bs}$ and given a group j situation A is at least as good as B so that $I_{jA}\leq I_{jB}$. Following are a number of intuitive properties that a measure of group differential, d or $d(I_{as},I_{bs})$ should satisfy.

Normalization (Axiom N): At a basic level, the measure of group differential should lie between zero and unity, $d\varepsilon[0,1]$. At a fundamental level the measure should have a minimum and a maximum such that 0=no group-differential and 1=highest group-differential.

Strong Monotonicity (Axiom M): The measure of group differential should be such that it is higher (lower) if one of the groups remaining constant at a particular level of failure; the other changes so that the absolute gap increases (decreases). Mathematically, $d(I_{aA},I_{bA})>d(I_{aB},I_{bB})$ when $I_{aA}=I_{aB}$ and $I_{bA}<I_{bB}$. Weak monotonicity means, $d(I_{aA},I_{bA})\geq d(I_{aB},I_{bB})$ when $I_{aA}=I_{aB}$ and $I_{bA}<I_{bB}$. Two corollaries of strong monotonicity are axioms of minimality and maximality.

Minimality (Axiom M_{min}): The measure of group differential should be higher than its minimum value if there is some group differential. Mathematically, $d>0$ if $(I_{as}-I_{bs})>0$.

Maximality (Axiom M_{max}): The measure of group differential should be lower than its maximum value if the group-differential is less than the highest. Mathematically, $d<1$ if $(I_{as}-I_{bs})<1$.

Difference based level sensitivity (DBLS) (Axiom D): The measure of group differential should be such that it is more pronounced if the difference level persists at a lower level of failure. Mathematically, if $I_{aA}-I_{bA}\geq I_{aB}-I_{bB}=h$; $h>0$, then the DBLS axiom requires that $d(I_{aA},I_{bA})>d(I_{aB},I_{bB})$.

Ratio based level sensitivity (RBLS) (Axiom R): The measure of group differential should be such that it is more pronounced if the ratio level persists at a lower level of failure. Mathematically, if $I_{aA}/I_{bA}\geq I_{aB}/I_{bB}=k$; $k>0$, then the RBLS axiom requires that $d(I_{aA},I_{bA})>d(I_{aB},I_{bB})$. RBLS is a stricter condition than DBLS, if $I_{aA}/I_{bA}=I_{aB}/I_{bB}$ then $I_{aA}-I_{bA}<I_{aB}-I_{bB}$.

III. MEASURES OF GROUP DIFFERENTIAL

Some of the differential measures with regard to a failure indicator discussed in literature are:

$$d_1 = I_a - I_b \tag{1}$$

$$d_2 = I_a^{\delta} - I_b^{\delta}; \; 0 < \delta < 1 \tag{2}$$

$$d_3 = 1 - I_b / I_a \tag{3}$$

$$d_4 = 1 - I_b^{\alpha+\beta} / I_a^{\alpha}; \; \alpha > 0, \beta \geq 0 \tag{4}$$

Mishra (2008) indicates that d_1 satisfies DBLS in a weak sense, d_2 satisfies DBLS strongly, d_3 satisfies RBLS in weak sense, and d_4 satisfies RBLS strongly. Keeping in mind that RBLS is a stricter condition for failure indicators, d_1 and d_2 would not be considered as serious contenders of a differential measure. The measure of d_3 satisfies RBLS weakly and also fails the strong monotonicity axiom at $I_b = 0$. We have d_4 that satisfies RBLS strongly but fails normalization at a fundamental level when there is no differential between sub-groups, $0 < I_a = I_b < 1$. Further, in d_4 the comparison between two situations is dependent on the subjective choice of α and β parameters and as in the previous case it also fails the strong monotonicity test. It is a measure that takes us out of the non-frying pan to the fire. The problems are addressed by a proposed alternative,

$$d_5 = (1 - I_b / I_a) * (1 - I_b) \tag{5}$$

The measure of d_5 satisfies the level sensitivities and normalization axioms but still fails the strong monotonicity, particularly the maximality version when $I_b = 0$. In fact, it is quite intuitive to show that at $I_b = 0$ the RBLS and maximality axiom cannot be satisfied together. RBLS indicates that for the same ratio (in this case zero) as level decreases (in this case I_a) then d should increase. Whereas maximality indicates that if value for one sub-group is constant (in this case $I_b = 0$) then a decrease in the value of the other sub-group, I_a, should lead to a decrease in d. Table 1 indicates the applicability of axioms to various differential measures.

TABLE 1
APPLICABILITY OF AXIOMS TO VARIOUS DIFFERENTIAL MEASURES

Measure	Axioms					
	N	M	M_{min}	M_{max}	D	R
$d_1 = I_a - I_b$	Yes	Yes	Yes	Yes	Yes (weakly)	No
$d_2 = I_a^\delta - I_b^\delta$	Yes	Yes	Yes	Yes	Yes	No
$d_3 = 1 - I_b/I_a$	Yes	Yes (weakly)#	Yes	Yes (weakly)#	Yes	Yes (weakly)
$d_4 = 1 - I_b^{\alpha+\beta}/I_a^\alpha$	Yes (Basic)$	Yes (weakly)#	Yes	Yes (weakly)#	Yes	Yes
$d_5 = (1 - I_b/I_a)*(1 - I_b)$	Yes	Yes (weakly)#	Yes	Yes (weakly)#	Yes	Yes

Note: # fails at $I_b = 0$; $ satisfies normalization at a basic level, $d_4 \varepsilon [0,1]$, but fails it at a fundamental level because at no differential, $0 < I_a = I_b < 1$, $d_4 > 0$. Further note that comparison between two situations in d_4 would be dependent on α and β parameters.

TABLE 2
COMPARING VARIOUS GROUP DIFFERENTIAL MEASURES USING INFANT MORTALITY RATE DATA FROM SELECTED INDIAN STATES

Cases	Situations	I_a	I_b	d_1	d_2	d_3	d_4	d_5
Case 1	Karnataka, 2003	0.052	0.051	0.0010	0.0022	0.0192	0.0221	0.0183
I_{aA}-I_{bA}=I_{aB}-I_{bB}	Orissa, 2003	0.083	0.082	0.0010	0.0017	0.0120	0.0145	0.0111
Case 2	Assam, 2003	0.070	0.035	0.0350	0.0775	0.5000	0.5017	0.4825
I_{bA}/I_{aA}=I_{bB}/I_{aB}	Assam, 1990	0.078	0.039	0.0390	0.0818	0.5000	0.5016	0.4805
Case 3	Kerala, Rural 2003	0.012	0.012	0	0	0	0.0044	0
I_{aA}=I_{bA} & I_{aB}=I_{bB}	West Bengal, Rural 2003	0.048	0.048	0	0	0	0.0030	0

Notes: I_a and I_b denote infant mortality converted to the 0-1 range for sub-groups a and b respectively; d_1, d_2, d_3, d_4 and d_5 denote the five differential measures discussed in the text; d_2 has been computed for $\delta=0.5$; d_4 has been computed for $\alpha=1$ and $\beta=0.001$. In all cases, situations A and B are indicated in the first and second rows respectively. Sub-groups a and b refer to female and male respectively in cases 1 and 3, and rural and urban respectively in case 2.

Sources: *Sample Registration System Statistical Report 2003*, Report No. 2 of 2005, Registrar General, India, New Delhi. *Vital Statistics of India 1990 Based on the Civil Registration System*, Office of the Registrar General, India, Ministry of Home Affairs, New Delhi.

IV. EMPIRICAL ILLUSTRATION

We use infant mortality rate (IMR) data of selected Indian states, the same as in Misrha (2007), for empirical illustration. Case 1 is equal difference case, $I_{aA}-I_{bA}=I_{aB}-I_{bB}$, where d_1 satisfies DBLS weakly, whereas other measures (d_2, d_3, d_4, and d_5) satisfy it strongly. Case 2 is equal ratio case, $I_{bA}/I_{aA}=I_{bB}/I_{aB}$, where d_1 and d_2 do not satisfy RBLS, whereas d_3 satisfies it weakly and d_4 and d_5 satisfy it strongly. Case 3 illustrates no group differentiation, $I_{aA}=I_{bA}$ & $I_{aB}=I_{bB}$, where d_4 gives a non-zero positive value indicating a failure of the normalization axiom at a fundamental level whereas other measures (d_1, d_2, d_3, and d_5) satisfy it.

V. CONCLUDING REMARKS

The paper discusses about measures of group differentials for failure indicators. It identifies the limitations of the measures in the literature and proposes an alternative which satisfies the axioms of level sensitivity and normalization. It also does away with the subjectivity associated in the choice of parameters in some existing measures. An empirical illustration using data for infant mortality rate from selected Indian states shows the advantages of the proposed alternative. For future work, providing a differential measure for attainment indicators would be useful. These measures can be used to evaluate success in some of the Millennium Development Goals.

REFERENCES

Kakwani, N. (1993): Performance in Living Standards: an International Comparison, *Journal of Development Economics*, 41 (2): 307-336.

Mishra, Srijit (2008): On Measuring Group-Differentials Displayed by Socio-economic Indicators: an Extension, *Applied Economics Letters*, 15(12): 935-938, http://www.informaworld.com/10.1080/13504850600972238, (accessed 28 September 2007). IGIDR working paper version of this paper is available at http://www.igidr.ac.in/pdf/publication/WP-2006-005.pdf.

Mishra, U. S. and Subramanian, S. (2006): On Measuring Group-Differentials Displayed by Socio-economic Indicators, *Applied Economics Letters*, 13 (8): 519-521.

Sen, Amartya (1976): Poverty: an Ordinal Approach to Measurement, *Econometrica*, 44 (2): 219-231.

4

Status and Trend of Human Development in North East Region of India

Purusottam Nayak[1]

I. INTRODUCTION

The development and growth of a nation depends upon proper utilization of its human resources. To utilize these resources, there is a need to convert human beings into human resources. Since the basic objective of development of a nation is to improve the welfare of the people, every nation strives hard not only to increase her wealth and productive resources but also to ensure better standard of living of her citizens by providing them with adequate food, clothing, house, medical facilities, education, et cetera. However, technical considerations of the means to achieve human development and the use of statistical aggregates to measure national income and its growth have at times obscured the fact that the primary objective of development is to benefit people. National income figures, though useful for many purposes, neither reveal its composition nor its real beneficiaries. Of course, people want higher incomes as one of their options; it is neither the sum total of human life nor the end in itself. Thus expansion of output and wealth is only a means; end of

---

[1] Department of Economics, School of Economics Management and Information Sciences, North-Eastern Hill University, Shillong, Meghalaya, India, E-mail: nehu_pnayak@yahoo.co.in

development is the welfare of human beings. To measure the welfare of the people UNDP (1990), in its first Human Development Report (HDR), introduced the concept of human development and its measurement. It was introduced as a composite measure of economic progress and human welfare and intended to be a better substitute to Per Capita Income (measure) that could neither capture nor exhibit exact level of development of human beings nor that of nations. The measure since then has been popularly known as human development index.

The primary purpose of the HDR has been to assess the state of human development across the globe and provide a critical analysis of a specific theme each year. It combines thematic policy analysis with detailed country data that focus on human well-being, not just economic trends (Griffin, 2002). Since the publication of the first report, four composite indices for human development have been developed — the Human Development Index (HDI), the Gender-related Development Index (GDI), the Gender Empowerment Measure (GEM), and the Human Poverty Index (HPI). Each report also focuses on a highly topical theme in the current development debate, providing path-breaking analysis and policy recommendations. The HDI aims to capture the attention of policy makers, media and NGOs and to draw their attention away from the more usual economic statistics to focus instead on human outcomes, not economic data, asking why what is achieved in one country is far from the reach of another. Nevertheless, the HDI is not enough to measure a country's level of development. The concept of human development is much broader than can be captured in the HDI, or any other of the indices (GDI, GEM and HPI). The HDI, for example, does not reflect political participation or gender inequalities.

Development experience in the past underlined the need for paying a close attention to the link between economic growth and human development because many fast growing and developing countries having high Gross National Product

(GNP) growth rates failed to reduce the socio-economic deprivation of substantial sections of their population. At the same time some low-income countries achieved high levels of human development by skillfully using the available means to expand basic human capabilities. Countries like Viet Nam, Georgia, Indonesia and Jamaica having relatively very low per capita Gross Domestic Product (GDP) [Purchasing Power Parity (PPP) US $ 3071, 3365, 3843 and 4291 respectively] could achieve medium levels of human development (0.733, 0.754, 0.728 and 0.736 respectively) whereas Botswana and South Africa in spite of having very high per Capita GDP (PPP US $ 12,387 and 11,110) achieved relatively lower level of human development (0.654 and 0.674) (see Table 1). Therefore, there was a need for shifting our emphasis from per capita GDP to HDI.

TABLE 1
PER CAPITA GDP AND HUMAN DEVELOMENT IN INDIA AND ABROAD

Country	Per Capita GDP (PPP US $)	HDI Value	HDI Rank
Iceland	36,510	0.968	1
Norway	41,420	0.968	2
Mauritius	12,715	0.804	65
Georgia	3365	0.754	96
Sri Lanka	4595	0.743	99
Maldives	5261	0.741	100
Jamaica	4291	0.736	101
Indonesia	3843	0.728	107
South Africa*	11,110	0.674	121
INDIA	3452	0.619	128

Source: UNDP (2007)

In the last two decades, the governments of various nations for planning purposes have used HDI very widely. Various scholars and organizations have also undertaken a number of research studies using the index to focus the magnitude of human development of various sections of society in different countries. This has helped a lot in formulating plans for improving the life of the neglected sections of the societies in different countries. Keeping all these points in view the present study is undertaken on the status and progress of human development in a backward region like North-East India comprising eight States, which is predominantly a region of tribal people.

II. MEASUREMENT OF HUMAN DEVELOPMENT

Though HDI was proposed by UNDP in 1990, many criticisms were raised against its construction and robustness in the subsequent periods. As a result some improvements were brought out in its construction in the subsequent reports of UNDP in 1991, 1994 and 1999. It is now in its present form as a composite index of three basic components of human development, viz., longevity, knowledge and standard of living. Longevity is measured by life expectancy. Knowledge is measured by a combination of adult literacy having one-third weight and mean years of schooling with two-third weight. Standard of living is measured by purchasing power, based on real GDP per capita adjusted for the local cost of living (PPP US $). The HDI sets a minimum and a maximum for each dimension and then shows where each country stands in relation to these scales. It is expressed in terms of a numerical value between 0 and 1. The scores for the three dimensions are then averaged in an overall index. The latest formula used for the first two individual indicators {Life Expectancy Index (LEI) and Education Index (EI)} is as follows:

$$\text{LEI or EI} = \frac{X_i - Min(X_i)}{Max(X_i) - Min(X_i)}$$

The income indicator (GDP Index) is calculated using the following formula:

$$GDPI = \frac{Log(X_i) - Log\{Min(X_i)\}}{Log\{Max(X_i)\} - Log\{Min(X_i)\}}$$

Finally, the HDI is calculated by taking the average of these three indices (LEI, EI and GDPI). For the construction of the dimension indices maximum and minimum values have been fixed as per UNDP (2003) as given below:

SCALING NORMS OF HDI
(Used by UNDP)

Indicators	Maximum Value [Max(X_i)]	Minimum Value [Min(X_i)]
Life Expectancy at Birth (Years)	85	25
Adult Literacy Rate (in percentage)	100	0
Combined Gross Enrolment Ratio (in percentage)	100	0
GDP Per Capita (PPP US $)	40,000	100

In this regard, GoI (2002a) brought out some changes in the formula of HDI. A composite health index consisting of life expectancy with a weight of 65 per cent and infant mortality rate with a weight of 35 per cent was proposed. Similarly, in case of composite index on educational attainment, while literacy rate was given a weight of 35 per cent, the indicator capturing intensity of formal education (based on current enrolment rates in successive classes at school level) was assigned 65 per cent weight. In case of indicator on economic attainment namely, inequality adjusted per capita consumption expenditure, an adjustment for inflation over the period was made to make it amenable to inter-temporal and inter-spatial comparisons. The maximum and minimum values for each dimension as used in GoI (2002a) are as follows:

SCALING NORMS OF HDI
(Used by Planning Commission of India)

Indicators	Maximum Value [Max (X_i)]	Minimum Value [Min (X_i)]
Life Expectancy at Age 1 (years)	80	50
Infant Mortality Rate (per thousand)	-	20
Literacy Rate (for 7 +Years)	100	0
Adjusted Intensity of Formal Education	7	0
Per Capita monthly Consumption Expenditure in Rupees (at 1983 prices)	325	65

III. OVERVIEW OF LITERATURE

There are two types of literatures available on human development - one on the methodological aspects and the other on empirical evidence.

As far as methodological aspect is concerned numerous efforts have been made to remedy the defects of the traditional measure of economic development and to suggest composite indicators that could serve as either complements or alternatives to this [Adelman and Morris (1973); Morris, (1979)].

Since the publication of first HDR the trend has been towards improvement of the method of measurement of human development and so far there have been three successive attempts in this regard in 1991, 1994 and 1999 by UNDP.

Few important works on human development which could not be reviewed for want of its access to individual papers are Desai, (1991); Jain, (1991); Kelley, (1991); McGillivray, (1991); Tilak, (1991); Haq, (1995); Anand and Sen (1995); Pal and Kant (1993); Srinivasan, (1994); Streeten, (1994); Baker, (1997); Hicks, (1997); Sagar and Najam (1998); Bardhan and Klasen (1999); Nagar and Basu (2000); Chakravarty, (2000); Sen, (2000); Alkire, (2002); Chaubey, (2002); Gasper, (2002); Bose, (2004). The important empirical works in the literature on human development in the context of India that are readily available are reviewed in the following paragraphs.

Dalal (1991) pointed out that Indian development goals have been in tune with the Human Development Report. There has however been a significant failure in the implementation of well-constructed policies as a result of lack of political will and administrative inefficiency. Kumar (1991) ranked 17 Indian major States by constructing the HDI using UNDP's methodology. He compared the rankings of these states with the rankings of the countries appeared in the report of UNDP. The absence of disaggregated data on health and life expectancy for the union territories and the North Eastern States of India prevented him in the computation of the HDI for these regions. The subsequent study (Kumar, 1996) revealed that States like Haryana and Punjab despite being relatively high-income States were facing the problem of serious gender inequality in basic capabilities. There were 13 countries in the world that had a lower value of GDI than that of the States like Bihar and Uttar Pradesh, which pointed to the seriousness of the problem of human development at the global level.

Vyasalu and Vani (1997) conducted a study of human development in Karnataka using HDI. While making concluding remarks they suggested that sustained political support to an across-the-board improvement in each district was essential if the HDI was to show improvement. Zaidi and Salam (1998) in their study correlated various indices denoting life expectancy, educational attainment and real GDP per capita to other parameters of the economies of 15 major States of India for finding out the causes of varying values of these indicators in different States. The study revealed that public expenditure had a more close association with educational attainment than it had with life expectancy as the latter is influenced by multiplicity of factors like heredity, race, climatic and environmental factors apart from public expenditures on health, nutrition and sanitation.

Viswanathan (1999) in her study, for the State of Madhya Pradesh, highlighted the fact that higher incomes do not always yield higher human development, and that higher human development does not always mean equal benefit to men and women. The study of NCAER (1999) conducted in 1994 revealed that although relative differentials existed, absolute deprivation was high in most parts of rural India. Among the social groups, the poor spent disproportionately large amounts on health and education.

NIRD (1999) conducted a study for the major states of India for the years 1961, 1971, 1981 and 1987-88. The study revealed that human development scores had gone up in all the states over time. The poverty-stricken States like Bihar and U.P. were at the lower rung and Gujarat made considerable progress on HDI. The ranking of States on HDI changed significantly during the last three decades. Gender discrimination was conspicuous in 14 States except Kerala and Karnataka. Rao (2000) made an attempt to bring out the insights provided by the human development report for the State of Karnataka. His study revealed that the State was lagging behind even in achieving what is regarded as minimum essential norms of human development.

Mahanty (2000) conducted a study with an alternative set of indicators for Andhra Pradesh for the years 1982-83, 1987-88 and 1992-93 using five different methods of index. He found that while the pattern of human development was relatively stagnant, some districts were lagging behind. Government of India (GoI, 2002a) compiled the HDI, GDI, and HPI for the entire country. However, the data for North Eastern States were prepared by taking the data of Assam (one of the big State in the region) as a representative one.

For the first time HDR 2003 devoted an entire chapter on human development to the North East India that busted some popular myths, particularly on literacy rates and the status of women. The report identified several factors that had contributed to the depressing and dismal situation in the region (UNDP, 2003). Vijaybhaskar et al. (2004) in their study while highlighting the key findings of the HDR of the state of Tamil Nadu mentioned that though the state had registered considerable progress in literacy and reduction of poverty it had failed miserably in arresting inter-district and intra-regional differences across gender and caste in human development achievements.

Fukuda-Parr (2007) in his study while mentioning the idea of development as expansion of capabilities and freedoms which is widely recognized as 'breakthrough' in the field of development economics stated that the capability perspective emphasizes a diverse set of means other than income in removing capability deprivation or improving human well-being. He further stated that the capability approach not only accords importance to economic growth and incomes for removing poverty, but also analyzes how other factors, including access to economic facilities and social opportunities such as employment, education and health, and the action of the people themselves, can affect poverty. He mentioned that the human development approach is based on the concept of development as capability expansion. While reviewing the World Bank's analysis of poverty he analyzed the extent to which the World Bank publications reflect the human development approach in the way that poverty is defined, its causes analyzed, and the process of poverty reduction understood. He explored how concepts of capability and human development have influenced global debates about poverty. He showed in his paper that there has been a substantial shift to using capability perspective though the income perspective continues to dominate.

Kannan and Pillai (2007) in their paper sought to provide a comprehensive meaning to the notion of social security from the point of view of human development and human rights, which are complementary perspectives. To them the core concerns of social security are perceived in terms of deficiency or capability deprivation and adversity of shocks arising out of contingencies and eventualities. The human development perspective emphasizes the need to address poverty manifested in various forms of deprivations rather than a single measure of income or consumption deficiency. They concluded by saying that human development paradigm stands on the premise that everyone has a right to development, where development is seen as removal of all 'un-freedoms' from all possible vulnerabilities, and the rights involve non-negotiable correlative obligations on the part of the State as the highest epitome of collectivity.

Malhotra (2007) in his paper analyzed the usefulness of UNDP's human development index for measuring development at the country level. By considering the example of India's National Human Development Report 2002, he showed how innovations in concepts and methodology could make the globally used UNDP approach more useful in measuring human attainments and provided a more effective tool in guiding policy and strategic framework for implementing a human development approach at the country level. He further stated that there is always a need to bring about a certain consensus on the use of the human development approach in India in general, and the framework for identifying appropriate indicators and building composite human development indices at the state level, in particular.

Nayak and Thomas (2007) conducted an in-depth study on human development by constructing HDI for all the seven districts of the state of Meghalaya. They analyzed the status and trend of human development and deprivation in

Meghalaya vis-à-vis other leading States in the country using both primary and secondary data. The study revealed a low level of human development in the state accompanied with considerable degree of unevenness between rural and urban areas, across different districts and also between genders in the State.

Many scholars in India and abroad have studied the link between human development and economic growth. Anand and Ravallion (1993) viewed development indicators or social outcomes as aggregate of individual capabilities and found that GNP and life expectancy are significantly and positively related. Aturpane, Glewwe and Isenman (1994) in their empirical work observed that economic growth is negatively related to infant mortality rate. Similarly taking three income decomposed health aggregates - life expectancy, infant mortality and prenatal mortality, Bidani and Ravallion (1995) found that overall per capita health spending has a positive effect on life expectancy at birth and infant mortality rate of the poor people. Geetarani (1995) found that economic progress in India is one of the important factors that determine the level of human development. Zaidi and Salam (1998) reported a high positive correlation between NSDP per capita and enrolment in higher education. The empirical findings of Chakraborty (1997) based on non-parametric approach revealed that dependency of life expectancy on income is tethered to time and space; income explains life expectancy only below a certain range and that range is moving up over time. Some studies confirmed the positive relationship between human development and economic growth using time-series data for developing nations. Ranis, Stewart and Ramirez (2000), in their study outlined two chains: from economic growth to human development and from human development to economic growth. Boozer, Ranis, Stewart and Suri (2003) while exploring the dual relationship between economic growth and human development urged that economic growth is just a means of human development while human development reinforces economic growth. Strong complementarities between investments in human development and attained sustained economic growth were emerged in the study of Muysken, Yetkiner and Ziesemer (2003). In the endogenous growth model, Schaper (2003) found that investment in education is able to enhance economic growth and income equality depending upon the way of financing it. Dholakia (2003) in his study examined the trends in regional disparity in India's economic and human development over the past two decades. Findings suggested a two-way causality between the two. The structure of the relationship varied over time when human development indicators were the cause and the PCI was the effect, but in the reverse causality case the structure of the equations was found to be stable over time. Estimation revealed that HDI positively influenced PCI with a lag of about eight years whereas PCI affected the HDI within two years. World Bank (2004) by using mortality statistics of India documented that both household living standards and national income levels have a positive effect on the reduction of infant mortality rate (under age 1). Drawing attention on a series of advanced studies in human capital theory, basic needs as well as welfare approach, Ranis and Stewart (2005) viewed that in most cases economic growth and human development run parallel.

The review of literature on human development reveals that very few studies have been undertaken to focus on the status and trend of human development of the north eastern region using human development index. Therefore, the present paper in this regard is a humble attempt with the main objectives of testing the following hypotheses:

1. Human development and its growth in North East India are too low as compared to many countries of the world.
2. There exists yawning gap between females and males; the rural-urban gap and State-wise variation is significant over time in the region.

III. GENERAL SCENARIO IN NORTH EASTERN REGION

North Eastern Region of India having a population of 39.04 million is basically a region consisting of eight States, namely Arunachal Pradesh, Assam, Manipur, Meghalaya, Mizoram, Nagaland, Sikkim and Tripura. Among these eight States four States are having tribal population in majority, specifically Mizoram (94.5 percent), Nagaland (89.1 percent), Meghalaya (85.9 percent) and Arunachal Pradesh (64.2 percent) (Table 2). The region had a literacy rate of 65.8 percent as against the all India average of 65.2 percent. However, literacy rate varied from State to State in the region from a lowest figure of 54.7 percent (Arunachal Pradesh) to the highest figure of 88.5 percent (Mizoram). Per capita net State Domestic Product in the States varied from lowest figure of INR 1675 in Assam to highest figure of INR 3571 in Arunachal Pradesh and average of INR 2223 in the region in the year 1997-98 at 1980-81 prices. Per Capita Monthly Consumption Expenditure (PCMCE) was as low as INR 147.52 in 2000 at 1983 prices. Assam had the lowest PCMCE of INR 99.81 as against highest PCMCE of INR 228.04 in Nagaland. The below poverty line (BPL) people in this region was 34.7 per cent in 2000 as against a national average of 26.1 per cent. Highest percentage of BPL people was estimated in Sikkim (36.6 percent) and lowest percentage in Mizoram (19.5 percent).

IV. HUMAN DEVELOPMENT IN INDIA AND NORTH EASTERN REGION

According to the 18th Human Development Report (UNDP, 2007), which includes data for 175 United Nations (UN) member countries, India has a long way to go achieve a decent level of human development. When Norway has a HDI values of 0.968, 27 other countries in the world are having HDI values above 0.9 and 70 countries are placed in 'high human development' $(HDI > 0.8)$, the corresponding figure for India is as low as 0.619 (Table 1). Though India is a fast growing developing nation she is placed in the 128th rank at the global level. Even small neighboring countries in Asia like Mauritius (0.804), Sri Lanka (0.743), Maldives (0.741) and Indonesia (0.728) have surpassed India. The country has been witnessing a very poor growth in human development. The HDI value in the country during 1975 is from 0.411 to increase to only 0.476 in 1985 and further to 0.619 in 2005. Thus, the country has witnessed an annual growth of merely 1.7 per cent on an average in a period of three decades[2].

The findings of the Planning Commission, Government of India on the magnitude and growth of human development has been quite different from that of the UNDP probably because of differences in their methodology of estimation. HDI value, which was estimated as 0.302 in 1981, improved to 0.381 in 1991 and subsequently to 0.472 in 2001 (GoI, 2002a). When UNDP estimates showed a relatively high human development (0.619) with low annual growth (1.7 per cent), estimates of Planning Commission showed a low human development (0.472) with a high annual growth (2.3 per cent) over time (GoI, 2002a).

Rural-urban disparity was quite low in 1981 (0.179) and 1991 (0.171), which instead of improving got deteriorated and it stood at 0.204 in 2000 (Table 3, 4 and 5). Gender disparity continued to be at a staggering rate. When male literacy rate was 75.6 per cent female literacy was 54.0 percent in 2001. Besides, there have been a wide spread disparity across the States in the country. The HDI varied between highest values of 0.638 in case of Kerala to the lowest value of 0.365 in Bihar.

---

[2] The figure was estimated by the author using data from *Human Development Report 2007-08*, UNDP (p.236) (HDI in 1975 and 2005 are 0.411 and 0.619).

TABLE 2
GENERAL INFORMATION ON NORTH EAST INDIA

State/Country	Total Population (in million)	Percentage of ST Population	Literacy Rate (Percentage)	Per Capita NSDP	PCMCE	Percentage of BPL
Arunachal Pradesh	1.09	64.2	54.74	3571	129.38	33.47
Assam	26.64	12.4	64.28	1675	99.81	36.09
Manipur	2.39	34.2	68.87	1948	130.88	28.54
Meghalaya	2.31	85.9	63.31	1804	145.65	33.87
Mizoram	0.89	94.5	88.49	NA	202.99	19.47
Nagaland	1.99	89.1	67.11	NA	228.04	32.67
Sikkim	0.54	20.6	69.68	NA	117.52	36.55
Tripura	3.19	31.1	73.66	2117	125.92	34.44
N.E Region	39.04	26.9	65.77	2223	147.52	34.69
INDIA	1027.02	-	65.20	2840	111.28	26.10

Note: 1. Population and literacy figures refer to the year 2001.
2. Per Capita NSDP and Per Capita MCE refer to the years 1997-98 and 1999-2000 respectively.
3. Percentage of people below poverty line refers to the year 1999-2000.

Source: GoI (2002b)

TABLE 3
HUMAN DEVELOPMENT IN NORTH EAST INDIA IN 1981

State/Country	Rural	Urban	Combined	Disparity
Arunachal Pradesh	0.228	0.419	0.242	0.191
Assam	0.261	0.380	0.272	0.119
Manipur	0.440	0.553	0.461	0.113
Meghalaya	0.293	0.442	0.317	0.149
Mizoram	0.381	0.558	0.411	0.177
Nagaland	0.295	0.519	0.328	0.224
Sikkim	0.302	0.515	0.342	0.213
Tripura	0.264	0.498	0.287	0.234
INDIA	0.263	0.442	0.302	0.179

Source: GoI (1992)

TABLE 4
HUMAN DEVELOPMENT IN NORTH EAST INDIA IN 1991

State/Country	Rural	Urban	Combined	Disparity
Arunachal Pradesh	0.300	0.572	0.328	0.272
Assam	0.326	0.555	0.348	0.229
Manipur	0.503	0.618	0.536	0.115
Meghalaya	0.332	0.624	0.365	0.292
Mizoram	0.464	0.648	0.548	0.184
Nagaland	0.442	0.633	0.486	0.191
Sikkim	0.398	0.618	0.425	0.220
Tripura	0.368	0.551	0.389	0.183
INDIA	0.340	0.511	0.389	0.171

Source: GoI (2002a)

As far as North East India is concerned the situation has been no different. During 1981 HDI value varied from the lowest figure of 0.242 in Arunachal Pradesh to the highest figure of 0.461 in Manipur. Similarly in 1991 the lowest and highest figures were 0.328 (Arunachal Pradesh) and 0.548 (Mizoram). The region witnessed further improvements in the last decade of the twentieth century. Assam witnessed the lowest HDI value of 0.362 and Mizoram the highest value of 0.552.

TABLE 5
HUMAN DEVELOPMENT IN NORTH EAST INDIA IN 2000

State/Country	Rural	Urban	Combined	Disparity
Arunachal Pradesh	0.379	0.622	0.411	0.243
Assam	0.330	0.613	0.362	0.283
Manipur	0.404	0.640	0.455	0.236
Meghalaya	0.390	0.671	0.436	0.281
Mizoram	0.473	0.687	0.552	0.214
Nagaland	0.477	0.738	0.515	0.261
Sikkim	0.396	0.571	0.411	0.175
Tripura	0.397	0.656	0.434	0.259
INDIA	0.380	0.584	0.435	0.204

Source: Estimated by the author

There has been a yawning gap between urban and rural areas. Human development in rural areas of the region has been consistently lower than that of the urban areas. The rural-urban disparity index varied from the lowest figure of 0.113 in Manipur to the highest figure of 0.234 in Tripura in 1981. The situation did not improve much in 1991 and also in 2000. In 2000, the highest disparity was observed in Assam (0.283) and lowest in Sikkim (0.175). The position of Meghalaya in this regard is worth mentioning. Her rank in rural-urban disparity deteriorated over time. Though Meghalaya occupied 3rd rank among all the States in the region in 1981, hers deteriorated to last (8th) rank in 1991 and subsequently to 2nd last in 2000.

Contrary to popular perceptions, the status of women in the region has been far from being on an equal footing with that of men. Particularly gender disparity has been consistently very high in Tripura and Assam (Table 6). It was lower in three states, namely, Manipur, Meghalaya and Nagaland in the year 1981 as compared to all India average situations. In 1991 only two states such as Manipur and Meghalaya were better off. Extent of gender disparity has been varying widely from one state to another in the region. Surprisingly when gender disparity has been decreasing over time in all the States in the region it has deteriorated in Nagaland.

TABLE 6
GENDER DISPARITY INDICES IN NORTH EAST INDIA

State/Country	Year	
	1981	1991
Arunachal Pradesh	0.537	0.776
Assam	0.462	0.575
Manipur	0.802	0.815
Meghalaya	0.799	0.807
Mizoram	0.502	0.770
Nagaland	0.783	0.729
Sikkim	0.643	0.647
Tripura	0.422	0.531
INDIA	0.620	0.676

Source: GoI (2002a)

V. CONCLUSION

Indian economy in spite of being a fast growing developing economy and pursuing the policy of liberalization and globalization since early eighties has not been able to achieve much on account of human development and welfare. Human development index is below 0.62 in India and much below in its North Eastern Region. Rural-urban disparity, gender disparity and uneven human development across the States in the region are quite significant. The disturbing trend of increasing gender disparity in Nagaland and escalating rural-urban gap, particularly in the States of Assam and Meghalaya is a matter of concern. Therefore, there is an urgent need for taking appropriate action in this regard.

REFERENCES

Adelman, I. and Morris, C. T. (1973): *Economic Growth and Social Equity in Developing Countries,* Stanford University Press, Stanford.

Alkire, S. (2002): Dimensions of Human Development, *World Development,* 30 (2): 181-205.

Anand, S. and Sen, A. (1995): Gender Inequality in Human Development: Theories and Measurement, HDR Office, *Occasional Paper No.19*, UNDP, New York.

Anand, S. and Ravallion, M. (1993): Human Development in Poor Countries: On the Role of Private Incomes and Public Services, *Journal of Economic Perspectives*, 7 (1): 133-150.

Aturpane, H., Glewwe, P. and Isenman, P. (1994): Poverty, Human Development and Growth: An Emerging Consensus, *American Economic Review*, 84 (2): 144-249.

Baker, J. (1997): Poverty Reduction and Human Development in the Caribbean, *World Bank Discussion Paper No. 366*, World Bank, Washington D.C.

Bardhan, K. and Klasen, S. (1999): UNDP's Gender-Related Indices: A Critical Review", *World Development*, 27 (6): 985–1010.

Bidani, B. and Ravillion, M. (1995): Decomposing Social Indicators Using Distributional Data, http://www_wds.worldbank.org/external/default/WDSContent services, accessed on 22 June 2006.

Boozer, M., Ranis, G., Stewart, F. and Suri, T. (2003): Paths to Success: The Relationship between Human Development and Economic Growth, Discussion Paper No. 874, Economic Growth Center, Yale University, http://www.econ.yale.edu/~egcenter/, accessed on the 15th May 2006.

Bose, A. (2004): HDRs: Some Reflections, *Economic and Political Weekly*, 39 (4): 323-325.

Chakraborty, I. (1997): Living Standard and Economic Growth: A Fresh Look at the Relationship through the Non-parametric Approach, http://cds.edu/download_files/wp283.pdf, accessed on the 15th 2006.

Chakravarty, S.R. (2003): A Generalized Human Development Index, *Review of Development Economics*, 7 (1): 99-114.

Chaubey, P.K. (2002): The Human Development Index: A Contribution to its Construction, *Indian Journal of Economics*, 83 (328): 95-100.

Dalal, K.L. (1991): *Human Development- An Indian Perspective*, Har-Anand Publications, New Delhi.

Desai, M. (1991): Human Development: Concept and Measurement, *European Economic Review*, 35 (2-3): 350-357.

Dholakia, R.H. (2003): Regional Disparity in Economic and Human Development in India, *Economic and Political Weekly*, 38 (39): 4166-4172.

Fukuda-Parr, Sakiko (2007): Has the Human Development Approach Influenced Policy? The Case of World Bank Flagship Reports", *Indian Journal of Human Development*, 1 (1): 153-159.

Gasper, D. (2002): Is Sen's Capability Approach an Adequate Basis for Considering Human Development? *Review of Political Economy*, 14 (4): 435-461.

Geetarani, P. (1995): Human Development in India: A District Profile, *Arthavijnana*, 41 (1): 9-30.

Government of India (GoI) (2002a): *National Human Development Report 1991*, Planning Commission, New Delhi.

GoI (2002b): *Basic Statistics of North Eastern Region*, North Eastern Council, Ministry of Home Affairs, Shillong.

Griffin, Tom (2002): UNDP Approach on Development, Human Rights and Indicators, Proceedings of the International Seminar on *"Statistics and Human Rights"*, organized by the European Commission and Munich Centre for Economic, Environmental and Social Statistics at Brussels, Belgium, 27-29 November, 2002. http://epp.eurostat.ec.europa.eu/pls/portal/docs/PAGE/ PGP_DS_COOP/PGE_DS_COOP_03/TAB59144315/TAB59

144831/REPORT-FINAL.PDF, accessed on the 3rd Feb February 2008.

Haq, M.U. (1995): *Reflections on Human Development,* OUP, New York.

Hicks, D.A. (1997): The Inequality Adjusted Human Development Index: A Constructive Proposal, *World Development,* 25 (8): 1283-1298.

Jain, L.C. (1991): Human Development in Rural India – A Blue Print, In K.L Dalal (ed.) *Human Development - An Indian Perspective,* Haranand Publications, and New Delhi.

Kannan, K.P. and Pillai, N. V. (2007): Conceptualizing Social Security in a Human Development and Rights Perspective, *Indian Journal of Human Development,* 1 (1): 33-54.

Kelley, Allen C. (1991): The Human Development Index: Handle with Care, *Population and Development Review,* 17 (2): 315-324.

Kumar, A.K. Shiva (1991): UNDP's Human Development in India - A Computation for Indian States, *Economic and Political Weekly,* 26 (41): 2343-2345.

Kumar, A.K. Shiva (1996): UNDP's Gender-Related Development Index – A Computation for Indian States, *Economic and Political Weekly,* 31 (14): 887-895.

Mahanty, G. (2000): Human Development in Andhra Pradesh: A District Level Analysis, *Indian Journal of Labour Economics,* 43 (2): 349-360.

Malhotra, R. (2007): Human Development Measures: From Advocacy to Policy Monitoring at Country Level, *Indian Journal of Human Development*, 1 (1): 103-127.

McGillivray, M. (1991): The Human Development Index: Yet another Redundant Composite Development Indicator, *World Development*, 19 (10): 1461-1468.

Morris, D.M. (1979): *Measuring the Condition of the World's Poor: The Physical Quality of Life Index*, Pergamon Press, Elmsford, NY.

Muysken, J., Yetkiner, H. and Ziesemer, T. (2003): Health, Labour Productivity and Growth, In Hagemann and Seiter (eds.) *Growth Theory and Growth Policy*, Routledge, London, 187-206.

Nagar, A.L. and Basu, S. R. (2000): *Weighting Socio-Economic Indicators of Human Development*, ICSSR Project Report submitted to NIPFP, New Delhi.

Nayak, P. and Thomas, E. D. (2007): *Human Development and Deprivation in Meghalaya*, Akansha Publishing House, New Delhi.

National Council of Applied Economic Research (NCAER) (1999): *India Human Development Report- A Profile of Indian States in the 1990's*, Oxford University Press, New Delhi.

National Institute of Rural development (NIRD) (1999): *India Rural Development Report 1999: Regional Disparities in Development and Poverty*, Hyderabad.

Pal, S.P. and Kant, D. K. (1993): An Alternative Human Development Index, *Margin*, 25(2).

Ranis, G. and Stewart, F. (2005): Dynamic Links between the Economy and Human Development, http://www.un.org/esa/desa/papers/2005/wp8_2005pdf, accessed on the 27th March 2006.

Ranis, G., Stewart, F. and Ramirez, A. (2000): Economic Growth and Human Development, *World Development*, 28 (2): 197-219.

Rao, V.M. (2000): Towards Human Development: Glimpses from India and Selected State", *Indian Journal of Labour Economics*, 43 (2): 327-338.

Sagar, A.D. and Najam, A. (1998): The Human Development Index: A Critical Review, *Ecological Economics*, 25 (3): 249-264.

Schaper, C. (2003): Growth and Distribution Effects of Education Policy in an Endogenous Growth Model with Human Capital Accumulation, In Hagemann and Seiter (eds.) *Growth Theory and Growth Policy*, Routledge, London, 136-155.

Sen, A. (2000): A Decade of Human Development, *Journal of Human Development*, 1 (1): 17-23.

Srinivasan, T.N. (1994): Human Development: A New Paradigm or Reinvention of the Wheel, *American Economic Review*, 84 (2): 238-243.

Streeten, P. (1994): Human Development: Means and Ends, *American Economic Review*, 84 (2): 232-237.

Tilak, J.B.G. (1991): Human Development Index of India, *IASSI Quarterly*, 10 (2): 132-138.

United Nations Development Program (UNDP) (1990): *Human Development Report 1990*, Oxford University Press, New York.

UNDP (2003): *Human Development Report 2003*, Oxford University Press, New York.

UNDP (2007): *Human Development Report 2007/2008*, Oxford University Press, New York.

Vijayabhaskar M., Swaminathan, P., Anandhi, S. and Balagopal, G. (2004): Human Development in Tamil Nadu, *Economic and Political Weekly*, 39 (8): 797-802.

Viswanathan, R. (1999): Human Development Report for Madhya Pradesh – Some Hidden Truths, *Economic and Political Weekly*, 34 (22): 1314-1315.

Vyasalu, V. and Vani, B. P. (1997): Development and Deprivation in Karnataka: A District Level Study, *Economic and Political Weekly*, 32 (46): 2970-1975.

Zaidi, N.A. and Salam, M.A. (1998): Human development in India: an Inter-state Comparison, *Indian Journal of Economics*, 78 (371).

World Bank (2004): *Attaining the MDGs in India*, Washington DC.

5

A Note on Human Development Indices with Income Equalities

S K Mishra[1]

I. INTRODUCTION

Sarker et al. (2006) argued that Human Development Index (HDI) should include income equality measures (EQ) in addition to the three measures of life expectancy (LE), education (ED) and per capita gross domestic product at the purchasing power parity with the US $ (PCI), conventionally incorporated into it. They computed the per capita income distribution-adjusted composite index (DAPCHDI) of human development and showed that the ranking of countries on the basis of this type of HDI (that includes income distribution as one of the component indices) differed substantially from the ranking calculated in the *Human Development Reports* (HDR) of United Nations Development Program (UNDP). They suggested, therefore, that within-country income distribution should be given its due importance in international comparison of countries.

Sarker et al. (2006) used data on life expectancy, educational index and per capita income from the Human Development Report of UNDP for 2004. They also constructed an index to measure equality in distribution of per

---

[1] Department of Economics, School of Economics Management and Information Sciences, North-Eastern Hill University, Shillong, Meghalaya, India, E-mail: mishrasknehu@hotmail.com

capita income based on the information on Gini coefficients of income distribution available in the HDR for various years. They used the Gini coefficients data over a span of 13 years (1990–2002). Under the constraints of data availability on income distribution, they chose 125 countries for construction of distribution-augmented HDI. The indices were subjected to the principal component analysis (PCA) and two composite indices of Human Development, the one is Principal Components based Human Development index (PCHDI) without incorporating equality index and the other (DAPCHDI) with its inclusion were obtained. They also noted the following points:

- Against the equal HDR weights for every index ($1/3 \approx 0.333$), the principal component weights for life expectancy, education and per capita income in the PCHDI were 0.36, 0.32 and 0.32 respectively. These weights were 0.30, 0.25 and 0.25 for the DAPCHDI. Since the latter also includes the equality index, the residual (0.20) weight was assumed by this additional variable. These weights sum up to unity.
- Due to change in weights assigned to different indices to make their linear aggregate (the composite index of HDI), the ranks of different countries in PCHDI and DAPCHDI were notably different.

II. THE PRESENT STUDY

The objective of this piece of work is twofold. First, to re-compute the DAPCHDI with the data given by Sarker et al. (2006) in their paper to compare our composite index with theirs. The HDR 2005 or the HDR 2006 adds little to the HDR 2004 database. Secondly, the present paper compute a slightly different DAPCHDI by a new method, which, unlike the principal component analysis that aims at maximizing the sum of squared coefficients of correlation between the composite index and the constituent variables, maximizes, instead, the sum of absolute coefficients of correlation between the composite index and the constituent variables. These are called New Human Development Index based on Norm 1 (maximization of sum of absolute correlation coefficients) (NHDI$_1$) and New Human Development Index based on Norm 2 (maximization of sum of squared correlation coefficients) (NHDI$_2$).

Haq (2003) noted that there is no *a priori* rationale for assigning different weights to different constituent indices. Each dimension of development is important, but the importance of each dimension may be different for developed and developing countries. Hence, he pleaded for equal weights on the principle of insufficient reason to discriminate among the constituent indices. In a hurry to abandon income as a sole measure of development, the protagonists of human development resorted to extreme pragmatism. On the other hand, the PCA, a blindly empiricist method, has a tendency to undermine poorly correlated variables and instead favour highly correlated variables to make a composite index (Mishra, 2007a and 2007b). A comparison of the principal component index with the one constructed by maximizing the sum of absolute correlation coefficients has revealed that the latter is an inclusive index (giving due weights to poorly correlated variable too) while the principal component index is largely elitist, favoring highly correlated variables and undermining the poorly correlated ones (Mishra, 2007c).

III. A FORMAL DESCRIPTION

It has been mentioned that the PCA makes a composite index such that the sum of squared coefficients of correlation between the composite index and the constituent variables is maximized. On the other hand, the new (inclusive) method (adopted in this paper) maximizes the sum of absolute coefficients of correlation between the composite index and the constituent variables. Formally, if $I = Xw = \sum_{j=1}^{m} w_j x_{ij}; \ i = 1, 2, ..., n$ is the composite index,

x_j; $j = 1, 2, ..., m$ are the constituent variables (such as the life expectancy index, educational index, et cetera) and $r(I, x_j)$ is the coefficient of correlation between I and x_j then,

(1). I (PCA) is obtained by maximizing $\sum_{j=1}^{m} r^2(I, x_j)$ or $\sum_{j=1}^{m} |r(I, x_j)|^2$ or $\left[\sum_{j=1}^{m} |r(I, x_j)|^2\right]^{1/2}$

(2). I (new method) is obtained by maximizing $\sum_{j=1}^{m} |r(I, x_j)|$

These measures relate to the Minkowski norm, L_p, for p=2 and p=1 respectively. The I (PCA) may be obtained by maximizing the above measure directly by some suitable method of non-linear optimization or by the traditional method (finding largest eigenvalue and the associated eigenvector of the correlation matrix of constituent variables, etc). However, I (new method) must be obtained by direct maximization.

IV. FINDINGS

We have maximized the quantities directly (Mishra, 2007d) by the differential evolution method of global optimization to obtain I (PCA) and I (new method) from the four indices, namely life expectancy (LE), education (ED), per capita income (PCI) and equality index (EQ). The data for 125 countries, given by Sarker et al. (2006) are reproduced in Table 1 here. We also reproduce the HDR 2004 ranks (R_1), PCHDI ranks (R_2) and values as well as the DAPCHDI ranks (R_3) and values obtained by Sarker et al (2006). It may further be noted that computation of I (PCA) by the traditional method gives the same correlation coefficients (loadings) to variables (LE, ED, PCI and EQ) as does the direct optimization method.

TABLE 1
COMPOSITE INDICES OF HUMAN DEVELOPMENT IN SELECT COUNTRIES OBTAINED BY DIFFERENT METHODS

Select Countries	Ranks by Different Methods					Human Development Indices: Different Aspects				Composite Indices of HDI			New Indices	
	R_1	R_2	R_3	R_4	R_5	LE	ED	PCI	EQ	PC HDI	DAPC HDI	$NHDI_2$	$NHDI_1$
Norway	1	1	1	1	1	0.90	0.99	0.99	0.96	0.96	0.96	0.96	0.96
Sweden	2	2	2	2	2	0.92	0.99	0.93	0.98	0.95	0.95	0.95	0.95
Canada	3	3	11	11	11	0.90	0.98	0.95	0.81	0.94	0.91	0.92	0.91
Netherlands	4	6	10	8	10	0.89	0.99	0.95	0.82	0.94	0.92	0.92	0.92
Australia	5	4	14	13	14	0.90	0.99	0.94	0.76	0.94	0.90	0.91	0.90
Belgium	6	5	3	3	3	0.90	0.99	0.94	0.98	0.94	0.95	0.95	0.95
United States	7	7	23	20	26	0.87	0.97	0.98	0.64	0.94	0.88	0.89	0.87
Japan	8	8	4	4	5	0.94	0.94	0.93	0.98	0.94	0.95	0.94	0.95
Luxembourg	9	10	9	10	9	0.89	0.91	1.00	0.86	0.93	0.92	0.92	0.92
Ireland	10	14	18	16	17	0.86	0.96	0.98	0.75	0.93	0.89	0.90	0.89
Switzerland	11	9	12	12	12	0.90	0.95	0.95	0.81	0.93	0.91	0.91	0.90
Austria	12	11	8	9	8	0.89	0.96	0.95	0.87	0.93	0.92	0.92	0.92
United Kingdom	13	12	17	17	19	0.88	0.99	0.93	0.74	0.93	0.89	0.90	0.89
Finland	14	13	6	6	6	0.88	0.99	0.93	0.94	0.93	0.93	0.93	0.94
Denmark	15	15	5	5	4	0.86	0.98	0.96	0.99	0.93	0.94	0.94	0.95
France	16	16	13	14	13	0.90	0.96	0.93	0.81	0.93	0.91	0.91	0.90
New Zealand	17	17	19	19	21	0.89	0.99	0.90	0.74	0.93	0.89	0.90	0.88

	18	18	7	7	7	0.89	0.95	0.94	0.91	0.93	0.92	0.92	0.92
Germany	18	18	7	7	7	0.89	0.95	0.94	0.91	0.93	0.92	0.92	0.92
Spain	19	19	15	15	15	0.90	0.97	0.90	0.82	0.92	0.90	0.91	0.90
Italy	20	20	21	21	23	0.89	0.93	0.93	0.74	0.92	0.88	0.89	0.88
Israel	21	21	24	23	24	0.90	0.94	0.88	0.76	0.91	0.88	0.88	0.87
Singapore	22	23	30	29	32	0.88	0.91	0.92	0.61	0.90	0.84	0.86	0.83
Greece	23	22	26	25	27	0.89	0.95	0.87	0.76	0.90	0.87	0.88	0.87
Hong_Kong_China_(SAR)	24	24	32	30	33	0.91	0.86	0.93	0.59	0.90	0.84	0.85	0.83
Portugal	25	25	28	27	28	0.85	0.97	0.87	0.69	0.89	0.85	0.86	0.85
Slovenia	26	26	16	18	16	0.85	0.96	0.87	0.91	0.89	0.89	0.90	0.90
Korea_Rep_of	27	27	22	24	22	0.84	0.97	0.86	0.84	0.89	0.88	0.88	0.88
Czech Republic	28	28	20	22	18	0.84	0.92	0.84	0.97	0.87	0.89	0.88	0.89
Argentina	29	29	47	45	49	0.82	0.96	0.78	0.40	0.85	0.76	0.78	0.75
Estonia	30	30	34	34	34	0.78	0.98	0.80	0.72	0.85	0.82	0.83	0.82
Poland	31	31	29	31	29	0.81	0.96	0.78	0.84	0.85	0.85	0.85	0.85
Hungary	32	32	25	26	20	0.78	0.95	0.82	1.00	0.85	0.87	0.87	0.89
Slovakia	33	33	27	28	25	0.81	0.91	0.81	0.96	0.84	0.87	0.86	0.87
Lithuania	34	35	33	33	31	0.79	0.96	0.77	0.83	0.84	0.84	0.84	0.84
Chile	35	34	60	49	64	0.85	0.90	0.77	0.30	0.84	0.73	0.75	0.71
Uruguay	36	36	43	43	44	0.84	0.94	0.73	0.56	0.84	0.78	0.79	0.77
Costa Rica	37	37	45	44	47	0.88	0.87	0.75	0.52	0.84	0.77	0.78	0.76
Croatia	38	38	31	32	30	0.82	0.90	0.77	0.89	0.83	0.84	0.84	0.84
Latvia	39	39	36	35	35	0.76	0.95	0.75	0.82	0.82	0.82	0.82	0.82
Mexico	40	40	66	63	72	0.81	0.85	0.75	0.35	0.80	0.71	0.73	0.70
Trinidad and Tobago	41	41	46	47	45	0.77	0.87	0.76	0.65	0.80	0.77	0.77	0.76

Bulgaria	42	42	40	39	40	0.77	0.91	0.71	0.83	0.80	0.80	0.80	0.80
Malaysia	43	45	63	58	63	0.80	0.83	0.75	0.46	0.79	0.73	0.74	0.71
Russian Federation	44	46	57	48	55	0.69	0.95	0.74	0.54	0.79	0.74	0.75	0.74
Macedonia TFYR	45	44	35	36	36	0.81	0.87	0.70	0.91	0.79	0.82	0.81	0.82
Panama	46	43	73	67	79	0.83	0.86	0.69	0.31	0.79	0.70	0.71	0.68
Belarus	47	47	39	40	39	0.75	0.95	0.67	0.86	0.79	0.80	0.80	0.81
Albania	48	48	38	38	38	0.81	0.89	0.65	0.91	0.78	0.81	0.80	0.81
Bosnia and Herzegovi	49	49	37	37	37	0.82	0.84	0.68	0.95	0.78	0.82	0.81	0.82
Venezuela	50	50	64	65	66	0.81	0.86	0.67	0.47	0.78	0.72	0.73	0.71
Romania	51	51	42	41	42	0.76	0.88	0.70	0.87	0.78	0.80	0.79	0.80
Ukraine	52	53	41	42	41	0.74	0.94	0.65	0.89	0.78	0.80	0.79	0.80
Saint Lucia	53	52	54	51	57	0.79	0.88	0.66	0.60	0.78	0.74	0.75	0.73
Brazil	54	54	81	78	81	0.72	0.88	0.73	0.25	0.77	0.67	0.69	0.65
Colombia	55	55	80	77	80	0.78	0.84	0.69	0.29	0.77	0.67	0.69	0.66
Thailand	56	56	58	57	59	0.74	0.86	0.71	0.59	0.77	0.73	0.74	0.73
Kazakhstan	57	57	44	46	43	0.69	0.93	0.68	0.84	0.76	0.78	0.78	0.78
Jamaica	58	58	49	50	51	0.84	0.83	0.61	0.70	0.76	0.75	0.75	0.74
Armenia	59	59	52	54	54	0.79	0.90	0.57	0.70	0.75	0.75	0.74	0.74
Philippines	60	60	67	66	68	0.75	0.89	0.62	0.53	0.75	0.71	0.71	0.70
Turkmenistan	61	61	62	61	60	0.70	0.93	0.63	0.64	0.75	0.73	0.73	0.73
Paraguay	62	62	82	81	85	0.76	0.85	0.64	0.30	0.75	0.66	0.67	0.64
Peru	63	64	78	74	78	0.74	0.86	0.65	0.45	0.75	0.69	0.70	0.68
Turkey	64	63	59	60	58	0.76	0.80	0.69	0.66	0.75	0.73	0.73	0.73
Azerbaijan	65	65	51	56	53	0.78	0.88	0.58	0.73	0.75	0.75	0.74	0.74

Jordan	66	66	53	53	50	0.76	0.86	0.62	0.74	0.75	0.75	0.74	0.74
Tunisia	67	67	61	62	61	0.79	0.74	0.70	0.66	0.75	0.73	0.73	0.72
China	68	68	69	69	69	0.76	0.83	0.64	0.56	0.74	0.71	0.71	0.70
Georgia	69	69	55	59	56	0.81	0.89	0.52	0.73	0.74	0.74	0.73	0.73
Dominican Republic	70	71	76	73	76	0.70	0.82	0.70	0.50	0.74	0.69	0.70	0.68
Sri Lanka	71	70	50	52	48	0.79	0.83	0.60	0.78	0.74	0.75	0.74	0.75
Ecuador	72	72	70	70	71	0.76	0.85	0.60	0.58	0.74	0.71	0.71	0.70
Iran Islamic Rep of	73	73	71	71	70	0.75	0.74	0.70	0.60	0.73	0.70	0.71	0.70
El Salvador	74	74	83	83	87	0.76	0.75	0.65	0.38	0.72	0.65	0.66	0.64
Guyana	75	75	77	75	75	0.64	0.89	0.63	0.59	0.72	0.69	0.70	0.69
Uzbekistan	76	76	48	55	46	0.74	0.91	0.47	0.94	0.71	0.76	0.74	0.76
Algeria	77	77	65	68	62	0.74	0.69	0.68	0.76	0.70	0.72	0.71	0.72
Kyrgyzstan	78	78	56	64	52	0.72	0.92	0.46	0.89	0.70	0.74	0.73	0.74
Indonesia	79	80	68	72	65	0.69	0.80	0.58	0.78	0.69	0.71	0.70	0.71
Viet Nam	80	79	72	76	67	0.73	0.82	0.52	0.74	0.69	0.70	0.70	0.70
Moldova Rep of	81	81	74	79	73	0.73	0.87	0.45	0.74	0.69	0.70	0.69	0.69
Bolivia	82	82	84	84	82	0.64	0.86	0.53	0.56	0.68	0.65	0.66	0.65
Honduras	83	84	91	90	90	0.73	0.74	0.54	0.34	0.67	0.61	0.61	0.59
Tajikistan	84	85	75	80	74	0.73	0.90	0.38	0.77	0.67	0.69	0.68	0.69
Nicaragua	85	83	90	91	91	0.74	0.73	0.54	0.34	0.67	0.61	0.61	0.59
Mongolia	86	86	85	85	84	0.64	0.89	0.47	0.57	0.66	0.65	0.65	0.64
South Africa	87	88	94	92	95	0.40	0.83	0.77	0.25	0.66	0.57	0.60	0.57
Egypt	88	87	79	82	77	0.73	0.62	0.61	0.78	0.66	0.68	0.67	0.68
Guatemala	89	89	89	88	89	0.68	0.65	0.62	0.48	0.65	0.62	0.62	0.61

A Note on Human Development Indices with Income...

Morocco	90	90	87	87	88	0.72	0.53	0.61	0.67	0.62	0.64	0.63	0.63
Namibia	91	91	108	103	111	0.34	0.79	0.69	0.00	0.60	0.47	0.51	0.47
India	92	92	86	86	83	0.64	0.59	0.55	0.82	0.60	0.64	0.63	0.65
Botswana	93	93	105	100	105	0.27	0.76	0.73	0.17	0.57	0.49	0.52	0.50
Ghana	94	94	88	89	86	0.55	0.65	0.51	0.87	0.57	0.63	0.62	0.64
Cambodia	95	95	92	93	92	0.54	0.66	0.50	0.65	0.57	0.58	0.58	0.59
Papua New Guinea	96	96	99	99	101	0.54	0.57	0.52	0.43	0.54	0.52	0.52	0.52
Lao People's Dem Rep	97	97	95	94	94	0.49	0.64	0.47	0.72	0.53	0.57	0.56	0.58
Swaziland	98	100	113	107	113	0.18	0.74	0.64	0.21	0.51	0.44	0.47	0.45
Bangladesh	99	98	93	95	93	0.60	0.45	0.47	0.83	0.51	0.58	0.56	0.58
Nepal	100	99	97	97	97	0.58	0.50	0.44	0.73	0.51	0.55	0.54	0.56
Cameroon	101	102	102	102	100	0.36	0.64	0.50	0.56	0.49	0.51	0.51	0.52
Pakistan	102	101	96	96	96	0.60	0.40	0.49	0.81	0.50	0.56	0.55	0.57
Lesotho	103	106	117	114	118	0.19	0.76	0.53	0.17	0.48	0.41	0.44	0.42
Uganda	104	103	101	101	99	0.34	0.70	0.44	0.60	0.49	0.51	0.51	0.52
Zimbabwe	105	107	114	111	114	0.15	0.79	0.53	0.30	0.48	0.44	0.46	0.45
Kenya	106	104	104	104	103	0.34	0.74	0.39	0.56	0.48	0.50	0.50	0.51
Yemen	107	105	98	98	98	0.58	0.50	0.36	0.80	0.48	0.55	0.53	0.55
Madagascar	108	108	107	108	110	0.47	0.60	0.33	0.50	0.47	0.47	0.47	0.47
Nigeria	109	110	112	112	112	0.44	0.59	0.36	0.43	0.46	0.46	0.46	0.46
Mauritania	110	109	100	105	102	0.45	0.42	0.52	0.68	0.46	0.51	0.50	0.52
Gambia	111	111	103	106	104	0.48	0.40	0.47	0.70	0.45	0.50	0.49	0.51
Senegal	112	112	106	109	106	0.46	0.39	0.46	0.63	0.44	0.48	0.47	0.48
Guinea	113	113	109	110	107	0.40	0.37	0.51	0.65	0.43	0.47	0.46	0.48

Tanzania U Rep of	114	114	110	113	109	0.31	0.62	0.29	0.70	0.40	0.46	0.45	0.48
Cote d Ivoire	115	115	116	116	116	0.27	0.47	0.45	0.55	0.39	0.42	0.42	0.44
Zambia	116	116	121	120	120	0.13	0.68	0.36	0.39	0.38	0.38	0.39	0.39
Malawi	117	117	119	119	119	0.21	0.66	0.29	0.44	0.38	0.39	0.39	0.40
Central African Rep	118	118	124	123	124	0.25	0.43	0.41	0.21	0.36	0.33	0.34	0.33
Ethiopia	119	119	111	115	108	0.34	0.39	0.34	0.87	0.36	0.46	0.44	0.48
Mozambique	120	121	118	118	117	0.22	0.45	0.39	0.67	0.35	0.41	0.41	0.43
Guinea-Bissau	121	120	120	121	121	0.34	0.39	0.33	0.51	0.35	0.38	0.38	0.39
Burundi	122	122	115	117	115	0.26	0.45	0.31	0.80	0.34	0.43	0.42	0.45
Mali	123	123	122	122	122	0.39	0.21	0.37	0.44	0.33	0.35	0.34	0.35
Burkina Faso	124	124	123	124	123	0.35	0.16	0.40	0.49	0.31	0.34	0.34	0.35
Niger	125	125	125	125	125	0.35	0.18	0.35	0.44	0.30	0.32	0.32	0.33

Source: Sarker et al. (adapted from HDRs of UNDP); PCI is named as GDP in HDR/Sarker et al. Computed by the author

The HDI indices computed are $NHDI_2$ (principal component) and $NHDI_1$ (new method) and the ranks obtained by different countries are R_4 and R_5 respectively. These HDI indices too are presented in Table 1. Note that ranks are based on more accurate $NHDI_2$ and $NHDI_1$ figures than what are presented in the Table 1.

In this analysis, the constituent indices of HDI obtain different weights and are differently correlated with their composite HDI indices. These weights and correlation coefficients are given in Table 2 and Table 3 respectively.

It may be noted that $NHDI_1$ trades off SSR only slightly to assign higher weights to EQ index. In exchange, the weights of LE, ED and PCI are reduced. Overall, $NHDI_1$ weights are more egalitarian than the $NHDI_2$ weights. Finally, in the Table 4 below we present the matrix of correlation coefficients (based on Table 1) among and across different ranks and composite HDI measures.

TABLE 2
WEIGHTS ASSIGNED TO THE CONSTITUENT INDICES BY DIFFERENT METHODS

Indices	LE	ED	PCI	EQ
DAPCHDI	0.30	0.25	0.25	0.20
$NHDI_2$	0.270909751	0.275588551	0.289481714	0.164019853
$NHDI_1$	0.239643184	0.258695275	0.265657700	0.236003815

Source: Calculated by the author

TABLE 3
CORRELATION OF COMPOSITE HDI INDICES WITH DIFFERENT CONSTITUENT INDICES

Index	LE	ED	PCI	EQ	SAR	SSR
$NHDI_2$	0.92363	0.87038	0.89030	0.56782	3.2521	2.7257
$NHDI_1$	0.9140	0.8459	0.8658	0.6396	3.2654	2.7099

SAR=Sum of Absolute correlation coefficients; SSR=Sum of Squared correlation coefficients
Source: Calculated by the author

TABLE 4
CORRELATION MATRIX OF DIFFERENT RANKS AND HDI INDICES OBTAINED BY DIFFERENT METHODS

Ranks/ HDI Indices	Ranks obtained by Different Methods					HDI Indices obtained by Different Methods			
	R1	R2	R3	R4	R5	PC HDI	DA PC HDI	NHDI$_2$	NHDI$_1$
R1	1.00	0.99	0.96	0.97	0.95	-0.97	-0.95	-0.96	-0.94
R2	0.99	1.00	0.96	0.97	0.95	-0.97	-0.95	-0.96	-0.94
R3	0.96	0.96	1.00	0.99	0.99	-0.94	-0.98	-0.98	-0.98
R4	0.97	0.97	0.99	1.00	0.99	-0.95	-0.98	-0.98	-0.98
R5	0.95	0.95	0.99	0.99	1.00	-0.93	-0.98	-0.97	-0.98
PCHDI	-0.97	-0.97	-0.94	-0.95	-0.93	1.000	0.971	0.983	0.962
DAPCHDI	-0.95	-0.95	-0.98	-0.98	-0.98	0.971	1.000	0.997	0.998
NHDI$_2$	-0.96	-0.96	-0.98	-0.98	-0.97	0.983	0.997	1.000	0.995
NHDI$_1$	-0.94	-0.94	-0.98	-0.98	-0.98	0.962	0.998	0.995	1.000

Source: Calculated by the author

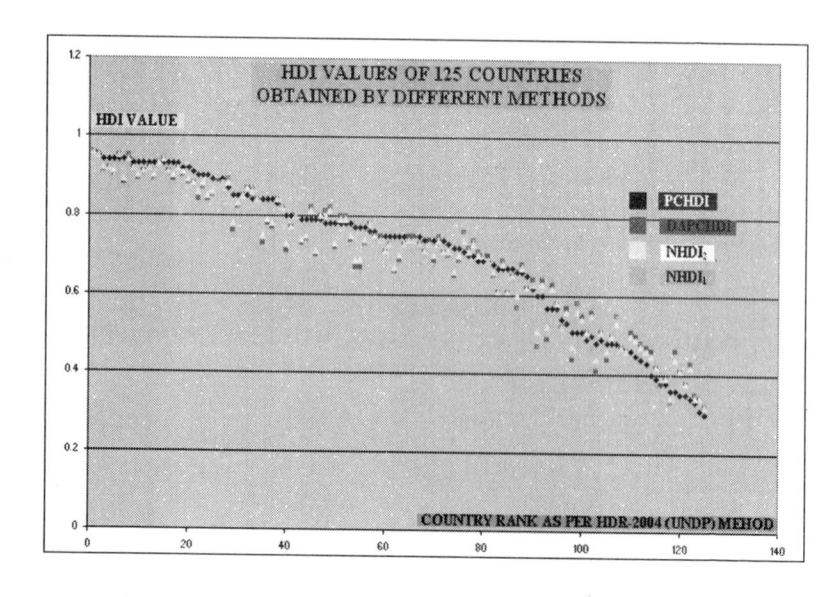

V. CONCLUDING REMARKS

The Human Development Reports assign subjective (or arbitrary) weights to indices of life expectancy, education, and income. Inclusion of equality index to HDI naturally raises the question as to the weight to be assigned to it. It is also required to reduce the weights assigned to other indices. An attempt may be made to obtain weights by the principal component analysis. However, the principal component analysis has a tendency to undermine the variables with weaker correlation coefficients. It may be elitist in favoring the highly correlated indices. Variance or explanatory power of a composite index cannot be the sole guide to assign weights. Representation of individual indices in the composite HDI also matters. The HDR has taken an extreme stand of assigning equal weights to all indices and suffers from an excessive bias to pragmatism. However, the new method of obtaining weights and constructing an HDI suggested by us is inclusive in nature, which takes care of weakly correlated indices also and gives them proper representation in the composite Human Development Index.

REFERENCES

Haq, Mahbub ul (2003): The Birth of the Human Development Index, In *Readings in Human Development*, S. Fukuda-Parr and A. K. Shiva Kumar (eds.), Oxford University Press, New Delhi.

Mishra, S. K. (2007a): Construction of an Index by Maximization of the Sum of its Absolute Correlation Coefficients with the Constituent Variables, http://ssrn.com/abstract=989088.

Mishra, S. K. (2007b): A Comparative Study of Various Inclusive Indices and the Index Constructed by the Principal Components Analysis, http://ssrn.com/abstract=990831.

Mishra, S. K. (2007c): Socio-Economic Exclusion of Different Religious Communities in Meghalaya, http://ssrn.com/abstract=992122.

Mishra, S. K. (2007d): A FORTRAN Computer Program for Construction of Composite Indices: Alternative to the Indices obtained by the Principal Components Analysis, http://www1.webng.com/economics/make-indices.html.

Sarker, S., Biswas, B. and Soundrs, P.J. (2006): Distribution-Augmented Human Development Index: A Principal Component Analysis, www.usu.edu/cob/econ/graduatestudents/documents/papers/developmentpaper.pdf.

6

Regional Planning, National Development and Conflict Resolution

Manas Chatterji[1]

I. INTRODUCTION

Regional planning starts with the basic assumption of the existence of political, geographic, economic and social regions within a nation or a group of nations. Climate and soil differences are pronounced in different parts of a country demanding different types of economic and social development. Historical reasons, political situations, language differences, ethnic diversities and most important the economic considerations all dictate that we choose a smaller area and decide the optimum planning strategy. In the beginning it may appear that this policy of treating a portion of the space (district, metropolitan area, river basin, State or a combination of States, etc.) as the proper planning unit, goes against the very formulation of overall national plans and the concept of national unity. But this does not have to be that way. A national plan cannot take into account the best possible strategy for regional development in its broad framework. On the other hand, a regional plan by its very definition possesses some question of inter-regional conflict. Whereas these conflicts are often over-emphasized and used against the concept and implementation or regional plans, enough is not

---

[1] School of Management, Binghamton University, Binghamton. New York, E-mail: mchatter@binghamton.edu.

said about how we can resolve these conflicts through inter-regional cooperation and at the same time maximize the potentialities of development of respective regions. It is true the benefits of this type of cooperation are often preached by politicians in different regions. But in reality it is seldom pursued primarily due to the absence of scientific studies which can show how this cooperation will lead to increased benefits for the interested regions and the nation as a whole. The objective of this paper is to discuss some of the analytical techniques that can be applied for such a purpose.

It is not suggested that the conflicts between regional and national goals do not exist in the developed countries. We can cite many examples in the case of Europe, United States and U.S.S.R and other countries where this is quite serious. This has been accentuated recently by the environmental and energy crises. Although in this paper we are primarily interested in the case of a developing country, namely India, we would like to present an example in the field of environmental conflict and the way we can deal with it.

One of the problems arising in environmental management and planning is the allocation of responsibility for cleaning up the environment. This problem arises at the international, national, and regional levels. The developing countries argue against any established standard of goods based on environmental consideration. According to them, the developed countries of the world have indiscriminately destroyed the balance in nature and they should assume the major responsibility for any regulation that needs to be imposed. Further, in the name of environment, the growth rate of economies of the developing countries might be substantially reduced were they required to abide by world-wide standards on pollutant emissions.

When we come to the question of pollution on regional level, it can be argued, say in the case of water pollution, that an upstream region pollutes the river and thus intensifies the pollution problem of the downstream regional community. Similarly, in the case of air pollution, the polluted air of one industrialized region can move to another area. The question is then, what should be the basis of sharing the responsibility for cleaning and managing the environment?

The problem is not simple. Nonetheless, it is necessary to attack it. In what follows, we wish to employ a balanced regional input-out-put model to begin to identify responsibility for pollution generation and control, especially when the several regions are contained within a single nation. While what we present can only be a beginning at analysis of this problem, it does provide some insights which may be useful, especially for developing regions where resources may permit the construction of only a national input-output table for environmental research purposes.

II. NOTATIONS

Consider a set of U regions in the nation. Each region produces n goods, of which m goods are useful goods and the remaining $n-m$ goods are pollutants generated by the production of the m useful goods. Each of the useful goods is classified as local, regional, or national.

According to the well-known classification of balanced regional input-output, some commodities like aircraft and motor vehicles are national, since their production and consumption balance only within the nation as a whole. They can be transported over great distances since they have a low weight to value ratio. There are other goods which like cement are designated *regional;* their supply and demand balance within the region as well as the nation since their transportability is restricted due to weight and other factors. There are still other goods which like soft drinks, shoe repair services, etc., are *local;* their supply and demand balance in the local area as well as in the region and in the nation. While we can list three classes of commodities, we shall set down only two classes in order to keep our analysis simple. (The reader can extend the model set down below to three classes following the standard procedures in the literature).

The idea of balanced regional input-output need not be limited to environmental problems. It is well known that there are some regions in India which produce the basic raw materials which are being used for the production of consumer goods that are demanded in different regions of the country. The question that naturally arises is what should be the proper share of these respective regions in terms of the division of the national wealth? It is often argued that the resources of one region are being utilized to produce goods for consumption in another area. It is not suggested that these accusations are always well founded. We are only saying that some new information may be obtained by applying this model.

	Useful Goods	Pollutants
Goods No.	1, 2, ... h, h+1, ... m	M+1, m+2, ... n
	Balanced in the region	Balance in the nation

There are U regions, A, ...J, K, L, ...U. The national outputs of regional, national and pollutants are denoted by

$$X_r = \begin{bmatrix} x_1 \\ \cdot \\ \cdot \\ \cdot \\ x_h \end{bmatrix} \quad \longleftarrow \text{Regional}$$

$$X_n = \begin{bmatrix} x_{n+1} \\ \cdot \\ \cdot \\ \cdot \\ x_m \end{bmatrix} \quad \longleftarrow \text{National}$$

$$X_t = \begin{bmatrix} x_{m+1} \\ \cdot \\ \cdot \\ \cdot \\ x_n \end{bmatrix} \leftarrow \overline{Pollutant}$$

The total output vector is given by
$$X = \begin{bmatrix} X_R \\ X_N \\ X_T \end{bmatrix}$$

In a similar fashion the national final demand vectors are denoted by

$$Y_r = \begin{bmatrix} Y_1 \\ \cdot \\ \cdot \\ \cdot \\ Y_h \end{bmatrix} \leftarrow \overline{Regional}$$

$$Y_n = \begin{bmatrix} Y_{n+1} \\ \cdot \\ \cdot \\ \cdot \\ Y_m \end{bmatrix} \leftarrow \overline{National}$$

$$Y_t = \begin{bmatrix} Y_{m+1} \\ \cdot \\ \cdot \\ \cdot \\ Y_n \end{bmatrix} \leftarrow \overline{Pollutant}$$

Y_T denoted the acceptable levels of pollution generated by the productive processes.

The total final demand vector is denoted by

$$Y = \begin{bmatrix} Y_R \\ Y_N \\ Y_T \end{bmatrix}$$

For the jth region (j=A, ..., J, K, L, ...U) the corresponding notations for the outputs are $_jX_R$, $_jX_N$, $_jX_T$, and $_jX$ and the symbols for the final demand are $_jY_R$, $_jY_N$, $_jYT$, and $_jY$.

Following the usual definition of input-output analysis, we set:

$$a_{rr} = \begin{bmatrix} a_{11} & a_{12} & \cdots & a_{1h} \\ \cdot & \cdot & \cdots & \cdot \\ \cdot & \cdot & \cdots & \cdot \\ \cdot & \cdot & \cdots & \cdot \\ a_{h1} & a_{h2} & \cdots & a_{hh} \end{bmatrix}_{hXh}$$

$$a_{rn} = \begin{bmatrix} a_{1,h+1} & \cdot & \cdot & a_{1m} \\ \cdot & \cdot & \cdot & \cdot \\ \cdot & \cdot & \cdot & \cdot \\ \cdot & \cdot & \cdot & \cdot \\ a_{h,h+1} & \cdot & \cdot & a_{hm} \end{bmatrix}_{hX(m-h)}$$

In the a_{RR} partition the matrix pertains to the interrelations of industries producing regional goods. Here the coefficients (say $a_{rr'}$; r, r'= 1, ..., h) denote the input of regional good r per unit output of regional good r' (produced by sector r'). In the a_{RN} partition the input-out put coefficient, say $a_{rn'}$ (r = 1, 2, ..., h; n = h+1, ..., m) denotes the input of rth (regional) industry per unit output of nth (National) industry. We also have

$$a_{Nr} = \begin{bmatrix} a_{n+1,1} & \cdot & \cdot & \cdot & a_{h+1,h} \\ \cdot & & \cdot & & \cdot \\ \cdot & & & \cdot & \cdot \\ \cdot & & & & \cdot \\ a_{m1} & \cdot & \cdot & \cdot & a_{mh} \end{bmatrix}_{(h-h)X1}$$

$$a_{NN} = \begin{bmatrix} a_{n+1,h+1} & \cdot & \cdot & \cdot & a_{n+1,m} \\ \cdot & & \cdot & & \cdot \\ \cdot & & & \cdot & \cdot \\ \cdot & & & & \cdot \\ a_{m,h+1} & \cdot & \cdot & \cdot & a_{mm} \end{bmatrix}_{(m-h)X(m-h)}$$

In the a_{NR} partition, the input-output coefficients (say a_{nr}; n = h+1, ... m; r = 1, ..., h) denote the input of nth (national) industry per unit output of the rth (regional) industry. In the partition a_{NN} the input-output coefficients (say $a_{nn'}$; n, n' = h+1, ..., m) denote the input required of the nth industry (National) for the unit production of nth (national) industry.

Let

$$a_{rt} = \begin{bmatrix} a_{1,m+1} & \cdot & \cdot & \cdot & a_{1n} \\ a_{2,m+1} & \cdot & & & a_{2n} \\ \cdot & & & & \cdot \\ \cdot & & & & \cdot \\ \cdot & & & & \cdot \\ a_{h,m+1} & \cdot & \cdot & \cdot & a_{hn} \end{bmatrix}_{hX(n-m)}$$

In a$_{RT}$ the input-output coefficients (say a$_{rt}$; r = 1, 2, ..., h; t = m, ..., n) denote input of rth regional industry per unit of pollutant abating activity t. Let

$$a_{NT} = \begin{bmatrix} a_{h+1,m+1} & \cdot & \cdot & \cdot & a_{h+1,n} \\ \cdot & & & & \cdot \\ \cdot & & & & \cdot \\ \cdot & & & & \cdot \\ a_{m,k+1} & \cdot & \cdot & \cdot & a_{mn} \end{bmatrix}_{(m-h)X(n-m)}$$

In a$_{NT}$ the input-output coefficients (say, a$_{nt}$; n = h+1, ..., m; t = m+1, ..., n) denote the input requirement from nth (national) industry per unit output of tth pollutant abating industry. Let

$$a_{Tr} = \begin{bmatrix} a_{m+1,1} & \cdot & \cdot & \cdot & a_{m+1,h} \\ \cdot & \cdot & \cdot & \cdot & \cdot \\ a_{n1} & \cdot & \cdot & \cdot & a_{nh} \end{bmatrix}_{(n-m)Xh}$$

In a$_{TR}$ the input-output coefficients (say a$_{tr}$; t = m+1, ..., n; n = 1 ... h) denote the output of pollutant t by unit output of regional good r. Further,

$$a_{tn} = \begin{bmatrix} a_{m+1,h+1} & \cdot & \cdot & \cdot & a_{m+1,m} \\ \cdot & \cdot & & & \cdot \\ \cdot & & \cdot & & \cdot \\ \cdot & & & \cdot & \cdot \\ a_{n,h+1} & \cdot & \cdot & \cdot & a_{nm} \end{bmatrix}_{(n-m) \times (m-h)}$$

In a_{TN} the input-output coefficients (say a_{tn}; $t = m+1$, ..., n, h = h+1, ..., m) denote the output of pollutant t by unit level of output of the national industry n. Finally,

$$a_{TT} = \begin{bmatrix} a_{m+1,m+1} & \cdot & \cdot & \cdot & a_{m+1,n} \\ \cdot & \cdot & & & \cdot \\ \cdot & & \cdot & & \cdot \\ \cdot & & & \cdot & \cdot \\ a_{n,m+1} & \cdot & \cdot & \cdot & a_{nn} \end{bmatrix}_{(n-m) \times (n-m)}$$

In a_{TT} the input-output coefficients (say a_{tt}, $t = m+1$, ..., n; $t = m+1$, ..., n) denote the output of pollutant t per unit of activity of pollutant abating industry t.

The Balanced Model

The complete input-output matrix is given by

$$C = \begin{bmatrix} a_{RR} & a_{RN} & a_{RT} \\ a_{NR} & a_{NN} & a_{NT} \\ a_{TR} & a_{TN} & a_{TT} \end{bmatrix} = \begin{bmatrix} R^A \\ N^A \\ T^A \end{bmatrix}$$

The inverse matrix is $(I-G)-1 = M = \begin{bmatrix} R^{A^R} & R^{A^N} & R^{A^T} \\ N^{A^R} & N^{A^N} & N^{A^T} \\ T^{A^R} & T^{A^N} & T^{A^T} \end{bmatrix}$

III. THE MODEL

With this framework it is possible to construct a model through which we can assign the responsibility for each region for cleaning up the pollution resulting from the production of regional and national goods in different regions. Let us explain the above statement with the help of an artificial example. Consider the consumption of national goods (say consumer goods) in New Delhi. These goods may have been produced in some place, say, in Bombay. Further, for the production of these goods, inputs were required from and produced in other regions. The cost of cleaning the pollution that has been produced directly and indirectly in different regions so that final consumption in New Delhi can take place should be shared by the consumers in New Delhi. From this static model this share can be determined[2]. The developed countries can afford to have inter-regional conflicts since they have higher standards of living and a fair amount of homogeneity with respect to language, ethnic back- ground et cetera of the population and its mobility. But this is much too serious for a developing country like India.

One of the basic problems facing the developing countries of the world is the low standard of living of its people. What is more disheartening is that the growth rate of income of these countries barely keeps up with the rate of population growth. The reasons for this are many. Among

---

[2] M. Chatterji, "On the Use of Balanced Regional Input-Output Model for Environmental Planning" *International Journal of Regional Science*, Vol. 1, No.1; for a dynamic formulation of the model see M. Chatterji, "A Dynamic Balanced Regional Input-Output Model of Pollution Control," Paper presented in the Third Advanced Studies Seminar on Regional Science, Univ. of Karlsruhe, Karlsruhe, Germany, August 1974.

these are poor natural environments, severe climatic conditions, niggardly endowment of resources, past social and cultural development and restrictive religious practices. All these factors confine the production far within the maximum possible frontier lending to low output. Frequently this results in a vicious circle of low output, high propensity to consume, low savings and capital accumulation. The situation is further complicated by political in- stability and internal conflicts.

Many of these countries, however, are trying to reverse the trend by relying on national economic planning. It consists in formulating economic and social goals for the people at a future date, expressing them in quantifiable money values and suggesting most efficient strategies to attain these goals with the available internal and external resources. There have been many experiments and numerous studies on the theory and practices of national planning are available in economic literature. However, over the years, it has been increasingly realized that national planning is not leading to a balanced development of the country. One of the reasons is that in most economic planning strategies, we abstract the notion of space. We are thinking in terms of one point economy and trying to devise policies so that economic growth is optimal over time. But in reality, we do not live in a one-point economy. All parts of a country do not have the same characteristics with respect to resource orientation, manpower, economic, social and political history. Some areas are urban, others rural. Some had an earlier start in economic growth to begin with. The situation is further complicated by the existence of different languages, ethnic groups and conflicting regional interest. So particular attention is needed for specific areas and regions. That does not mean that the country should be divided into smaller areas each having a separate planning authority. What is needed along with a national framework is a series of interconnected regional plans consistent with national plans.

The situation is basically the same in all the so-called poor countries, especially those countries, which were under the foreign rule for a long time. Examples are Pakistan, Vietnam, Indonesia (Java *vs* other islands), Burma and Thailand (capital cities and rice growing areas *vs* up-country), Brazil (North-east and Central-South area), etc. The general pattern is economic disparity between the capital or port city and the rest of the country. Look at the economic history of any of these countries. Industrialization typically has started at a few focal points (mostly port cities). These points were deemed convenient to the rulers and were not necessarily optimum locations. In addition to economic development, these points obtained an earlier start with respect to education, health care facilities and all other benefits and deterrents of western civilization. The case for Calcutta, Bombay and Madras in India are good illustrations.

The regional dimension of Indian planning problems is too well- known to be emphasized. In India, the claim for a regional development is based on several considerations. Geographically, the country comprises a vast area with significant variations in its natural endowment. Climatic and -soil differences are very pronounced in different parts of the country demanding different patterns of economic development. From the economic standpoint, the factors of production are not equally distributed. Capital and enterprises are available in large measures in certain states enabling them to steal a march over the others in exploiting the available resources. There are also glaring differences in social welfare, as the total quantum of the socially necessary work is not equitably distributed over the entire country due to the unevenness of its economic development.

Although India, through her five year plans, is trying to raise the standard of living of her people, it is becoming increasingly clear that the problem here is not to select a strategy that will maximize the rate of growth since this maximum can only be modest due to resources restrictions.

The real question is distributional i.e., how to distribute the growth spatially and amongst different income groups. Fortunately, Indian people by tradition are patient. They are prepared to wait, particularly when they see fair distribution of benefits. Two of the basic ingredients of the economic and social transformation in India are international peace and inter-regional cooperation. In both lies the importance of regional planning. One of the impediments in the process of economic developments of many countries is continued tension due to occasional wars and conflicts. In the case of the Indian subcontinent, evidences of such disruptions abound. With the recent recognition of Bangladesh by Pakistan, a new era in South Asia has unfolded. Let us look at the countries of South Asia. These are India, Pakistan, Bangladesh, Burma, Ceylon, Afghanistan, and Nepal. Afghanistan has serious border disputes with Pakistan but it is also a Muslim country having strong similarities with Pakistan with respect to geography, culture and social system. Bangladesh, though a Muslim country has strong cultural and sentimental ties with India (particularly W. Bengal) but it does not want to be dominated by a big country such as India, and rightly so. The same is true of smaller countries like Burma and Ceylon. Pakistan, in spite of its recent war with India will greatly profit if it cooperates with India. India with a large Muslim minority and stupendous problems 1of economic and social development is the last country to afford constant tensions in the subcontinent and risk another war costing a billion rupees. It will be naive to suggest that everything is rosy and problems don't and will not exist. Politics is a treacherous game. What is emphasized, hower, is that peace, goodwill to cooperate and common interests can also be powerful forces. Efforts should be made to emphasize the common good and benefits of cooperation and find objective peaceful ways to solve the problems through comprehensive regional plans. But the question is how? It is true that the decision to cooperate and give and take are made by the politicians but there is considerable scope of preparing scientific studies showing how cooperation leads to benefits. What is suggested here (which, I am afraid, may not be feasible at this point of political reality) is to formulate a comprehensive regional plan for the South-Asian region on the pattern of ECM or at least coordinate the national plans of these countries. I know that it will take years for such an effort to be fruitful or it may never materialize. But if we can show the benefits of regional cooperation through our studies, this process can be accelerated. When we consider the question of inter-regional cooperation within a nation, the problem is more crucial for the very existence of the" nations, but probably easier to handle.

It is a common complaint that while Indian plans are basically sound, it is too centralized, it is imposed from above. The real question, as Mahatma Gandhi pointed out, is to involve the people. Decision making process should be decentralized in such a way that the integrity of the country is not endangered. Centre-State relations have attained significance in recent years when parties with different ideologies were controlling the central government and a number of key states. The future of democracy in India will be very much determined by the harmonious functioning of these relations and the participation of the people as a whole in the decision making at different levels. A strong central government is necessary to protect the integrity of the country and fight against the disruptive elements. On the other hand, decentralization of decision making is a must to allow the broad participation of organizations at different levels and the people at large. The question then is to choose the optimum amount of decentralization in decision making with respect to international, national, regional, inter-regional, state and local decisions. For this purpose, we can start with a model of a four-fold symmetrical tree-like hierarchical system with the central government at the top with four states in each (Nagaland can be combined with Assam). For each state, four sub-regions are defined on local units. These units can be a group of districts, or geographical subdivisions like east, west, south, north or some special interest groups. It is not necessary that this structure has to be symmetrical with four branches. For the sake of simplicity it can be assumed to be so. Thus, these four orders involving eighty-five nodes are numbered 1, 2, ...85.

For each of these nodes a mass vector having k components is defined. The components of this mass vector denote characteristics of a node with respect to social, political, and economic attributes. A system of distances between the members of the same order and between different orders with respect to a particular component of the mass vector is devised. These masses and distances are used in the calculation of potentials as follows:

$$_iV^e = \sum_{j=1}^{n} G_j W_{je} (M_{je})^\beta d_{ije}$$

Where G, β, b are constant, M_{je} is the mass of the jth node with respect to e^{th} component and W_{je} is the corresponding weight. d_{ije} is the distance between (i, j) with respect to e^{th} component however defined.

This potential is defined at the following levels:
1. of the zones at the centre;
2. amongst the zones ;
3. of the states at the zone ;
4. of the states at the centre ; and
5. of the local units at the state

Next, the following decision matrix involving international, national, regional, and inter-regional, state and local decisions is defined.

Type of Decision ↓	Authority			
	Centre	Zone	State	Local
International	r_{IC}	0	r_{IS}	0
National	r_{CC}	r_{ZC}	r_{CS}	r_{CL}
Regional and Interregional	r_{ZC}	r_{ZZ}	0	0
State	r_{SC}	0	r_{SS}	r_{SL}
Local	0	0	r_{LS}	r_{LL}

Any element, r_{ij}, in the matrix denotes the percentage of i the type (international, national, etc.) of decision left to j^{th} order (center, zone, etc.). Multiplying the potential generated at each order by the percentage of decisions made at each order and summing over all the orders, we get what may be called *participation potential*.

Next, we consider the costs of decentralization. These costs are grouped into the following categories:
1. cost of misjudgment;
2. bureaucratic cost;
3. cost of communication;
4. cost of the lack of integration;

These costs will change with different degrees of decentralization. The problem is, then, to choose that amount of decentralization for which the participation is maximum with given costs. Again, the parameters of the potential and cost functions will change over time with the growth of literacy rate, per capita income, etc., and the problem becomes dynamic in nature[3].

Another vexing problem in the centre-state relation is the question of resource allocation. It has been often argued that allocation should be made according to population. This becomes unacceptable to those states from where a major

---

[3] For details of such a model see, Chatterji, M (1970): A Scheme of Decentralized Decision-Making in India, *Indian Journal of Public Administration,* 16(4).

portion of the central tax income comes. However, it may be argued that the so-called industrial states are in a better position *now* since it had an earlier start during British rule. Again, a state with low per capita income (relative to national average) can claim extra attention in the name of balanced regional growth. Although it is to be realized that the concept of optimum allocation plan based on the productivity of capital cannot be applied as a rule of thumb, every state cannot have everything since the total amount of available resources is fixed. One thing is certain that a single variable like population cannot and should not determine the allocation. Other variables like capital-output ratio, savings-income ratio, per capita income, locational advantage, defence need, capacity of one state to bear- its own burden, level of managerial skill, and other relevant norms should be considered. For this purpose a dynamic programming model of the following type can be used.

$$\text{Maximize} \sum_{L=r,s} \sum_{i=1,2} p_i^{-L}(N) X_i^{L(N)}$$

Subject to:

$$X_1^L(t+1) \leq X_1^L(t) + \theta_1^L(t)(y_1^r + y_1^s)t \leq X_2^I(t+1) \leq \theta_2^L(t)(y_2^r + y_{2t}^s)$$

for some $\theta_i^r(t) + \theta_i^s(t) = 1, \theta_i^r(t), \theta_i^s(t) \geq 0$; I = 1, 2.

and $(y_1^L, Y_2^L) \varepsilon f_1(X_1^L, X_2^L)t$; t = 0, 1, ..., N-1.

where
X_1^L = Amount of capital used in region L

X_2^L = Amount of material good used in regional L

Y_1^L = Amount of investment good produced in region L and

Y_2^L = Amount of material good produced in region L

Amongst these restrictions we can include the inter-regional input-out-put relations, transportation system and other social, political and economic constraint. There is only one kind or investment good I which can be moved between locations without transport inputs and only two locations, region r and s. θ is ratio of investment good allocated to region r and p^L $(L= r, s)$ is the efficiency prices of capital in region L. This model can be extended to m regions and n goods[4]. Another important case that is often mentioned but rarely implemented is the inter-state cooperation. We have few studies that utilize the techniques of conflict resolution and social sciences that can show how inter-state cooperation can lead to benefit of both the parties. For this purpose the feed-back system of inter-regional input-output analysis and recently developed concepts of growth points can be effectively utilized. A case in point is the sharing of river water by two regions. The water of a river can be used for different purposes in different regions. Again, the benefits that accrue due to the efficient use in one area can be transmitted to the other part and a chain re- action can be generated to speed up the process of development. This will also stop the force of separatist interest of any particular state. How the benefit is increased through cooperation can be explained by the following example.

Consider two contiguous states; W. Bengal *(A)* and Bihar *(B)* sharing a common a river basin (say Damodar River Basin area). Sup- pose they are interested in a joint development of the area. Two aspects of this development are (l) the generation of power (2) irrigation and flood prevention. Let us say each one has 10 million rupees to invest. The regional planning authority in *A* may estimate π^a – the rate of growth of its income for a combination of his own investment and that of *B*. For example, in Figure 1, *A* may estimate for

---

[4] For details see M. Fujita. "Optimum Growth in Two-Region, Two-Good I Space Systems: The Final State Problem," *Journal of Regional Science*, Vol. 13, No.3, 1973. Also see Isard, W. and P. Liossatos, "Space Time Development and a General Transfer Principle Papers," *Regional Science Association*, Vol. III, 1973.

itself an annual increase of gross regional product of INR 1.59 million (π^a) if it were to undertake a program of INR 2.5 million in irrigation and INR 7.5 million in power generation when B divides his investment equally between 1 and 2. Each contour line of Figure 1 denotes all combinations A's and B's expenditure program which yield A the specified level π^a (average annual increase in A's gross regional product). The contour line may be called A's π possibility curve.

FIGURE 1

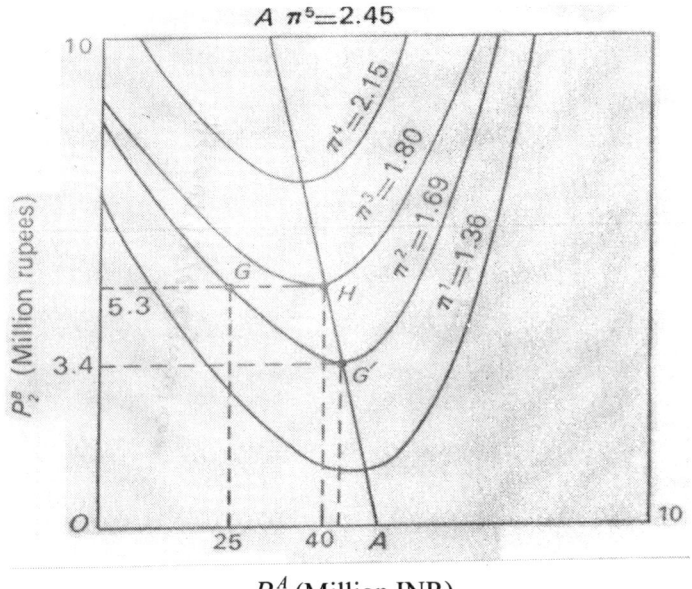

A $\pi^5 = 2.45$

P_2^B (Million rupees)

$\pi^4 = 2.15$
$\pi^3 = 1.80$
$\pi^2 = 1.69$
$\pi^1 = 1.36$

P_2^A (Million INR)

If we examine Figure 1, we see that as we move vertically along A's possibility surface the value of π^a increases. This means that as B undertakes more investment in irrigation, A profits more since it can divert more investment in power generation and its agriculture income increases simultaneously since B's investment in irrigation indirectly benefits him. (Assume that *B's* investment in irrigation prevents floods *A* and supplies steady water through canals.) Again for any given expenditure program of *B*, say INR 5 million, we observe that 7t/J steadily increases up to a certain point and steadily decreases beyond that point. This relationship signifies that up to a certain point a rupee invested in irrigation tends to have a greater impact on *A's* gross regional product than a rupee invested in electricity generation. Similar arguments can be made for *B*.

When the two states are not cooperating then the equilibrium situation may be depicted by Figure 2.

FIGURE 2

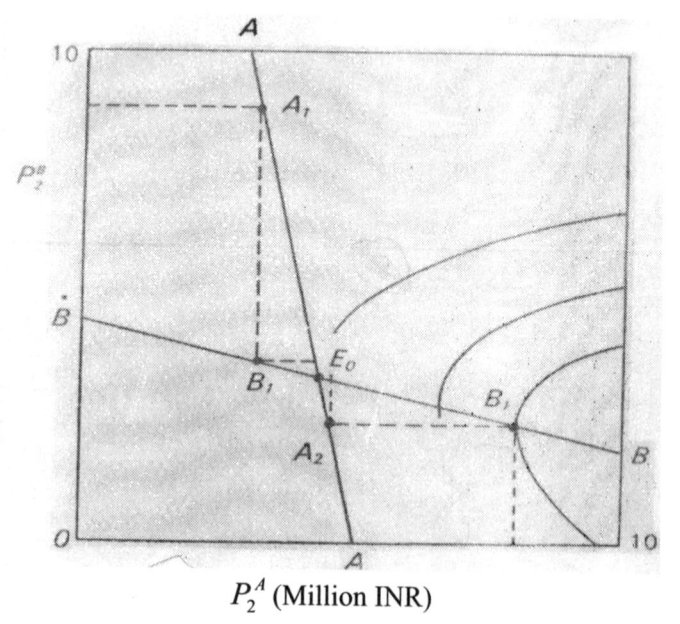

P_2^A (Million INR)

If the initial proposals of the regions are P_2^a = INR 8 million and P_2^b = INR 9 million, then *A's* response to *B's* initial proposal and *B's* response to *A's* initial proposal are designated A₁ and B₁ respectively. But once these new proposals have been announced, A will respond to B_I with a new proposal A_I, and B will respond to A_I with B_I and so on. The process will continue until the equilibrium point E_o. It is seen that although states A and B have reached a stable equilibrium at E_o both regions could do better. Both could increase their levels of π simultaneously if they get together and agree to shift their program proposals to some point in the shaded area of Figure 3. As a first step, each state comes to realize that the relevant range for bargaining over possible joint programs is given by points on arc TT. The point at which the compromise will be made depends upon the cooperative arrangement. Suppose we assume the following:

1. In negotiating a joint decision, each region will have full power to veto any proposal.
2. No joint regional investment decision will be proposed that involves investment shifts exceeding any regions shift limit.
3. On any move a set of compatible proposals must be reached which will then form the base for the next move.
4. No state will be asked to agree to a compromise proposal which does not yield it a 7t that is at least equal to that achieved by its and the other state's proposals.

With these principles, a better solution E_n will emerge as shown in Figure 4. Thus, this example shows how cooperation amongst the two can lead them to better levels than the independent action[5].

---

[5] The arguments and the statements are heavily drawn from: (i) Walter Isard and Tony Smith, "*A* Practical Application of Game Theoretical Approaches to Arms Reduction (and to Goal Determinations among Regional Planning Authorities)" *Regional Science Association Papers*, Vol. VV, 1966. (ii) Walter Isard: "Game Theory, Location Theory, and Industrial Agglomeration", *Regional Science Association Papers* XVIII, Vienna Congress, 1966. (iii) Walter Isard and Tony Smith, "Location Games with Applications to Classic Location Problems," *Regional Science Association Papers*. (iv) W. Isard and T. Smith, "On the Resolution of Conflicts among Regions of a System," *Regional Science Association Papers* XVII, 1966.

FIGURE 3

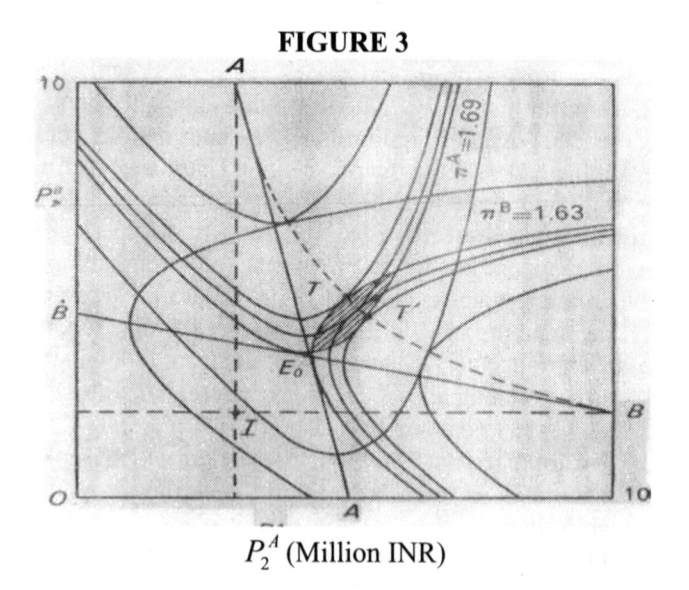

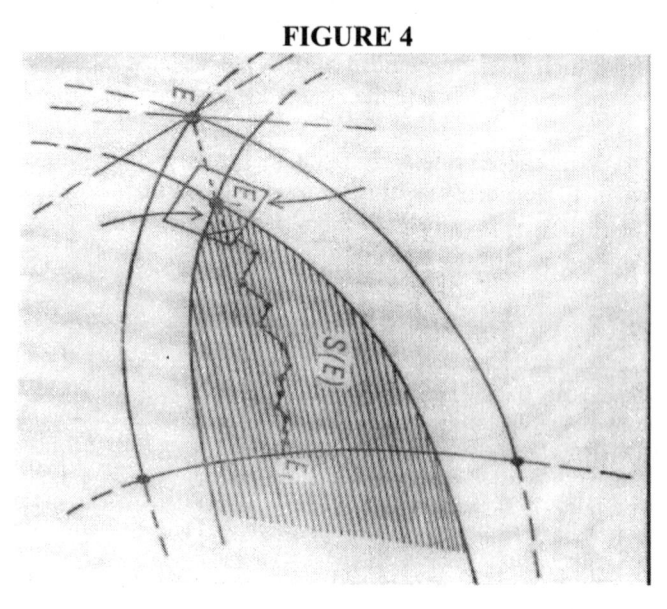

P_2^A (Million INR)

FIGURE 4

It is often seen that when there is some outstanding quarrel between two states, the progress of reconciliation is quite slow. Same is true in the case of conflicts among different groups. In this case, the Central Government can act as a third party and through pressures and rewards it can keep the process moving. In this connected three-person-game theoretical approaches can be utilized profitably.

Like any other country in the world, conflict situations exist in India on international, national, regional, inter-regional, state, local, and group levels. On the positive side, there also exists an underlying unity of the Indian people through the common heritage, goodwill and determination to solve these conflicts in the framework of democratic society.

Talking of conflicts and dissensions, these positive aspects should not be forgotten. In fact, they should be emphasized while steps are taken to resolve the conflicts. The efforts in this direction will ultimately result in all-round social and economic development of India and will set an example in the family of nations.

IV. CONCLUSION

In this paper, I have discussed in a small way the scope of applying conflict resolution researches in regional planning in India emphasizing the need of objective scientific studies to explore the benefits of cooperation. This does not undermine the importance of the use of descriptive and historical research. In essence, these two are complementary. Nor is it implied -that these models solve the problem. But I do believe that they may throw some new insights and point to some objective steps which will help the political leaders at all levels and people at large to pursue the paths of peace true to their ancient tradition and teachings of the Father of the Nation.

REFERENCES

Acarya, B.K. (1965): India and China, *Indian and Foreign Review,* 2(2): 9-10, 19-20.

Aiyar, S.P. (1967): Union-State Relations in India: A Post-Election View, *United Asia*, 19: 80-90.

Alvares, Peter (1965): Kashmir and Power Balance in Asia, *Janata,* 20 (43): 3-4, 6.

Bandyopadhyaya, Jayantanuju (1967): Sino-Soviet Rift and India, *Shakti*, 4 (2): 14-23.

Baranwal, G.S. (1965): Role of Union Government in Financing the Development of Uttar Pradesh, *Prajna,* 11 (1): 190-195.

Berelson, B. and Steinder, Gary (1966): *Human Behavior: An Inventory 01 Scientific Findings,* Harcourt, Brace and World, Inc., New York.

Boulding, Kenneth (1966): Towards a Theory of Peace, In Roger Fisher (ed.), *Inter- national Conflict and Behavioral Science,* Basic Books, New York.

Boulding, Kenneth (1965): The British Press and the War with Pakistan, *Vidura,* 2 (4): 11-18.

Boulding, Kenneth (1965): The British Press on the India-Pakistan Conflict, *Foreign Affairs Report,* 14 (12): 161-170.

Catell, R. B. (1950): *An Introduction to Personality Study,* Hutchinson's University Library, London and New York.

Chelyshev, E. (1967): Friendship Benefits Both Countries, *Amity*, 4 (2-3): 5-9.

Chopra, R. N. (1965): Administrative Organization for Regional Development: The Experience of Punjab, *Indian Journal of Public Administration*, 11 (4): 737-4.

Dandavate, M.R (1967): Common Bonds of Nationalism, *Janata*, 22 (37): 5-6.

Datta, Abhijit and Bhattacharya, Mohit (1967): Functional Approach to Indian Federalism - Case Study of Urban Development, *Indian Journal of Public Administration*, 13: 283-298.

Dutt, Vidya Prakash (1966): China and Indo-Pakistani Relations, *International Studies*, 8 (1-2): 126-133.

Dwivedy, Surendranath (1967): New Relationship between the Centre and States, *Janata*, 22 (8): 2.

Gangal, S. C. (1966): The Commonwealth and Indo-Pakistani Relations, *International Studies*, 8 (1-2): 131-149.

Ghatate, Narayan Madhav (1966): Disarmament in India's Foreign Policy, 1947-1965, Unpublished Ph. D. Dissertation, American University.

Gulati, Hans Raj (1967): India and Pakistan: Their Mutual Antagonism, *Janata*, 22 (35): 7-8.

Guha, Samar (1966): When East Bengal Breaks Off, *Janata*, 21 (2): 7-8, 12.

Gupta, Sisir (1966): India's Policy towards Pakistan, *international Studies*, 8 (1-2): 29-48.

Isard, W. and Smith, T. (1965): *A Practical Application of Game Theoretical Approach to Arms Reduction*, *Peace Research Society Papers*, IV.

Jena. B. B. (1965): Jurisdictional Contradictions in State Organisms in India, *Indian Journal of Political Science*, 27 (4): 30-36.

Jha, C. S. (1967): Non-alignment in a Changing *World, Indian and Foreign Review*, 4 (23): 9-11, 17-19.

Kapur, Harish (1966): The Soviet Union and the Indo-Pakistan Relations, *International Studies*, 8 (1-2): 150-157.

Karanakaram, K. P. (1966): China in India's International Relations, *China Report*, 2 (6): 35-39.

Lakdawala, Dansukhlal Tulsidas (1967): *Union-State Financial Relations*, Lalvani Publication House, Bombay.

Misra, K. P. (1965): The Indo-Pakistan Conflict, *Africa Quarterly*, 5 (3): 203-217.

Mohan, Surendra (1967): Regionalism-Unresolved Dilemma, Janata, 22 (37): 3, 15.

Nath. V. (1966): Region for Planning, *Indian Journal of Public Administration*, 12 (1): 1-17.

Prabhakar,Purushottam (1967): Indo-Japanese Cooperation: Need For New Openings, *Foreign Affairs Reports*, 16 (10): 6-10.

Ramachandran, G. (1966): Union State Relations in Finance and Planning, *Indian* i *Journal of Public Administration*, 12 (3): 378-388.

Rao, P. Chandrasekhara (1965): Indo-Pakistan Agreement on the Rann of Kutch: Form and Contents, *Indian Journal of International Law*, 5 (2): 176-185.

Rath, P. K. (1965): Governmental set-up in the States of the Indian Union-Some Aspects of its Working, *Indian Journal of Political S'cience*, 27 (4): 18-22.

Ray, Amal (1966): *Inter-governmental Relations in India: A Study of Indian Federalism*, Asia Publishing House, Bombay.

Ray, Asmini K. (1966): Pakistan as a Factor in Indo-Soviet Relations, *Economic and Political Weekly*, 1 (12): 503-06.

Ray, Jayant Kumar (1966): India and Pakistan as Factors in Each Other's Foreign Policies, *International Studies*, 8 (1-2): 49-63.

Richardson, L.F. (1960): *Arms and Insecurity*, The Bon Wood Press, Pittsburgh.

Sastry, S. V. S. (1967): The Case for Nonalignment, *Indian and Foreign Review*, 4 (8): 18-19.

Seth, Nareshavern Dayal (1966): India's Policy Towards China and Pakistan in the Light of Kautilya's Arthasastra, *Modern Review*, 120 (3): 200-203.

Singh, Balgit (1955): The United States and the India-Pakistan Conflict, *Parliamentary Studies*, 9 (12): 15-19.

Singh, Gopal (1967): India's Relations with Pakistan, *Parliamentary Studies*, 11 (5): 11-13.

Sinha, Shyam Nandan (1967): Union-state Relations in a New Key, *AICC Economic Review*, 19 (8): 625-629.

Smoker, Paul (1967): The Arms Race as an Open and Closed System, *Peace Research Society Papers,* VII.

Srinivasan, N. (1966): Union State Relations in Agricultural Development, *Indian Journal of Public Administration.* 12 (3): 389-406.

Tripathi, P. K. (1965): Legislative Relations between the Union and the States and Educational Planning, *Indian Advocate,* 5 (3- 4): 4-12.

Vaidyanathan, R. (1966): Some Recent Trends in Soviet Policies towards India and Pakistan, *International Studies,* 12 (3): 429-447.

Zhukov, Yuri (1967): India and the Struggle for World Peace, *Indian and Foreign Review,* 4 (24): 10-13.

7

Age-structured Human Capital Dynamics and Economic Growth: A Note on Interdependence, Coordination and Welfare

Tapas Mishra[1]
Mamata Parhi[2]

I. INTRODUCTION

Humans lead the race among other living beings with respect to their ability to think, generate ideas and transform imagination into reality. Ideas evolve, new ideas replace the old ones and new socio-economic orders are then established as 'changes' are facilitated by the pace of diffusion in the space-time domain. Two important notes can be uncovered from the above. *First*, ideas and imaginations are embodied in nature, which under certain socio-economic and infrastructural conditions generate innovations. Innovations diffuse over time and space and often trigger long term growth swings over centuries. *Second*, economies' 'demand-supply' rule of

---

[1] International Institute for Applied Systems Analysis (IIASA), Schlossplatz, Laxenburg, Austria & University of Wales, Swansea, UK. E-mail: t.k.mishra@swansea.ac.uk
[2] BETA-Theme, Universit'e Louis Pasteur, Strasbourg 1, 61, Avenue de la Foret Noire, F-67065 Strasbourg Cedex, France & University of Wales, Swansea, UK. E-mail: m.parhi@swansea.ac.uk

resource allocation and distributions is invariably limited by the state and speed of innovations. As a matter of fact, although educated and trained minds (broadly defined as people with higher education) have proclivity for innovation, its pace may be severely constrained by the distribution of education within various population age groups. A country with higher proportion of younger people with higher education (i.e., secondary education and more) is often assumed to generate more resources than the ones with smaller proportions. Thus, the distribution of education across age-structured population matters more for economic growth than with its aggregate dynamics. The above provides a glimpse of the origin, relevance and extension of human capital as a propeller of economic growth.

An imposing feature of human capital is that it induces non-decreasing returns to scale to production. Decreasing and/or constant returns to scale appears in the traditional production function, e.g., Cobb-Douglas type represented by: $Y = AK^{\alpha}L^{\beta}$. Here the production (Y) is a function of physical capital, labor, and technical change, denoted respectively by K, L and A. Additionally, α represents the share of capital in the production of one unit of output, Y. Labor's share is presented by β. Various degrees of returns to scale occur when the combined value of $\alpha + \beta$ exceeds, is less than or equal to unity. In Cobb-Douglas type specification with labor and physical capital, decreasing returns to scale to labor and capital occurs when their marginal productivities decline over time in the absence of any qualitative improvement of their efficiencies. Indeed, the latter assumes intrinsic value to the modern growth theory. By embedding efficiency to labour input, for instance, its negative trend of marginal productivity can be reversed or kept constant: As a labourer enhances his efficiency through special training and education, his productivity per unit of output increases, hence the marginal productivity of labor becomes positive. Similarly the marginal productivity of capital[3] can also be enhanced by improving its efficiency through technological embodiment and replacement over its life cycle. This way, the combined proportion of labor (here the efficient labor or productive labor or human capital) and capital (i.e., $\alpha + \beta$) can be greater than unity, thus exhibiting increasing returns to scale. It is this addition of an input's character which is important for sustainable economic growth. Sustainability requires that the responsible inputs of the production technology continuously improves its efficiency in the production space and contribute to (a possibly monotonic) increase in the total value over time. Therefore, without an efficiency embodiment to labour through education, it would not be possible to reverse the trend of declining marginal productivity. This summarizes the idea of the recently developed 'endogenous growth theory' (Romer, 1986; Rebelo, 1991).

While theoretical development in human capital theory has witnessed remarkable progress since Romer (1986), its development in empirical testing is not far reaching. Rather it is often vexed with critical questions of the presence and/or absence of stochastic trend in output. Popular test of endogenous growth involves unit root, cointegration and error correction analysis among the co-moving variables in an economy. As evident from numerous such applications (e.g., Lau, 1995, 2001) since Nelson and Plosser (1981), the empirical tests are conducted in the time dimension and hardly corroborate the dynamic impact of spatial variations. Accumulation of a production factor can occur both in time and space. However, possibly due to complex methodological and empirical application, testing of endogenous growth in space has not been explicitly conducted. The spatial testing is

---

[3] Adam Smith defined four types of fixed capital: (1) useful machines, instruments of the trade; (2) buildings as the means of procuring revenue; (3) improvements of land and (4) human capital. In line with recent growth theoretic tradition, we will emphasize on physical capital in terms of machines, instruments, etc., and the human capital.

not our point of interest in this piece of research although we will come across the implications and necessity of such testing in the ensuing sections.

Our basic argument in this chapter lies in delineating the importance of age-structured human capital in endogenous economic growth. And in this context, we intend to stress on the relevance of 'space' for accumulation of human capital on economic growth. Note that 'space' can be defined both in the relational and geographical sense. As will be evident from the discussions below, we would superimpose geographical space to get a better result of the relational structure. On the basis of a defined geographical space, we will show theoretically that an international cooperation in human capital policy would improve aggregate welfare of nations. An empirical test will be conducted next to provide evidence of dynamic spatial correlation of economic growth across countries due to their human capital accumulation pattern and externalities. The plan of this chapter is as follows. In Section 2, we discuss the origin of the theory of human capital and its implications in growth theory. A policy coordination game in line with the cooperative game theory is proposed in Section 3 and shown how knowledge spillovers can generate positive growth momentums in adjoining countries and how policy coordination is welfare improving for the participating nations. Section 4 presents the econometric specification required for the empirical model. In Section 5, we discuss data characteristics. Section 6 presents empirical results and Section 7 provides concluding remarks.

II. AGE-STRUCTURED HUMAN CAPITAL: THEORY AND EMPIRICS

The origin of human capital as a concept can be traced to the early the days of Adam Smith. In general, human capital and the productive power of labor are often argued to be both dependent on the division of labor and the greater part of the skill, dexterity, and judgement with which it is any where directed, or applied. In short, there is a complex relationship between the division of labor and human capital. Smith saw human capital as skills, dexterity (physical, intellectual, psychological, etc) and judgment[4]. The use of the term in the modern neoclassical economic literature dates back to Jacob Mincer's pioneering article "Investment in Human Capital and Personal Income Distribution" in The *Journal of Political Economy* in 1958. The pioneering development occurred in the research of Mincer and Gary Becker of the Chicago School of economics. In this view human capital is similar to physical means of production, e.g., factories and machines. That is, one can invest in human capital (via education, training, medical treatment) and one's outputs depend partly on the rate of return on the human capital one owns. Thus, human capital is a means of production into which additional investment yields additional output. An important element of human capital is knowledge which is gained through higher education and training. The development of knowledge is physically captured by innovations. By the basic property of knowledge (that it is expandable and self generating with use and it is transportable and shareable), human capital accumulation in one location generates externalities which tend to migrate to other locations. This way, countries' growth processes are (dynamically) correlated by human capital development across spatial locations and over time. Methodological and conceptual definitions and implications of human capital abound in economic growth theory, however, in this chapter we will not divulge to elaborating such arguments. Rather, we will stress on their summary idea that human capital - whether segregated from labor with productive capabilities or treating them as a bundle which is embodied in nature - refers to the efficiency gain in the labour input. In either case, human capital is

---

[4] Furthermore, human capital can be acquired through formal schooling and on-the-job training.

assumed to generate sustainable production through non-constant returns to scale.

Traditionally, the theory and empirics of human capital in economic growth and development has stressed on decomposing aggregate population growth into the growth of its components, e.g., the growth of population age-structures. The total population of a nation generally comprises of population of young age (0-14), working age (15-64) and retired cohorts (64+). The provision of education and efficiency achievement for the young age population and its continuation afterwards (to secondary and tertiary level for population age 15 or more) actually sets the initial condition needed for a nation's high growth momentum. The general understanding is that once the young age population with standard education reaches the working age, they are already endowed with higher knowledge needed for innovation, assimilation of ideas and adaption in order to generate sufficient resources for the economy for sustainability. This approach has been recently employed in empirical endogenous growth testing by e.g., Barro (1991), Kelley and Schmidt (2001), Crenshaw et al. (1997), and Mishra and Diebolt (forthcoming), Azomahou and Mishra (2008) among others. Theoretical modeling leading to the explicit treatment of demographic decomposition to the rates of growth return in the long run due to rate of schooling has been documented by Boucekkine et al. (2002) and the references therein. Lindh and Malmberg (2007), Creso-Cuaresma and Mishra (2008) provide analysis for using age-structure population and human capital for economic growth forecasts. From spatial perspective, Parhi and Mishra (2008) study the effect of age-structured human capital on dynamic growth correlations, while Azomahou, Diebolt and Mishra (forthcoming) use age-structure population information to construct a demographic distance function and show its effect on growth interdependence among sets of geographically clustered countries.

The underlying idea in the mentioned research is that age-structure human capital provides a clear scientific basis for unraveling growth dynamics (either in space or time or both) than the aggregate human capital concept. By decomposing human capital with age specification, as the authors argue, one is able to identify the explicit dynamics of demographic changes, their productivity patterns and the (cross-) effects they exert on economic growth over time and across country locations. For instance, as the degree of educational status increases from primary to secondary and tertiary, the productivity of population age groups 15-29, 30-49 and 50-64 also increases. Through knowledge accumulation and gained experience, the efficiency and thus the return to growth also accelerate. This generates a productivity cycle within a national boundary. However, the peaked productivity of a nation due to high stock of educated personnel always increases the transferability chance across borders through tradable and non-tradable goods and services and very often through migration.

Assuming that human capital can be generated through education and training and that embodied knowledge is transferable across national boundaries, question may arise whether economic growth across countries are correlated and/or interdependent and whether such interdependence is due to human capital accumulation dynamics among them. If so, would a joint policy program enhance individual and collective economic welfare? Empirically, one may ask what type of econometric specification can lead to a test of dynamic spatial interdependence across countries. To answer these questions, we provide an endogenous growth theoretic model in the next section and propose a dynamic game between countries due to knowledge spillovers and weigh its effects on growth and welfare. We build a recursive growth model with human capital (spillover effects across countries through productivity shocks) in endogenous growth theoretic setting. It is shown that cooperation in age-structured human capital policy development lead to higher aggregate social welfare than under isolation. On an interesting note it is also shown how volatility in cross country growth (international persistence of output) could be modeled via human capital differences. In the next section we design a spatial econometric model to test for spatial interdependence of economic growth due to human capital accumulation.

III. THEORETICAL SPECIFICATION: RECURSIVE GROWTH MODEL WITH INTERNATIONAL HUMAN CAPITAL SPILLOVERS

(a) Deterministic setting

As eked out before, the idea that an economy could be in balanced growth equilibrium when its production technology is homogeneous of degree one, or greater than one in the accumulable factor (such as human capital) is the basic foundation of endogenous growth theory (see, Romer, 1986). Interestingly, due to high integratedness of world economies, countries' growth processes are dynamically correlated. The correlation, in most likelihood, occurs in the accumulative factor for the simple reason that positive growth synergies from across the border is often encouraged by the neighboring economies to provide momentum or a push of their own economy along the long-run growth path. Negative externalities are often guarded across spatial locations and policies are designed to arrest their free movements in space. Since international movement of shocks could result in diminishing and sometimes skewed growth pattern in different locations, stringent policies are often adopted or sought for to safe-guard economies from spatially persistent shocks. However, since positive growth externalities are often presaged to improve individual as well as collective welfare, policy cooperation in enhancing the development of such growth agenda is often encouraged at international levels.

The interdependence in countries' growth and policy cooperation with respect to human capital can be modeled in two ways. First, a cooperative game theoretic framework can be employed to show that under certain incentive constraints, cooperation of economies with respect to human capital development and demographic policy would be a superior strategy to achieve aggregate welfare. Since countries would not wish to be chaotically affected by strategies adopted in the neighborhood (by some other countries) and would like to maintain that sum of individual payoffs be equal the value of the grand coalition. And no coalition has a value greater than the sum of its members' payoffs. The concept of 'core' and stability of core under cooperative game theory can be applied. We do not follow this line of argument in this chapter although it has been preserved for future research.

The second strategy, which we follow here is based on a recursive formulation of a stochastic growth model with international spillover effects of human capital accumulation at locations, say i and j where $i, j = 1, \ldots, N$. Basically, the framework is based on the idea that growth occurs from international externalities in the production of knowledge. To elucidate, consider two symmetrical economies, $i, j \in \{1, 2\}$[5]. Agent produces and consumes single commodity and allocates a fixed time endowment between leisure and investment in human capital. The agent derives utility from the consumption of output, c_t and incurs disutility[6] from the amount of time spent on non-leisure activities, here the proportion of time

---

[5] The assumption of symmetry is neither binding nor unrealistic. Because in a clustered geographic location, say, Europe, Asia, Africa, etc., countries share common demographic and socio-economic traits. By similar and symmetric economies here we mean that the demographic processes governing the economies are the same and that the production technologies in these economies are similar.

[6] In the strict sense of the term, the latter cannot be said to be disutility per se as the accumulated human capital helps the agent in future period to be more productive and earn more for consumption.

devoted for development of human capital, λ_{it} in the following equations. The model can be developed both in a deterministic and stochastic setting. Under stochasticity, we can add preference and output shocks to the model specification where both shocks are assumed to be independently and identically distributed with mean and constant variance. Given the objective of this chapter, it would suffice to describe a model under deterministic setting so that international policy cooperation can be studied under a fairly non-chaotic dynamic setting.

The expected inter-temporal utility function defined for each agent i is

$$U_i = E_0 \sum_{t=0}^{\infty} \beta^t [\log(c_{it}) + \zeta \log(1 - \lambda_{it})] \qquad (1)$$

Where E_0 is the conditional expectations operator, $\beta \in (0, 1)$ is a discount factor. The optimization problem for each agent is described by

$$\underset{\{c_{it}, \lambda_{it}, h_{i,t+1}\}_{t=1}^{\infty}}{\text{Max}} U_i = E_0 \sum_{t=0}^{\infty} \beta^t [\log(c_{it}) + \zeta \log(1 - \lambda_{it})] \qquad (2)$$

s.t.
$$c_{it} = (1 - \rho_{it}) h_{it} \qquad (3)$$
$$h_{i,t+1} = A(h_{it} \lambda_{it}^{\alpha}) g_{it}^{\gamma} H_{it}^{\psi} H_{jt}^{1-\alpha-\tau-\psi} \qquad (4)$$

where $\zeta > 0$, $\rho_{it} \in (0, 1)$ is the flat tax rate, λ_{it} is the time spent on investing in human capital. g_{it} is public expenditure. Equation 3 implies that consumption is equal to the disposable income. The latter is given by income from human capital accumulation less flat rate income taxes levied on hit. Revenues from taxation are used by the government to finance the provision of public goods and services. To generate perpetual growth we assume constant returns to scale production technology so that production function is linearly homogeneous in human capital, h_{it}.

Equation 4 defines the human capital accumulation dynamics as in Blackburn and Ravn (1993). α, γ, ψ ∈ (0, 1), α + γ + ψ ∈ (0, 1). A > 0. Average (aggregate) human capital stock is H. In the equation, H_{it} captures spillover effects of human capital within the same country, whereas H_{jt} indicates the aggregate stock of human capital abroad as reflecting a system of imperfect property rights in the acquisition and transmission of knowledge across countries (see Tamura, 1991). Thus, the inter-connectedness among countries (which forms the empirical foundation of the paper) is modeled through cross-country spillovers in the accumulation of human capital. In the empirical section of the chapter we will come across this type of interconnectedness where it is captured by the correlatedness among error terms in a spatial vector autoregressive model (SVAR). The SVAR is assumed to be a function of human capital accumulation dynamics at country locations.

The government's budget constraint is given by:

$$g_{it} = \tau_{it} H_{it} \tag{5}$$

where we assume that government in each economy has a monopoly in taxing domestic income. Now, the government's objective is to choose a sequence of tax rates which *maximizes* the welfare of the representative agent *subject* to private equilibrium behavior and cooperation or non-cooperation. The Bellman value function for each country is:

$$V(h_{it} g_{it} \tau_{it} H_{it} H_{jt} = \max_{\{\lambda_{it}, h_{i,t+1}\}} \{\log((1-\rho_{it})h_{it}) + \zeta \log(1-\lambda_{it}) + \beta E_0 V(h_{it+1} g_{it+1}, \rho_{it+1}, h_{it+1}, h_{jt+1})\} \tag{6}$$

The value function V (.) exists and satisfies usual conditions of uniqueness, concavity and differentiability. To obtain the solutions each agent forecasts the time paths of ρ_{it}, g_{it}, H_{it}, H_{jt} by the sequences

$\{\tau_{it}\}_{t=0}^{\infty}, \{g_{it}\}_{t=0}^{\infty}, \{\rho_{it}\}_{t=0}^{\infty}, \{H_{it}\}_{t=0}^{\infty}, \{H_{jt}\}_{t=0}^{\infty}$.

The balanced growth equilibrium for each economy is captured by differentiating the value function with respect to λ_{it} and gives rise to the following relationship:

$$\frac{\zeta}{1-\lambda_{it}} = \frac{\alpha\beta E_0 V'(h_{it+1} \mid g_{it+1}, \rho_{it+1}, H_{it+1}, H_{jt+1})h_{it+1}}{\lambda_{it}} \quad (7)$$

$$V'(h_{it+1} \mid g_{it+1}, \rho_{it+1}, H_{it+1}, H_{jt+1}) =$$
$$\frac{1}{h_{it+1}} + \frac{\alpha\beta E_0 V'(h_{it+2} \mid g_{it+2}, \rho_{it+2}, H_{it+2}, H_{jt+2})h_{it+2}}{h_{it+1}} \quad (8)$$

where $V'(h_{it+s|.}) = \partial V(h_{it+s,.})/\partial h_{it+s}$. Combining we arrive at

$$\frac{\lambda_{it}}{1-\lambda_{it}} = \frac{\alpha\beta}{\zeta}(1 + \frac{\zeta\lambda_{it+1}}{1-\lambda_{it+1}}) \quad (9)$$

establishing that $\lambda_{it} = \lambda_{jt} = \lambda \in (0, 1)$. The implication is that government in each country invests the same constant amount of time in human capital production and the investment is independent of growth and policy. In particular,

$$\lambda = \frac{\alpha\beta}{\alpha\beta + \zeta(1-\alpha\beta)} \quad (10)$$

The equilibrium growth rate of aggregate human capital in each economy for any given tax rate is given by:

$$\frac{H_{it+1}}{H_{it}} = \Delta_{it}(\lambda_{it}, \rho_{it}) = A\left(\frac{H_{jt}}{H_{it}}\right)^{1-\alpha-\gamma-\psi} \lambda_{it}^{\gamma} \lambda^{\alpha} \qquad (11)$$

which follows from Equations 4, 5 and 10.

Assuming same amount of initial human capital for i and j, and if taxes are identical for i and j, each country experiences the common rate of growth such that $H_{it+1}/H_{it} = H_{jt+1}/H_{jt} = H_{t+1}/H_t$ where

$$H_{t+1}/H_t = \Delta(\lambda_t, \rho_t) = A\rho^{\gamma}\lambda^{\alpha} \qquad (12)$$

Apparently, $(\lambda_t, \rho_t) > 0$. The implication of this equilibrium is as follows. Under non-stochastic shocks (i.e., without any preference or technology shocks, to say) the endogeneity of growth is due to constant returns to human capital accumulation in equilibrium. The expression also says that under different equilibrium policy (for example, under cooperation or strategic cooperation in human capital) the choice and distribution of λ and ρ plays pivotal role in the extent and consequence of cooperative programs.

We now define the equilibrium policy under cooperation, strategic cooperation and non-cooperation. Since the problem is to choose a sequence of tax rates optimizing an intertemporal trade-off between current and future consumption, the problem becomes interesting with cross-country interdependence with human capital and demographic shocks spillover effects. Growth in each country is determined by tax policies in both countries. The solution to the problem is the equilibrium of a dynamic game between governments: Cooperative or noncooperative (isolationist and strategic). Following Blackburn and Ravn (1993), an isolationist government takes as given the production of human capital in other countries. Strategic government implies that government in each country takes account of the effect of own policy on the production of human capital in other country locations. Finally, under cooperation, government in each country chooses a tax strategy (that is cooperates) to maximize a joint welfare function taking account of the effect of policy action in other locations as well as the effects of human capital externalities. Thus under non-cooperation, the each government maximizes its own welfare function taking as given the tax strategy of other governments, while under cooperation a joint welfare function is maximized. We want to show that higher social welfare accrue under cooperation when countries either in the geographical cluster or correlated by economic openness. Under the above definition of cooperation and non-cooperation, the modified objective functions are as follows:

1. Noncooperative: Isolationist:

$$V(H_{it}, H_{jt}) = \max_{\{\rho_{it}, H_{i,t+1}\}} \{\log((1-\rho_{it})H_{it}) + \beta V(H_{it+1}, H_{jt+1})\} \tag{13}$$

2. Noncooperative: Strategist:

$$V(H_{it}, H_{jt}) = \max_{\{\rho_{it}, H_{i,t+1}, H_{j,t+1}\}} \{\log((1-\rho_{it})H_{it}) + \beta V(H_{it+1}, H_{jt+1})\} \tag{14}$$

3. Cooperative:

$$V(H_{it}, H_{jt}) = \max_{\{\rho_{it}, \rho_{jt}, H_{i,t+1}, H_{j,t+1}\}} \{\phi \log((1-\rho_{it})H_{it}) + (1-\phi)\log((1-\rho_{it})H_{it}) + \beta V(H_{it+1}, H_{jt+1})\} \tag{15}$$

For the above three cases (Equations 13-15) the equilibrium policy can be derived by maximizing each objective function subject to the government budget constraint, initial human capital and the human capital production function described before. Solving for the first order conditions of the three value functions we find that optimal tax rate is constant and same for each country: $\rho_{it} = \rho_{jt} = \rho \in (0,1)$. (The details of the proof are available upon request).

Isolationist: $\rho = \dfrac{\gamma\beta}{1-\beta(\alpha+\psi)}$ (16)

Strategist:
$$\rho = \dfrac{\lambda\beta[1-\beta(\alpha+\lambda+\psi)]}{\lambda\beta[1-\beta(\alpha+\lambda+\psi)]+(1-\beta)[1+\beta-2\beta(\alpha+\lambda+\psi)]}$$ (17)

Cooperative: $\rho = \dfrac{\gamma\beta}{1-\beta(1-\gamma)}$ (18)

From the above after some algebra we get:
$\rho(isolationist) < \rho(strategist) < \rho(cooperative)$
$\rightarrow \Delta(isolationist) < \Delta(strategist) < \Delta(cooperative)$

This proves that countries gain more under cooperation than under non-cooperation. Therefore, a joint policy program in human capital development would maximize aggregate welfare.

Given that $\Delta_{it}(\lambda_{it},\rho_{it}) > 0$ and that countries growth processes are interconnected by openness, a small increase in one country's growth by human capital development program will increase other country's growth. That is, countries growth programs are supermodular. The conjecture can be qualified by applying the single crossing property of supermodularity. In the ordinal form it says that an increase in the value of the objective function due to a rise in one of the variables is preserved after the rise of any other variable. In the differentiable or cardinal version it means that the marginal gain with respect to one variable is nondecreasing in the other variables. In our case, a rise in human capital increases the value of the objective function of domestic economy and also improves upon the value function of other economies (due to human capital externality - which is mostly positive). For own economy, the marginal gain due to a rise in human capital is nondecreasing in other variables, such as raw labor and physical capital in the production. Using complementarity theory we can formulate a stochastic objective function[7] (the production function with human capital and physical capital) denoted by say, $F(K,H)$ function F: S × A → R is increasing difference in the argument (K,H) if and only if F(K',H') − F(K',H) ≥ F(K,H') − F(K,H) ∀K' > K, H' > H.

(b) Stochastic setting

Under stochastic growth model, Δ can be a function of stochastic parameters, viz., preference shocks (Ω_1), technology shocks (Ω_2), and stochastic demographic shocks (Ω_3). Depending on the interest, the growth program can be designed such that either (Ω_1) and (Ω_2) or (Ω_2) and (Ω_3) can enter the optimization program described in equations 1-4. If preference and technology shocks enter the model, then consumption can be described by (Ω_{1tct}). The output y_t can be given by

$$y_t = \Gamma(\Omega_{2t}, h_t) \qquad (19)$$

Note that we may or may not consider raw labor input for production - the choice largely depends on our choice given the objective specification. Finally, under stochastic demographic system and productivity shocks, we introduce

---

[7] The investigation of this property by proving complementarity of growth processes and establishing strategy proofness of the core is beyond the scope of this paper. This is preserved for future investigation

labor input N_t along with h_t such that the production function becomes:

$$y_t = \Gamma(\Omega_{2t}, N_t h_t) \qquad (20)$$

In the equation above N_th_t is a composite production input that measures efficiency units of time spent on working. N_t as it evolves according to the following:

$$N_t = (1 + n_t)N_{t-1} \qquad (21)$$

where n_t is population growth. Demographic system, like any other physical system is often subject to endogenous and/or exogenous shocks which might render more than mere short-run mean-converging effect on long-run growth of the interacting economy. To capture this, we follow Mishra and Diebolt (2007) and Mishra (2006) to characterize n_t with a fractal process where it evolves as a long-memory mechanism:

$$(1 - LD)^d \Phi(L) n_t = \Theta(L) \varepsilon_t \qquad (22)$$

L is the lag operator and the shock propagation mechanism is defined by power series expansion:

$$(1-L)^d = \sum_{j=0}^{\infty} \frac{\Gamma(J-d)}{\Gamma(J+1)\Gamma(-d)} L^j \qquad (23)$$

$\Phi(L) = (1 + \phi_1 L + ... + \phi_p L^p)$ and $\Theta(L) = (1 - \theta_1 L - ... - \theta_q L^q)$ are autoregressive (AR) and moving average (MA) polynomials respectively. The persistent shock in the demographic system could be due to non-stationary Markovian transition from one state of the demographic system to the other mainly due to non-linear interaction with economic system and frequent exogenous shocks imparting long-run non-mean converging effects. Analytical expression of production function with stochastic long-memory demographic system can be found in Mishra (2006), however, this exact expression is not required for the purpose here. A compact expression of the production function however can be obtained which may appear as:

$$y_t = \Gamma(\Omega_{3t}, N_t h_t) \tag{24}$$

Let's assume that $\Omega_{1t} \sim N(\mu\Omega_1, \sigma^2_{\Omega_1})$, $\Omega_{2t} \sim N(\mu\Omega_2, \sigma^2_{\Omega_2})$ and $\Omega_{3t} \sim N(\mu\Omega_3, \sigma^2_{\Omega_3})$. Then under the described stochastic production functions and solving the optimization problem (equations 1-4) we can arrive at the expression of human capital accumulation similar to equation 12. However, Δ will now contain stochastic elements, the distribution of which are described as above such that $\Delta(\lambda_t, \rho_t)$ are replaced by $\Delta(\Omega_{it}, \Omega_{jt})$ where i, j correspond to preference, technology shocks, and stochastic demographic shocks and where *i* different than *j*.

Proposition 1 *Given that $\Delta(\Omega_{it}, \Omega_{jt}) > 0$ an increase or decrease in stochastic exogenous shock in one economy induces spatial persistence of declining (mean-preserving) magnitude in other locations. That is, growth shocks are correlated by human capital policy program and are spatially persistent related to the distant measure.*

Proof of proposition 1: The proof of this conjecture can be laid in two steps. First we show how for a domestic economy growth and volatility are correlated. Next, under the built-in structure of a spatial production function, we show how spatial persistence may occur and why countries should cooperative in joint policy program. To prove the first point let's expand $\Delta(\Omega_{it}, \Omega_{jt}) > 0$ by a second order Taylor series approximation. Denoting this expression by $\Delta(.)$, the Taylor expansion gives:

$$\Delta(.) \approx \Delta(\mu\Omega_i, \mu\Omega_j) + \Delta_1(\mu\Omega_i, \mu\Omega_j)(\Omega_{it} - \mu\Omega_i) +$$
$$\Delta_2(\mu\Omega_i, \mu\Omega_j)(\Omega_{jt} - \mu\Omega_j) + \frac{1}{2}\Delta_{11}(\mu\Omega_i, \mu\Omega_j) \quad (25)$$
$$(\Omega_{it} - \mu\Omega_i)^2 + \frac{1}{2}\Delta_{22}(\mu\Omega_i, \mu\Omega_j)(\Omega_{jt} - \mu\Omega_j)^2$$

The expected value of this is:

$$E[\Delta(.)] = \Delta(\mu\Omega_i, \mu\Omega_j) + \frac{1}{2}\Delta_{11}(\mu\Omega_i, \mu\Omega_j)\sigma^2_{\Omega_i}$$
$$+ \frac{1}{2}\Delta_{22}(\mu\Omega_i, \mu\Omega_j)\sigma^2_{\Omega_j} \quad (26)$$

Where $\Delta_i(.) = \frac{1}{2}\Delta_{ii}(.)$. As per the expression above an increase in $\sigma^2_{\Omega_i}$ (or $\sigma^2_{\Omega_j}$) will increase (decrease) $E(h_{t+1}/h_t)$ depending on whether $\Delta_i(.) >$ or < 0. Intuitively, if $\Delta_i(.)$ is convex (concave), the gain in learning as a result of favorable shock more (less) than compensates the loss in learning as a result of unfavorable shock so that, on the average, growth is increased (decreased) by a mean-preserving spread in the distribution of shocks. To prove spatial persistence of growth and volatility we require a spatial production function where the interconnectedness among countries is represented by common demographic process and human capital accumulation. A detailed description of the model will follow in the following section. However, for the present purpose we state the production function as: $Y_{i,t+1} = \alpha_i Y_{i,t} + \sum_{j \neq i}^{N} f_i[D_t(i,j)]Y_{j,t}$, where growth at country location i and at period $t+1$ is a function of its own past growth as well growth in the neighboring countries based on a distance function defined by $D_t(i,j)$. The property of the distance metric will be explored shortly, however, in our case it could represent the distance between say $E(h_{t+1}/h_t)_i$ and $E(h_{t+1}/h_t)_j$ (i, j represent two countries). It depends on the similarity in the use of human capital in the production of output. The spatial production function specification indicates that since countries' growth processes are correlated with respect to human capital appropriation in output production, a technology and/or demographic shock is likely to persist to spatial locations over time with some lag.

IV. THE ECONOMETRIC SPECIFICATION: A SPATIAL VECTOR AUTOREGRESSIVE APPROACH

Our econometric specification embodies a dynamic structure in the form of a panel vector autoregressive (VAR) model on growth rates of GDP per capita, where the structure of the error term allows for a general type of spatial correlation across countries. This setting allows us to quantify the effect of human capital distance on the diffusion of shocks to GDP per capita among countries in the sample. The econometric specification and the estimation method used are based on Chen and Conley (2001) and Conley and Dupor (2003). The model is characterized by spatio-temporal links in the process of economic growth, where the spatial dimension is based on a distance measure constructed using human capital data. The results for different potential measures of human capital distance, which were computed using a new data set that comprises information on demographic structure and educational attainment across countries of the world, are reported below.

A spatial VAR growth model

We describe economic growth in a semi parametric spatial VAR framework. Let $\{Y_{i,t} : i = 1,...,N; t = 1,...,T\}$ denote the sample realizations of the growth variable for N countries at locations $\{s_{i,t} = i = 1,...,N; t = 1,...,T\}$. Now, let D_t be a stacked vector of distances between the $\{s_{i,t}\}_{i=1}^{N}$ defined for two points i and j as $D_t(i,j) = \|s_{i,t}; s_{j,t}\|$ with $\|\cdot\|$ denoting the Euclidean norm. Then,

$$D_t = [D_t(1,2)...D_t(1,N), D_t(2,3)...D_t(2,N), D_t(N-1,N)]' \in \Re^{\frac{N(N-1)}{2}}$$

Moreover, the distances are assumed to have a common support $(0, d_{max}) \forall t, i \neq j$. We assume that the growth of a given country denoted at $t+1$ denoted $Y_{i,t+1}$ will depend not only on its own past (home externalities), but also nonparametrically on the performance of its neighbors (spatial spillovers effects). Given the history $\{Y_{t-1}, D_{t-1} l \geq 0\}$, our specification is given by

$$Y_{i,t+1} = \alpha_i Y_{i,t} + \sum_{j \neq i}^{N} f_i [D_t(i,j)] Y_{j,t} \qquad (27)$$

where the α_i parameters describe the strength of externalities generated by home growth, f_i are continuous functions of distances mapping from $(0, \infty)$ to $\Re^l$. One interesting feature in this specification is that it does not assume an a-priori parametric specification of neighborhood structure as usually done in parametric spatial models.

Let us denote $Z_t = Y_{1,t}, Y_{2,t}...Y_{N,t}) \in \Re^N$ as a vector stacking $\{Y_{i,t}\}_{i=1}^N$. Following Chen and Conley (2001), we model the joint process $\{(Z_t, D_t) : t = 1,...,T\}$ as a first order Markov process which designs the evolution of Z_t according to the following nonlinear Spatial Vector Autoregressive Model (SVAR):

$$Z_{t+1} = A(D_t)Z_t + \varepsilon_{t+1} \quad \varepsilon_{t+1} = Q(D_t)u_{t+1} \qquad (28)$$

where $A(D_t)$ is a $N \times N$ matrix whose elements are functions of human capital distances between countries. We assume that u_{t+1} is an i.i.d. sequence with $E(u_{t+1}) = 0$ and $V(u_{t+1}) = I_N$. It follows that the conditional covariance matrix of ε_{t+1} is $E(\varepsilon_{t+1}, \varepsilon'_{t+1}) = Q(D_t)Q(D_t)' := \Omega(D_t)$ which is also a function of distances. In the specification (28), the conditional mean $A(D_t)$ and the conditional covariance $\Omega(D_t)$ are of importance and have to be estimated. More structure will be imposed on these objects in order to allow estimation.

1. Structure on conditional means.

From (28), the conditional mean of $Y_{i,t+1}$ given $\{Z_{t-l}, D_{t-l}, l \geq 0\}$ is modeled as

$$E[Y_{i,t+1}\{Z_{t-l}, D_{t-l}, l \geq 0\}] = \alpha_i Y_{i,t} + \sum_{i \neq j}^{N} f_i[D_t(i,j)]Y_{j,t} \qquad (29)$$

where as pointed out above, the f_i are continuous functions mapping from $(0, \infty)$ to $\Re^l$. Notice that this conditional mean turns out to be relation (29). As a result, it follows that the conditional mean of Z_{t+1} given $\{Z_{t-1}, D_{t-1} l \geq 0\}$ is $A(D_t)Z_t$.

$$A(D_t) = \begin{pmatrix} \alpha_1 & f_1[D_t(1,2)] & \cdots & f_1[D_t(1,N)] \\ f_2[D_t(2,1)] & \alpha_2 & \cdots & f_2[D_t(2,N)] \\ \cdot & \cdot & & \cdot \\ \cdot & \cdot & & \cdot \\ \cdot & \cdot & & \cdot \\ f_N[D_t(N,1)] & f_N[D_t(N,2)] & \cdots & \alpha_N \end{pmatrix} \quad (30)$$

It can be interesting in practice to model the α_i parameters and the f_i functions as having features in common across i.

2. Structure on conditional covariance

The conditional covariance of Z_{t+1} given $\{Z_{t-1}, D_{t-1} l \geq 0\}$ is modeled as

$$\Omega(D_t) = \begin{pmatrix} \sigma_1^2 + \gamma(0) & \gamma[D_t(1,2)] & \cdots & \gamma[D_t(1,N)] \\ \gamma[D_t(2,1)] & \sigma_2^2 + \gamma(0) & \cdots & \gamma[D_t(2,N)] \\ \cdot & \cdot & & \cdot \\ \cdot & \cdot & & \cdot \\ \cdot & \cdot & & \cdot \\ \gamma[D_t(N,1)] & \gamma[D_t(N,2)] & \cdots & \sigma_N^2 + \gamma(0) \end{pmatrix} \quad (31)$$

where $\gamma(.)$ is assumed to be continuous at zero and is k-dimensional isotropic covariance function[8]. The choice of γ

---

[8] Isotropy means that the stationary random field (with indices in $\Re^k$) that generates the process is directionally invariant.

ensures that $\Omega(D_t)$ is positive definite for any set of interpoint distance D_t and any values of the $\sigma_i^2 \geq 0$. Yaglom (1987: 353–354) showed that an isotropic covariance function has a representation as an integral of a generalized Bessel function. The representation of γ is analogous to the spectral representation of time-series covariance functions.

Estimation strategy

For simplicity, we assume that the distance function D_t is exogenous, i.e., determined outside the relation (28). We are interested in the shape of functions f_i and γ specified above. Chen and Conley (2001) propose a semi-parametric approach based on the cardinal B-spline sieve method. This approach uses a flexible sequence of parametric families to approximate the true unknown functions. The cardinal B-spline of order m, B_m on compact support $[0, m]$ is defined as

$$B_m = \frac{1}{(m-1)!} \sum_{k=0}^{m} (-1)^k \binom{m}{k} [\max(0, x-k)]^{m-1} \qquad (32)$$

Hence, $B_m(x)$ is a piecewise polynomial of the highest degree $m-1$. Then, the functions of interest f_i and Φ can be approximated by

$$f_i(y) \approx \sum_{j=-\infty}^{\infty} a_j B_m(2^n y - j) \qquad (33)$$

and

$$\Phi(y) \approx \sum_{j=-\infty}^{\infty} b_j B_m(2^n y - j) \qquad (34)$$

where the index j is a translation and the index n provides a scale refinement. The coefficients a_j and b_j are allowed to differ across these approximations. As n gets larger more $B_m(2^n y - j)$ are allowed and this in turn improved the approximation. Moreover, since B_m is nonnegative, a non-decreasing and nonnegative approximation of Φ can be obtained by restricting the coefficients b_j to be non-decreasing and nonnegative.

The estimation is performed in two-steps sieve least squares. In the first step, least square (LS) estimation of α_i and $f_i, i = 1,...,N$ is based on conditional mean (30) and sieve for f_i using the minimizations problem.

$$(\hat{\alpha}_i, T, \hat{f}_i, T) = \underset{(\hat{\alpha}_i, \hat{f}_i) \in \Re \times F_i T}{\arg\min} \frac{1}{T} \sum_{t=1}^{T} \{Y_{i,t+1} - (\alpha_i Y_{i,t} + \sum_{j \neq i} f_i[D_t(i,j)]Y_{j,t})\}^2 \quad (35)$$

where $F_{i,T}$ denotes the sieve for f_i (see Chen and Conley, 2001). Let us denote $\hat{\varepsilon}_{i,t+1} = (\hat{\varepsilon}_{1,t-1},...\hat{\varepsilon}_{N,t+1})$ as the LS residuals following from the first stage:

$$\hat{\varepsilon}_{i,t+1} = Y_{i,t+1} - (\hat{\alpha}_{i,t} Y_{i,t} + \sum_{j \neq i} \hat{f}_{i,T}[D_t(i,j)]Y_{j,t}) \quad (36)$$

Then, in the second step, sieve estimation for σ^2 and $\gamma(.)$ based on the conditional variance (31), sieve for γ and fitted residuals $\hat{\varepsilon}_{i,t+1}$ is obtained as

$$(\hat{\sigma}_T^2, \hat{\gamma}_T) = \underset{(\sigma^2, \gamma) \in (0,\infty)^N G}{\arg\min} \sum_{t=1}^{T-1} \sum_i \{\hat{\varepsilon}_{i,t+1}^2 - (\sigma_i^2 + \gamma(0))\}^2 + \sum_i \sum_{j \neq i} \{\hat{\varepsilon}_{i,t+1}\hat{\varepsilon}_{j,t+1} - \gamma(D(i,j))\}\}^2 \quad (37)$$

where G_T denotes the sieve for γ. Chen and Conley (2001) derived the $\sqrt{T}$ limiting normal distributions for the parametric components of the model. The author also suggested a bootstrap method for inference as the point wise distribution result for the nonparametric estimators $\hat{f}$ and $\hat{\gamma}$ is not provided. Moreover, the asymptotic covariance is computationally demanding.

The model proposed above is estimated using data on GDP per capita growth as the Y_{it} variable and measures of the demographic distribution of human capital in order to specify the locations $s_{i,t}$. This allows us to assess and quantify the effect of (di)similarity in the demographic distribution of human capital on the transmission of shocks to income across countries. It should be noticed that this nonparametric approach is a departure from typical spatial econometric models in which a parametric form of dependence is assumed (see, e.g., Anselin and Griffith, 1988 or Case, 1991). The spatial model as described above puts restrictions on comovement across countries that are different from those of typical factor models. In this case, the covariance across variables is mediated by a relatively low dimensional set of factors as in, for example, Quah and Sargent (1993) and Forni and Reichlin (1998).

V. DATA AND DISTANCE DEFINITIONS

The real GDP per capita series, measured in thousand constant dollars in 2001 international prices, are extracted from the Penn World Table Version 6.2 (Heston et al. 2006), while the age-structured human capital data is sourced from International Institute for Applied Systems Analysis and Vienna Institute of Demography's (IIASA-VID) newly constructed data base on educational attainments taking into account dynamic demographic developments (see Lutz et al.

2007a, 2007b). The time frame is 1970-2000 with annual frequency in all cases. Some specific characteristics of the educational attainment data are in order. This human capital data set was produced in a joint effort by the International Institute for Applied Systems Analysis (IIASA) and the Vienna Institute of Demography (VID) and improves enormously on previously available data on education in several respects. In contrast to most earlier attempts to improve data quality, which were concentrated on raising more empirical information or using economic perpetual inventory methods and interpolation, such as the contributions of, for example, Barro and Lee (2001), de la Fuente and Domenech (2006) or Cohen and Soto (2001), this latest attempt is based on demographic back-projections and exploits for the first time differences in mortality across education levels[9]. Most importantly, this data set allows a cross-classification of education data by age groups (in age intervals of five years), and thus allows us to obtain estimates of the full demographic distribution of educational attainment[10].

As compared to the existing datasets by Barro and Lee, De la Fuente and Domenech as well as Cohen and Soto, the IIASA-VID data reflect explicitly the fact that mortality differs by level of education and have education categories that are consistent over time. The dataset also provides the full educational attainment distribution by five-year age groups. Indeed, most economic growth regressions so far approximated human capital by one variable giving the mean years of schooling of the population above age 25.

This indicator includes all elderly people beyond retirement age and therefore shows a much slower pace of

---

[9] The importance of these mortality differentials is highlighted by Cohen and Soto (2001), for instance. For a detailed description of the methodology used to reconstruct the data see Lutz et al. (2007a, 2007b).
[10] See Crespo Cuaresma and Lutz (2007) for evidence on the importance of the demographic dimension for explaining differences in income and income growth across countries.

improving average human capital than age-specific indicators for younger adults. In addition, the full distribution of educational attainment categories by age allows for important empirical studies about the relative importance of primary education as compared to secondary and tertiary in the course of development.

Two types of human capital distance measures have been used in this study: The first distance measure (D_1) is based on the secondary education attainment level of the age-structured population for males, females and total population. Distances are defined as the Euclidean distance between country locations which are in turn defined as vectors in R^3 whose elements are the average proportions of population in an age group (three age groups are considered: 14-29, 30-49 and 50-64) with completed secondary education. Country locations $s_{i,t}$ are then identified with D_1. Thus, two countries are close in the sense of D_1 if the proportion of human capital in the age-structured population for two countries is same, distant, otherwise.

The second measure of economic distance (D_2) is based on country-specific elasticities of economic growth to human capital, which is calculated by estimating a standard Cobb-Douglas production function where human and physical capital are used as inputs. The estimates were obtained from a pooled data set of five-year averages by regressing the growth rate of GDP per capita on the average investment rate, the change in years of education for the adult population and the initial level of GDP per capita (the education data is sourced from IIASA-VID and the rest of the variables are from the Penn World Table Version 6.2).

Country-specific estimates of the parameter attached to the human capital variable were then used as elasticities in the construction of the distance matrix. In this case, country locations $s_{i,t}$ are then identified with D_2. Two countries are close in the sense of D_2 if they utilize approximately same quantity of human capital in production. While the former induces productivity effects as the stock of human capital at each demographic level exerts varying productivity effects across country locations, the latter induces a scale effect in the economies (affecting production through knowledge creation). Time non-varying distance is assumed for simplicity, which could be reasonable, given the slow paced demographic changes.

Based on the contiguity matrix of economic distance, we estimate a SVAR model to infer on complementarities in growth, their nature of interdependence and trace the source of fluctuations (in our case differences in the human capital accumulation in different countries). The list of countries in each group (namely, Asia, Africa, Europe, and Latin America and Offshore) is described in Table 1. The number of countries comprising each group complies with our estimation requirement that the cross-section dimension is dominated by the time dimension.

Figures 1 to 8 present the histograms of the different distance measures for the sample at hand. Distance plots based on the shares of age-structured human capital for the four country sub-groups are presented in Figures 1 and 2. Similarly, Figures 3 and 4 depict distance plots based on the input share of human capital in production for each country. Further disaggregation is made for the male population (Figures 5 and 6) and for the female population (Figures 7 and 8) based on the proportion of age-structured human capital for each sex in the total population.

VI. EMPIRICAL RESULTS

This section discusses the estimation results of the SVAR model outlined above for the different groups of countries and two alternative human capital distance measures.

TABLE 1: LIST OF COUNTRIES

Asia	Africa	Europe	Lat America offshore
Bahrain	Benin	Austria	Argentina
Bangladesh	Burki Faso	Belgium	Australia
Cambodia	Cameroon	Bulgaria	Bolivia
China	Central Africa Republic	Denmark	Brazil
Hong Kong	Chad	Finland	Canada
India	Cote d'Ivoire	France	Chile
Indonesia	Egypt	Germany	Colombia
Iran	Gabon	Greece	Costa Rica
Japan	Ghana	Hungary	Cuba
Jordan	Guinea	Ireland	Dom Republic
Malaysia	Kenya	Italy	Ecuador
Nepal	Madagascar	Netherlands	El Salvador
Pakistan	Malawi	Norway	Guatemala
Philippines	Mali	Poland	Honduras
Singapore	Mauri9tius	Portugal	Mexico
S. Korea	Morocco	Romania	New Zealand
Sri Lanka	Mozambique	Spain	Panama
Syria	Namibia	Sweden	Paraguay
Thailand	Niger	Switzerland	Peru
Turkey	Nigeria	UK	USA
Vietnam	South Africa	-	Uruguay
	Togo		
	Uganda		
	Zambia		
	Zimbabwe		
N=21	N=25	N=20	N=21

The coefficient estimates for α and σ^2 based on the two measures of distance can be found in Tables 2 and 3. Note that $\hat{\alpha}$ values in the two tables are the average estimates over countries for a given region. The significance of the coefficients can be gauged by calculating the corresponding pooled t-ratio. Table 2 reports the parameter estimates of the SVAR using the demographic-economic distance matrix calculated by taking the average of the age shares over four decades for each country enlisted in each region.

The significance of the averaged estimate of α is indicative for the presence of autocorrelation for the region under investigation. From Table 2 it is evident that the $\hat{\alpha}$ for each region is not particularly large, however, Europe and Latin America and Offshore countries exhibit significant estimates of α. The same conclusion holds for Table 3 where the distance measure is based on appropriation of human capital in the production of one unit of output. The averaged conditional variances $(\hat{\alpha}^2)$ for each region described by idiosyncratic components (α_i^2) are also presented. While the results for α appear very consistent across estimations with different distance measures, some relevant differences appear in the point estimates of the average variance. This gives us a first indication concerning the fact that the two measures give rise to potentially different covariance dependence structures in the error term, an issue which will be assessed directly by the estimates of the γ function.

Figures 9 to 24 present the plots of the estimates of the f and γ functions with respect to the respective distance metrics in different subsamples. In each case the solid line is the point estimate of f or γ plotted over the range of distances in our sample. The crosses correspond to a 95 per cent bootstrap confidence interval around the estimate.

TABLE 2: PARAMETER ESTIMATES $\hat{\alpha}$ AND $\hat{\sigma}^2$ WITH AGE-STRUCTURED HUMAN CAPITAL SHARES.

	$\hat{\alpha}$		$\hat{\sigma}^2$		
Regions	Coef.	Std-Dev.	Coef.	Std-Dev.	Obs.
Africa	0.0281	0.1418	0.0052	0.0018	1716
Asia	0.1810	0.1361	0.0063	0.0023	1452
Europe	0.2126	0.1268	0.0008	0.0003	924
Latin America and Offshore	0.2244	0.1404	0.0016	0.005	1144

TABLE 3: PARAMETER ESTIMATES $\hat{\alpha}$ AND $\hat{\sigma}^2$ WITH INPUT SHARE OF HUMAN CAPITAL IN PRODUCTION

	$\hat{\alpha}$		$\hat{\sigma}^2$		
Regions	Coef.	Std-Dev.	Coef.	Std-Dev.	Obs.
Africa	0.0272	0.1414	0.0039	0.0020	1716
Asia	0.1852	0.1373	0.0037	0.0020	1452
Europe	0.2158	0.1288	0.0008	0.0003	924
Latin America and Offshore	0.2305	0.1400	0.0005	0.0005	1144

The results for Europe (Figures 9 to 12) present evidence of significant spatial effects depending on the human capital distance, although the nature of the channel identified differs across metrics. Using the age-structured human capital distance (Figure 10), we notice that the point estimates for f appear positive and significant for relatively short distances. A significant non-linear pattern is also observed, with the effect leveling out at an increasing rate as distance increases. We therefore show evidence of complementarity in the growth process which is regulated by the similarity in the demographic distribution of the human capital stock and the importance of human capital in the production process. For large distances, the effect is still positive but highly non-linear and imprecisely estimated. No significant spatial effects appear in the covariance structure using this measure of distance, with a $\hat{\gamma}$ function which is significant only at zero distance. It is noticeable that, when disaggregating data by gender, this effect is only captured by the distance based on female population.

The situation is more revealing as we look at the γ function. The estimated shape of the γ function as plotted in Figure 9 (right side) shows the expected pattern: the covariances of the residuals between countries are monotonically decreasing with distance. The effect is not present in a significant manner if the demographic metric is used, as shown in Figure 10. It should be noticed that the estimates presented in the figures are those of γ divided by the country variance estimates. This normalization would render an estimate of the spatial correlation if the shock variances were identical across countries. Notice that the magnitude of the estimates of γ is quite large for the first distance metric and small but positive and constant for the latter. Using the former, there is strong evidence that shocks in our VAR model are spatially correlated as a function of distance in the specification which uses the elasticity measure to define the space metric.

Figures 13 and 14 present significant spatial persistence for the defined two measures of economic distance in the Asian group. For both distance measures, the f functions are significant. For elasticity-based measures, the f function is positive on the average, most importantly at the higher distances, assuming a peak in the middle. With the human capital distribution based measure, the f function is negative and significant on average for most distances. Being 17 labor-dominant economies, the Asian countries' production function can assume striking similarity based on the amount of input used for production. Thus, the elasticity-based distance measure can reveal more about the interdependence nature of Asian economies, although the distribution of human capital across age and gender (Figures 15 and 16) is a good indicator of demographic similarity. Putting the results together, we observe a weak form of spatial autocorrelations based on the proposed distance metrics. Importantly, a still highly non-linear pattern of the f function is observed for all distance measures across gender and aggregate population, which reinforces the evidence found in the European case.

Latin America and offshore countries also exhibit spatial persistence due to the defined distance measures although the degree of persistence appears to be low in magnitude (Figures 21 and 22). The f functions in Figures 21 and 22 depict different patterns and appear thus to be sensitive to the distance metrics used. The f function responds non-linearly to the distance variation due to demography-based human capital share (Figure 22) such that significant spatial autocorrelation can be discerned at most distances. With respect to the distinction of the male and female population's contribution to spatial volatility in these regions (Figures 23 and 24), we find no significant differences in both f and γ functions.

For African countries (Figures 17 and 18), however, no significant spatial persistence patterns are discerned. However, as expected the γ functions in Figures 17 and 18 indicate that the residual variances from the regression decline with distances. Similar conclusions follow for male and female populations in this region (Figures 19 and 20). Summing up, for most country groups the growth processes are observed to be complementary and the corresponding stochastic error terms in these countries can also be explained as functions of economic distances.

VII. CONCLUSIONS

In this chapter we underlined the contribution of human capital in countries growth processes by fully capturing the effect of international spillovers. Explicit role of demographic system has been allowed to determine the pace of economic growth over time and across spatial locations. Our theoretical model specification showed that due to high interconnectedness of countries in the wake of globalization, faster movement of productivity shocks and stochastic demographic disturbance require that countries cooperate in the growth programs and design joint policy in demographic and human capital development. Welfare under cooperation was also shown to beget higher social welfare than under non-cooperative paradigm. From econometric perspective, we designed an empirically testable spatial growth framework which is related to a distance metric with respect to human capital appropriation. We aimed at the quantification of cross-country growth spillovers based on human capital similarity measures where the recently developed IIASA-VID human capital database was used. We employed a multivariate semi-parametric spatial time series model where the coefficients of the vector autoregressive structure and of the covariance of the error terms were modeled as a function of the economic distance between countries. At a broader level, we were motivated by the fact that unveiling the determinants of the interaction patterns of output growth in a spatial setting would lend an additional dimension of testing endogenous economic growth in space. In keeping up with our objective, we investigated the spatial dynamics of human capital accumulation for four geographically clustered set of countries, viz., Asia, Africa, Europe and Latin America and Offshore countries.

The overall finding is that there is a significant degree of cross-country growth volatility and that it is attributed to shock correlation based on human capital similarity. In this respect, national growth processes are complementary to each other with respect to the proposed distance metric (based on the proportion of age-structured human capital growth or elasticity of human capital in the production). The results stress on the evaluation of the potential advantages of cross-national cooperation in demographic and educational policy programs.

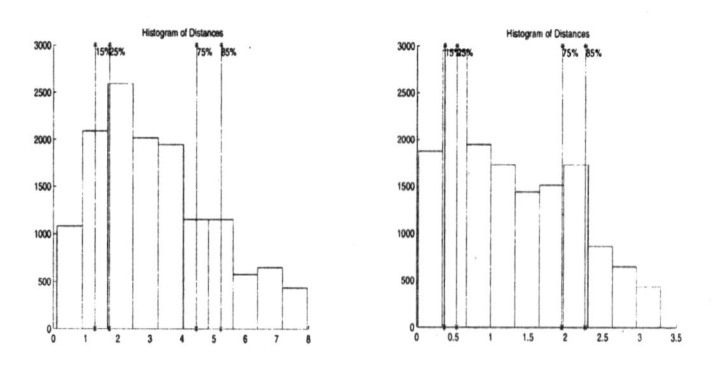

Figure 1: Histogram of distances based on aggregate population on age-structured human capital share: Africa (left), Asia (right)

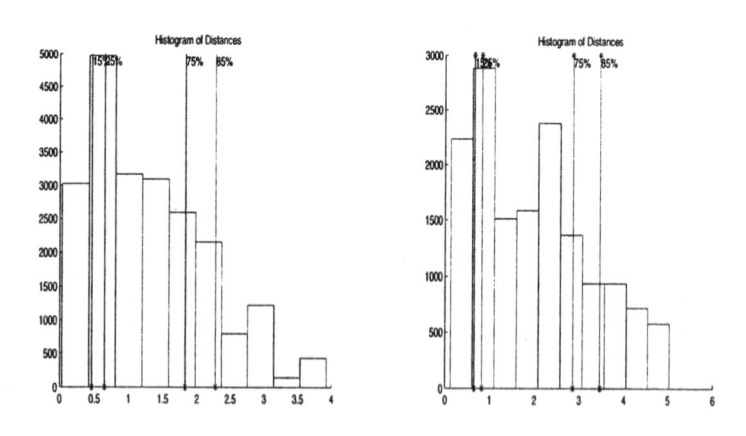

Figure 2: Histogram of distances based on aggregate population on age-structured human capital share: Europe (left), Latin America and Offshore (right)

Age-structured Human Capital Dynamics and Economic... 165

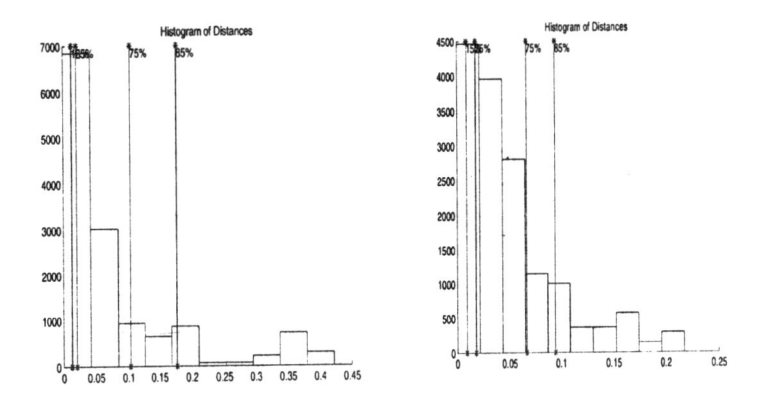

Figure 3: Histogram of distances based on aggregate population on elasticity of human capital share: Africa (left), Asia (right)

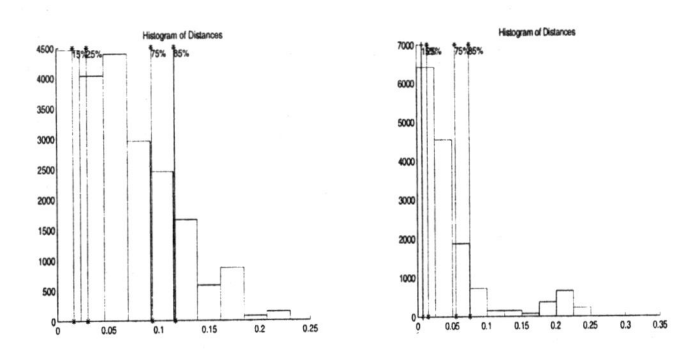

Figure 4: Histogram of distances based on aggregate population on elasticity of human capital share: Europe (left), Latin America and Offshore (right).

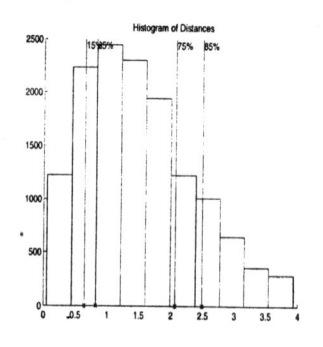

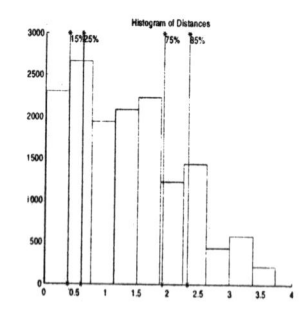

Figure 5: Histogram of distances based on male population on age-structured human capital share: Africa (left), Asia (right)

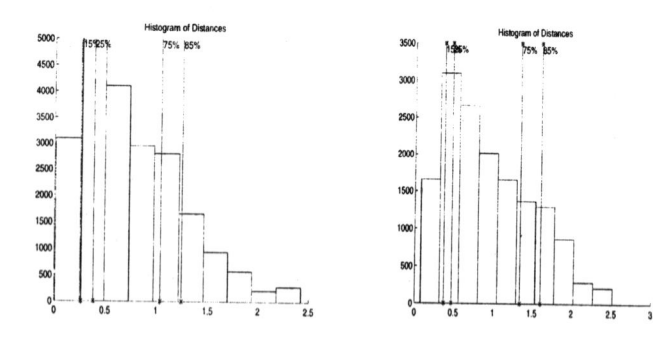

Figure 6: Histogram of distances based on male population on age-structured human capital share: Europe (left), Latin America and Offshore (right)

Age-structured Human Capital Dynamics and Economic... 167

Figure 7: Histogram of distances based on female population on age-structured human capital share: Africa (left), Asia (right)

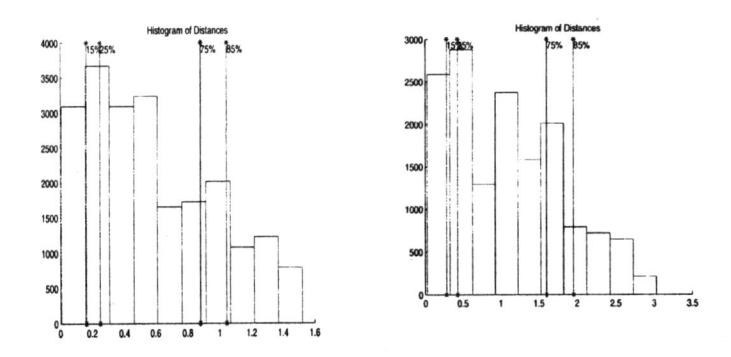

Figure 8: Histogram of distances based on female population on age-structured human capital share: Europe (left), Latin America and Offshore (right)

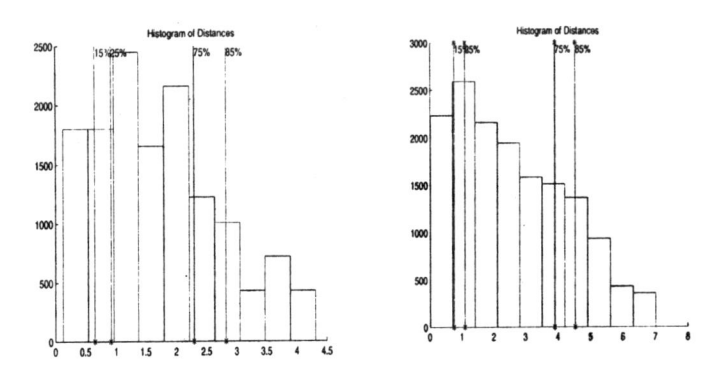

Figure 9: Conditional mean ($\widehat{f}$ [left]) and covariance ($\widehat{\gamma}$ [right]) functions based on elasticity measure: Total Population for Europe

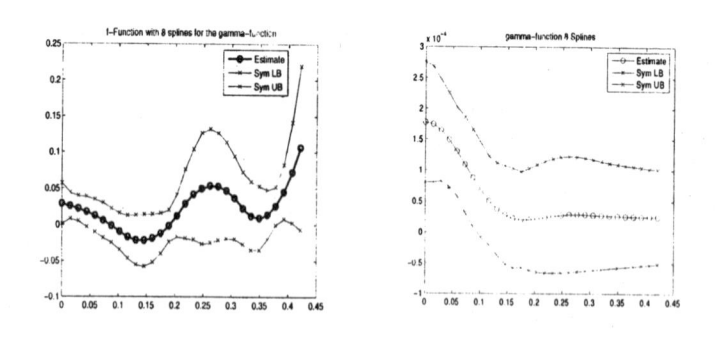

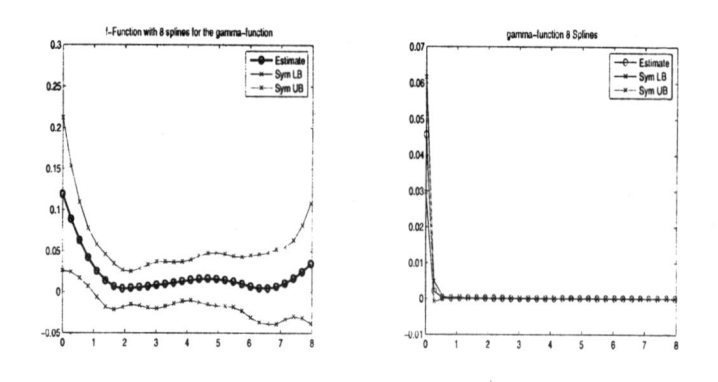

Figure 10: Conditional mean ($\widehat{f}$ [left]) and covariance ($\widehat{\gamma}$ [right]) functions based on demography based human capital share: Total Population for Europe

Figure 11: Conditional mean ($\hat{f}$ [left]) and covariance ($\hat{\gamma}$ [right]) functions based on demography based human capital share: Male Population for Europe

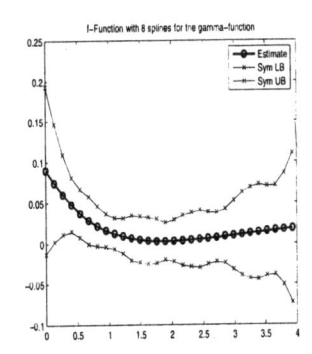

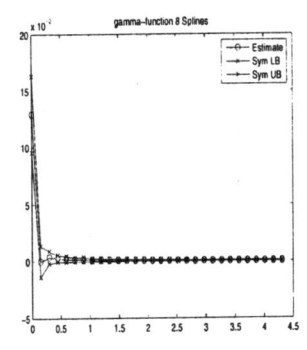

Figure 12: Conditional mean ($\hat{f}$ [left]) and covariance ($\hat{\gamma}$ [right]) functions based on demography based human capital share: Female Population for Europe

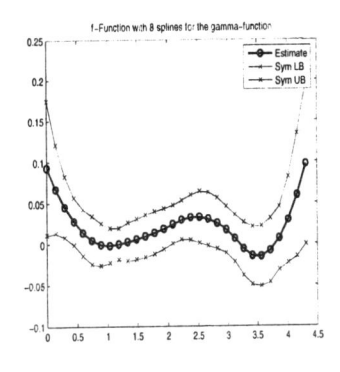

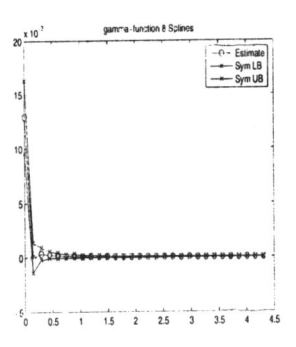

Figure 13: Conditional mean ($\hat{f}$ [left]) and covariance ($\hat{\gamma}$ [right]) functions based on elasticity measure: Total Population for Asia

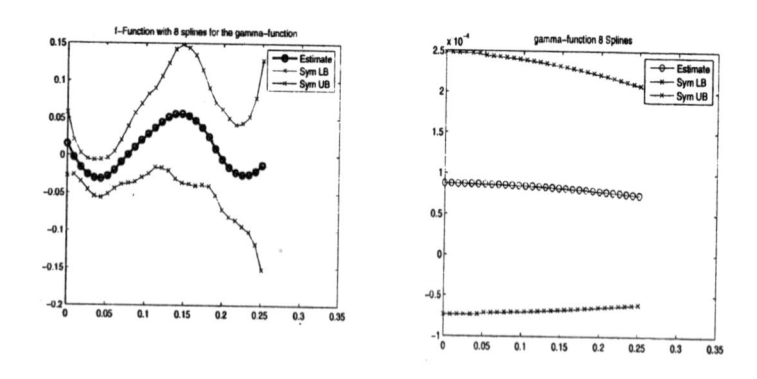

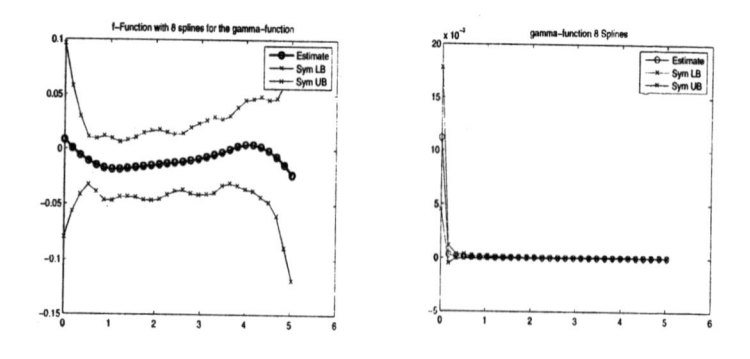

Figure 14: Conditional mean ($\hat{f}$ [left]) and covariance ($\hat{\gamma}$ [right]) functions based on demography based human capital share: Total Population for Asia

Figure 15: Conditional mean ($\hat{f}$ [left]) and covariance ($\hat{\gamma}$ [right]) functions based on demography based human capital share: Male Population for Asia

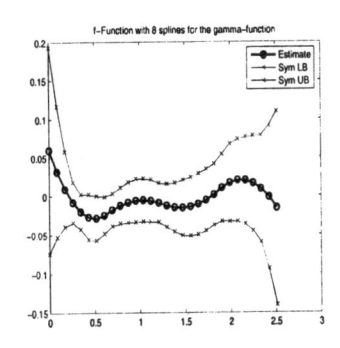

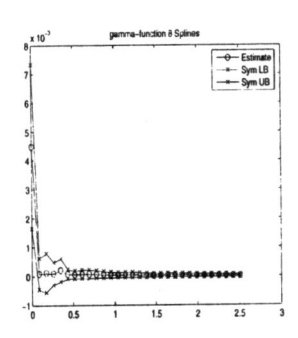

Figure 16: Conditional mean ($\hat{f}$ [left]) and covariance ($\hat{\gamma}$ [right]) functions based on demography based human capital share: Female Population for Asia

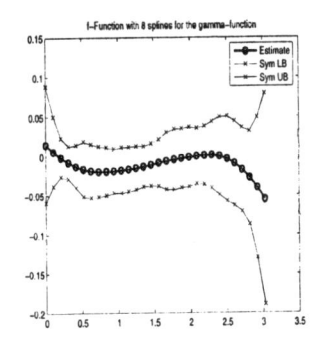

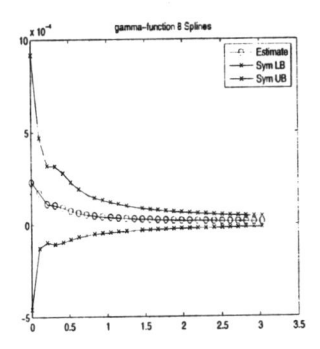

Figure 17: Conditional mean ($\hat{f}$ [left]) and covariance ($\hat{\gamma}$ [right]) functions based on elasticity measure: Total Population for Africa

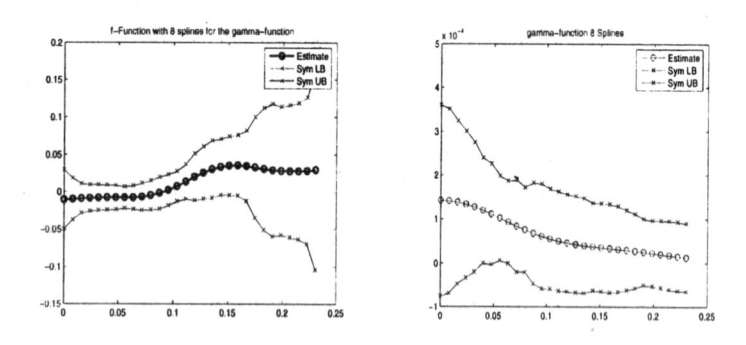

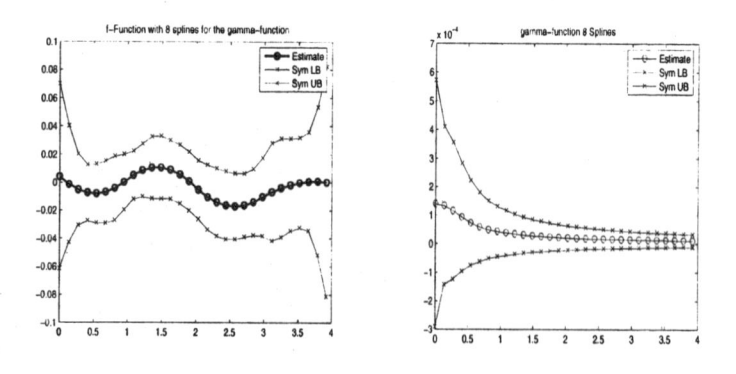

Figure 18: Conditional mean ($\hat{f}$ [left]) and covariance ($\hat{\gamma}$ [right]) functions based on demography based human capital share: Total Population for Africa

Figure 19: Conditional mean ($\widehat{f}$ [left]) and covariance ($\widehat{\gamma}$ [right]) functions based on demography based human capital share: Male Population for Africa

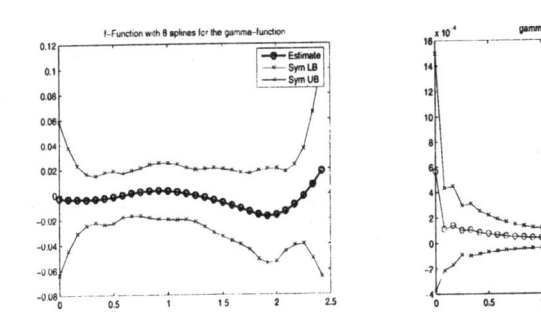

Figure 20: Conditional mean ($\widehat{f}$ [left]) and covariance ($\widehat{\gamma}$ [right]) functions based on demography based human capital share: Female Population for Africa

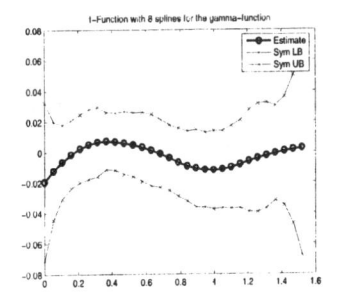

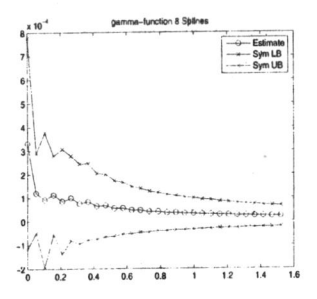

Figure 21: Conditional mean ($\hat{f}$ [left]) and covariance ($\hat{\gamma}$ [right]) functions based on elasticity measure: Total Population for Latin America and Offshore

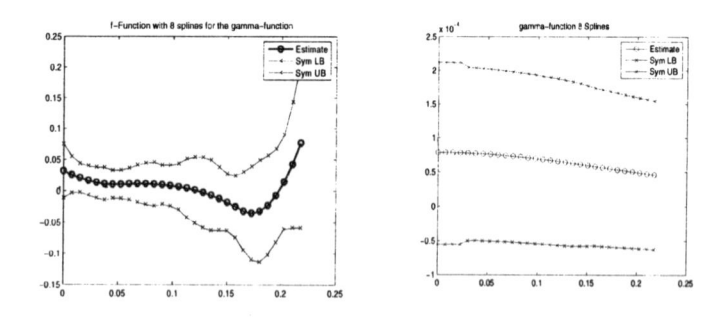

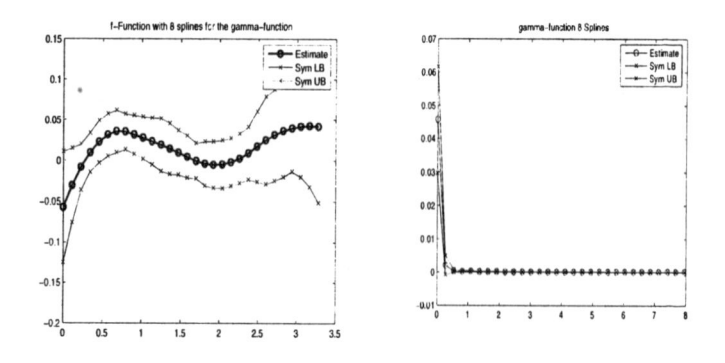

Figure 22: Conditional mean ($\hat{f}$ [left]) and covariance ($\hat{\gamma}$ [right]) functions based on demography based human capital share: Total Population for Latin America and Offshore

Figure 23: Conditional mean ($\hat{f}$ [left]) and covariance ($\hat{\gamma}$ [right]) functions based on demography based human capital share: Male Population for Latin America and Offshore

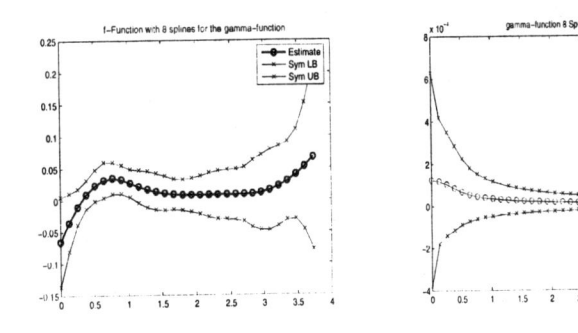

Figure 24: Conditional mean ($\hat{f}$ [left]) and covariance ($\hat{\gamma}$ [right]) functions based on demography based human capital share: Female Population for Latin America and Offshore

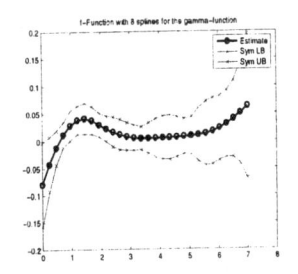

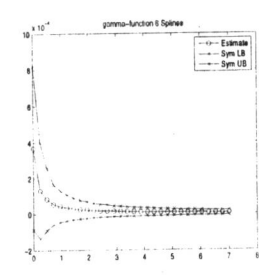

REFERENCES

Anselin, L. and D.A. Griffith (1988), "Do spatial effects really matter in regression analysis?" Papers of the Regional Science Association, 25: 11-34.

Azomahou, T. and T. Mishra (2008), "Age dynamics and economic growth: An analysis in a nonparametric setting", Economics Letters, Elsevier, vol. 99(1), pages 67-71, April.

Azomahou, T., C. Diebolt, and T. Mishra (forthcoming), "Spatial persistence of demographic shocks and economic growth", Journal of Macroeconomics.

Barro, R.J. (1991), "Economic Growth in a Cross section of Countries," Quarterly Journal of Economics, 106: 407-44.

Barro, R. and J.W. Lee (2001), "International measures of schooling years and schooling quality", American Economic Review, Papers and Proceedings, 53: 541-563.

Benhabib, J. and M. Spiegel (1994), "The role of human capital in economic development: Evidence from aggregate cross-country data", Journal of Monetary Economics, 34: 143-173.

Benhabib, J. and M. Spiegel (2005), "Human capital and technology diffusion", pp. 935-966 in P. Aghion and S. Durlauf (eds.), Handbook of Economic Growth. New York: Elsevier.

Blackburn, K. and M.O. Ravn (1993), "Growth, human capital spillovers and international policy coordination", The Scandinavian Journal of Economics, 95(4), 495-515.

Boucekkine, R., D. de la Croix, and O. Licandro (2002), "Vintage Human Capital, Demographic Trends, and Endogenous Growth," Journal of Economic Theory, 104: 340-375.

Case, A.C. (1991), "Spatial patterns in household demand", Econometrica, 59: 953-965.

Chen, X. and T.G. Conley (2001), "A new semiparametric spatial model for panel time series", Journal of Econometrics, 105: 59-83.

Cohen, D. and M. Soto (2001), Growth and Human Capital: Good Data, Good Results, CEPR Discussion Paper, No. 3025. London: Centre for Economic Policy Research.

Conley, T.G. and B. Dupor (2003), "A spatial analysis of sectoral complementarity", Journal of Political Economy, 111(2): 311-352.

Crenshaw, E., A. Ameen, and M. Christenson (1997), "Population Dynamics and Economic Development: Age Specific Population Growth and Economic Growth in Developing Countries, 1965 to 1990," American Sociological Review 62(6):974-984.

Crespo Cuaresma, J. and W. Lutz (2007), "Human Capital, Age Structure and Economic Growth: Evidence from a New Dataset", IIASA Interim Report IR-07-011. Laxenburg, Austria: International Institute for Applied Systems Analysis.

Crespo Cuaresma, J. and T. Mishra (2007), "Human Capital, Age Structure and Growth Volatility", IIASA Interim Report IR-07-31. Laxenburg, Austria: International Institute for Applied Systems Analysis.

Crespo Cuaresma, J. and T. Mishra (2008), "The Role of Education Data for Economic Growth Forecasts", IIASA Interim Report IR-03-08, 2008. Laxenburg, Austria: International Institute for Applied Systems Analysis.

De la Fuente, A. and R. Domenech (2006), "Human capital in growth regressions: How much difference does data quality make?" Journal of the European Economic Association, 4: 1-36.

Forni, M. and L. Reichlin (1998), "Let's get real: A factor analytical approach to disaggregated business cycle dynamics", Review of Economic Studies, 65: 453-473.

Hall, R.E. and C.I. Jones (1999), "Why do some countries produce so much more output per worker than others?" Quarterly Journal of Economics, 114: 83-116.

Heston, A., R. Summers, and B. Aten (2006), Penn World Table Version 6.2. Philadelphia: Center for International Comparisons of Production, Income and Prices at the University of Pennsylvania.

Horvath, M.T.K. (1998), "Cyclicality and sectoral linkages: Aggregate fluctuations from sectoral shocks", Review of Economic Dynamics, 1: 781-808.

Horvath, M.T.K. (2000), "Sectoral shocks and aggregate fluctuations", Journal of Monetary Economics, 45: 69-106.

Kelley, A.C. and R.M. Schmidt (2001), "Economic and Demographic Change: A Synthesis of Models, Findings and Perspectives," in 'Birdsall N, Kelley A. C, Sinding, S (eds) Demography Matters: Population Change, Economic Growth and Poverty in the Developing World.' Oxford University Press, 2001.

Lau, S-H. P. (1999), "I(0) In, Integration and Contegration Out: Time Series Properties of Endogenous Growth Models," Journal of Econometrics, 93, 1-24.

Lindh, T. and B. Malmberg (2007), Demographically Based Global Income Forecasting up to the Year 2050. International Journal of Forecasting, 23: 553-567.

Long, J.B. and C. I. Plosser (1983), "Real business cycles", Journal of Political Economy, 91: 39-69.

Lucas, R. (1988), "On the mechanics of economic development", Journal of Monetary Economics, 22: 3-42.

Lutz, W., A. Goujon, and A. Wils (2007a), "The population dynamics of human capital accumulation", in Population Aging, Human Capital Accumulation and Productivity Growth, edited by A. Prskawetz, D. Bloom, and W. Lutz. A special issue of Population and Development Review, Vol. 33. New York: Population Council.

Lutz, W., A. Goujon, S. K.C., and W. Sanderson (2007b), Reconstruction of Populations by Age, Sex and Level of Educational Attainment for 120 Countries for 1970-2000, IIASA Interim Report IR-07-002. Laxenburg, Austria: International Institute for Applied Systems Analysis. 20

Mankiw, N.G., D. Romer, and D.N. Weil (1992), "A contribution to the empirics of economic growth", Quarterly Journal of Economics, 107(2): 407-437.

Mishra, T. and C. Diebolt (2007), "Demographic Volatility and Economic Growth: Convention and Beyond", Quality & Quantity: International Journal of Methodology, Springer publication. Forthcoming.

Mishra, T. (2006), "Dynamics of Demographic Change and Economic Development", Doctoral Dissertation, Dept. of Economics, Catholic University of Louvain, Belgium. Mimeo.

Nelson, R. and E. Phelps (1966), "Investment in humans, technological diffusion, and economic growth", American Economic Review, Papers and Proceedings, 56: 69-75.

Nelson, C.R. and C.I. Plosser (1982), "Trends and random walks in macroeconomic time series," Journal of Monetary Economics, 10, 139-162.

Quah, D. and T.J. Sargent (1993), "A dynamic index model for large cross sections", pp. 285-306 in J.H. Stock and M.W. Watson (eds.), Business Cycles, Indicators, and Forecasting. Chicago: University of Chicago Press.

Parhi, M. and T. Mishra (2008), "Spatial Growth Volatility and Age-structured Human Capital Dynamics in Europe", BETA Discussion Paper, No. 4, 2008, Louis-Pasteur University, France.

Romer, P.M. (1986), "Increasing Returns and Long-run Growth," Journal of Political Economy 94:1002-1037.

Tamura, R. (1991), "Income convergence in an endogenous growth model", The Journal of Political Economy, 99(3), 522-540.

Yaglom, A.M. (1987), Correlation Theory for Stationary and Related Random Functions, Vols. I and II. New York: Springer.

Abramovitz, M. (1986), "Catching Up, Forging Ahead and Falling Behind," Journal of Economic History, 46, pp. 385-406.

Baillie, T. R. and T. Bollerslev, (1994), "The Long Memory of the Forward Premium," Journal of International Money and Finance, 13, 555-571.

Barro, R.J. (1991), "Economic Growth in a Cross section of Countries," Quarterly Journal of Economics, 106: 407-44.
Barro R.J. and X. Sala-I-Martin (1992), "Convergence," Journal of Political Economy, 100, pp.223-251.

Barro R.J. and X. Sala-I-Martin (1995), Economic Growth, McGraw-Hill, Inc., New York.

Birdsall N., A.C. Kelley, and S. Sinding ed. (2001), Demography Matters: Population Change, Economic Growth and Poverty in the Developing World. Oxford University Press.

Bloom, D. and D. Canning, (2001), "Cumulative Causality, Economic Growth, and the Demographic Transition," in Demography Matters: Population Change, Economic Growth and Poverty in the Developing World, 2001 edited by N. Birdsall, A.C. Kelley, and S. Sinding. Oxford University Press.

Boucekkine, R., D. de la Croix, and O. Licandro (2002), "Vintage Human Capital, Demographic Trends, and Endogenous Growth," Journal of Economic Theory, 104: 340-375.

Boucekkine, R., D. de la Croix, and D. Peeters (2005), "Early literacy achievements, population density and the transition to modern growth," Mimeo, Department of Economics, Catholic University of Louvain, Belgium.

Burkett, J.P., C. Humblet, and L. Putterman (1999), "Preindustrial and Postwar Economic Development: Is There a Link?" Economic Development and Cultural Change volume 47, p.471.

Crafts, N. (1987), "Cliometrics, 1971-1986: A Survey," Journal of Applied Econometrics, 2, pp. 171-192.

Crenshaw, E., A. Ameen, and M. Christenson (1997), "Population Dynamics and Economic Development: Age Specific Population Growth and Economic Growth in Developing Countries, 1965 to 1990," American Sociological Review 62(6):974-984.

Darn´e, O. and C. Diebolt (2004), "Unit Roots and Infrequent Large Shocks: New International Evidence on Output," Journal of Monetary Economics, 51, pp. 1449-1465.

Dasgupta, P. (1995), "The Population Problem: Theory and Evidence," Journal of Economic Literature, Vol. XXXIII: 1879-1902.

Diebolt, C. and V. Guiraud (2000), "Long Memory Time Series and Fractional Integration: A Cliometric Contribution to French and German Economic and Social History," in : Historical Social Research. An International Journal for the Application of Formal Methods to History (University of Cologne, Center for Historical Social Research), 25 (3/4), 4-22.

Galor, O. (2005), The Transition from Stagnation to Growth, in the Handbook of Economic Growth, North Holland, 171- 293.

Geweke, J. and S. Porter-Hudak (1983), "The Estimation and Application of Long Memory Time Series Models," Journal of Time Series Analysis, 221-238.

Gil-Alana, L.A. (2003), "A Fractional Integration Analysis of the Population in Some OECD Countries," Journal of Applied Statistics, Vol.30, No.10: 1-13.

Goldin, C. (1995), "Cliometrics and the Nobel," Journal of Economic Perspectives, 9, pp. 191-208.

Granger, C. W. G. and R. Joyeux (1980), "An introduction to long memory time series models and fractional differencing," Journal of Time Series Analysis, 1, 15-29.

Heston, A., R. Summers and B. Aten (2002), Penn World Table Version 6.1, Center for International Comparisons at the University of Pennsylvania (CICUP).

Kelley, A.C. and R.M. Schmidt (1995), "Aggregate Population and Economic Growth Correlations: The Role of the Components of Demographic Changes," Demography, 32: 543-555.

Kelley, A.C. and R.M. Schmidt (2001), "Economic and Demographic Change: A Synthesis of Models, Findings and Perspectives," in 'Birdsall N, Kelley A. C, Sinding, S (eds) Demography Matters: Population Change, Economic Growth and Poverty in the Developing World.' Oxford University Press, 2001.

Kim, C.S. and P.C.B. Phillips, (2000), "Modified Log Periodogram Regression," Working Paper, Yale University.

Lindh, T. and B. Malmberg (2000), "Can age structure forecast inflation trends?" Journal of Economics and Business, Vol. 52, Issues 1-2, 31-49.

Lucas, R. (1988), "On the Mechanics of Economic Development," Journal of Monetary Economics 22:3-42.

Maddison, A. (2004), Total Economy Database from Groningen Growth and Development Centre. http://www.ggdc.net/index-dseries.html.

Malmberg, B. and T. Lindh (2005), "Demographically-based Global Income Forecasts up to 2050," Forthcoming in International Journal of Forecasting.

McCloskey, D. (1987), Econometric History, Macmillan, London.

Mishra, T. (2006), "Dynamics of Demographic Change and Economic Development," Catholic University of Louvain Doctoral Dissertation, Belgium.

North, D. (1994), "Economic Performance Through Time," American Economic Review, 84, pp. 359-368.

Ramsey, F. (1928), "A Mathematical Theory of Saving," Economic Journal, 38, pp. 543-559.

Romer, P.M. (1986), "Increasing Returns and Long-run Growth," Journal of Political Economy 94:1002-1037.

Romer, P.M. (1990), "Endogenous Technological Change," Journal of Political Economy, 98, pp. S71-S102.

Solow, R.M. (1956), "A Contribution to the Theory of Economic Growth," Quarterly Journal of Economics 70(1): 65-94.

Temple, J. (1999), "The New Growth Evidence," Journal of Economic Literature, 37, pp. 112-156.

Wright, G. (1971), Econometric Studies of History, in: M. Intriligator (Ed.), Frontiers of Quantitative Economics, North-Holland, Amsterdam, pp. 412-459.

8

Human Development in India: Issues and Challenges

Mihir K. Mahapatra[1]
Rajesh Raj S. N.[2]

I. INTRODUCTION

Human development (HD) that encompasses quality of life, the level of well being and access to basic social services, is an input as well as a key ingredient in the development process. HD is development that not only generates economic growth but distributes its benefits equitably; regenerates the environment rather than destroying it; empowers people rather than marginalizing them (UNDP, 1994). It is now fully recognised that the ultimate end of all development strategies must be people and their welfare: and economic growth is only a means towards that end (Haq, 1993). Thus the basic objective of the development process is to enlarge the range of choices available to the people who should include in addition to income and employment aspects such as health, education, physical environment, human dignity and freedom. The inherent message is that the usual indicator of income level of a country may not truly reflect the level of human development achieved by that country. A comparison of income and human development levels of different countries bears testimony to the above assertion. For instance, Canada

---

[1] Goa Institute of Management, Goa, India, E-mail: mihir@gim.ac.in
[2] Centre for Multi-Disciplinary Development Research (CMDR), Dharwad, Karnataka, India, E-mail: rajeshraj.natarajan@gmail.com

has 8 times the per capita income of Sri Lanka in 2003, but less than three times its infant mortality (UNDP, 2005). Similarly, the per capita income of United Arab Emirates (UAE) in 2003 was 9 times higher than that of Viet Nam, but only around three times in terms of infant mortality. USA ranks fourth in the world in terms of per capita income in 2003, but 34th based on its infant mortality rate (UNDP, 2005). In essence, there exists severe disparity between economic and social progress in many countries highlighting the uneven distribution of benefits of economic growth. Taking cognizance of the low level of human development indicators, the United Nations fifty-fifth session has developed 8 Millennium Development Goals to be achieved by 2015. Some of these goals are eradication of extreme poverty and hunger, achievement of universal primary education, promotion of gender equity and empowerment of women, reduction of child mortality, improvement of maternal health, combating HIV/AIDS, Malaria and other Diseases, reducing by half the proportion of people without sustainable access to safe drinking water and ensuring environmental sustainability.

India, the largest home to people in the world after China, has a very low level of human development. The recent human development index estimated for 2006 by UNDP puts India in the 127th position among 177 countries with HDI score of 0.602. This is much lower as compared to the highest HDI score of 0.963. The HDI value has declined from 0.611 in 2005 to 0.602 in 2006 and this is reflected by the decline in the HDI rank by 'one' unit during the said period. This fall in HDI has to be seen against the country's elevation to a higher growth path in the recent times[3]. No doubt, this composite national scenario is a sum total of state-level experiences.

---

[3] Between 1992 and 2002, the gross domestic product (GDP) of India grew at a rate of 6 per cent, much above the growth rate of 5.2 percent registered during 1982-1992 (Kelkar, 2006). Such a faster growth is observed in the per capita GDP too (Kelkar, 2006).

Available evidence points to the case of divergence rather than convergence among Indian states. The National Human Development Report of India (2001) reports drastic differences in human development among the states in India and there has been no reduction of such disparities between the BIMARU states and few better performing states. Against this backdrop, the paper makes an attempt to examine the level of human development in India vis-à-vis the neighbouring countries with different levels of development. Given the fact that the level of human development varies considerably across Indian states, an attempt has been also made to assess the inter-state variation in human development by focusing on the major states of India. In order to identify the determining factors of Human Development, the paper has focussed on healthcare scenario both in the country and major states.

The paper is organised as follows: with a brief introduction in section I, section II deals with a comparative analysis of human development in India vis-à-vis its neighbouring countries over time. This section also presents a comparative analysis of level of human development across major states in India during 1981-2001. Identifying wide disparity in levels of human development, an attempt has been made in section III to examine the crucial factors determining human development levels in a comparative perspective by focusing on the performance of healthcare sector. The section also delves in detail the progress of healthcare sector in India by focusing on the performance of key healthcare indicators over time. Section IV identifies the key factors that determine the performance of health sector in India. The summary and conclusion have been discussed in section V.

II. HUMAN DEVELOPMENT IN INDIA VIS-À-VIS SELECTED COUNTRIES

Human development is defined as the process of enlarging people's choices in terms of knowledge, health and longevity, and levels of income. These choices can be translated to acquire knowledge, to lead a long and healthy life; and to have access to resources needed for a decent standard of living. From Table 1 it is evident that the there has been consistent improvement in HDI score over the years-a rise in index value by about 0.2 during 30 years since 1975. In spite of the progress, the level of human development achieved by India is much lower than that of some of the neighbouring countries (both developed and developing countries) barring Pakistan. Moreover, India has to go a long way to catch up with some of the Asian countries including Singapore as the latter has achieved HDI score of 0.92 in 2005 while it is 0.62 in India.

TABLE 1
TRENDS IN HUMAN DEVELOPMENT INDEX ACROSS COUNTRIES

Year	China	India	Singapore	Pakistan	Malaysia	Sri Lanka
1975	0.525	0.412	0.725	0.363	0.615	0.607
1980	0.558	0.438	0.761	0.386	0.659	0.649
1985	0.594	0.476	0.784	0.419	0.695	0.681
1990	0.627	0.513	0.822	0.462	0.721	0.705
1995	0.683	0.546	0.861	0.492	0.76	0.729
2003	0.755	0.602	0.907	0.527	0.796	0.751
2004	0.768	0.611	0.916	0.539	0.805	0.755
2005	0.777	0.619	0.922	0.551	0.811	0.743

Note: Rank of China, India, Singapore, Pakistan, Malaysia and Sri Lanka in HDI is 81, 128, 25, 136, 63 and 99 respectively in 2005.
Source: UNDP's Human Development Reports, various issues.

Human Development in Major States of India

There has been consistent progress in the level of human development in India with a relatively better achievement during the 1990s as compared to the 1980s as evident from rise in index score by about 0.08 and 0.09 in the 1980s and 1990s respectively. In spite of considerable improvement in the Index score across major states in India during 1981-2001, wide disparity among the states remains the cause for concern. Analysis of the relative performance of each state does not reflect any outstanding progress. For instance, Kerala consistently maintained the first rank while the BIMARU states have failed to improve its rank during the last two decades (1981-2001).The index score of BIMARU states is close to 60 per cent of that achieved by some of the best performing states (Table 2).

TABLE 2
HUMAN DEVELOPMENT INDEX OF MAJOR STATES IN INDIA

State	1981 Index Value	Rank	1991 Index Value	Rank	2001 Index Value	Rank
High Income							
Gujarat	0.36	4	0.431	6	0.479	6
Haryana	0.36	4	0.443	5	0.509	5
Maharashtra	0.363	3	0.452	4	0.523	4
Punjab	0.411	2	0.475	2	0.537	2
Middle Income							
Andhra Pradesh	0.298	9	0.377	9	0.416	10
Karnataka	0.346	6	0.412	7	0.478	7
Kerala	0.5	1	0.591	1	0.638	1
Tamil Nadu	0.343	7	0.466	3	0.531	3
West Bengal	0.305	8	0.404	8	0.472	8
Low Income							
Bihar	0.237	14	0.308	14	0.367	14
Madhya Pradesh	0.245	13	0.328	12	0.394	12
Orissa	0.267	10	0.345	11	0.404	11
Rajasthan	0.256	11	0.347	10	0.424	9
Uttar Pradesh	0.255	12	0.314	13	0.388	13
INDIA	**0.302**		**0.381**		**0.472**	
Minimum	0.2		0.3		0.4	
Maximum	0.5		0.6		0.6	
Min/Max(%)	47.4		52.1		57.5	
C.V. (%)	21.9		37.3		15.5	

Note: Ranking of States in the descending Order
Source: Government of India (2002)

III. HUMAN DEVELOPMENT AND HEALTHCARE SCENARIO

Health Scenario: India vis-à-vis other Countries

The extent of improvement in human development is primarily determined by the progress achieved in the health indicators though the contribution of other factors cannot be undermined. From Table 3 it is evident that the performance of the country is not quite promising in the selected key health indicators as compared to other developing countries. In life Expectancy at birth (defined as the number of years a new born infant would live if prevailing patterns of age-specific mortality rates at the time of birth were to stay the same throughout the child's life) there has been substantial improvement over the years yet the country is still lagging behind the neighbouring countries especially China and Sri Lanka (Table 3). The under-five mortality rate (defined as the probability of dying between birth and exactly five years of age, expressed per 1,000 live births) in India has come down by close to half in about one and a half decades since 1990.

Of late, it hovers around 74 and this is more than 5 times the rate prevailing in Sri Lanka (14) and about 3 times that of China. Similarly, there has been considerable progress in reducing the infant mortality rate (defined as the probability of dying between birth and exactly one year of age, expressed per 1,000 live births)- a fall by 24 points in one and a half decades. But it is around 5 times higher than that of Sri Lanka and close to 3 times that of China. The Maternal Mortality Rate in India is about 9 and 10 times higher than that of Sri Lanka and China respectively.

The foregoing analysis paints a disappointing healthcare picture in the country as compared to some of the neighbouring countries, implying ample scope for further improvement. Again, there is wide disparity in the performance of the health indicators between the rich and the poor. From Table 4 it is evident that both the infant mortality rate and under-five mortality rate among the poorest 20 per

TABLE 3
SURVIVAL, PROGRESS AND SETBACKS: INDIA VIS-À-VIS NEIGHBOURING COUNTRIES

Country	Life Expectancy at Birth 2000-05	Under-five Mortality Rate (per 1,000 live births) 1990	Under-five Mortality Rate (per 1,000 live births) 2005	Infant Mortality Rate (per 1,000 live births) 1990	Infant Mortality Rate (per 1,000 live births) 2005	Maternal Mortality Rate (per 1 lakh live births) 2005
China	72	49	27	38	23	45
India	**62.9**	**123**	**74**	**80**	**56**	**450**
Nepal	61.3	145	74	100	56	830
Pakistan	63.6	128	99	96	79	320
Sri Lanka	70.8	23	14	19	12	58
Bangladesh	62	144	73	96	54	570
South Asia	62.9	126	80	84	60	NA

Source: UNDP (2007) and Government of India (2008) N.A.: Not Available

cent of total population is much higher as compared to the richest 20 per cent. For instance, 97 infants belonging to the poorest 20 per cent of the total population die per 1000 live births before completing their first birth day. This is much lower (38 per 1000 live births) in case of the richest 20 per cent.

The persistence of this trend can be analysed by considering access to health infrastructure and level of poverty though other major factors do play a vital role. With respect to birth attended by skilled health personnel, a wide disparity is noticed between the poor and rich households. A total birth attended by skilled health personnel in case of the poorest 20 per cent of the total households is 16 per cent while it is 84 per cent for the richest 20 per cent households. The inequality in access to health care is also evident from the percentage of one-year old children fully immunized against major diseases including Polio, Measles and so on. Similarly, on account of persistence of extreme poverty, the children in low income bracket do not have access to nutritious food and therefore, the growth in height is much lower in the said group as compared to the richest one.

TABLE 4
INEQUALITIES IN MATERNAL AND CHILD HEALTH IN INDIA: 1998

Births attended by skilled health personnel (%)		One-year-olds fully immunized (%)		Children under height for age (% under age 5)		Infant mortality rate (per 1000 live births)		Under-five mortality rate (per 1,000 live births)	
Poorest 20%	Richest 20%	Poorest 20%	Richest 20%	Poorest 20%	Richest 20%	Poorest 20%	Richest 20%	Poorest 20%	Richest 20%
16	84	21	64	25	17	97	38	141	46

Note: The survey was conducted in 1998
Source: UNDP (2006)

Determining Factors of Health Care Scenario

The dismal performance of the country in health care scenario is determined by several factors including growth of income, level of poverty, access to health care, availability of water for consumption or water scarcity, extent of deficit in sanitation, regional disparity, provision of health infrastructure and so on. Some of the factors that determine mortality rate include access to safe drinking water, sanitation and nutritious food. 'The human rights to water entitle everyone to sufficient, safe, acceptable, physically accessible and affordable water for personal and domestic use (UN General Comment No. 15 on the right to water, 2002)'[4]. 'For individuals, for households and for whole societies access to clean water and sanitation is the one of the foundations for progress in human development (UNDP, 2006)'.

Access to clean water and sanitation can reduce the risk of child dying by as much as 50 per cent while clean water can reduce deaths due to typhoid. In this context, it needs to be mentioned that water borne diseases like Typhoid fever, Cholera and Diarrhoea are the biggest killer of children. Diarrhoea has been identified as the second biggest killer of children next to acute respiratory track infections. Globally the disease kills more people than Tuberculosis or Malaria.

As regards access to clean water, one in five people living in the developing world (some 1.1 billion) do not have access to it while some 2.6 billion people (almost half the total population of developing countries) do not have access to adequate sanitation (UNDP, 2006).

As regards India, percentage of people with sustainable access to improved sanitation has improved from 14 per cent to 33 per cent during one and a half decades since 1990 (Table 5). But this is much lower than that of the world average (59 per cent) and average for the Medium Human Development Countries (51 per cent). However, with respect to access to improved water resources the performance of India is marginally higher than that of World average (83 per cent) and average for the Medium Human Development Countries.

---

[4] Quoted in UNDP's Human Development Report, 2006.

TABLE 5
WATER SANITATION AND NUTRITIONAL STATUS

Country/Region	Population with sustainable access to Improved Sanitation (%)		Population with sustainable access to improved water resource (%)		Population undernourished (% of total)	
	1990	2004	1990	2004	1990-92	2001-03
India	**14**	**33**	**70**	**86**	**25**	**20**
Developing Countries	33	49	71	79	20	17
East Asia and the Pacific	30	50	72	79	17	12
South Asia	18	37	72	85	25	20
High human development	94	97	98	99	NA	NA
Medium Human development	34	51	74	83	19	15
Low human development	28	35	45	52	32	32
High Income	-	-	100	100	-	-
Middle Income	46	61	78	84	15	11
Low income	22	38	64	76	27	23
World	49	59	78	83	20	17

Source: UNDP (2006) N.A.: Not Available

The second crucial issue that deserves priority is the commitment made by the government to health care services especially with respect to child mortality. No doubt, there has been enough progress in immunizing the children against major diseases during the last few years but there is still ample scope to improve the scenario. In 2004, 73 per cent of one year old baby are fully immunized against Tuberculosis while it is 56 per cent for Measles (Table 6). The figures are not on par with the achievement made by the Medium Human Development countries. Even it is much lower than that of World average.

TABLE 6
COMMITMENT TO HEALTH AND SERVICE

(in percentage)

Country	One year old fully immunized Against Tuberculosis in 2004	Against Measles in 2004	Birth attended by skilled health personnel 1996-2004
India	**73**	**56**	**43**
Developing Countries	84	74	59
East Asia and the Pacific	92	83	86
South Asia	78	62	38
High human development	95	93	99
Medium human development	86	76	65
Low human development	74	64	39
High Income	88	92	99
Middle Income	94	87	87
Low income	77	64	41
World	84	76	63

Source: UNDP (2006)

To reduce death rate especially child mortality, the importance of birth attended by skilled health personnel cannot be undermined. During 1996-2004, 43 per cent of the child birth was attended by skilled health personnel though it is 99 per cent in High human development countries and 65 per cent in Medium Human Development countries (Table 6).

Health Care Scenario in India

Health is not the mere absence of disease or infirmity as good health confers on a person or groups freedom from illness and ability to realize its potential (Srinivasan, 2004). Health care refers to activities directed towards preserving and enhancing the physical and mental well being of people. This justifies the need to focus on healthcare so as to improve the productivity of the individuals and hence, increase in national income of the country. In this context, it needs to be mentioned that healthcare covers not only medical care but also all aspects of pro-preventive care including nutrition. The progress in the improvement in healthcare is determined by a series of factors including growth of the economy, success in reducing poverty, reduction in regional inequality in access to health care, improvement in quality of health care, investment on health with focus on health infrastructure and so on. Improvement in health scenario is contingent upon the success in reducing population growth with focus on reduction in mortality, burden of diseases, improvement in nutrition services and literacy rate, women empowerment, access to health care service and so on.[5] Some of the issues especially key achievements in health have been addressed in this part.

Key Demographic Indicators

One of the key demographic indicators that determines health scenario is population growth. With acceleration in growth of population it will be extremely difficult to ensure

---

[5] In this context, Srinivasan (2004) argues that ideal health care system should satisfy four criteria: universal access to adequate level and access without excessive burden, fair distribution of financial costs for access and fair distribution of burden in rationing care and a constant search for improvement to a more just system, training providers for competence, empathy and accountability and special attention to be vigilantly provided to vulnerable groups (children, aged, disabled and women).

improvement in healthcare by the government. From Chart 1 it is evident that Natural Growth Rate (NGR) of population has consistently declined during the last three and a half decades. But the extent of decline was relatively much higher (3.2 points) during the 1990s (a fall from 20.5 to 17.3 per 1000 population during 1980 to 1990) as compared to the 1970s and1980s. The NGR has declined by 1.1 points (from 17.2 to 16) during 2000 to 2006.

In order to identify the causes of variation in natural growth rate over the years, progress in reducing both birth rate and death rate has been taken into account. The extent of decline in birth rate is relatively more during the 1990s followed by 1980s and 1970s as it declined in absolute number by 4.4 points (30.2 in 1990 to 25.8 in 2000) during the 1990s, 3.6 points during 1971-1980 and 3.1 points during 1980-90. In contrast, the extent of decline in death rate remained more or less the same during the 1990s and the subsequent period (1991-2006) as evident from Chart 1. This implies that on account of substantial decline in birth rate during the 1990s the natural growth of population came down considerably. However, a substantial decline in death rate was noticed during the 1980s (a fall in 2.7 points from 12.4 to 9.7 during 1980-1990) and 1970s (a fall by 2.5 points). The extent of decline in both the birth rate and death rate has slowed down during 2000-2006 as the birth rate has declined by 2.3 points while death rate dropped by 1.3 points during the said period. In fact, it may not feasible to reduce the death rate considerably as it is as low as 7.5 per 1000 population.

In spite of progress in containing the growth of population, the disparity in birth rate and death rate between rural and urban area is still persisting as the birth rate in rural areas remains much higher than that of the urban areas (Chart 2). This can be essentially on account of certain social and economic factors including higher level of poverty and illiteracy leading to increase in number of child births, lack of unawareness about family planning and so on. The same trend is noticed in death rate though the extent of disparity between the rural and urban areas has come down over the years primarily on account of immunization of children, abolition of certain diseases including small pox, improvement in health infrastructure, access to safe drinking water and sanitation, and development of health awareness among the households.

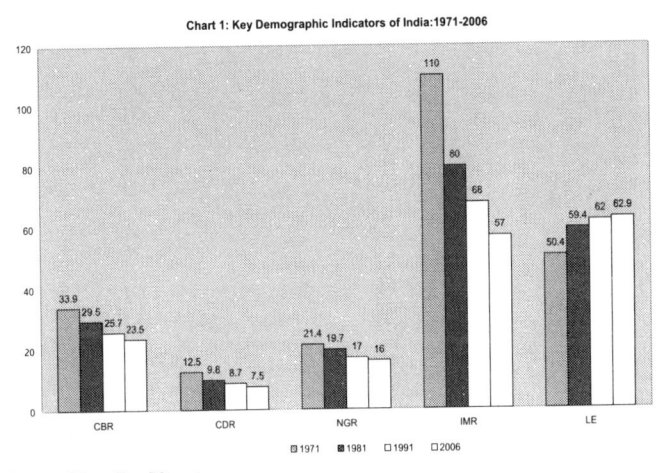

Chart 1: Key Demographic Indicators of India:1971-2006

Indicator	1971	1981	1991	2006
CBR	33.9	29.5	25.7	23.5
CDR	12.5	9.6	8.7	7.5
NGR	21.4	19.7	17	16
IMR	110	80	66	57
LE	50.4	59.4	62	62.9

Mortality Indicators

The foregoing analysis reveals that crude death rate has comedown over the years and it hovers around 8.7 in the recent past with no significant decline during almost last one decade (Chart 3). In this context, some of the crucial issues that deserve priority include high Infant Mortality Rate (IMR) and Maternal Mortality Rate. Of late, more children are surviving infancy and young childhood (GoI, 2007). The IMR (defined as number of child births before completing their first birth day per 1000 live births) has come down by 53 points (from 110 in 1971 to 57 in 2006) during the last three and a half decades. However, it is much higher as compared to some of the developed and developing countries. Again, IMR is relatively higher in rural areas as compared to the urban areas (Table 7). As per NFHS-3 (2007) the prospects of children living until age of 5 are better than what was noticed earlier but it is disheartening to learn that more than one in 18 children die within the first year of life and more than one in 13 die before reaching the age of 5 (GoI, 2007).

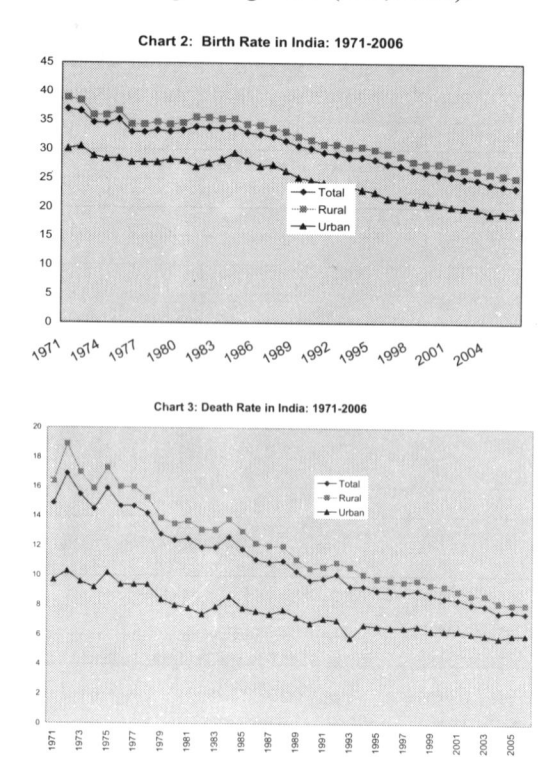

Chart 2: Birth Rate in India: 1971-2006

Chart 3: Death Rate in India: 1971-2006

The persistence of this unhealthy trend can be on account of lack of access to safe drinking water, sanitation and health infrastructure, prevalence of closely spaced birth and limited success in children immunization, and reduction in poverty. The risk of infant death can be reduced to some extent by preventing closely spaced birth. As per NFHS-3 (2007) IMR is 86 for births less than 2 years apart, 50 for births 24-35 months apart, and 30 for births 36-47 months apart. Of late, 28 per cent of births have been spaced less than 2 years despite lower chance of survival of these births (GoI, 2007).

TABLE 7
MORTALITY INDICATORS IN INDIA 1986 - 2006

AREA	INDICATORS	1986	1990	1995	1999	2002	2006
Rural	Crude Death Rate	12.2	10.5	9.8	9.0	8.7	8.1
	Infant Mortality Rate	105.0	86.0	80.0	75.0	69.0	62.0
	Neo-Natal Mortality Rate	65.5	57.4	52.3	49.0	43.5	NA
	Post-Natal Mortality Rate	39.1	28.9	27.5	26.0	25.8	NA
	Peri-Natal Mortality Rate	51.8	51.7	47.6	47.0	38	NA
	Still Birth Rate	10.5	11.9	9.3	11.0	9.1	NA
Urban	Crude Death Rate	7.6	6.8	6.6	6.0	6.1	6.0
	Infant Mortality Rate	62.0	50.0	48.0	44.0	40.0	39.0
	Neo-Natal Mortality Rate	36.2	30.9	29.2	28.0	23.8	NA
	Post-Natal Mortality Rate	25.8	19.5	19.0	16.0	15.8	NA
	Peri-Natal Mortality Rate	32.7	34.0	31.2	30.0	23.1	NA
	Still Birth Rate	9.0	11.0	8.8	8.0	6.9	NA
Combined	Crude Death Rate	11.1	9.7	9.0	9.0	8.1	7.5
	Infant Mortality Rate	96.0	80.0	74.0	70.0	63.0	57.0
	Neo-Natal Mortality Rate	59.8	52.5	48.1	45.0	39.6	NA
	Post-Natal Mortality Rate	36.6	27.2	25.9	24.0	23.8	NA
	Peri-Natal Mortality Rate	48.1	48.4	44.6	44.0	35.1	NA
	Still Birth Rate	10.2	11.8	9.2	10.0	8.6	NA

Sources: (i) Government of India (2006): Health Information in India 2005.
(ii) Registrar General (2007): Sample Registration Bulletin.

As per NFHS-3 (2007) 44 per cent of children in 12-23 months are fully vaccinated against common infectious diseases (Tuberculosis, Diphtheria, Pertussis, Tetanus, Polio and Measles). There has been little improvement in fully vaccination coverage between NFHS-2 (1998-99) and NFHS-3 (2005-06) as it went up from 42 per cent to 44 per cent during the said period. As regards, Polio vaccination, there has been improvement by about 15 percentage points (a rise from 63 to 78 per cent) during the period between NFHS-2 and NFHS-3. However, 22 per cent children still have not received three doses of Polio Vaccine. Again, there is wide disparity across the states. For instance, there has been substantial improvement in Polio vaccination in Bihar, Chattisgarh, Jharkhand, Sikkim and West Bengal while vaccination coverage worsened in Andhra Pradesh, Gujarata, Maharashtra, Punjab and Tamil Nadu during the said period. The success of vaccination differs depending on the level of development (rural versus urban), level of income and between sex. For instance, the children in the urban area belong to households in general category and in the high income bracket are more likely to receive all vaccination. It is disheartening to note that the gender disparity in the extent of vaccination is still prevailing as boys (45 per cent) are more likely than girls (43 per cent) to be fully vaccinated. Besides, there is widespread prevalence of underweight children in India- the highest in the world. The underweight children in India are nearly double that of Sub-Saharan Africa (World Bank, 2006). Further, there is significant inequalities in under nutrition across states, socio-economic groups- girls, rural areas, the poorest, the SC and STs and the inequality has gone up during the 1990s. 'In India, child malnutrition is mostly the result of high levels of exposure to infection and inappropriate infant and young child feeding and caring practices, and has its origins almost entirely during the first two to three years of life. However, the commonly held assumption is that food insecurity is the primary or even sole cause of malnutrition. Consequently, the existing response to malnutrition in India has been skewed towards food based intervention and has placed little emphasis on schemes addressing the other determinants of malnutrition (World Bank, 2006)'. The persistence of this unhealthy trend will have adverse impact on health, education, productivity and therefore, a major obstacle to human development and economic growth.

Maternal Death

The persistence of severe maternal death remains a key concern for the planners and economists as it is a crucial indicator that measures success in providing clinical health service to the poor. India accounts for one-fifth of the total number of maternal death around the globe (DFID, 2007). Taking cognizance of the high maternal death, the Millennium Development Goals stressed on reduction of Maternal Mortality Ratio by three quarters. This needs to be achieved by 2015.[6] For protection of Women from the risk of Maternal Mortality, the government of India launched Janani Suraksha Yojana (JSYA) along with National Rural Health Mission in 2005.

In Maternal death, the performance of Indian economy does not seem to be quite promising as compared to some of the neighbouring countries including China and Sri Lanka (Table 1). The Maternal Mortality Ratio (defined as the number of female deaths from pregnancy related causes per 1 lakh live births) figures for India hovers around 340 during 1997-2003 with wide disparity across the states; the highest in Uttar Pradesh (553) and the lowest in Kerala (136).

The Registrar General of India attempted to estimate maternal death based on large scale survey, covering 4,484 maternal deaths among 13 lakh births in over 11 lakh homes

---

[6] Achieve target of *200 maternal deaths per lakh of live births by 2007* and 109 per lakh of live births by 2015.

during 1997-98, 1999-2001 and 2001-03[7]. The maternal mortality ratio (MMR) per 1 lakh live births declined from about 400 in 1997-98 to about 300 in 2001-03 in India. But there is skepticism about achieving the MDG target of 109 by 2015. Among the states, about two-thirds of maternal deaths occur in few states (Bihar, Jharkhand, Orissa, Madhya Pradesh, Chattisgarh, Rajasthan, Uttar Pradesh, Uttaranchal and in Assam) and this is pronounced in rural area. Low level of education among females enhances the risk of maternal death appreciably (Registrar General, 2006)

Among the causes of maternal death, hemorrhage accounts for 37 per cent of the total followed by sepsis and abortion each account for 11 per cent and 8 per cent respectively (Chart 4). Presence of trained health attendants reduces mortality significantly. For instance, six in every 10 women in rural West Bengal give birth with no skilled health personnel present (GoI, 2007). Besides, good nutrition is the key to reducing mortality rates. Malnutrition and early Pregnancy stunts women's' growth and smaller women experience a higher incidence of birth complications. To reduce maternal mortality significantly, efforts need to be made to empower women so as to ensure their involvement in the decision making process. The reduced social, cultural and economic status of Indian Women inhibits them from adequate access to health facilities, and thus compromises them with their nutritional status (DFID, 2007).

IV. KEY DETERMINING FACTORS OF HEALTH SCENARIO

The success of any economy in improving healthcares scenario is influenced by a number of factors including growth of per capita income, poverty ratio, literacy rate, and public

---

[7] 'The surveys in 1997-98, 1999-2001 and 2001-03 have used retrospective or continuous recording of maternal deaths, with generally consistent definitions (SRS: 2006)'.

expenditure on health, nutrition, water and sanitation, provision of health infrastructure and so on. With the improvement in literacy rate there can be development of health consciousness and therefore, improvement in healthcare scenario is feasible. There has been improvement in literacy rate in India during the last couple of decades as it has gone up by 9 percentage points (from 43.6 to 52.2 per cent) and 13 percentage points (52.2 to 65.4 per cent) during 1991-2001. However, the level of literacy is relatively low in BIMARU states especially in Bihar (50.9 per cent in 2001) while it is as high as 90.9 per cent in Kerala. The persistence of wide disparity in literacy rate can have adverse impact on healthcare scenario in the country.

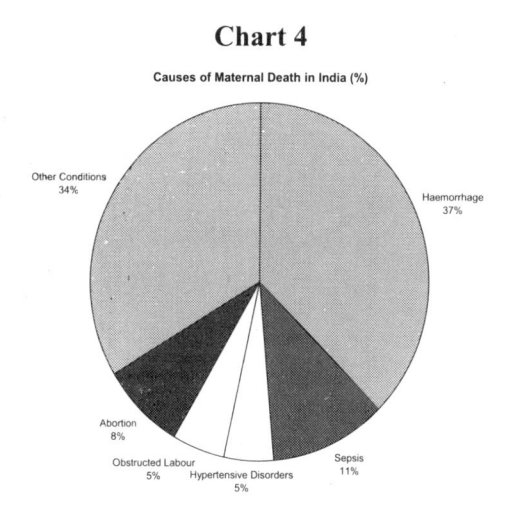

Chart 4

Causes of Maternal Death in India (%)

- Other Conditions 34%
- Haemorrhage 37%
- Abortion 8%
- Obstructed Labour 5%
- Hypertensive Disorders 5%
- Sepsis 11%

The second crucial economic factor that influences the health scenario is the incidence of poverty. As regards level of poverty, around 28 per cent of the total population live below poverty line in 1999-2000. No doubt, there has been consistent decline in poverty ratio but extent of disparity has not come down drastically over the years. About 46 per cent of the total population live below poverty line in Orissa and Bihar in

1999-2000 though it is about 12 per cent in Punjab and Haryana. Third, there seems to be a positive correlation exists between health care scenario and per capita income as improvement in income offers ample scope to increase expenditure on healthcare. There has been improvement in growth of income during the reforms period as compared to pre-reforms period. Of late, the economy is growing between 8-9 per cent and hence, improvement in health care scenario during the reforms period could be partly the outcome of the growth in per capita income.

Public Expenditure on Health

One of the crucial factors that determine the health scenario is the public expenditure on health especially for preventive health if not curative or promotive. Around two-third of health care expenditure is private household's expenditure especially out-of-pocket expenditure. The contribution of state government (15.2 per cent), Union government (5.2 per cent) and third-party insurance and employers (3.3 per cent) together account for 23.7 per cent and the local governments and foreign donors contribute 1.3 per cent (World Bank, 1993). From Table 8 it is evident that total health spending as percentage of Gross Domestic Product (GDP) is about 5 per cent in India in 2001. This is much lower than that of South Africa, Brazil, China and Russia. The per capita expenditure on Health is much lower in the country as compared to Mexico and some of the developed countries including Malaysia. Health expenditure as percentage of total expenditure in India is about 18 per cent in 2001. In this context, the performance of Indian economy is not quite promising as compared to the selected neighbouring countries barring Myanmar. For instance, public expenditure on health as percentage of total expenditure is as high as 90 per cent in Maldives and 57 per cent in Thailand (Table 9). The public investment on Health, family welfare and Indian Systems of Medicine and Homoeopathy by the Centre, state and Union

Territories as percentage of developmental expenditure hovers around 3 per cent during the last half a century (from First five year plan to the Tenth Five year Plan) though it had increased to about 4 per cent during the Ninth and Tenth Five year Plan periods (Chart 5).

TABLE 8
HEALTH SPENDING IN INDIA AND COMPARATOR COUNTRIES, 2001

Country	GDP Per capita	Total Spending as a percentage of GDP	Public Health Spending as a percentage of GDP	Private Health Spending as a percentage of GDP
Pakistan	420	4.1	0.9	3.2
India	**460**	**4.9**	**0.9**	**4.0**
Indonesia	690	2.7	0.6	2.1
China	890	5.3	1.9	3.4
Russia	1750	5.3	3.8	1.5
Thailand	1940	3.7	2.1	1.6
South Africa	2820	8.8	3.7	5.1
Brazil	3070	8.3	3.4	4.9
Malaysia	3330	2.5	1.5	1.0
Mexico	5530	5.4	2.5	2.9

Source: World Bank (2003)

The slow growth in public expenditure on Health is the outcome of substantial increase in current consumption during the 1990s. One of the factors that have contributed significantly to the deteriorating fiscal health of the Union government and state economy is the 'Fifth Pay Commission Recommendations' for the government employees. The substantial upward revision of salary and pension outgo together has resulted in decline in developmental expenditure especially the social sector expenditure. From Table 10 it is evident that public expenditure on healthcare to GSDP ratio has declined during 1990-2002 across the states with wide variation. For instance, public expenditure on health as percentage of GSDP decline by more than 40 per cent in a rich income state (Gujarat) while the extent of decline remains between 20-30 per cent in some of the BIMARU states (Table 10). A comparative analysis of public expenditure on health during 1990-96 and 1996-2002 reveals that for all states public health expenditure to GSDP ratio declined significantly during the first period. Again, it went down during the second period except for Andhra Pradesh, Madhya Pradesh, Orissa, Maharashtra, Punjab and West Bengal, thereby reflecting non-prioritization of healthcare expenditure by the government over the years (Bhat and Jain, 2006).

TABLE 9
PUBLIC EXPENDITURE ON HEALTH AS PERCENTAGE OF TOTAL EXPENDITURE, 2001

Country	Health Expenditure
India	17.9
Bhutan	90.6
Maldvies	83.5
Republic of Korea	73.4
Thailand	57.1
Sri Lanka	48.9
Bangladesh	44.2
Nepal	29.7
Indonesia	25.1
Myanmar	17.8

Source: Bhat and Jain (2006)

Chart 5 Investment on Health, Family Welfare ISM&H in Public Sector, Centre, State and Union Terriitories as % of Total Developmental Expenditure

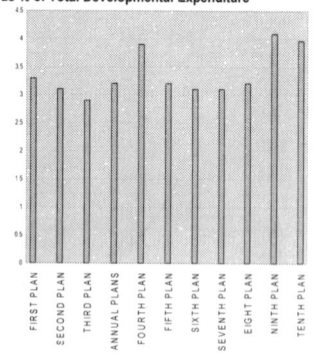

TABLE 10
DECLINE IN PUBLIC HEALTH CARE EXPENDITURE TO GSDP RATIO: 1990-2002

(in Percentage)

Extent of decline	States
More than 40	Gujarat
Between 30-40	Andhra Pradesh, Karnataka, Kerala, Uttar Pradesh, Tamil Nadu
Between 20-30	Orissa, West Bengal, Bihar, Maharashtra, Rajasthan
Less than 20	Madhya Pradesh, Punjab, Assam

Source: Bhat and Jain (2006)

Health Infrastructure in the Public Sector

The development of healthcare scenario is influenced by Health infrastructure. Access to healthcare infrastructure especially skilled manpower determines the health scenario. In this context, population served by one government allopathic doctor can be taken into account. During 2000-05, around 14,000 people are served by one allopathic government doctor with wide variation across the states. Among the selected states, about 24,000 people are served per one government allopathic doctor in Uttar Pradesh while it is the lowest (7200) in Punjab (Chart 6).

Chart 6 Health Manpower in India 2000-05

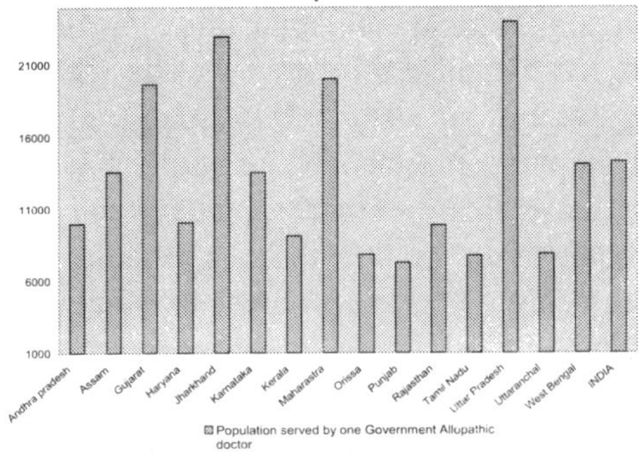

V. SUMMARY AND CONCLUDING OBSERVATIONS

To sum up, the Indian economy has consistently improved the HDI score during the last few decades but it has to go a long way to catch up with some developed economies. The improvement in absolute performance failed to take the economy to the comfort zone as it occupies 127th rank in the recent past. This reflects that in spite of absolute improvement the relative performance of the economy is not quite outstanding. Coming to the performance of the major states, it is noticed that there has been improvement in HDI score during the 1980s and 1990s. But this is noticed along with persistence of wide disparity across the states especially BIMARU states vis-à-vis some of the middle income and developed states.

To identify the proximate determinants of the level of human development, the paper focussed on 'health care scenario'. Some of the key health care indicators do not reflect promising result as compared to some of the developing countries. This is primarily on account inadequate effort made to improve access to health infrastructure and access to both safe drinking water and sanitation. With the implementation of the Union Fifth Pay Commission recommendation, there has been substantial growth in current consumption and thereby it left little scope for the state governments to increase expenditure on social sector especially health care expenditure. By introducing Fiscal Responsibility Act the state governments have managed to improve the fiscal scenario in the recent past. But to sustain this trend can be extremely difficult as implementation of the sixth Pay Commission recommendation is likely to increase salary and pension outgo substantially. Overall, in the absence of adequate effort to improve health care scenario, progress in Human development does not seem to be feasible as it can have adverse impact on education and level of poverty. With the given resource constraint, the state government can explore the possibility of having Public-Private Partnership to develop health infrastructure.

REFERENCES

Bhat, Ramesh and Jain, N. (2006): Analysis of Public and Private Healthcare Expenditures, *Economic and Political Weekly*, 41 (1): 57-68.

DFID (2008): *Maternal Health Strategy*, Pan Africa Strategy Department, South Asia Division, Europe, Middle East and Americas Division, Policy and Research Division.

Government of India (GoI) (2002): *National Human Development Report 2001*, Planning Commission, New Delhi.

GoI (2007): National Family Health Survey-3, Ministry of Health and Family Welfare, New Delhi

GoI (2008): *Economic Survey: 2007-08*, Ministry of Finance, New Delhi.

Haq, Mahbub ul (1995): Reflections on Human Development, Oxford University Press, New York.

Registrar General (2006): *Maternal Mortality in India: 1997-2003, Trends, Causes and Risk Factors*, New Delhi.

Srinivasan, R. (2004): Healthcare Vision 2020, In *India vision 2020*, Planning Commission (Ed.), Planning Commission, Government of India.

United Nations Development Program (UNDP) (1994): *Human Development Report 1994*, Oxford University Press, New York.

UNDP (2005): *Human Development Report, 2005*, Oxford University Press, New York.

UNDP (2006): *Human Development Report, 2006*, Oxford University Press, New York.

UNDP (2007): *Human Development Report 2007/2008*, Palgrave Macmillan, New York.

World Bank (2003): *World Development Report 2004: Making Services Work for Poor People*, World Bank, Washington DC.

World Bank (2006): *India Undernourished Children: A Call for Reform and Action,* World Bank, Washington DC.

9

The Perspectives of Economic Growth and Social Insecurity on Human Development for Lagging States in India

Aswini Kumar Mishra[1]
Biswabas Patra[2]

I. INTRODUCTION

The central objective since the plan era in India has been to initiate a process of development, which will raise living standards and open out the people new opportunities for a richer and more varied life. It is a well-established fact that the varying state of human development across the regions, nations and states within a nation is mainly attributed to two different but complementary approaches namely; growth-mediated and support-led strategy. While the growth mediated strategy aims at promoting economic growth in order to improve public and private incomes, the support-led strategy envisages at wide-ranging public support in areas such as education, health care, employment provision, assets redistribution, and social assistance. It is a well-established fact that there is links between economic growth, social security and human development (though it is not automatic) (UNDP, 1996; Prabhu and Iyer, 1999; Prabhu, 2001; Dev,

---

[1] Indian Institute of Management Ahmedabad (IIMA), India, Email: mishra.aswini@gmail.com
[2] Nabakrushna Choudhury Centre for Development Studies (NCDS), Bhubaneswar, India, E-mail: biswabas.patra@gmail.com.

2002). It needs to be highlighted that the state of human development cannot be treated in isolation of the goal of achieving higher levels of economic growth and public provisioning of social security. As can be seen from Chart 1, the links is a bi-directional one. The links can be strengthened through sensible policy actions. In the long-run economic growth, social security and human development, generally, move together and tend to be mutually reinforcing. The National Human development Report 2001 shows considerable variations in the state of human development across the major states and expresses its concern for income poorer and poverty ridden states (henceforth would be termed as lagging states) for their very slow performance in development radars as reflected through very low value of Human Development Index (HDI) and relatively high value of human poverty index (HPI) since 1980s. Selected parameters of social attainments exhibit very abysmal performance of these states even at the dawn of this new millennium.

Against this backdrop, the primary objective of this paper is to analyze the economic performance as well as the extent of social insecurity across the major states with emphasis of lagging states in India and to show the interstate differences in the state of human development. The organization of the chapter is as follows. In the following section, we examine the economic performance of major states with particular reference to lagging states over a decade starting with early 1990s. Section III reflects some major dimensions and magnitude of social insecurity. An analysis of public provisioning of social security and its implications for human development is made in section IV. Following this, concluding observations have been made.

II. ECONOMIC PERFORMANCE AND HUMAN DEVELOPMENT IN INDIA

In its 1996 Human Development Report, the UNDP's study found that economic growth has a positive impact on several human development indicators reflected in its

CHART 1: ECONOMIC GROWTH, SOCIAL SECURITY AND HUMAN DEVELOPMENT

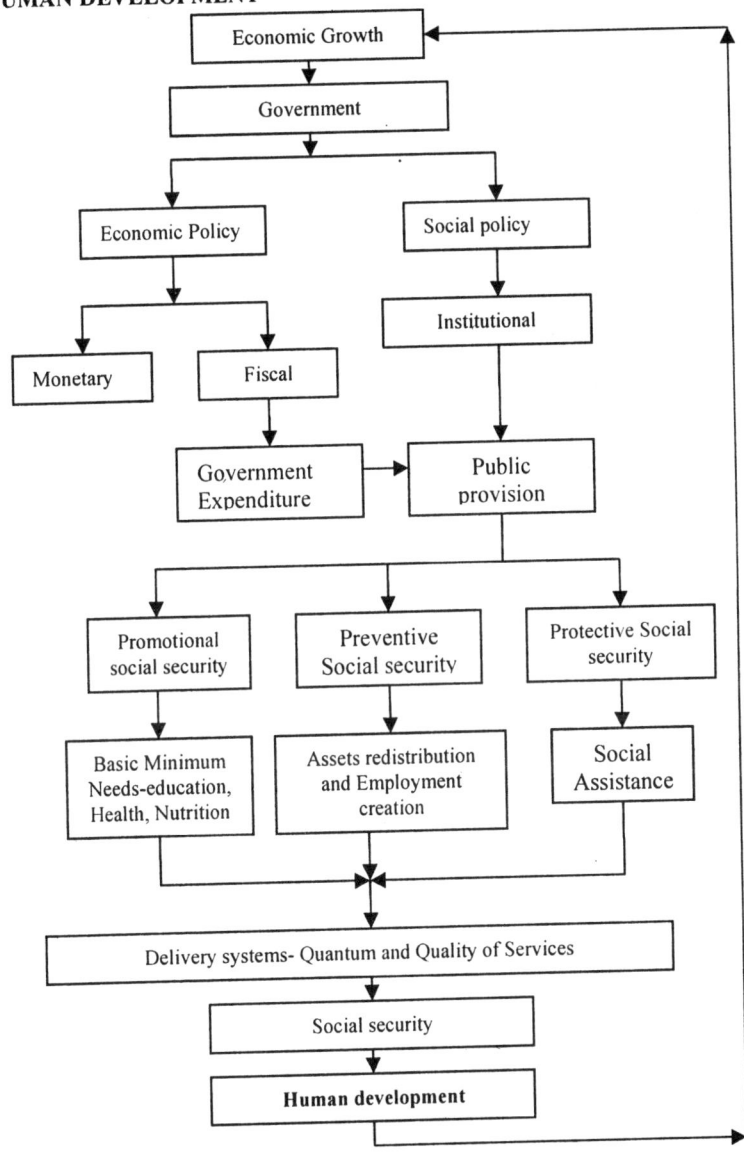

```
                    Economic Growth
                          ↓
                      Government
                     ↙          ↘
          Economic Policy    Social policy
              ↓                   ↓
         ↙       ↘           Institutional
     Monetary   Fiscal            ↓
                  ↓                ↓
          Government  →      Public
          Expenditure        provision
                     ↓    ↓    ↓
        ┌────────────┼─────────┬──────────┐
   Promotional    Preventive         Protective Social
   social security  Social security    security
        ↓               ↓                  ↓
   Basic Minimum    Assets redistribution  Social
   Needs-education, and Employment        Assistance
   Health, Nutrition   creation
                     ↓
        Delivery systems- Quantum and Quality of Services
                          ↓
                   Social security
                          ↓
                   Human development
```

Source: Prabhu and Iyer (1999), Prabhu (2001)

magnitude of HDI. Many states in our country also reveal the same fact.

It is found from the National Human Development Report 2001 (GoI, 2002) that the richer states (like Punjab, Haryana), on the average, have higher magnitude of HDI compared to the middle-income states (like Karnataka, Tamilnadu) and similarly the latter have higher magnitude of HDI compared to the poorer states (like Orissa, Bihar). This is not to say, however, that economic growth will invariably and automatically translate into human development if other important factors are not in place. Now the links from growth to human development can be set through the influence of household activity and spending on human development, and the influence of government policies and expenditures.

Considering the first part, a family's income has a positive effect on educational status, health achievements and nutritional conditions. Such activities as education and health contribute to growth in the economy through the improvements in people's productive capacity, such as higher skills and better health (Hayami, 2000). So, in this way, income is an important means to enhance capabilities and, this would in turn help in expanding a person's ability to be more productive and earn a higher income and help him to emancipate from poverty.

At the State level in India, there are major differences in Socio-economic dimensions of development, such as size of the economy, population, physical infrastructure, agro-climatic conditions, et cetera. However, great regional inequality exists within India in terms of population and income across the states (and the union territories) as is visualized from Table 1 for selected years. For these selected years, Maharashtra is the largest State in terms of its Gross State Domestic Product (GSDP) share relative to the all states (and union territories excluding Mizoram state for which data is not available at 1993-04 prices). It contributes 14 to 15 per cent of the total GSDP in all three different reference years. Next to it, Uttar

Pradesh, the most populous state and its share varies between 10 to 11 percent (Mishra and Patra, 2006). The third position is occupied by Tamil Nadu, Andhra Pradesh and West Bengal have alternated their position in successive years as the difference in their contributions to the total was found to be marginal one. But what is surprising that the share of states like Assam, Orissa, Madhya Pradesh to GSDP is gradually decreasing even though, it is small compared to their population size.

On the whole, in addition to these States, 10 other states, which together constitute the major states, contribute about 90 percent of the total GSDP as well as population. Therefore, it is important to know their variation separately. To be more specific, these 15 major states are grouped into three major categories - (i) High Income States (HIS) comprising of Gujarat, Haryana, Maharashtra and Punjab (ii) Middle Income States (MIS) comprising of Andhra Pradesh, Karnataka, Kerala, Tamil Nadu and West Bengal, and (iii) Low Income States (LIS) comprising of Assam, Bihar, Madhya Pradesh, Orissa Rajasthan and Uttar Pradesh. However, looking at the share of population and GSDP among these three sub-categories of states, greater inequality is found to be exist between HIS and LIS, which is rather surprising - as found from the Table 1. But what is more important here to mention that greater equality between population and GSDP share is found among middle income states taken together.

Though, GSDP measures the size of the "Economic Cake" of a State, it remains silent about its distribution amongst the inhabitants. In order to know its distributional aspect, per capita income is generally used. Therefore, another way of looking at the economic inequality is the trend in per capita income. Therefore, 15 major states are ranked in ascending order of their per capita NSDP (see Table 2).

TABLE 1
POPULATION AND GSDP (AT 1993-94 PRICES) AND THEIR SHARE IN SELECTED YEARS

(in percentage)

Sl. No.	State	Share in GSDP in 1993-94	Share in Population in 1993-94	Share in GSDP in 1997-98	Share in Population in 1997-98	Share in GSDP in 2000-01	Share in Population in 2000-01
01	Andhra Pradesh	7.82	7.82	7.19	7.65	7.94	7.42
02	Assam	2.05	2.65	1.76	2.63	1.64	2.59
03	Bihar	3.08	7.68	2.75	7.84	3.20	8.04
04	Gujarat	6.65	4.88	7.57	4.84	6.97	4.92
05	Haryana	2.99	1.97	2.91	2.01	3.06	2.05
06	Karnataka	5.55	5.30	5.70	5.24	6.43	5.15
07	Kerala	3.56	3.37	3.37	3.27	3.46	3.14
08	Madhya Pradesh	5.13	5.78	4.92	5.85	4.52	5.88
09	Maharashtra	15.32	9.37	15.23	9.42	14.35	9.43
10	Orissa	2.51	3.71	2.35	3.65	2.17	3.59
11	Punjab	4.09	2.39	3.80	2.39	3.79	2.39
12	Rajasthan	4.46	5.26	5.28	5.37	4.78	5.48
13	Tamil Nadu	7.78	6.47	8.07	6.25	8.36	6.08
14	Uttar Pradesh	10.88	15.71	10.35	15.94	9.82	16.15
15	West Bengal	7.22	8.04	7.52	7.96	7.87	7.84
16	All States and UTs*	100.00	100.00	100.00	100.00	100.00	100.00
17	Share of Major States	89.10	90.40	88.76	90.31	88.35	90.15
18	HIS	32.61	20.58	33.25	20.65	31.88	20.84
19	MIS	35.85	34.29	35.88	33.64	38.55	32.87
20	LIS	31.54	45.13	30.87	45.71	29.57	46.29

Note: * does not include Mizoram State
Source: **Central Statistical Organisation, New Delhi.**

It is revealed from the Table 2 that, Punjab stood at the top position in terms of highest per capita income, whereas, Bihar got its position at the bottom level through out the reference period. It is rather surprising that excepting few years, the top positions were pre occupied by HIS and next to them are MIS and LIS respectively. But what is more important to mention here that, the mean per capita income difference among these states is gradually increasing particularly between HIS and LIS. Between 1993-94 and 2002-03 the per capita income difference between HIS and LIS rose from Rs. 6,400 to 9,300 and the gap in mean per capita income difference between MIS and LIS increased by more than twice, i.e., from Rs.2, 600 to 5,600.

Inter-state comparisons of growth performance based on GSDP, Net State Domestic Product (NSDP) and per capita NSDP at constant prices have been worked and are presented in Table 3. A perusal of the data from the Table 3 reveals that between 1993-94 and 2002-03 the compound annual growth rate of GSDP in real terms for the 15 major states was 5.2 percent. However, the variation in growth rates among these states was substantial. The relatively better performers with growth rates well in excess of the average were Karnataka, West Bengal, Haryana Gujarat, Andhra Pradesh, Bihar, Rajastan and Tamil Nadu. Four of these states are belong to the category of MIS. The probable reason for this could be the growth of tertiary sector and more particularly the booming Information Technology (IT) sector in these Southern States. The same eight states are also found to be the best performers, with growth rates in excess of the average NSDP growth (which turned out to be 4.97 percent). All LIS except Bihar witnessed a NSDP growth of about four per cent or less.

Though the economic performance as measured by the growth of GSDP / NSDP, which shows whether a state is growing faster than its neighbouring states, but it does not capture the growth of population. Therefore, it is pertinent to visualize the growth in real per capita income. Compared to an average growth of per capita income of 3.07 percent per annum as witnessed by these 15 major states, only six states are found to have crossed that ladder, namely, West Bengal, Karnataka, Andhra Pradesh, Tamil Nadu, Kerala and Haryana. Again, the southern states, which mainly constitute the MIS, performed well ahead of the 15 major states average level.

TABLE 2
RANKING OF MAJOR STATES IN TERMS OF PER CAPITA INCOME AT 1993-94 PRICES (IN ASCENDING ORDERS)

Sl. No.	State	1993-94	1994-95	1995-96	1996-97	1997-98	1998-99	1999-00	2000-01	2001-02	2002-03
01	Andhra Pradesh	8	8	8	8	6	8	8	8	8	7
02	Assam	4	4	4	4	4	4	4	4	4	4
03	Bihar	1	1	1	1	1	1	1	1	1	1
04	Gujarat	12	12	13	13	13	13	12	11	12	12
05	Haryana	13	13	12	12	12	12	13	13	13	13
06	Karnataka	9	9	9	10	10	10	10	10	10	10
07	Kerala	10	10	10	9	9	9	9	9	9	9
08	Madhya Pradesh	6	5	5	5	5	5	5	5	5	5
09	Maharashtra	14	14	15	14	15	14	15	14	14	15
10	Orissa	2	2	2	2	2	3	3	2	3	3
11	Punjab	15	15	14	15	14	15	14	15	15	14
12	Rajasthan	5	7	6	6	8	6	6	6	6	6
13	Tamil Nadu	11	11	11	11	11	11	11	12	11	11
14	Uttar Pradesh	3	3	3	3	3	2	2	3	2	2
15	West Bengal	7	6	7	7	7	7	7	7	7	8

Source: Central Statistical Organization, New Delhi.

TABLE 3
GROWTH RATE OF DIFFERENT PARAMETERS BETWEEN 1993-94 AND 2002-03 (AT 1993-94 PRICES)

Sl. No.	State	GSDP Growth	NSDP Growth	PCY Growth
01	Andhra Pradesh	5.61	5.51	4.38
02	Assam	2.49	2.28	0.78
03	Bihar	5.65	5.63	2.97
04	Gujarat	5.79	5.15	3.04
05	Haryana	5.86	5.66	3.1
06	Karnataka	7.1	6.93	5.35
07	Kerala	4.8	4.71	3.83
08	Madhya Pradesh	3.92	3.69	1.52
09	Maharashtra	4.89	4.57	2.57
10	Orissa	3.73	3.62	2.2
11	Punjab	4.25	4.1	2.31
12	Rajasthan	5.46	5.08	2.46
13	Tamil Nadu	5.31	5.18	4.15
14	Uttar Pradesh	3.76	3.41	1.09
15	West Bengal	7.03	7.11	5.54
16	All-India (CSO)	6.1	6.02	4.06
17	All States and UTs*	5.54	5.33	3.36
18	All States*	5.41	5.18	3.25
19	15 Major States	5.19	4.97	3.07
20	HIS	5.13	4.75	2.7
21	MIS	6.05	5.79	4.7
22	LIS	4.21	3.95	1.68

Source: CSO, New Delhi.

The above analysis shows that the share of lagging states in total GSDP has gradually come down and on the other hand, growth performance of these states was very low at the beginning of the new millennium. Therefore, in order to keep pace with other states in terms of the state of human development, these states have to put greater emphasis on growth-mediated strategy. With this now turn to examine the extent of social insecurity and the public provisioning for it.

III. DIMENSIONS AND MAGNITUDE OF SOCIAL INSECURITY

Dev and Ravi (2007) found that nearly 115 million people out of 315 million poor people in India are extremely poor. The reason for such high magnitude is obvious, as these people are most often not being reached by current development policies, and whose situation might have deteriorated even in comparison with other poor people. Now the obvious question arises who are the extremely/ chronically poor. However, the extremely poor are not a homogenous group. Extreme poverty clearly affects people in many different situations. In specific contexts there are differing sets of factors associated with chronic poverty, and the causes of chronic poverty vary from region to region, household to household and person to person. As Chronic Poverty Research Centre (CPRC) points out that there are various combinations of structural factors (labour and product markets, caste, geographic location), life cycle factors (widowhood, household composition, disability, being young or elderly) and idiosyncratic factors (ill health, impairment) and common shocks (like natural disasters) create and maintain the poverty of some while giving others the chance to avoid or escape it.

The Chronic Poverty Report 2004-05, based on panel data, identifies some of the typical characteristics of chronic poverty in India. The panel data (1970/71-1981/82) shows that in rural India the casual agricultural laborers (56.3 per cent) followed by cultivators (26.9 per cent) constitute the largest segment in the category of always being poor. These can be put into the category of *working poor*. Nevertheless, as mentioned above most of the unemployable (like the old and the handicapped, the widows, the orphans) - owing to life cycle contingencies or exigencies - and henceforth considered as *non - working poor* also falls into this category. The aged, widows, physically challenged obviously constitute the most vulnerable section (also the orphans) of the population of any society. They are assumed to be in the trap of perennial poverty and are vulnerable to social stigmatization, to have limited access to and control over economic resources, and may have the inability to work (physically / mentally). They are quite often deprived of social, economic and civic rights and are vulnerable to social neglect. Moreover, while there are some rays of hope for the extremely / chronically working poor to move out of poverty with conventional anti-poverty programs, it seems quite difficult to make these non - working extremely / chronically poor especially the aged, the infirmed, the invalid to move out of poverty. Moreover, as National Human Development Report 2001 (GoI, 2002) points out that societies, cultures and nations have often been evaluated on the basis of how they have been treating their elderly, the children, the disabled and the deprived in course of their development.

Though it is beyond the scope of the paper to go into detail in examining the extent of vulnerability being faced by these particular groups, nevertheless these are some of the appalling features of these people in India:

Aged
- In India, in the year 2001 over 76 million (exactly 76.62 million) were in the age group of 60+. This population is expected to go up to 173 million by the year 2026 and a whopping of 324 million by the year 2050 (GoI, 2006a).
- 90 per cent of older persons are from the unorganized sector, with no social security at the age of 60 (http://www.helpageindia.org/ageingScenario.php).
- 30 per cent of older persons live below the poverty line and another 33 per cent just marginally over it (*ibid.*).

- About 52 per cent of the aged in India are economically fully dependent on others and their size at present is estimated to be to the tune of 34.4 million during the year 2004 (GoI, 2006b).

Widows
- In India, in the year 2001 there were over 34 million (exactly 34.3 million) widows and the incidence of widowhood was 6.91per cent (GoI, 2006a).
- In India, 70 per cent of the head of the households are widow, which are strongly linked with poverty (*ibid.*).
- The World Bank report *Voices of the Poor* (2000) cites that widows here are assumed an economic burden on the household: 'They are wholly dependent on their family for care and support as they do not have any earnings of their own.
- A study estimates that at the all-India level, widows had 82 per cent higher mortality rate than married women of 45 and above years of age (Bhat, 1998).

People with Disabilities
- The Chronic Poverty Research Centre has identified disability as one of the characteristics of the 'very poor' or chronic poor.
- Elwan (1999) estimates that 20per cent of the world's poorest people are disabled.
- There were 21.9 million persons with disabilities as per the Census 2001 in India (GoI, 2006a).

A research study in India finds that the percentage of households living below the poverty line to be significantly higher (54-62 per cent) when the household has a person with a disability-as opposed to 36-51 per cent for households without disabilities (Harris-White, 1999).

The dimensions of social insecurity and vulnerability of working poor and non-working poor can well be exemplified. While the former are vulnerable to transient poverty arising out of market conditions, the latter mostly face chronic poverty due to what may be called structural factors.

Moreover, their vulnerability increases when non-market risks or exogenous shocks are imposed on them. In the above analysis, we also have explained some of major dimensions of insecurity and vulnerability of these working as well as non-working poor in the state vis-à-vis other states to ascertain the relative position of the state. Table 4 shows some major dimensions of social insecurity across the major states in India. A perusal of data from the above table shows that the proportion of these core vulnerable groups is relatively high in lagging states.

IV. PUBLIC PROVISIONING OF SOCIAL SECURITY AND ITS IMPLICATIONS FOR HUMAN DEVELOPMENT

As mentioned in our introductory part, there is a link from social security to human development via support-led strategy. The two are inter-related and one leads the other (but not always). Government action can add to the material resources for human development. This is because, human development, among other things, requires considerable investment in education, health and nutrition whose provision is considered to be the responsibility of the government as these have intrinsic values and spill over effects. Moreover, the more inclusive the reach of basic education, and health care, the more likely it is that even the potentially poor would have a better chance of overcoming penury (Sen, 1999).

Poverty eradication has been an important goal of development policy since the inception of planning in India. Various anti-poverty; employment generation and basic services programs have been in operation for decades. These are targeted mainly at persons who are able to work but remain unemployed for lack of employment opportunities. But as mentioned above, there are certain classes of people who are unable to work and earn their livelihood (due to life-cycle factors). In their case eradication of destitution and hunger calls for social protection measures involving direct income transfers by way of social assistance. This protective aspect aims at maintaining or preventing a decline in living standards in general and in basic conditions in particular (Guhan, 1993).

TABLE 4
DIMENSIONS OF SOCIAL INSECURITY AND THEIR CORRELATES AND SPECIFIC POVERTY INDICATORS IN MAJOR STATES OF RURAL INDIA

Sl. No	States	Proportion of SC and ST to Total Population (PROPSCST)	Old Age Dependency Ratio (ODR)	Incidence of Widowhood (IWH)	Widows as % of Ever Married Female Population (WFP)	Ratio of Widows to Widowers (WTOWDR)
		(1)	(2)	(3)	(4)	(5)	(6)
1	Andhra Pradesh	26.83	13.80	9.15	15.04	5.53
2	Assam	20.28	10.60	6.71	13.85	4.09
3	Bihar*	23.08	12.85	4.12	9.68	2.27
4	Gujarat	28.50	12.60	6.83	12.10	3.01
5	Haryana	21.36	14.55	5.47	9.92	2.32
6	Himachal Pradesh	29.92	15.80	7.85	13.97	3.79
7	Jammu and Kashmir	22.16	12.31	4.07	8.92	1.95
8	Karnataka	26.80	14.16	9.41	16.49	6.27
9	Kerala	12.32	16.72	10.15	16.85	8.46
10	Madhya Pradesh*	43.46	14.08	6.49	11.86	2.65
11	Maharashtra	24.35	18.41	8.48	14.61	5.31
12	Orissa	41.80	14.95	7.72	14.23	3.97
13	Punjab	33.04	17.04	5.93	10.56	2.26
14	Rajasthan	33.40	13.65	5.96	10.84	2.80
15	Tamil Nadu	25.37	14.81	10.05	16.55	4.55
16	Uttar Pradesh*	23.49	14.60	4.88	9.44	1.59
17	West Bengal	34.05	11.54	7.98	14.28	7.16
	INDIA	**28.33**	**14.11**	**6.91**	**12.56**	**3.27**
	Coeff. of Var.	28.20	14.06	27.18	20.67	49.46

Contd...

% of Non-Working Disabled Population (NWDP)	Proportion of Marginal Workers Seeking / Available for Work (MWSAFW)	AL as % of Main Workers (ALMW)	MW as % of TW (MWTW)	Proportion of Dependent among Aged NW (PDAANW)	Proportion of Dependent among Disabled NW (PDEDNW)
(7)	(8)	(9)	(10)	(11)	(12)
61.99	43.26	41.42	18.44	68.96	57.02
67.02	30.63	10.42	27.94	58.75	56.16
65.26	21.96	40.74	29.44	62.20	59.15
60.97	23.10	26.28	25.87	74.93	58.08
65.64	19.93	12.81	29.95	46.78	49.26
57.76	18.91	2.01	36.56	63.17	56.90
64.53	23.07	5.00	36.31	54.03	51.81
62.05	17.28	26.37	21.40	74.72	58.83
74.31	49.64	15.84	21.81	50.11	54.60
60.35	23.48	25.36	29.43	71.09	57.20
62.94	26.62	33.32	19.84	71.31	57.39
66.85	34.28	25.49	35.87	58.40	54.51
70.96	27.05	18.74	17.49	57.98	56.30
59.56	18.51	6.92	29.69	76.97	60.18
53.54	31.99	36.39	18.62	66.28	49.81
66.62	20.68	17.58	30.07	56.38	52.34
66.07	40.98	27.60	26.42	61.25	52.52
63.85	26.56	26.41	26.06	63.79	55.55
7.70	34.28	55.44	23.61	14.15	5.89

Contd...

Proportion of Disabled to total Population (PDTTP)	Proportion of Elderly to total Population (PETTP)	Proportion of Poor (2004-05) (HCR)	Proportion of Extremely Poor (2004-05) (EP)
(13)	(14)	(15)	(16)
1.90	8.13	10.85	2.8
2.02	5.86	23.05	4.96
2.14	6.55	43.06	14.65
2.27	7.31	19.76	5.04
2.26	7.93	13.41	2.91
2.64	9.31	12.5	1.95
3.01	6.76	4.81	0.64
1.89	8.28	23.73	3.83
2.75	10.52	12.27	3.91
2.30	7.43	38.17	14.72
1.83	10.24	30.36	11.25
2.81	8.58	47.76	25.16
1.85	9.82	9.55	1.04
2.56	6.99	18.91	3.39
2.71	9.23	22.96	5.04
2.07	6.59	34.06	11.14
2.35	7.35	28.49	7.41
2.21	**7.74**	**29.18**	**9.64**
16.11	**17.20**	**53.50**	**91.35**

Note: Extremely poor are those persons whose per capita consumption is less than 75 per cent of state-specific poverty line

Source: Col.(2) to Col(13), GoI (2006a); Col.(15) and Col(16) Dev and Ravi (2007)

India is a federal State. The Constitution of India assigns the responsibility for social security concurrently to the Union and the States. The subject is, therefore, placed in the Concurrent List (List III of the Seventh Schedule) of the Constitution. The items on List III relevant to social security are: Social security and social insurance, employment and unemployment; Welfare of labour, including conditions of work, provident funds, employers' liability, workmen's compensation, invalidity and old age pensions and maternity benefits.

Till now, the much awaited Social Security Bill for the Unorganized Workers has not been placed in the Parliament which could serve the social security needs of more than 430 millions working poor people at present. A review of plan documents indicates how fitful and feeble the reference to the social security for the unorganized non-working poor has been. There is, as a matter of fact, no policy on social security, no plan for social security and the Five Year Plans (FYPs) are practically silent about this important aspect. Several other experts have expressed similar views. After forty years of plan development, the 8th FYPs recognized the need for suitable organizational arrangements for providing *a minimum measure of social security* for the unorganized workers; and as a follow up measure the central government introduced a *National Social Assistance Program* (NSAP) in the year 1995.

The *Report of the Working Group on Social Protection Policy – NSAP and Associated Programs*, Government of India (2006) observes, "The NSAP was intended to be a significant step towards fulfillment of the *Directive Principles* in Article 41 of the Constitution". The program included for the time being three benefits, namely, old age pension (NOAPS[3]), family benefit (NFBS[4]) and maternity benefit (NMBS[5]) recently renamed as Janani Suraksha Yojana (JSY). It was obviously envisaged that more such benefits would be added in due course to extend protection against other cases of undeserved want.

In the year 2006, the assistance under NOAPS was enhanced to Rs.200. In the year 1998, the rate of maternity benefit was raised to Rs.500 per pregnancy and the rate of family benefit due to natural causes was raised to Rs.10, 000,

---

[3] National Old Age Pension Scheme: Rs.75 per month per beneficiary.
[4] National Family Benefit Scheme: Rs 5000 in case of death due to natural causes and Rs.10, 000 in case of accidental death of the primary breadwinner of the bereaved household.
[5] National Maternity Benefit Scheme: Rs.300 per pregnancy up to the first two live births.

the quantum of benefit in the event of death due to accident remaining the same. In the year 2000, a new scheme called Annapurna Scheme was added providing for supply of 10 kgs of food grains free of cost to those senior citizens who were eligible for old age pension but had remained uncovered under the National Old Age Pension Scheme.

Evaluation studies find that NSAP has in fact reached the target segment. Achievement rates are also increasing over the years. Benefits offered under the program have met the objective as laid down in the program. However, the program now needs to re-look into the numerical ceiling norms, provide provision for updating below poverty line list, clearly define responsibility among the various functionaries involved in the implementation, ensure timely release of benefit and lay greater emphasis on publicity and awareness generation. Moreover, barring a few states namely Kerala, Tamil Nadu and Maharashtra, which have adequate provisions of protective/preventive social security, in other states more particularly in lagging states the schemes/programmes for the destitute being, run in an ad hoc and piecemeal manner. It may be underlined that the provisioning of social security from the human development perspectives is well recognized and well documented. Even in industrially advanced countries, where the priority have been growth-mediated strategies are allocating more than one-fourth of their budgetary resources towards it. In principle, governments in richer states could give more support to human development, as more funds are available. But this is not the only constraint for poorer states. Poorer states with their effective expenditure management can divert more resources for social security from unproductive uses and thereby can raise the magnitude of social indicators of human development. Thus, mobilizing resources for productive uses enhance social security and human development.

V. CONCLUSIONS

The perusal of above discussions revealed that the growth performance is sluggish in case of lagging states and so also there has been very inadequate provisioning of social security in these states. It has its effects on human development. The challenges to overcome this grim situation necessitate effective mobilization of resources for poverty reduction and social development, which are as great as ever. The role of public sector as well as private sector is sought for creating favorable infrastructure environment. The former has to act as a catalyst in the development process.

REFERENCES

Bhat, P.N. Mari (1998): Widowhood and Mortality in India, In Chen, Martha (ed.), *Widows in India*, Sage Publications, New Delhi.

Hayami, Yujiro (2000): *Development Economics - From the Poverty to the Wealth of Nations*, Oxford University Press, New York.

Sen, Amartya (1999): *Development as Freedom*, Oxford University Press, New Delhi.

Government of India (GoI) (2002): *National Human Development 2001*, Planning Commission, New Delhi.

GoI (2006a): *Population Projections for India and States 2001-2026 (Revised December 2006)*, Census of India 2001, Office of the Registrar General and Census Commissioner, New Delhi.

GoI (2006b): *Report No. 507 - Morbidity, Health Care and the Condition of the Aged*, NSS 60th round (January –June 2004), National Sample Survey Organization, New Delhi.

Dev, S. Mahendra and C. Ravi (2007): Poverty and Inequality: All-India and States, 1983-2005, *Economic and Political Weekly*, 42(6): 509-521.

Dev, S. Mahendra (2002): Growth mediated and Support-led Social security in the Unorganized Sector in India, *The Indian Journal of Labour Economics*, 45 (2): 219-42.

Elwan, Ann (1999): Poverty and Disability: A Survey of the Literature, Discussion Paper Series No. 9932, Social Protection Unit, The World Bank, Washington D.C.

Guhan, S. (1993): Social Security for the Poor in the Unorganized Sector: A Feasible Blueprint for India, In K.S.Parikh and R.S. Sudarshan (Eds.) *Human Development and Structural Adjustment*, Macmillan, Madras, 203-237.

Harris-White, Barbara (1999): On to a Loser: Disability in India, In B. Harris-White and S. Subramanian (eds.), *Ill fare in India: Essays on India's Social sector in Honour of S. Guhan'*, Sage Publications, New Delhi.

Mishra, Aswini Kumar and Biswabas Patra (2006): Spatial Dimensions of Economic Growth in India, *Vision*, 26(3): 49-57.

Prabhu, K. Seeta and S. V. Iyer (1999): Financing Social Security in India: A Human Development Perspective, *The Indian Journal of Labour Economics*, 42 (3): 519-33.

Prabhu, K. Seeta (2001): Socio-Economic Security in the Context of Pervasive Poverty: A Case Study of India, *Indian Journal of Labour Economics,* 44(4): 519-558.

United Nations Development Program (UNDP) (1996): *Human Development Report*, Oxford University Press, New York, 66-85.

World Bank (1994): *World Development Report*, Washington D.C.

10

Environment, Human Development and Economic Growth of Indian States after Liberalisation

Sacchidananda Mukherjee[1]
Debashis Chakraborty[2]

I. INTRODUCTION

The economic reform process initiated in 1991 has played a major role in shaping India's overall as well as its sub-regional economic growth. First, the unshackling of domestic industries, coupled with the shift towards export-oriented economic philosophy caused an industrialisation drive across the Indian States. Second, the easing of FDI approval system provided ample scope for States with enterprising governments to strike their own growth curves by encouraging investment and thereby ensuring industrialisation within their territories. Third, in the post-1991 period the policy objective of achieving balanced growth no longer remained a driving concern, and thus enhanced the possibility of increasing industrial concentration in strategic locations.

Enhanced economic growth (EG) is likely to raise the general level of human development (HD) in the current

---

[1] WWF-India Secretariat, New Delhi, E-mail : smukherjee@wwfindia.net
[2] Indian Institute of Foreign Trade (IIFT), New Delhi, India, Email: debashis@iift.ac.in

period, which in turn may influence future EG potential positively. However, increasing industrialisation or urbanisation on the other hand, if not associated with requisite level of governance, can considerably influence the environmental sustainability of a region in question (Maiti and Agrawal, 2005). The adverse impact could either come through natural resource depletion and/or adverse health consequences of environmental degradation, e.g., air or water pollution (Brandon and Hommann, 1995).

It can be further argued that with increasing level of HD, public awareness on environmental sustainability increase in a particular State, which in turn will influence its pattern of governance.[3] In other words, States with higher HDI should ideally be ranked higher in terms of environmental performance. The relationship between economic growth, measured through per capita net state domestic product (PCNSDP), and environmental performance might be more complex in nature. In general, higher income level is conducive for ensuring higher HD, and therefore should ideally be favourable for maintaining environmental sustainability (World Bank, 2006). However, some States might also choose to grow in the short run by hosting a number of environmentally damaging but fast-growing industries within their territories, with obvious consequences on local environment.

Globally, the environmental regulation-avoiding attitude of producers often leads to concentration of polluting industries in locations characterised by lax environmental norms ('Pollution Haven Hypothesis - PHH'). Usually it is argued that the developed country producers relocate their polluting units in newly industrialising developing countries

---

[3] Jalan et el. (2003) show that raising the level of schooling of woman in an urban household from 0 to 10 years approximately doubles willingness to pay for improved drinking water quality.

(Eskeland and Harrison, 2003).[4] Similarly within a country, relocation along that line from 'cleaner' States to the 'dirtier' States may be noticed for various reasons (Dastidar, 2006).[5]

Working with the Indian scenario, while negative environmental performance by transnational corporations during 1980s (Jha, 1999) and higher FDI inflow in relatively more polluting sectors in the post-liberalisation period have been reported (Gamper-Rabindran and Jha, 2004); several studies rejected the existence of PHH (Dietzenbacher and Mukhopadhyay, 2007; Jena et el., 2005). In long run the PHH may or may not become a reality in some Indian States. However, that is beyond the scope of the current exercise.

The efficiency of environmental governance and pollution-abatement is currently a much-researched area (Costantini and Salvatore, 2006; Kathuria and Sterner, 2006; Sankar, 1998). The intervention of Supreme Court in India has been quite successful in this regard (Antony, 2001; World Bank, 2006), although the limitation of that approach has also been highlighted (Venkatachalam, 2005).[6] Programs like joint forest management (JFM) can also be mentioned here, with direct involvement of stakeholders, which has helped natural

---

[4] Gallagher (2004) cautioned that without environmental laws, regulations, and the willingness and capacity of enforcement, trade-led growth will lead to increase in environmental degradation.

[5] Maharashtra is the biggest producer of electronic waste in India; however the more hazardous recycling of these products (e.g., extraction of copper, gold, breaking-up of cathode-ray tubes etc.) is actually undertaken in Delhi. This particular choice of recycling location comes from the fact that the extracted materials are important inputs for the copper and gold business in Moradabad and Meerat respectively, both close to Delhi (Dastidar, 2006).

[6] For instance, through setting up of the Local Area Environmental Committees (LAECs) with the active participation of the local people for inspection, monitoring of day-to-day development in hazardous waste affected sites; the Supreme Court Monitoring Committee (SCMC) on hazardous waste has ensured strict compliance of the *Hazardous Wastes (Management and Handling) Rules, 1989* on the part of the industries or any other agency involved in hazardous waste generation, collection, treatment and disposal.

resource management to a great extent (CBD, undated; Balooni, 2002)[7].World Bank (2006) has noted that India's environmental institutions and regulatory regime need to be strengthened through incentives to the industries complying with greener norms on one hand and devolution of more powers to local governments on the other. In addition, Chopra and Gulati (1997) argued that strengthening property rights can also arrest environmental degradation.

Apart from the internal factors like economic liberalisation, external factors have also influenced the environmental scenario in India significantly. Trade and Environment remained an important issue for discussion at the WTO forums since the inception of the multilateral body in 1995 and standard-setting has been a continuous process. Indian firms, especially doing business in sectors like textile, marine products, leather, chemicals etc., have often complained that the environmental compliance norms for exporting to EU and US are too stringent (Chakraborty and Singh, 2005). Nonetheless, owing to sanctions and regular factory visits by importing country officials, the compliance level in India has increased over the years for several industries (Tewari and Pillai, 2005; Sankar, 2006; Schjolden, 2000), with obvious positive implications on the domestic environment.

In this background, on the basis of a secondary data analysis, the current paper attempts to analyze the relationship of environmental quality with human development and economic growth separately for 14 major Indian States over 1991-2004. For a closer analysis of the impact of the reform element on environmental quality of the States, the sample period is divided into two sub-periods - Period A (1990–1996) and Period B (1997–2004) respectively. This period marks an evolving attitude of the country towards environment, although in a gradual

---

[7] Sankar (1998) argues that the government may ensure participation of community based organisations in management of local commons as well as in the enforcement of environmental laws and rules.

manner.[8] The paper is organised as follows. A brief literature survey on environmental sustainability, human development and economic growth is followed by the discussion on the methodology adopted in this paper, the results and the policy observations respectively.

II. LITERATURE REVIEW
Environmental Sustainability

Determining the appropriate methodology for arriving at meaningful environmental indices is a debated research question (Ebert and Welsch, 2004; Zhou et el., 2006). It has generally been observed that using a composite environmental index summarises the environment condition of a region or country or state,[9] and is more meaningful than individual indicators (Rogers et al., 1997; Adriaanse et al., 1995; Adriaanse, 1993, Esty et al., 2005; Jones et el., 2002; Mukherjee and Kathuria, 2006). However the methodology and selection of variables for construction of environmental index vary considerably across these studies.

In Table 1, we look at the relationships between Environmental Performance Index (EPI), HDI and Per Capita GDP for a few select economies. The Environmental Performance Index (EPI) data is taken from the recent study by Esty et al. (2006), which constructs the index for 133 countries. The study is based on a compilation of 32 indicators classified into 6 environmental groups. HDI Scores and Ranks are taken from latest Human Development Report 2007 (UNDP, 2007), which ranks 177 countries on the basis of their

---

[8] India introduced *Environment (Protection) Act* and *Hazardous Waste (Management and Handling) Rules* in 1986 and 1989 respectively and became a member of *Basel Convention* in 1992. However, the national rules on hazardous waste were brought into conformity with Basel norms only in 2000 (Sharma, 2005; Divan and Rosencranz, 2002).

[9] It is argued that environmental degradation or pollution level cannot by merely measured by actual emissions of certain hazardous materials; but other factors influencing its spread and intensity also need to be considered (Mukherjee and Kathuria, 2006).

HDI Score. It is observed from the table that the countries having higher HDI scores (e.g., New Zealand) are generally characterised by higher values of EPI as well. However, exceptions also exist – for instance Malaysia, despite having a medium HDI score, is characterised by a high EPI. The Per Capita GDP (in PPP USD) for the two countries is found to be higher in comparison with the remaining countries. On the other hand, the South Asian countries with medium HDI performance (e.g., India, Pakistan) have also performed moderately on the EPI front. The countries further down the HDI list (e.g., Niger) are ranked lower in the EPI list as well. It has been observed that the relationships between (1) HDI score and EPI score and (2) Per Capita GDP and EPI Score of the South East and South Asian countries show a non-linear pattern (Mukherjee and Chakraborty, 2007).

Relationships between Environmental Quality and Economic Growth

The literature on the relationship between Per Capita Income (PCI) or the PCNSDP in case of States within a country, and pollution or environmental degradation generally attempts to verify the existence of an inverted U-shaped curve in the PCI vs. pollution plane ('Environmental Kuznets Curve'). The relationship implies that with the rise in PCI, environmental degradation continues up to a certain level of PCI, but improves afterwards as with prosperity, countries shift to cleaner production technologies or spend more resources on pollution abatement (Esty and Porter, 2001-02; Andreoni and Levinson, 2001). Recent empirical studies show that while some local pollutants like Sulphur dioxide (SO_2), Suspended Particulate Matter (SPM), Carbon monoxide (CO) etc. support EKC hypothesis; other pollutants exhibit either monotonicity or N-shaped curve (Dinda, 2004; Stern, 1998). Studies based on both ambient concentration of pollutants (Baldwin, 1995; Grossman and Krueger, 1995; Selden and Song, 1994; Panayatou, 1993; Shafik and Bandyopadhyay, 1992; Pezzey,

1989) or the actual emissions of pollutants (Bruvoll and Medin, 2003; de Bruyn et el., 1998; Carson et el., 1997) also support the EKC hypothesis.

TABLE 1
ENVIRONMENTAL PERFORMANCE INDEX, HUMAN DEVELOPMENT INDEX AND PER CAPITA GDP – A CROSS COUNTRY VIEW

Country	Environmental Performance Index Score: 2006		Human Development Index Score: 2005		Per Capita GDP (PPP USD): 2005
Bangladesh	43.5	(125)	0.547	(140)	2,053
China	56.2	(94)	0.777	(81)	6,757
India	47.7	(118)	0.619	(128)	3,452
Indonesia	60.7	(79)	0.728	(107)	3,843
Malaysia	83.3	(9)	0.811	(63)	10,882
Myanmar	57.0	(88)	0.583	(132)	1,027
Nepal	60.2	(81)	0.534	(142)	1,550
Pakistan	41.1	(127)	0.551	(136)	2,370
Philippines	69.4	(55)	0.771	(90)	5,137
Sri Lanka	64.6	(67)	0.743	(99)	4,595
Thailand	66.8	(61)	0.781	(78)	8,677
Niger	25.7	(133)	0.374	(174)	781
New Zealand	88.0	(1)	0.943	(19)	24,996

Source: Esty et al. (2006), UNDP (2007).

It is argued that working with a composite indicator of pollutants, as a proxy of actual EQ scenario, scores over selection of a single pollutant in determination of the EKC relationship (Mukherjee and Kathuria, 2006), although only a handful of studies have adopted that approach so far. Jha and Bhanu Murthy (2001) created an Environmental Degradation Index (EDI) for 174 countries and compared that with the

Human Development Index (HDI) instead of the PCI. The study found an inverse link between EDI and HDI, which supported the existence of an inverted N-shaped global EKC rather than an inverted U-shaped one.

In Indian context, Mukherjee and Kathuria (2006) explored the EKC relationship for 14 major Indian States over 1990-2001 by considering 63 environmental variables, arranged under eight broad environmental groups. The ranking of the States on a constructed Environmental Quality Index (EQI) were determined by using the factor analysis method. The results indicate that the relationship between EQ and PCNSDP is slanting S-shaped, indicating that the economic growth has occurred in Indian States mostly at the cost of EQ. It was observed that except Bihar, all the States are on the upward sloping portion of the EKC. Kadekodi and Venkatachalam (2006) noted evidence of a strong linkage between various natural resources and environment with income and the status of livelihood and concluded that the causal relationship between poverty and environment works in both directions. The research has also highlighted the importance of poverty alleviation while minimising the human health and environmental costs of economic growth (Nadkarni, 2000; Nagdeve, 2007) and the possibility of entering into a long-run vicious circle of environmental degradation, greater inequality and lower growth (Dutt and Rao, 1996) in that process. However, Bhattacharya and Innes (2006) argued that the poverty-environment nexus (vicious-cycle) hypothesis does not hold in rural India.

Relationship between Environment and Human Well-being

It is observed from the literature on environmental impacts of structural adjustment program that if the victims of depletion and degradation of natural environment are not identified and compensated by the beneficiaries, the vulnerable sections face additional economic hardship, which may fuel inequality further (Dasgupta, 2001). It has been argued by

Boyce (2003) that, "social and economic inequalities can influence both the distribution of the costs and benefits from environmental degradation and the extent of environmental protection. When those benefit from environmentally degrading economic activities are powerful relative to those who bear the costs, environmental protection is generally weaker than when the reverse is true." The analysis suggests that socio-economic inequality leads to environmental inequality, which may consequently affect the overall extent of environmental quality. Therefore any attempt to reduce inequalities would eventually result in environmental protection (Sagar, undated).

It is increasingly believed that environmental problems should no longer be viewed as the side effects of development process. On the contrary, a new approach focusing on promotion of their integration need to be adopted (van Ginkel et al., 2001). The objective has been met through Target 9 of the United Nations' Millennium Development Goals (MDGs),[10] which demands that environmental conservation and conservation of natural resources from quantitative depletion and qualitative degradation, should be an integral part of any economic and development policy.

Melnick et al. (2005) highlight the critical importance of achieving environmental sustainability to meet the MDGs with respect to poverty, illiteracy, hunger, gender inequality, unsafe drinking water and environmental degradation. They argue that achieving environmental sustainability requires carefully balancing human development activities while maintaining a stable environment that predictably and regularly provides resources and protects people from natural calamities.

---

[10] "Integrate the principles of sustainable development into country policies and programs and reverse the losses of environmental resources" - Target 9 of the UN's MDGs.

Relationship between Economic Growth and Human Development

The literature suggests a two-way relationship between EG and HD, implying that nations may enter either into a virtuous cycle of high growth and large HD gains, or a vicious cycle of low growth and low HD improvement (Ranis, 2004). It is also observed that higher initial level of HD corresponds to positive effects on institutional quality and indirectly on EG (Costantini and Salvatore, 2006). The study by Agarwal and Samanta (2006) involving 31 developing countries, observed that EG is not correlated with social progress, structural adjustment or governance. Nevertheless, all of them might have an impact on the EQ within a country like India, where a two-way causality between EG and HD is observed, indicating possibilities of vicious cycles (Ghosh, 2006), which might have environmental repercussions.

The UNDP annually publishes an extensive analysis of global HD situation in the Human Development Report (HDR) along with country rankings. However, it is often argued that the UNDP's HD indicators are perhaps too narrow in nature, and inclusion of certain important socio-economic variables would enrich the analysis further. The Latent Variable Approach adopted by Nagar and Basu (2001) involving 174 countries confirms that with inclusion of additional socio-economic variables, the alternate HD rankings differ significantly from the official UNDP ranking.

While India's HD ranking remained in the low HD category throughout nineties, in 2002 it graduated to medium HD category with the HDI score of 0.577, as compared to the corresponding figure of 0.439 in 1990. India's global HDI rank has improved from 132 in 1999 to 127 in 2003.[11] Recently in association with UNDP, the Government of India has started analysing the State-wise HD status. The National Human

---

[11] In relative sense, India's position actually does not look that bad as UNDP considered 130 and 177 countries in 1990 and 2003 respectively.

Development Report (NHDR) 2001 (Government of India, 2002), brought out by the Planning Commission, is worth mentioning in this regard. While the report ranked Kerala, Punjab and Tamil Nadu as the toppers; Bihar, Madhya Pradesh and Uttar Pradesh were at the other extreme in HD scale. The alternate index developed by Guha and Chakraborty (2003), in line with Nagar and Basu (2001), however showed that inclusion of other socio-economic variables changes the State rankings to some extent. For instance, Tamil Nadu, ranked third by NHDR 2001, slides down the ladder to the eighth place according to the alternate index.

III. METHODOLOGY AND DATA

Environmental Quality Index (EQI)

The EQI for the States is postulated to be linearly dependent on a set of observable indicators and has been determined by adopting the HDI method, by putting the selected variables under eight broad environmental categories mentioned in Appendix 1. The idea is that all the 63 environmental variables, when combined, give a composite EQI of the States, unobservable otherwise. We assume X_{ij} to be the value of the ith indicator for j^{th} State of India with respect to X (or environmental quality), where X consists of a large number of indicators varying from 6 to 12 (see Appendix 2).

As defined earlier, X's are Air Pollution (AIRPOL), Indoor Air Pollution Potential (INDOOR), Green House Gases Emissions (GHGS), Pollution from Energy Generation and Consumption (ENERGY), Depletion and Degradation of Forest Resources (FOREST), Depletion and Degradation of Water Resources (WATER), Nonpoint Source Pollution Potential (NPSP) and Depletion and Degradation of Land Resources (LAND) respectively.

In line with the HDI method, we transform the indicators into their standardised form, by which the adjusted values of X_{ij} (i.e., EX_{ij}'s) to be used for the analysis become:

$$EX_{ij} = (X_{ij} - X_i^*)/(X_i^{**} - X_i^*) \text{ or}$$

$$EX_{ij} = (X_i^{**} - X_{ij})/(X_i^{**} - X_i^*)$$

where, X_i^* and X_i^{**} are the minimum and maximum values for the ith indicator of environmental quality X respectively.[12] Now, EQIX$_j$, i.e., the environmental quality index score for the jth State with respect to each individual environmental quality X (which constitutes of n number of indicators, n varies from 6 to 12), is arrived at by summing the EX$_{ij}$s over i by using the following formula:

$$EQIX_j = \frac{1}{n}\sum_{i=1}^{n} EX_{ij}$$

In a similar manner, EQI$_j$, i.e., the overall environmental quality index score for the jth State, is arrived at by summing the EX$_{ij}$s for all X over i by using the following formula:

$$EQI_j = \frac{1}{N}\sum_{i=1}^{N=63} EX_{ij} \forall X$$

The obtained EQIs measure the environmental well-being of the States, i.e., the States with higher score are characterised by cleaner environment. The EQI$_j$s (where j=1 to 14), thus arrived, is therefore used to obtain the rank of the jth State, where the States having higher EQI$_j$ are assigned higher rank.

Human Development Index (HDI)
Following the principle of the NHDR 2001 (Government of India, 2002) methodology, for calculation of the Human Development Index (HDI), we consider three

---

[12] The variables for which these two alternate formulas are used are specified at the end of Appendix 3.

variables, namely - inflation and inequality adjusted per capita consumption expenditure (X_1); and composite indicator of educational attainment (X_2) and composite indicator on health attainment (X_3). With this formulation, following the HDI method, the HDI score for the jth State is given by:

$$HDI_j = \frac{1}{3}\sum_{i=1}^{3} X_i$$

where, X_i represents the normalised values of the three indicators selected for construction of the HDI score, obtained by using the following formula:

$$X_i = (X_{ij} - X_i^*)/(X_i^{**} - X_i^*)$$

where X_{ij} refers to attainment of the ith indicator by the jth State and X_i^{**} and X_i^* are the scaling maximum and minimum values of the indicators respectively (i = 1 to 3).

Although UNDP considers real per capita GDP in PPP USD for generating the HDI, the NHDR 2001 (Government of India, 2002) has preferred total inflation and inequality adjusted per capita consumption expenditure of a State (i.e., Rural and Urban Combined) over that for the analysis. Here the monthly per capita consumption expenditure data obtained from NSSO for two periods (1993-94 and 1999-2000), adjusted for inequality using estimated *Gini* ratios, and further adjusted for inflation to bring them to 1983 prices by using deflators derived from State specific poverty line (Government of India, 2002). We follow the NHDR methodology in our analysis and consider total inflation and inequality adjusted per capita consumption expenditure of a State as an explanatory variable.

The composite indicator on educational attainment (X_2) is arrived at by considering two variables, namely literacy rate for the age group of 7 years and above (e_1) and Adjusted Intensity of Formal Education (AIFE) (e_2). The idea is that literacy rate being an overall ratio alone may not indicate the actual scenario, and the drop-out rate, needs to be incorporated in the formula. We consider the data on literacy rate for two periods, namely - 1991 and 2001. The AIFE data is used for two periods – 1993 and 2002. The following weightage is assigned for the two variables so as to determine the composite indicator:

$$X_2 = [(e_1 \times 0.35) + (e_2 \times 0.65)]$$

The Intensity of Formal Education (IFE) is estimated as weighted average of the enrolled students from Class I to Class XII (where weights being 1 for Class I, 2 for Class II and so on) to the total enrolment in Class I to Class XII. This is adjusted by proportion of total population in the age group 6-18 (Government of India, 2002). According to the formula suppose E_i be the number of children (rural and urban combined) enrolled in i^{th} standard in 2002, i= 1 for Class I to 12 for Class XII. Then Weighted Average of the Enrolment (WAE) from Class I to Class XII becomes:

$$WAE = \frac{\sum_{i=1}^{12} i \times E_i}{\sum_{i=1}^{12} i}$$

Now, let TE_i be the total enrolment of Children from Class I to Class XII in 2002. Then by definition, we have:

$$TE = \sum_{i=1}^{12} E_i$$

Hence, the IFE for children (rural and urban combined) in 2002 becomes:

$$IFE = \frac{WAE}{TE} \times 100$$

From the IFE, we can determine the Adjusted Intensity of Formal Education (AIFE) for children (rural and urban combined) in 2002 by using the following formula:

$$AIFE = IFE \times \frac{TE}{P_C}$$

Where P_C represents the Population of Children (rural and urban combined) in the age group 6 to 18 years in 2001.

The Composite indicator on health attainment (X_3) is arrived at by considering two variables, namely Life Expectancy (LE) at age one (h_1) and the reciprocal of Infant Mortality Rate (IMR) as the second variable (h_2). For h_1, which measures the life expectancy at age 1 (Rural and Urban Combined), the two data points considered for the two periods are 1990-94 and 1998-2002 respectively. On the other hand, the IMR (Per Thousand) data is considered for two periods, namely - 1992 and 2000. The following weightage is assigned for the two variables so as to determine the composite indicator used for calculation of the HDI:

$$X_3 = [(h_1 \times 0.65) + (h_2 \times 0.35)]$$

Economic Growth (EG)

Economic growth in the current analysis is measured by the PCNSDP of the States at constant (1993-94) prices. PCNSDP for the Period A is the average PCNSDP for the period 1993-94 to 1995-96 and for Period B, it is the average PCNSDP over 1997-98 to 1999-2000. The average is taken to smoothen out uneven fluctuations. To understand the size of the economy and growth pattern of each of the 14 States, we have classified the States into three categories with respect to their Gross State Domestic Product (GSDP) at constant 1993-94 prices, e.g., high income States (having GSDP: greater than 3rd Quartile), medium income States (GSDP: 1st to 3rd Quartile) and low income States (GSDP: less than 1st Quartile), for early

1990s (1993-96), late 1990s (1997-2000) and early years of new millennium (2001-2005).

Mukherjee and Chakraborty (2007) noted that during early 1990s (1993-96), on an average middle income states (e.g., Gujarat, Rajasthan and Karnataka) were growing faster than others. However, during late 1990s (1997-2000), except for low income States, growth rate slowed down, indicating a stagnation. On the other hand, during early 2000s (2000-2004), the difference in economic growth rate across the States having different level of income has gone down, and barring few exceptions (Rajasthan and West Bengal) both for low and medium income States the growth rate generally slowed down as compared to the late 1990s level.

Data

In order to obtain State level secondary information on environment and natural resources from published government reports and other databases for both the time periods selected in our analysis, i.e., Period A (1990-96) and Period B (1997-2004), the sample is restricted only to 14 major Indian States, namely - Andhra Pradesh (AP), Bihar (BH), Gujarat (GJ), Haryana (HR), Karnataka (KR), Kerala (KL), Madhya Pradesh (MP), Maharashtra (MH), Orissa (OR), Punjab (PB), Rajasthan (RJ), Tamil Nadu (TN), Uttar Pradesh (UP) and West Bengal (WB). Now the data available for various environmental indicators in India are not always necessarily compatible with the time period selected by us, given the varying date and frequency of their publication. To resolve this issue, we have chosen only those indicators with at least two observations, where one of these observations is located within the boundary of the two sample periods. The selected indicators have then been normalised using appropriate measures of size / scale of the States — geographical area, population and GSDP at current prices.

Here we need to distinguish between two key concepts, namely - endowment effect and efficiency in natural resource management effect. The depletion and degradation of natural resources and occurrence of environmental pollution is chiefly concerned with environmental management. On the other hand, the initial endowments of natural resources (forests, land and water) are determined by geographical, climatic and ecological factors. Quite understandably, the former is comparatively more influenced by human activities. By calculating the change in the natural resource position with respect to a base year we can isolate the two effects.[13] The current study focuses on the environmental management efficiency effect as well as the size effect of the States.

The data sources for our analysis on EQ and descriptions of the actual data series used to construct each group are listed in Appendix 1 and 2 respectively. A total of 63 variables have been selected for the analysis, placed under eight broad categories, which are summarised in Appendix 1.

For the analysis on education, we use the data available from the "*7th All India Educational Survey (AIES): All India School Education Survey (AISES)*", published by NCERT (2002). On the health front, IMR data is taken from Sample Registration System (SRS) Bulletins; Registrar General of India, New Delhi and LE data is taken from Indiastat database website (www.indiastat.com). The data on EG of the States is obtained from EPW Research Foundation Database Software and RBI's Database on Indian Economy.

---

[13] For instance, a higher index for Orissa as compared to Punjab by merely ranking the forest resources of the two States (by taking the percentage of geographical area under forests land) comes from the fact that Punjab possess very little of the selected variable to begin with. Therefore the analysis does not imply that forest conservation practices of the former are in any way better than the same of the latter. Ranking the change in their forest area (as a percentage of geographical area) during any two periods would be the ideal exercise for comparing their forest conservation practices.

IV. THE RESULTS
EQI

In Table 2, we present the EQ scores and rankings of the States for Period A, both for individual categories as well as for the composite index. It is observed that Kerala, Karnataka and Maharashtra were the toppers during this period, while Uttar Pradesh, Punjab and Haryana had been the laggards. Interestingly the topper Kerala, despite a good performance in AIRPOL, GHGS, ENERGY, WATER and NPSP, fared among the laggards in case of INDOOR, LAND and FOREST. Karnataka had good performance in case of AIRPOL and GHGS, while maintaining moderate performance in other categories. The third ranking of Maharashtra, an industrialised state, is justified by the fact that the State performed appreciably in several categories like INDOOR, GHGS, LAND and NPSP, however the performance with respect to ENERGY, WATER, FOREST and AIRPOL was not that satisfactory. Looking at the other extreme, we can see that the overall rankings of laggards like Haryana and Uttar Pradesh were influenced by their performance in sub-categories like LAND, NPSP etc. It is observed that while some major States like Madhya Pradesh (tenth) and West Bengal (ninth) placed in the lower segment, others like Gujarat (sixth) and Andhra Pradesh (seventh) had performed moderately well. Interestingly, a relatively poorer State, Orissa, obtained the fourth rank, owing to comparatively better performance in case of AIRPOL, ENERGY and WATER.

Table 3 provides the EQ scores and ranking of the States for Period B. As in the earlier case, we see that Kerala, Karnataka and Maharashtra retained their positions at the top (although the latter two interchange their positions), while Haryana, Bihar and Punjab now turned out to be the laggards. It is observed that the toppers improved their position in certain sub-categories (Kerala in AIRPOL, INDOOR, GHGS, FOREST; Karnataka in ENERGY, FOREST etc.). However, their performance deteriorated in certain key areas as well. For instance, the lower ranking of Karnataka in AIRPOL in Period B can be explained by rapid urbanisation, industrialisation and vehicular pollution. Its relative performance on WATER also raises concern. Among the states at the middle, Andhra Pradesh's performance in WATER is not satisfactory, and degradation in water bodies within its territory has already been highlighted (Reddy and Char, 2004). On the other hand the laggards continued to perform poorly in several sub-categories (e.g., Punjab – AIRPOL, GHGS, ENERGY, LAND, WATER and NPSP; Bihar - AIRPOL, INDOOR, GHGS, LAND, FOREST and NPSP; Haryana – ENERGY, LAND, WATER and NPSP). Energy management and forest conservation should be the first two priority areas for environmental management in Maharashtra. For Karnataka, conservation of land and water should be priority areas for environmental management.

We can compare the relative performance of the States on EQ scale during the two time periods looking at their ranks. It is observed that although the overall position of the better performing States remained unchanged, there had been some interesting movements of their ranking within the sub-categories. For instance, Maharashtra's rank declined in LAND and FOREST,[14] while it improved its performance in WATER. Karnataka had been subjected to greater variations - while its ranking improved in ENERGY and FOREST, but declined for AIRPOL, INDOOR and WATER. Kerala on the other hand improved its relative performance in a number of sub-categories (notably FOREST).[15] Nonetheless, its score got affected by the decline in its ranking in categories like

---

[14] Rithe and Fernandes (2002) argued that Maharashtra has achieved the current level of industrialisation at the cost of the loss of much of its forests. However, the findings of Kadekodi and Venkatachalam (2005) do not support this.

[15] Apart from the Government regulations, exporter firms increasingly adopted environment-friendly processes to comply with strict norms in export markets (e.g., marine industries in Kochi), which had a significant positive influence on the environment of the State.

TABLE 2
ENVIRONMENTAL QUALITY SCORES AND RANKS OF THE STATES: 1990-1996

	AIRPOL (1)	INDOOR (2)	GHGS (3)	ENERGY (4)	LAND (5)	WATER (6)	FOREST (7)	NPSP (8)	EQI SCORE (9)
Andhra Pradesh	0.876 (4)	0.320 (11)	0.685 (5)	0.524 (8)	0.592 (5)	0.535 (6)	0.506 (13)	0.489 (8)	0.544 (7)
Bihar	0.647 (8)	0.129 (14)	0.467 (11)	0.555 (7)	0.502 (10)	0.604 (5)	0.515 (12)	0.467 (11)	0.480 (11)
Gujarat	0.432 (12)	0.643 (3)	0.617 (7)	0.282 (13)	0.616 (4)	0.482 (9)	0.594 (6)	0.630 (2)	0.545 (6)
Haryana	0.783 (6)	0.574 (4)	0.494 (9)	0.450 (12)	0.183 (13)	0.381 (13)	0.671 (2)	0.333 (13)	0.475 (12)
Karnataka	0.912 (1)	0.435 (5)	0.901 (1)	0.673 (5)	0.535 (7)	0.516 (7)	0.573 (9)	0.541 (6)	0.607 (2)
Kerala	0.874 (5)	0.327 (10)	0.870 (3)	0.709 (3)	0.520 (8)	0.696 (3)	0.517 (11)	0.559 (5)	0.617 (1)
Madhya Pradesh	0.483 (11)	0.367 (8)	0.355 (13)	0.468 (10)	0.719 (1)	0.695 (4)	0.158 (14)	0.597 (4)	0.493 (10)
Maharashtra	0.653 (7)	0.715 (2)	0.697 (4)	0.473 (9)	0.652 (2)	0.514 (8)	0.581 (8)	0.599 (3)	0.605 (3)
Orissa	0.909 (2)	0.228 (12)	0.350 (14)	0.771 (1)	0.543 (6)	0.760 (1)	0.584 (7)	0.516 (7)	0.578 (4)
Punjab	0.644 (9)	0.803 (1)	0.427 (12)	0.274 (14)	0.181 (14)	0.244 (14)	0.840 (1)	0.267 (14)	0.456 (13)
Rajasthan	0.631 (10)	0.397 (7)	0.881 (2)	0.622 (6)	0.637 (3)	0.465 (10)	0.520 (10)	0.642 (1)	0.577 (5)
Tamil Nadu	0.896 (3)	0.412 (6)	0.656 (6)	0.458 (11)	0.513 (9)	0.381 (12)	0.612 (4)	0.478 (10)	0.525 (8)
Uttar Pradesh	0.152 (14)	0.222 (13)	0.600 (8)	0.682 (4)	0.363 (12)	0.447 (11)	0.620 (3)	0.478 (9)	0.443 (14)
West Bengal	0.248 (13)	0.357 (9)	0.473 (10)	0.758 (2)	0.369 (11)	0.699 (2)	0.611 (5)	0.442 (12)	0.508 (9)

Note: Figure in the parenthesis shows the rank for the State for corresponding environmental group
Source: Estimated by the authors.

TABLE 3
ENVIRONMENTAL QUALITY SCORES AND RANKS OF THE STATES: 1997-2004

STATES	AIRPOL (1)	INDOOR (2)	GHGS (3)	ENERGY (4)	LAND (5)	WATER (6)	FOREST (7)	NPSP (8)	EQI SCORE (9)
Andhra Pradesh	0.802 (3)	0.498 (7)	0.553 (5)	0.585 (5)	0.617 (3)	0.479 (9)	0.781 (9)	0.474 (9)	0.580 (6)
Bihar	0.433 (12)	0.141 (14)	0.428 (10)	0.574 (7)	0.436 (10)	0.675 (2)	0.480 (13)	0.422 (12)	0.455 (13)
Gujarat	0.310 (13)	0.718 (3)	0.547 (6)	0.231 (13)	0.653 (1)	0.539 (8)	0.769 (10)	0.599 (4)	0.564 (7)
Haryana	0.715 (5)	0.714 (4)	0.542 (7)	0.362 (10)	0.088 (14)	0.332 (13)	0.790 (7)	0.278 (14)	0.472 (12)
Karnataka	0.684 (6)	0.610 (6)	0.885 (1)	0.679 (3)	0.568 (7)	0.465 (11)	0.807 (5)	0.563 (6)	0.636 (3)
Kerala	0.791 (4)	0.467 (8)	0.882 (2)	0.644 (4)	0.534 (9)	0.541 (7)	0.942 (1)	0.598 (5)	0.656 (1)
Madhya Pradesh	0.510 (10)	0.453 (10)	0.302 (14)	0.349 (12)	0.647 (2)	0.689 (1)	0.230 (14)	0.627 (1)	0.497 (10)
Maharashtra	0.676 (7)	0.771 (2)	0.682 (4)	0.428 (9)	0.578 (6)	0.606 (5)	0.731 (11)	0.615 (2)	0.641 (2)
Orissa	0.823 (2)	0.189 (13)	0.381 (11)	0.745 (2)	0.612 (4)	0.673 (3)	0.864 (2)	0.527 (7)	0.593 (5)
Punjab	0.600 (9)	0.812 (1)	0.349 (13)	0.211 (14)	0.118 (13)	0.273 (14)	0.789 (8)	0.279 (13)	0.434 (14)
Rajasthan	0.670 (8)	0.459 (9)	0.807 (3)	0.564 (8)	0.603 (5)	0.470 (10)	0.804 (6)	0.614 (3)	0.606 (4)
Tamil Nadu	0.949 (1)	0.624 (5)	0.376 (12)	0.361 (11)	0.567 (8)	0.356 (12)	0.842 (3)	0.483 (8)	0.555 (8)
Uttar Pradesh	0.471 (11)	0.305 (12)	0.518 (8)	0.584 (6)	0.366 (11)	0.566 (6)	0.507 (12)	0.458 (10)	0.473 (11)
West Bengal	0.212 (14)	0.417 (11)	0.476 (9)	0.794 (1)	0.347 (12)	0.610 (4)	0.825 (4)	0.422 (11)	0.522 (9)

Note: Figure in the parenthesis shows the rank for the State for corresponding environmental group
Source: **Estimated by the authors.**

WATER.[16] Looking across categories, it is observed that Punjab and Uttar Pradesh experienced a sharp decline in their ranking in case of FOREST, indicating degradation on that front.

HDI

Table 4 provides the HDI scores and rankings of the States in the three sub-categories and the composite index for two periods, Period A and Period B. It is observed that while for the first period, Kerala, Punjab and Maharashtra were holding the top three positions; in the second period, Haryana had replaced Maharashtra at the top three. Looking at the sub-categories, it is observed that Kerala continued to perform well in all categories. Punjab performed comfortably in terms of consumption and health, but was in the mid-level on educational attainments. Looking at the other end of the distribution, we observe that Bihar, UP and MP were consistently at the bottom for most of the categories, which in turn leads to their poor overall HDI ranking.

Comparison of the relative performance of the States on HDI during the two time periods covered in our analysis shows interesting results. We observe that there had not been major changes in the overall HDI Score of the States, and in all cases their ranks changed by one unit only. Some changes in the relative positions of the States in terms of consumption can be noted, reflecting their relative growth pattern, but in case of education and health the relative positions of fifty percent of the States remained unchanged. We observe that the aggregate picture do not always show the dynamics of different components of HDI, e.g., for MP aggregate HDI Score had gone up from 0.072 to 0.132, however its consumption score had gone down from 0.052 to 0.000. A declining trend in the

---

[16] Nair (2006) noted that depletion of the groundwater table due to indiscriminate sand mining, shrinkage in natural forest cover and reclamation of wetland and paddy fields are major environmental challenges that Kerala is facing today.

HDI is noticed for AP as well. For MP, since health status remained unchanged it is only the improvement in education, which had driven its HDI score up. Movement in consumption expenditure is interesting; it had gone down both for poor States like Orissa (insignificant poverty reduction over NSSO 50th (1993-94) and 55th (1999-2000) round) and moderate performers like West Bengal (9 percent poverty reduction over NSSO 50th and 55th round). One reason may perhaps be that the decline in income inequality (*Gini* ratio) in these two States over 1993-94 to 1999-00 (Government of India, 2002) had been marginal.

EQI and PCNSDP

Figure 1 plots the EQI Scores and PCNSDP of the States during both Periods (postscript 1 and 2 denote periods A and B respectively), which suggests a convex relationship between the two. While the North-East corner of the Figure characterise States with both high EQI and PCNSDP, States placed in South-West corner represents those with worst performance on both counts. The States positioned in the North-West corner of the figure on the other hand indicates the States performing appreciably in terms of EQI, but not on PCNSDP. It is observed that Maharashtra retains its top position on both counts during the two periods. Bihar during Period B get grouped with UP at the South-West corner. Despite improvement in EQI Score, Orissa however remains at the bottom in terms of PCNSDP (i.e., below the first quartile line). Punjab and Haryana stay in the South-East corner of the Figure, implying their growth may have come at the cost of their environmental degradation. Karnataka, Kerala, Andhra Pradesh and Rajasthan improved their respective positions in both the fronts during Period B and are toppers among the medium income States. West Bengal, Tamil Nadu and Gujarat, the laggards among medium income States in terms of EQ, however improved their respective positions in both the fronts during Period B.

Environment, Human Development and Economic Growth... 255

TABLE 4
HDI SCORES AND RANKS OF THE STATES OVER THE SAMPLE PERIOD

States	Consumption Period A (1)	Consumption Period B (2)	Health Period A (3)	Health Period B (4)	Education Period A (5)	Education Period B (6)	HDI SCORE Period A (7)	HDI SCORE Period B (8)
Andhra Pradesh	0.338 (8)	0.196 (10)	0.300 (8)	0.410 (7)	0.136 (11)	0.344 (11)	0.258 (9)	0.317 (9)
Bihar	0.000 (14)	0.025 (13)	0.125 (11)	0.143 (11)	0.000 (14)	0.000 (14)	0.042 (14)	0.056 (14)
Gujarat	0.575 (5)	0.636 (4)	0.275 (9)	0.374 (9)	0.484 (4)	0.531 (4)	0.445 (6)	0.514 (6)
Haryana	0.610 (3)	0.792 (3)	0.499 (4)	0.614 (3)	0.366 (8)	0.497 (6)	0.492 (4)	0.635 (3)
Karnataka	0.295 (9)	0.402 (8)	0.466 (5)	0.481 (5)	0.371 (7)	0.478 (8)	0.377 (8)	0.454 (7)
Kerala	0.831 (2)	1.000 (1)	1.000 (1)	1.000 (1)	1.000 (1)	1.000 (1)	0.944 (1)	1.000 (1)
Madhya Pradesh	0.052 (12)	0.000 (14)	0.000 (14)	0.000 (14)	0.165 (10)	0.396 (9)	0.072 (12)	0.132 (13)
Maharashtra	0.459 (7)	0.490 (6)	0.549 (3)	0.570 (4)	0.541 (2)	0.710 (2)	0.516 (3)	0.590 (4)
Orissa	0.258 (11)	0.069 (11)	0.083 (12)	0.089 (13)	0.235 (9)	0.377 (10)	0.192 (10)	0.178 (11)
Punjab	1.000 (1)	0.907 (2)	0.765 (2)	0.837 (2)	0.414 (5)	0.505 (5)	0.726 (2)	0.750 (2)
Rajasthan	0.294 (10)	0.307 (9)	0.241 (10)	0.312 (10)	0.038 (13)	0.317 (12)	0.191 (11)	0.312 (10)
Tamil Nadu	0.489 (6)	0.583 (5)	0.366 (6)	0.454 (6)	0.517 (3)	0.658 (3)	0.457 (5)	0.565 (5)
Uttar Pradesh	0.039 (13)	0.054 (12)	0.050 (13)	0.134 (12)	0.073 (12)	0.238 (13)	0.054 (13)	0.142 (12)
West Bengal	0.583 (4)	0.441 (7)	0.358 (7)	0.383 (8)	0.378 (6)	0.486 (7)	0.440 (7)	0.437 (8)

Note: Figure in the parenthesis shows the rank for the State for corresponding category.
Source: Estimated by the authors

EQI and HDI

Figure 2 plots the EQI and HDI Scores of the States for the Periods (postscript 1 and 2 denote periods A and B respectively). While the North-East corner of the Figure characterise States with both high EQI and HDI scores, States placed in South-West corner represents those with worst performance on both counts. The States positioned in the North-West corner of the figure on the other hand indicates the States performing appreciably in terms of EQI, but not on HDI scale. It is observed that while Kerala retains its position in the North-East corner during both periods. Haryana, a top performer on HDI front, despite a marginal improvement in EQ still remains a poor performer. Punjab, another top performer in HDI, experienced a decline in EQI Score, primarily owing to overexploitation of natural resources (Bhullar and Sidhu, 2006). Looking at the South-West corner, it is seen that while the EQI Score had declined for Bihar, it had marginally increased for MP and UP. Orissa on the other hand maintains its position in the North-West corner during both periods. Though its performance marginally improved in EQ front, it performed poorly on HD scale (placed below the first quartile). AP and Rajasthan had improved their positions in both the fronts. As compared to Period A, the middle HD category States improved their positions in EQI during Period B. Broadly, the relationship between EQI Score and HDI Score is found to be slanting N-shaped owing to the divergence in performance of States like Punjab, Haryana and Kerala.

Testing the Existence of the Environmental Kuznets Curve (EKC)

For testing the EKC hypothesis, multivariate OLS regression models are estimated for individual environmental groups. Different variants of the models are estimated by assuming a non-linearity between PCNSDP and EQ. Apart from PCNSDP (in INR thousand at constant 1993-94 Prices);

FIGURE 1
PCNSDP Vs. EQI SCORE - PERIOD A AND PERIOD B

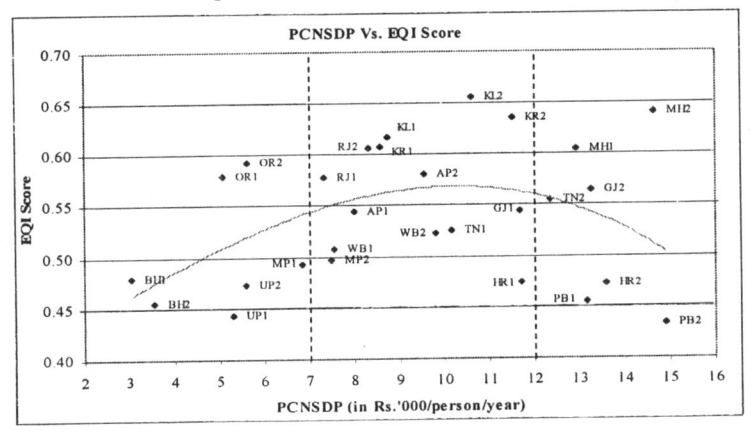

various other explanatory variables are introduced to capture the dynamic aspects of EQ. Tables 5 present the regression results which show a mixed picture: while non-linearity exist for a number of environmental groups like ENERGY, GHGS, LAND, NPS; linear relationship is observed for other groups like INDOOR, WATER and FOREST (See Appendix 3 for graphical representation of the obtained relationships between PCNSDP and various environmental groups). Similarly, with respect to controlling variables, it is observed that share of primary sector in GSDP (PRISHARE)[17] is negatively related to ENERGY, LAND, NPS and FOREST. This is because with the fall in share of primary sector in GSDP; pressure on land, water and forest resources goes down and EQ improves. With the rise in share of secondary sector in GSDP (SECSHARE),[18] ENRGY score falls and the same for WATER increases and as the share of tertiary sector improves, the scores of GHGs and

---

[17] Percentage share of Primary Sector in GSDP (at constant 1993-94 Prices), which includes Agriculture, Forestry and Logging and Fishing.
[18] Secondary sector includes Mining and Quarrying, Manufacturing and Construction.

WATER increase. The results imply that composition of income of a State has substantial impacts on its environmental quality. Increased share of workers in agriculture (AGRWRK) shows a mixed trend (positive for GHGS, INDOOR and NPS etc. and negative for LAND and AIRPOL). Population density (POPD) and level of urbanisation (URB) is generally showing a negative relationship with EQ.

FIGURE 2
HDI SCORE Vs. EQI SCORE – PERIOD A AND PERIOD B

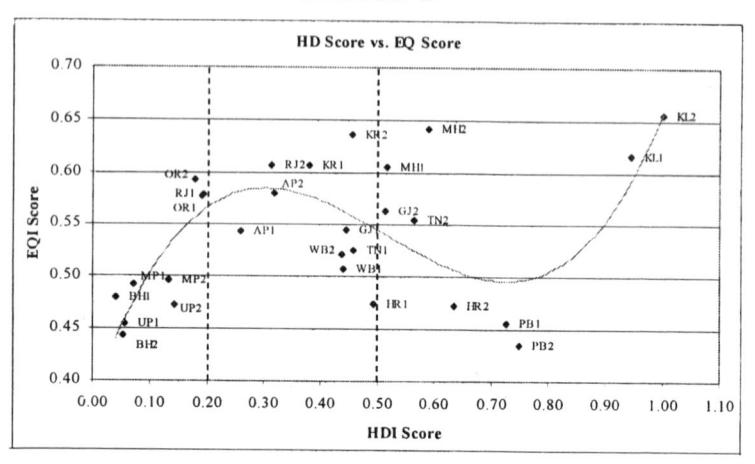

Relationship between HDI Score and Individual Environmental Groups

For analysing the relationship between the HDI score and composite indicator of individual environmental groups, we estimate different specifications of multivariate OLS regression models by assuming the presence of non-linearity. In addition, apart from HDI score, various other explanatory variables are introduced. From Tables 6, summarising the regression results for different variants of the models, it is observed that non-linearity exist for all the eight environmental groups (See Appendix 4 for graphical representation of the obtained relationships between HDI score and various environmental groups). The results show that investment in human development will have both direct and cumulative impacts on the natural resources conservation. In addition, with respect to controlling variables, it is observed that share of primary sector in GSDP (PRISHARE) is negatively related to most of the environmental groups, but positively related to INDOOR. The exception can be explained by the fact that the fall in PRISHARE leads to sophistication in domestic energy use, thereby improving INDOOR. With the rise in share of secondary sector in GSDP (SECSHARE), ENRGY and WATER score fall and the same for LAND and NPS increase. As the share of tertiary sector improves, the scores of GHGs, LAND and NPS improve. The findings indicate that composition of income of a State significantly influence its EQ. Like the EKC result, increased share of workers in agriculture (AGRWRK) shows a mixed trend (positive for FOREST, GHGS and INDOOR and negative for AIRPOL). Share of workers in non-agriculture (NAGRWRK) is negatively related to AIRPOL. Population density (POPD) generally shows a negative relationship with EQ (exception: ENERGY). The relationship between level of urbanisation (URB) and EQ however shows a mixed trend (positive for INDOOR, LAND and NPS and negative for ENERGY and FOREST).

V. POLICY CONCLUSIONS

A number of developing countries located in Asia, Africa and Latin America witnessed economic stagnation or crisis during eighties, and had to undergo structural adjustment in the subsequent period, either unilaterally or as part of policy package offered by external development agencies. Given the focus on growth in the short run, many developing countries created little room to accommodate environmental and natural resource concerns in their economic policy. A similar picture emerges if one analyses the cross-region scenario within a country as well. However, despite the attempts by various studies to evaluate different environmental parameters, determination of a composite overall environmental quality index is still lacking. The current study makes an attempt to bridge that gap by constructing an index of EQ for India by using 63 environmental indicators.

Based on inter- and intra-sectoral differences in economic activities, different States in India in the post-1991 period have different levels of stress on their natural resources. To understand the impacts of economic growth on environmental quality, the current analysis first constructs the environmental quality index for the 14 major Indian States and look for its possible relationship with economic growth. This paper also attempts to capture the relationship between environmental sustainability and human well-being – as measured by the Human Development Index. To capture the temporal aspects of environmental quality and to understand the dynamics of economic liberalisation process, the entire period of our study has been divided into two broad time periods – Period A (1990-1996) and Period B (1997-2004).

It is observed that different States possess different strengths and weaknesses in managing various aspects of EQ. For instance, while Maharashtra is in the second position in terms of EQI during period B, and fares satisfactorily in terms of INDOOR and NPSP; it's performance on ENERGY and FOREST is not that satisfactory. On the other hand, Punjab, the state at the bottom in terms of overall EQI and ENERGY and WATER, is actually topper for INDOOR. It also shows that there are scopes for the States to learn from each other about different aspects of environmental management. Therefore, adoption of a 'one-size-fits-all' National Environmental Policy at the country-level might have limited impact on the local environmental quality. In other words, individual States should adopt environmental management practices based on their local (at the most disaggregated level) environmental information. Furthermore, over time performance of an individual State varies across the environmental criteria, which shows that environmental management practices should take into account this dynamic nature of environment, and review their environmental status or achievement regularly.

The analysis on the relationship between economic growth and EQ does not reveal a very clear picture during the two time periods under consideration. For different States, the impacts of economic restructuring process, as adopted by them during 1990s, have affected the environmental quality differently. It is observed that while States like Maharashtra has performed well on both counts, growth in northern States like Punjab and Haryana has taken place mostly at the cost of EQ. On the other hand Orissa, despite being a low-income State, performed well during both period A and B in terms of EQ. The results indicate that laggards like Bihar and MP have also achieved their economic growth at the cost of their EQ. On the other hand a few States like Karnataka and Rajasthan have achieved economic growth and also maintained their environment well. The obtained results again indicate that individual States should adopt special environmental measures, based on their environmental impacts assessment of major economic activities, to achieve sustainable economic growth.

The formal testing for the existence of Environmental Kuznets Curve (EKC) through multivariate OLS regression models are estimated by assuming non-linearity in the relationship between PCNSDP and the composite score of the defined environmental sub-categories. It is observed that while for a few categories an inverted U-shaped relationship exists between PCNSDP and individual indicator of environmental quality (e.g., GHGS, LAND, ENERGY, NPS),[19] a linear

---

[19] However it goes against the popular EKC hypothesis, which shows inverted U-shaped relationship between PCI and environmental degradation (pollution) instead of environmental quality.

relationship exist for other categories (INDOOR, WATER, FOREST) and no relationship in case of AIRPOL. The absence of the EKC in the Indian framework can be explained by the mixed performance of the States across environmental groups – e.g., worse EQ for economically advanced Punjab and better EQ for economically lagging Orissa.

Estimation of multivariate OLS regression models between individual EQ Scores and HDI Score indicate presence of non-linear relationships (in most cases, slanting N-shaped and parabolic in case of FOREST). The results originate from the concentration of several States in low HDI-Low EQ category (Bihar, UP) and high EQ-mid HDI category (AP, Rajasthan) on one hand, and presence of the outliers like Orissa (high EQ-Low HDI) on one hand and Punjab and Haryana (high HDI-Low EQ) on the other. The result indicates the need to re-examine the methodology for calculating the HD achievements of the States. Perhaps, the HD ranking of States like Punjab and Haryana has been influenced too heavily by their high per capita consumption expenditure. Broad-basing the HD index by incorporating other social achievements might reveal interesting results.

A few policy issues need to be highlighted here. First, the increment in HD indicators and economic growth can effectively increase the demand for a better environment, and therefore provide a demand side solution to the problem of environmental sustainability. Second, in contrary to popular belief, industrial pollution is not the source of all the problems. In Punjab and Haryana, it seems that the thrust on agriculture is increasingly becoming a serious concern. Third, given the need to arrive at local State-level solutions, there seems to be enough scope to involve local communities with direct interest in certain initiatives (e.g., JFM). Fourth, it is difficult to comment on the choice of optimal level of income and its composition for a State, which would be in line with the objective of sustainable development. For instance, we observe a high level of EQ for a poor State like Orissa, which clearly is a result of unutilised resources. Fifth, as has been observed, improved governance can play a key role (e.g., Supreme Court intervention) in ensuring sustainable development, and there is increasing need for implementing that in environmentally vulnerable States. Finally, here we focus only on the economic growth of the Indian States during the two periods (1990-96 and 1997-2004) and look into its relationship with EQ. However, income inequality varies across Indian States and it has often been observed that inequality has increased in the post-reform period (Deaton and Dreze, 2002). An area of future research can be to analyse the relationship between income inequality of the States, their EQ and HD achievements.

Finally, a few limitations of the study are as follows. We have confined our analysis only to 14 major Indian States, the constraint being the availability of various secondary environmental information for both the time periods under consideration. Given the fact that a number of Indian States are currently in the process of preparing their environmental profile, one future area of research would be to extend the analysis to the remaining States. The analysis can be further extended by dividing the post-1997 period into more sub-groups, as permitted by availability of newer data points.

APPENDIX 1
DESCRIPTION OF THE ENVIRONMENTAL GROUPS AND DATA SOURCES

Groups	Description	Number of Variables	Data Sources*
AIRPOL	Air Pollution	6	8
INDOOR	Indoor Air Pollution Potential	9	2, 3, 13, 14
GHGS	Green House Gases Emissions	6	12, 15, 16
ENERGY	Pollution from Energy Generation and Consumption	6	2, 12, 14, 15
FOREST	Depletion and Degradation of Forest Resources	8	3, 4, 6, 10, 12, 15
WATER	Depletion and Degradation of Water Resources	12	1, 2, 3, 7, 9, 11
NPSP	Nonpoint Source Water Pollution Potential	10	1, 5, 7, 13
LAND	Pressure and Degradation of Land Resources	6	1, 3, 4, 7, 12
	Total	**63**	

Note: * - implies that details of the data sources are provided below

1	Centre for Monitoring Indian Economy, Mumbai: India's Agriculture Sector – Various Years
2	Centre for Monitoring Indian Economy, Mumbai: India's Energy Sector – Various Years
3	Centre for Science and Environment, New Delhi: State of India's Environment: The Citizens' Fifth Report (Part II: Statistical Database)
4	Central Statistical Organisation, Ministry of Statistics and

	Program Implementation, Government of India (GoI), New Delhi: Compendium of Environmental Statistics – 2000 and 2002
5	Department of Animal Husbandry, Dairying and Fisheries, Ministry of Agriculture, GoI, New Delhi: Livestock Census Data – 1992, 1997 and 2003
6	Forest Survey of India, Ministry of Environment and Forest, GoI, Dehradun: State of Forest Reports – 1997, 1999 and 2001
7	Ministry of Agriculture, GoI, New Delhi: Annual Report – Various Years
8	Central Pollution Control Board, Ministry of Environment and Forests, GoI, New Delhi: National Ambient Air Quality Monitoring Program Database – Various Years
9	Central Pollution Control Board, Ministry of Environment and Forests, GoI, New Delhi: National Rivers Water Quality Monitoring Program Database – Various Years
10	Ministry of Environment and Forests, GoI, New Delhi: The State of Environment – India: 1999 and 2001
11	Ministry of Water Resources, GoI, New Delhi: Annual Report – Various Years
12	Office of the Registrar General, Director of Census Operation, Ministry of Home Affairs, GoI, New Delhi: Census of India 2001 – CensusInfo India 2001 (Version 1.0) – Database Software
13	Office of the Registrar General, Director of Census Operation, Ministry of Home Affairs, GoI, New Delhi: Census of India 2001 – Tables on Houses, Amenities and Assets (Database Software)
14	The Energy and Resources Institute, New Delhi (TERI): TERI Energy Data Directory and Yearbook (TEDDY) – Various Years (Database Software)
15	Economic and Political Weekly Research Foundation (EPWRF), Mumbai: Domestic Product of State of India: 1960–1961 to 2000–2001, Database Software, 2003.
16	Garg, A. and P.R. Shukla (2002), *Emission Inventory of India*, Tata McGraw-Hill Publishing Company Limited, New Delhi.

APPENDIX 2
DESCRIPTIONS OF ENVIRONMENTAL GROUPS (VARIABLES) AND INDICATORS

AIR POLLUTION (12 indicators)
- Maximum Concentration of NO_2, SO_2 and SPM in Residential and Industrial Area ($\mu g/m^3$): 1990-1995 and 1996-2000 *

INDOOR AIR POLLUTION POTENTIAL (18 indicators)
- Monthly Per-Capita Expenditure (MPCE) on Fuel & Lighting (INR/month/head) Rural and Urban Areas: 1993-94 and 1999-2000 $
- Percentage of Rural Households using Bio-fuels (Firewoods and chips, Dung cake) as primary source of energy (Traditional & Commercial) for cooking (%): 1993-1994 and 1999-2000 *
- Percentage of Urban Households using Bio-fuels (Firewoods and chips) as primary source of energy (Traditional) for cooking (%): 1993-1994 and 1999-2000 *
- Percentage of Rural and Urban Households Do Not Have Access to Electricity: 1991 and 2001 *
- Achievement in Installation of Biogas Plants: Upto 1994-95 and Upto 2001-2002 $
- Kerosene as a Primary Source of Energy for Lighting for Rural and Urban Households (%): 1993-94 and 1999-2000 *

GREEN HOUSE GASES EMISSIONS (12 indicators)
- CO_2 Equivalent GHGs (CO_2, CH_4, N_2O) Emissions (Kg. /Person): 1990 and 1995 *
- CO_2 Equivalent GHGs (CO_2, CH_4, N_2O) Emissions (Tons/INR Lakh of GSDP at Constant 1980-81 Prices): 1990 and 1995 *
- CO_2 Equivalent GHGs (CO_2, CH_4, N_2O) Emissions (Tons/hectare of Reporting Area of Land Utilisation): 1990 and 1995 *
- Other GHGs (NOx, SO2) Emissions (Kg. /Person): 1990 and 1995 *
- Other GHGs (NOx, SO2) Emissions (Tons/INR Lakh of GSDP at Constant 1980-81 Prices): 1990 and 1995 *
- Other GHGs (NOx, SO2) Emissions (Tons/hectare of Reporting Area of Land Utilisation): 1990 and 1995 *

POLLUTION FROM ENERGY GENERATION AND CONSUMPTION (12 indicators)
- Annual Percentage Increase in Motor Vehicles Number (given

geographical area) during 1991-92 to 1995-96 and during 1995-96 to 2000-2001 *
- Average Per Capita Consumption of LPG, MG, Kerosene, HSD & LDO (in Kg. per person): 1993-94 to 1996-97 and 1997-98 to 2000-2001 *
- Average Petroleum Consumption (in tonnes) Per INR Lakh of GSDP (at constant 1993-94 Prices): 1993-94 to 1996-97 and 1997-98 to 2000-2001 *
- Average Thermal Electricity Generation as a Percentage of Total Electricity Generation (in percentage): 1990-91 to 1995-96 and 1996-97 to 1999-2000 *
- Average Electricity Consumption (in KwH) per INR Lakh of GSDP at Constant (1993-94) Prices: 1993-94 to 1995-96 and 1996-97 to 1999-2001 *
- Average Per Capita Consumption of Electricity (in KwH/Person): 1990-91 to 1995-96 and 1996-97 to 1999-2000 *

DEPLETION AND DEGRADATION OF FOREST RESOURCES (16 indicators)
- Change in Forest Cover (Dense and Open Forest) as Percentage of Geographical Area (in percentage points): 1995 to 1997 and 1999-2001 $
- Change in Per Capita Forest Cover (Dense Forest, Open Forest, Mangrove, Scrub) (in Hectare): 1995 to 1997 and 1999 to 2001 $
- Change in Recorded Forest Area as a Percentage of Total Geographical Area: 1997 to 1999 and 1999 to 2001 $
- Change in Common Property Forest Area@ as Percentage of Total Recorded Forest Area: 1997 to 1999 and 1999 to 2001 $
- Change in Common Property Forest Area@ as a Percentage of Geographical Area: 1997 to 1999 and 1999 to 2001 $
- Change in Per Capita Availability of Recorded Forest Area (Person/ha): 1997 to 1999 and 1999 to 2001$
- Change in Per Capita Availability of Common Property Forest Area (in Person/ha): 1997 to 1999 and 1999 to 2001$
- Change in Protected Area (National Park & Sanctuary) as a Percentage of Total Geographical Area: 1997 to 1999 and 1999 to 2001 $

Note: @ - Common Property Forest Area = Protected + Unclassed Forest Area

DEPLETION AND DEGRADATION OF WATER RESOURCES (24 indicators)
▪ Level of groundwater development (%): 1996 and 2004 *
▪ Percentage of Irrigated Area Irrigated by Surface Water Sources (Canals & Tanks): 1992-93 and 1998-99 $
▪ Inland Surface Water Resources (% of geographical area): 1995 and 2001 $
▪ Major & Medium Irrigation Potential Created (Developed) upto the end of the 8th Plan (1992-1997) as a Percentage of Ultimate Irrigation Potential of the State *
▪ Major & Medium Irrigation Potential Utilised as a Percentage of Irrigation Potential Created Upto March 1997 *
▪ Minor Irrigation Potential Created (Developed) upto the end of the 8th Plan (1992-1997) as a Percentage of Ultimate Irrigation Potential of the State *
▪ Minor Irrigation Potential Utilised as a Percentage of Irrigation Potential Created Upto March 1997 *
▪ Major & Medium Irrigation Potential Created (Developed) upto the end of the 9th Plan (1997-2002) as a Percentage of Ultimate Irrigation Potential of the State *
▪ Major & Medium Irrigation Potential Utilised as a Percentage of Irrigation Potential Created Upto March 2002 *
▪ Minor Irrigation Potential Created (Developed) upto the end of the 9th Plan (1997-2002) as a Percentage of Ultimate Irrigation Potential of the State *
▪ Minor Irrigation Potential Utilised as a Percentage of Irrigation Potential Created Upto March 2002 *
▪ Average Gross Irrigated as a Percentage of Total Cropped Area (%): 1992-93 to 1995-96 and 1996-97 to 1999-2000 *
▪ Average Area Irrigated more than Once as a Percentage of Gross Irrigated Area (in percentage): 1992-93 to 1995-96 and 1996-97 to 1999-2000 *
▪ Average Agricultural Consumption of Electricity (in KwH) Per INR Lakh of Agricultural GSDP at Constant (1993-94) Prices: 1993-94 to 1995-96 and 1996-97 to 1999-2001 *
▪ Number of Energised Pump sets Per Hectare of Gross Irrigated Area (No./ha): 1995-96 and 1999-2000 *
▪ Change in Number of Energised Pump sets Per Hectare of Gross Irrigated Area (No./ha)/: 1992-93 to 1995-96 and 1995-96 to

1999-2000 *
NON-POINT SOURCE WATER POLLUTION POTENTIAL (20 indicators)
- Population Density (Person Per Km^2 of Geographical Area): 1991 and 2001*
- Percentage of Rural and Urban Households Without Latrine: 1993 and 1998 *
- Average Fertilisers Consumption (Kg./hectare): 1992-93 to 1995-96 and 1996-97 to 2000-01 *
- Average Annual Rainfall (in mm): 1990-95 and 1996-2000 $
- Pesticides Consumption: (Kg./hectare) 1995-96 and 1999-2000 *
- Area under Pulses as a Percentage of Gross Cropped Area: 1990-91 and 2000-2001 $
- Livestock Per Head of Person (No. in Cattle unit Per Person): 1992 and 1997 *
- Poultry Birds per Head of Person (No. Per Person): 1992 and 1997 *
- Average Total Cropped Area as a Percentage of Reporting Area of Land Utilisation (in percentage): 1992-93 to 1995-96 and 1996-97 to 1999-2000 *
PRESSURE AND DEGRADATION OF LAND RESOURCES (12 indicators)
- Average Forest Area as a Percentage of Reporting Area of Land Utilisation (in percentage): 1992-93 to 1995-96 and 1996-97 to 1999-2000 $
- Average Non-Forest Common Property Land as a Percentage of Reporting Area of Land Utilisation (in percentage): 1992-93 to 1995-96 and 1996-97 to 1999-2000 $
- Average Non-Forest Common Property Land Per Capita (in ha/person): 1992-93 to 1995-96 and 1996-97 to 1999-2000 $
- Average Area Sown more than Once as a Percentage of Total Cropped Area (in percentage): 1992-93 to 1995-96 and 1996-97 to 1999-2000 *
- Average Gross Irrigated as a Percentage of Total Cropped Area (in percentage): 1992-93 to 1995-96 and 1996-97 to 1999-2000 *
- Land Degradation as a Percentage of Geographical Area: 1994 and 2001 *

Note: * - implies that for the environmental indicator we have used (Maximum – Actual) / (Maximum – Minimum) for standardisation.

$ - implies that for the environmental indicator we have used (Actual − Minimum) / (Maximum − Minimum) for standardisation.

APPENDIX 3
GRAPHICAL RELATIONSHIP BETWEEN PCNSDP AND VARIOUS COMPONENTS OF ENVIRONMENTAL QUALITY SCORES

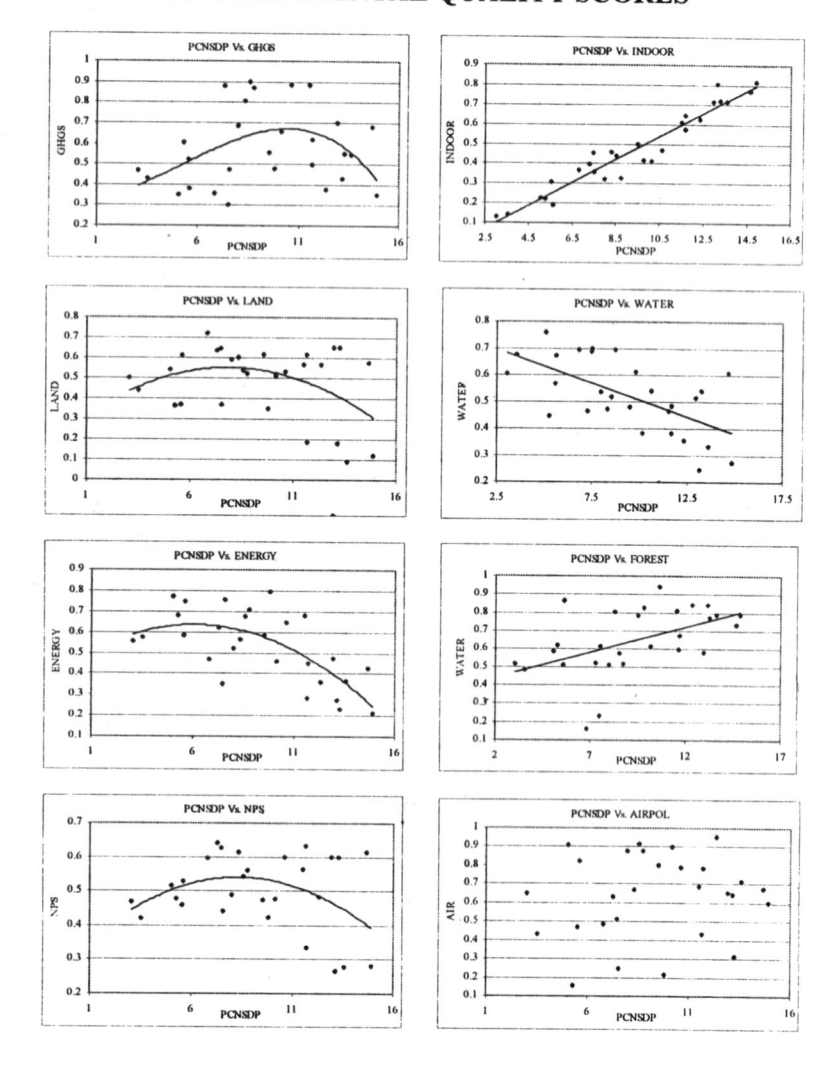

APPENDIX 4
GRAPHICAL RELATIONSHIP BETWEEN HDI SCORE AND VARIOUS COMPONENTS OF ENVIRONMENTAL QUALITY SCORES

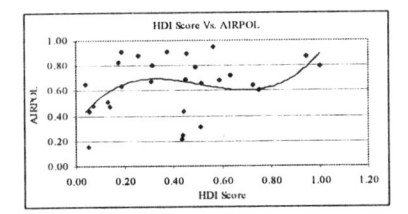

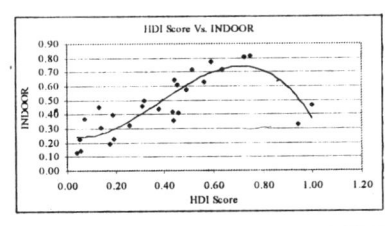

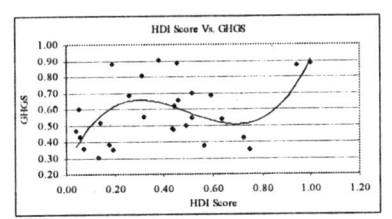

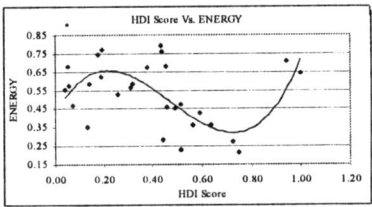

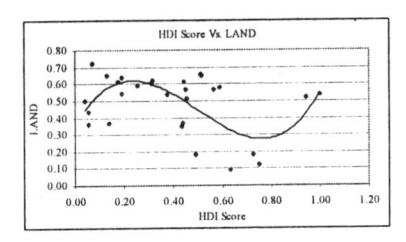

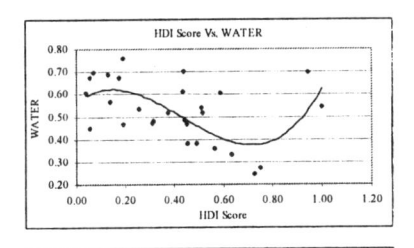

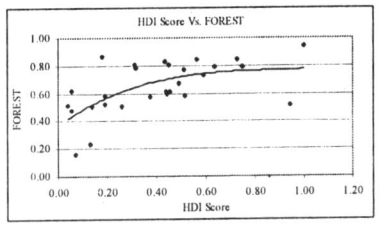

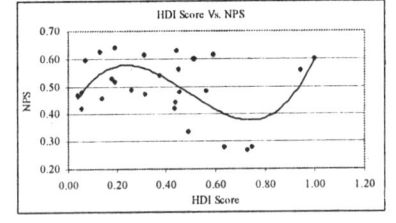

REFERENCES

Adriaanse, A. (1993): *Environmental Policy Performance Indicators: A Study of the Development of Indicators for Environmental Policy in the Netherlands*, SDU Publishers, The Hague.

Adriaanse, A., Bryant, D., Hammond, A.L., Rodeburg, E. and Woodward, R. (1995): *Environmental Indicators: A Systematic Approach to Measuring and Reporting on Environmental Policy Performance in the Context of Sustainable Development*, World Resources Institute, Washington D.C.

Agarwal, M. and Samanta, S. (2006): Structural Adjustment, Governance, Economic Growth and Social Progress, *Journal of International Trade and Economic Development*, 15 (3): 387 – 401.

Andreoni, J. and Levinson, A. (2001): The simple analytics of the Environmental Kuznets curve, *Journal of Public Economics*, 80 (1): 269–286.

Antony, M. J. (2001): *Landmark Judgements on Environmental Protection*, Indian Social Institute, New Delhi.

Baldwin, R. (1995): Does sustainability require growth? In *The Economics of Sustainable Development*, I. Goldin and L.A. Winters (Eds.), Cambridge University Press, Cambridge, UK.

Balooni, K. (2002): *Participatory Forest Management in India - An Analysis of Policy Trends amid Management Change*, Policy Trend Report 2002: 88-113, The Institute for Global Environmental Strategies (IGES), Japan.

Bhattacharya, H. and Innes, R. (2006): *Is There a Nexus between Poverty and Environment in Rural India?* Available at http://cals.arizona.edu/AREC/pubs/researchpapers/2006-05bhattacharyainnes.pdf

Bhullar, A.S. and Sidhu, R.S. (2006): Integrated Land and Water Use: A Case Study of Punjab, *Economic and Political Weekly*, 41 (52): 5353-5357.

Boyce, J.K. (2003): *Inequality and Environmental Protection*, Working Paper Series No. 52, Political Economy Research Institute, University of Massachusetts, Amherst, The Netherlands.

Brandon, Carter and Hommann, Kirsten (1995): The Cost of Inaction: Valuing the Economy-Wide Cost of Environmental Degradation in India, *Modelling Global Sustainability*, United Nations University, Tokyo.

Bruvoll, A. and Medin, H. (2003): Factors behind the Environmental Kuznets Curve: A Decomposition of the Changes in Air Pollution, *Environmental and Resource Economics*, 24 (1): 27–48.

Carson, R.T., Jeon, Y. and McCubbin, D.R. (1997): The Relationship between Air Pollution Emissions and Income: US data, *Environment and Development Economics*, 2 (4): 433–450.

Chakraborty, P. and Singh, J. (2005): *Leather Bound: A Comprehensive Guide for SMEs*, The Energy and Resources Institute, New Delhi.

Chopra, K. and Gulati, S.C. (1997): Environmental degradation and Population Movements: The Role of Property Rights, *Environmental and Resource Economics*, 9 (4): 383-408.

Convention on Biological Diversity (CBD) (undated): *Case study on Joint Forest Management (JFM) as an example of non-monetary positive incentive*, Available at: www.biodiv.org/doc/case-studies/inc/cs-inc-india-forest-en.doc

Costantini, V. and Salvatore, M. (2006): *Environment, Human Development and Economic Growth*, The Fondazione Eni Enrico

Mattei, Note di Lavoro Series, Available at: http://www.feem.it/NR/rdonlyres /CA11D877-29E3-462F-A591-7738FBD508F0/1891/3506.pdf

Dasgupta, P. (2001): Human Well-Being and the Natural Environment, Oxford University Press, New Delhi.

Dastidar, A. G. (2006): Maharashtra 'outsources' toxic e-waste to Delhi, *Hindustan Times*, 30 December.

Deaton, A. and Drèze, J. (2002): Poverty and Inequality in India: A Re-Examination, *Economic and Political Weekly*, 36 (37): 3729-3748.

de Bruyn, S.M., van den Berg, J.C.J.M. and Opschoor, J.B. (1998): Economic Growth and Emissions: Reconsidering the Empirical basis of Environmental Kuznets Curve, *Ecological Economics*, 25 (2): 161–175.

Dietzenbacher, E. and Mukhopadhyay, K. (2007): An Empirical Examination of the Pollution Haven Hypothesis for India: Towards a Green Leontief Paradox?, *Environment and Resource Economics*, 36 (4): 427-449.

Dinda, S. (2004): Environmental Kuznets Curve Hypothesis: a Survey, *Ecological Economics*, 49 (4): 431–455.

Divan, S. and Rosencranz, A. (2002): *Environmental Law and Policy in India: Cases, Materials and Statutes*, Second Edition, Oxford University Press, New Delhi.

Dutt, A.K. and Rao, J.M. (1996): Growth, Distribution and the Environment: Sustainable Development in India, *World Development*, 24 (2): 287-305.

Ebert, U. and Welsch, H. (2004): Meaningful Environmental Indices: a Social Choice Approach, *Journal of Environmental Economics and Management*, 47 (2): 270–283.

Eskeland, G.S. and Harrison, A.E. (2003): Moving to Greener Pastures? Multinationals and the Pollution Haven Hypothesis, *Journal of Development Economics*, 70 (1): 1-23.

Esty, D.C., Levy, M.A., Srebotnjak, T., de Sherbinin, A., Kim, C.H. and Anderson, B. (2006): *Pilot 2006 Environmental Performance Index*, Yale Center for Environmental Law and Policy and Center for International Earth Science Information Network (CIESIN), Available at: http://www.yale.edu/epi/2006EPI_Report_Full.pdf

Esty, D.C., Levy, M.A., Srebotnjak, T. and de Sherbinin, A. (2005): *Environmental Sustainability Index: Benchmarking National Environmental Stewardship*, Yale Center for Environmental Law and Policy, New Haven.

Esty, D.C. and Porter, M.E. (2001-02): *Ranking National Environmental Regulation and Performance: A Leading Indicator of Future Competitiveness?* Chapter 2.1, pp. 78-100, Harvard Business School, Global Competitiveness Report, http://www.isc.hbs.edu/GCR_20012002_Environment.pdf

Gallagher, K.P (2004): *Free Trade and the Environment: Mexico, NAFTA, and Beyond*, Available at: http://ase.tufts.edu/gdae/Pubs/rp/NAFTAEnviroKGAmerProgSep04.pdf

Gamper-Rabindran, S. and Jha, S. (2004): *Environmental Impact of India's Trade Liberalization*, Available at: http://unpan1.un.org/intradoc/groups/public/documents/APCITY/UNPAN024230.pdf

Ghosh, M. (2006): Economic Growth and Human Development in Indian States, *Economic and Political Weekly*, 40 (30): 3321-3329.

Government of India (2002): *National Human Development Report 2001*, Planning Commission, New Delhi.

Grossman, G.M. and Krueger, A.B. (1995): Economic Growth and the Environment, *Quarterly Journal of Economics*, 110 (2): 353–378.

Guha, A. and Chakraborty, D. (2003): Relative Positions of Human Development Index Across Indian States: Some Exploratory Results, *Artha Beekshan*, 11 (4): 166-181.

Jalan, J., Somanathan, E. and Chaudhuri, S. (2003): *Awareness and the Demand for Environmental Quality: Drinking Water in Urban India*, Economics Discussion Paper No. 03-05, Indian Statistical Institute, New Delhi.

Jena, P.R., Sahu, N.C. and Rath, B. (2005): Does Trade Liberalisation Create Pollution Haven? An Indian Experience', *International Conference on Environment and Development: Developing Countries Perspective*, Jawaharlal Nehru University, New Delhi.

Jha, R. and Bhanu Murthy, K.V. (2001): *An Inverse Global Environmental Kuznets Curve*, Departmental Working Papers: 2001–2002, Division of Economics, RSPAS, Australian National University, Canberra, Australia.

Jha, V. (1999): *Investment Liberalization and Environmental Protection: Conflicts and Compatibilities in the Case of India*, Occasional Paper No. 1, Copenhagen Business School. Copenhagen, Denmark.

Jones, L., Fredricksen, L. and Wates, T. (2002): *Environmental Indicators*, 5th edn., The Fraser Institute, Available at: http://www.fraserinstitute.ca/shared/readmore.asp?snav=pb&id=3 14.

Kadekodi, G. K. and Venkatachalam, L. (2006): *Human Development, Environment and Poverty Nexus in India*, Background Paper on Environment and Poverty, UNDP, New Delhi.

Kathuria, V. and Sterner, T. (2006): Monitoring and Enforcement: Is two-tier Regulation Robust? - A case study of Ankleshwar, India, *Ecological Economics*, 57 (3): 477-493.

Maiti, S. and Agrawal, P.K. (2005): Environmental Degradation in the Context of Growing Urbanization: A Focus on the Metropolitan Cities of India, *Journal of Human Ecology*, 17 (4): 277-287.

Melnick, D., McNeely, J., Navarro, Y.K., Schmidt-Traub, G. and Sears, R.R. (2005): *Environment and human well-being: a practical strategy*, UN Millennium Project, Task Force on Environmental Sustainability, Available at: http://www.unmillenniumproject.org/documents/Environment-complete-lowres.pdf

Mukherjee, S. and Chakraborty, D. (2007): Environment, Human Development and Economic Growth of Indian States after Liberalisation, *Making Growth Inclusive with Special Reference to Imbalance in Regional Development,* Department of Economics, Jammu University, Jammu and Kashmir.

Mukherjee, S. and Kathuria, V. (2006): Is Economic Growth Sustainable? Environmental Quality of Indian States after 1991, *International Journal of Sustainable Development*, 9 (1): 38-60.

NCERT (2002): *7th All India Educational Survey (AIES): All India School Education Survey (AISES)*, National Council of Educational Research and Training (NCERT), Ministry of Human Resource Development (MHRD), Government of India, New Delhi.

Nadkarni, M.V. (2000): Poverty, Environment, Development: a many Patterned Nexus, *Economic and Political Weekly*, 35 (14): 1184–1190.

Nagar, A.L., and Basu, S.R. (2001): *Weighing Socio-Economic Indicators of Human Development: A Latent Variable Approach*, Working Paper, National Institute of Public Finance and Policy, New Delhi.

Nagdeve, D.A. (2007): *Population Growth and Environmental Degradation in India*, Available at: http://paa2007.princeton.edu/download.aspx?submissionId=7192

Nair, G.K. (2006): *Water scarcity hits parts of south Kerala*, The Hindu Business Line, 31 March, Available at: http://www.thehindubusinessline.com/2006/03/31/stories/2006033101981900.htm

Panayatou, T. (1993): *Empirical Tests and Policy Analysis of Environmental Degradation at Different Stages of Economic Development*, Working Paper No. WP238, Technology and Employment Program, International Labour Office, Geneva.

Pezzey, J. (1989): *Economic Analysis of Sustainable Growth and Sustainable Development*, Environment Department Working Paper No 15, World Bank, Washington DC.

Ranis, G. (2004): *Human Development and Economic Growth*, Center Discussion Paper No. 887, Economic Growth Center, Yale University, Available at: http://www.econ.yale.edu/growth_pdf/cdp887.pdf

Reddy, M. S. and Char, N. V. V. (2004): *Management of Lakes in India*, Available at: http://www.worldlakes.org/uploads/Management_of_lakes_in_India_10Mar04.pdf

Rithe, K. and Fernandes, A. (2002): *Maharashtra's Tiger Troubles*, Available at: www.satpuda.org/maharashtratiger.doc

Rogers, P., Jalal, K.F., Lohani, B.N., Owens, G.M., Yu, C-C., Christia, M. and Dufournaud, J.B. (1997): *Measuring Environmental Quality in Asia*, Harvard University Press and ADB, London, UK.

Sagar, V. (undated): Inequality, Agricultural Sustainability and Environmental Degradation, Available at: http://www.sussex.ac.uk/Units/PRU/inequality_agricultural_sustain.pdf

Sankar, U. (2006): Trade Liberalization and Environmental Protection Responses of Leather Industry in Brazil, China and India, *Economic and Political Weekly*, 41 (24): 2470-2477.

Sankar, U. (1998): Laws and Institutions relating to Environmental Protection in India, Occasional Paper, Madras School of Economics, Chennai, Available at: http://www.mse.ac.in/pub/op_sankar.pdf

Schjolden, A. (2000): *Leather tanning in India: Environmental regulations and firms' Compliance*, F-I-L. Working Papers, No. 21, Available at: http://www.cicero.uio.no/media/1677.pdf

Selden, T.M. and Song, D.S. (1994): Environmental Quality and Development: is there a Kuznets Curve for Air Pollution Emissions?, *Journal of Environmental Economics and Management*, 27 (2): 147–162.

Shafik, N. and Bandyopadhyay, S. (1992): *Economic Growth and Environmental Quality: Time-Series and Cross-Country Evidence*, World Bank Policy Research Working Paper No. 904, World Bank, Washington DC.

Sharma, D.C. (2005): By Order of the Court: Environmental Cleanup in India, *Environmental Health Perspectives*, 113 (6): A394-A397.

Stern, D.I. (1998): Progress on the Environmental Kuznets curve, *Environment and Development Economics*, 3 (2): 175–198.

Tewari, M. and Pilai, P. (2005): Global standards and environmental compliance in India's leather industry, *Oxford Development Studies*, 33 (2): 245-267.

UNDP (2007): *Human Development Report 2007/2008 - Fighting Climate Change: Human Solidarity in a Divided World*, United Nations Development Program, New York, USA.

van Ginkel, H., Barrett, B., Court, J. and Velasquez, J. (eds.) (2001), *Human Development and the Environment: Challenges for the United Nations in the New Millennium*, United Nations University Press, Tokyo, Japan.

Venkatachalam, L. (2005): Damage Assessment and Compensation to Farmers: Lessons from Verdict of Loss of Ecology Authority in Tamil Nadu, *Economic and Political Weekly*, 40 (15): 1556-1560.

World Bank (2006): *India: Strengthening Institutions for Sustainable Growth*, Country Environmental Analysis for India, Washington D.C., Available at:
http://siteresources.worldbank.org/INDIAEXTN/Resources/295583-1176163782791/complete.pdf

Zhou, P., Ang, B.W. and Poh, K.L. (2006): Comparing Aggregating Methods for Constructing the Composite Environmental Index: an Objective Measure, *Ecological Economics*, 59 (3): 305-311.

11

Gender and Human Development

Liliane Bensahel[1], Steven Coissard[2], Asma Ben Lazrak[3]

I. INTRODUCTION

The report on the human development of the United Nations Development Program (UNDP) (1998) considers that the possessions must not be intrinsically valued but considered as the instruments of the realization of certain potentialities such as the health, the knowledge, the self-respect and the capacity to participate actively in the life of the community. It is so all the approach of the wealth that is reconsidered to allow new potentialities of development. "We live a conception of the wealth and the prosperity today which doubtless puts obstacle not only to a human and durable development instruments are simplistic, false and superficial and base themselves on a conception impoverished by the fact what is the wealth" (Meda, 2001).

A part of the imperatives of the durable development resumes these problems through the notions of human resources, (development of the individual and collective capacities), authorized capital and social durability

---

[1] Université de Grenoble, UPMF, CREPPEM, France, E-mail: liliane.bensahel@upmf-grenoble.fr.
[2] Université de Grenoble, CREPPEM et IDRAC, école de commerce, Lyon, France, E-mail :steven.coissard@upmf-grenoble.fr
[3] Université de Grenoble, UPMF, CREPPEM, France

(democracy, nearness, solidarity), of transmission in the future generations. One of the corollaries of the collective human development is to make of every individual an agent. "Define the individuals by their only relation in the good be - the one from which they benefit or acquire is an indispensable stage, but be held in this restrictive approach would be miss an essential dimension of the human personality. While seizing their capacity of initiative one recognizes the individuals as responsible. We are not only healthy or sick; we are also opened in actions or in position of refusal towards an action. It is an important distinction there which we have to keep present in the spirit and which, although elementary in its principle, must be respected in all its rigor, if we want to pull all the implications, and they are considerable, whether it is in the analysis or the practice" (Sen, 2000a).

The human development so became an important axis of the development of societies and indicators proposed by the World Bank testify of it. The indicator of Human Development developed by the UNDP in 1990 takes into account three elements (longevity and health, knowledge: rate of elimination of illiteracy in the adults, raw rate of schooling, and level of life). It is completed by three other indicators which seem to us important and which are the Indicator of Human Poverty (IPH) which clarifies the indicator of human development, the sex-specific indicator of human development (ISDH) which leans on the sociological disparities of sex and the Indicator of the participation of the women (IPF) which reports the insertion of the women in the public life. The gender is so integrated into the estimation of the development of nations. Indeed, the approach by the gender sends back to the manners men and women of which interact. Analyses in terms of gender so study the way societies distribute three roles between men and women, how men and women are invested in the various needs and in which the various programs and the projects of development are of the responsibility of the one or the other one or both sexes. They allow getting the elements of construction of a completely responsible society which can guarantee a more harmonious development and for which the peace is essential of the wealth. Today the approaches on the gender more were much interested in the conditions of life of the women because of their discrimination in a general way on the planet. This does not have to hide on one hand the necessity of taking into account the situation of the men and especially of analyzing the relation man-woman. We can, however, wonder about the notion of equality. The male and the feminine cannot become confused, as they are additional. The composed question is not that of their equality but the dissolution of the hierarchy as indicates it Françoise Heritier *"To want to reach the lack of differentiation between the sexes, it is not to take into account an one given with which the alive has to compose, namely the existence of the sexual difference ... The contemporary fight so that the women reach the freedom and the dignity of nobody has for object a political, intellectual and symbolic rebalancing of the categories which form the social to end in a more just situation and more coherent of our knowledge, and not in a reversal which would reproduce a system of disparities"*. The analysis of gender applied in social sciences constitutes a new epistemological datum which questions research methodologies. She allows wondering about statutes, roles of the woman and the man in the social stratification on one hand and on the impact of the relation man-woman in the collective situations.

Having presented the approach by the gender and the analyses concerning the human development, we shall examine the contributions of this approach by the participation of the women through the following elements: the economic, the education and the participation to institutions.

II. THE GENDER APPROACH: A SPECIFIC ANALYSIS

The discrimination based on the gender exists, in different degrees, in all the countries of the world. This disparity of the access to the legal, social and economic resources for the women also has strong negative repercussions on the whole society and the development of nations, because it notably affects the health and the good to be men, women and children. The annual report of the United Nations 2006 shows that if the women are not healthy or do not have access to the education or not the means to take care, it is the children who suffer from it. The economic liberalization comes along with an increase of the distances based on the sex. The women are the first victims of the poverty, the unemployment, and conflicts. In all the countries, the women are, at level of identical human resources, less indeed paid than the men or have no access to the highest jobs (the famous "glass ceiling"[4]).

The conference of Beijing so introduced the notion of gender and we notice the appearance of related notions used today to define analyses on the gender such as the gender mainstreaming or the empowerment. *"The equality man-woman supposes that men and women enjoy in conditions of equality of possessions, possibilities, resources and rewards to which the society attaches a value. The equality man-woman does not imply that men and women become identical, but that they have possibilities and equal chances in the existence. The interest for the equality man-woman and in the intensification of the power of the women does not presuppose a particular model of equality man-woman for all the societies and the cultures, but translates the concern to look to the men and to the women of the equal chances to choose that it is necessary to understand by equality man-woman and to allow them to work on it in a joint way"*. Surrounding areas of gender

---

[4] The term glass ceiling refers to situations where the advancement of a qualified person within the hierarchy of an organization is stopped at a lower level because of some form of discrimination, most commonly sexism or racism, http://en.wikipedia.org/wiki/glass_ceiling accessed on the 5th July 2008.

articulate around two big concepts, that of *mainstreaming* and around *empowerment*.

The mainstreaming leans on principles, which recommend a commitment and conceptions for the equality and of a more just society and by systems (strategies, policies, structures, mechanisms and tools). The mainstreaming about the honorable gender the specific characteristics of the place and the situation of the men and the women in the elaboration of the policies and the economic and social measures, their application but also the analysis of the incidences of any order which these measures could have on men and women. He supposes legislation, policies but also good knowledge of the gender relations, well-balanced participation of the men and the women in the public life. The mainstreaming of the gender consists of two approaches: the integrated approach and the participative approach. The first one is more connected to the notion of the equality of opportunity and the second is an awareness of relations between men and women. The current expressions of the "mainstreaming" is the principle of positive discrimination and parity. In most of the countries, the mainstreaming is there only for its stammering.

For Jacquet (1995), the concept of empowerment recovers the acquisition of the right for the word and for the social recognition. Eisen (1994) defines it as the way by which the individual increases his skills favoring the self-respect, the self-confidence, the initiative and the control. 'The empowerment contains four essential constituents: the participation, the competence, the self-respect and the consciousness criticizes (individual, collective, social and political consciousness)' (Le Bossé and Lavalée, 1993). McWhirter (1991) adds it social and community perspectives when the empowerment is situated at the collective or community level. It contributes then to the development of the community health by attitudes, the values, the capacities, the organizational structures and the leadership.

In this approach, the empowerment concerns mostly groups of persons without recognized power the often-unused forces of which it is important to strengthen. It is a question of returning the community capable of analyzing its situation of defining its problems and of resolving them so that it enjoys completely its rights. In the political perspective, the empowerment is the result, which allows to change the current structures and the relations of power between the different authorities, the speakers and the individuals (Sherwin, 1992). The empowerment should allow the persons living in conditions of poverty to go out durably of this condition by reducing their social, economic, political or psychological vulnerability. Its various levels of intervention concern the prosperity (satisfaction of the practical needs of the women), the equality in the access to the resources and the services, the conscious approach of the difference between sex and gender, collective participation of the women.), the participation (participation equals women in all the processes of decision), the control of the processes of decisions, wealth and profits).

The symbolic dimension of the social relations, which passes by the notion of "capacity" and "to be able to", is too often neglected. Sen (2000a) shows that the perception, by the very women, of the secondary character of their contribution affects their capacity of negotiation and thus dialogue, so contributing to immortalize the rules of a game in terms of "cooperative conflict" the exit of which reflects the male superiority.

Surrounding areas of gender meet, however, some difficulties:
- The measures taken by the international organizations or States following the demands led by the women in terms of parity makes the big part in "positive discrimination" of specific rights based on the biologic difference of the women. These measures are difficult to accept because they are passing and are not in itself an end. The ethics

of gender implies an appeal in the "right for the equality and not the equality of the rights or the right equals for all", independently of the real exercise of their freedom, beyond the normative principles.
- The generalization of the presentation of the situations and the behavior of the women and the men and the myths, which result from it, does not give a clear picture of the problem. Numerous specialists of the gender denounced this situation and its recovery by the international organizations to justify their policies.

III. AN ECONOMIC DEVELOPMENT BASED ON THE PROSPERITY

The modern approaches of the development integrate more and more the notion of prosperity of every individual. Since the beginning of the 1990s, in reason notably of the discharge of the reforms and the narrow economic perspectives, we begin to privilege a better balanced approach of the development, which includes at the same moment social and economic objectives without that some are subordinated to the others.

For Sen (2000b), the notion of prosperity is in relation with the capacity to act in a given space in particular in the possibility of getting itself the possessions, which it needs. He distinguishes two sorts of economic possessions:
- the "functioning", connected to the way of life which determines the custom of the possessions and confers them their utility; and
- the "Capabilities" or real capacities that one the individuals to reach the purposes that they chose. They do not become confused with the way of life.

The author suggests allocating to every constituent of the prosperity a weight of evaluation, which would be subjected to the public discussion to validate him or her. He recognizes the value judgment inherent to this method but he thinks that if the majority of the persons allow these indicators, they win in aptness. Perrin (2004) suggests to use the analysis of the value as methodology of economic evaluation by tracking down the functions characterized and by estimating the solutions by a note, what allows to organize into a hierarchy the acceptable propositions by appreciating the report function / cost of each.

This does not suppose to abandon the fight against the poverty. As such, it is advisable to mention Sherraden (1991)'s propositions. He thinks that the constitution of a patrimony is a means of fight against the poverty thanks to a public policy based on the social investment. This one could take the shape of an individual account of training and a fund for the childhood, which would allow the poor men to constitute a capital to face the chances of the life. For this author, the patrimony improves the stability of the households, favors the development of the human resources and the other active persons, gives one based necessities for the risk-taking, improves the personal efficiency, increases the social influence, increases the participation in the public life and this fact fights the exclusion, improves the prosperity of the descendants. The micro-credit participle in the development of the patrimony of the poor men.

The objectives of the Millennium Development Goals (MDGs) determined by United Nations had emphasized the urgency to reduce the disparities of sex. The Report on the development in the world in 2006 of the World Bank notes that in most of the developing countries, we can notice disparities of the chances in the field of the health, of the education, of the economic prosperity and of the political agency today. In the world, men and women do not reach really in the same way the resources and the opportunities, and this disparity is strengthened by standards and unegalitarian social orders. As a result the differences between the sexes continue from century to century. The inequity of the sexes, it is the archetype of the trapdoor with disparity. In the evaluation of the disparity of the chances, the education has a big intrinsic importance. It is also an important determining of the income of the individuals, their health (and that of their children), of their capacity to interact and to communicate with others. The disparities in education contribute to the disparities of the other fundamental constituents of the prosperity. He pursues that in most of the countries (with the weak incomes) the probability that a head of the family did not receive educational school is considerably more brought up than averages it when this head of the family is a woman. This disparity goes in certain countries until the preference for the male children and the elimination to the birth or during the pregnancy of the female children or an inattention towards these children, which pulls mortality more, rose for the girls. Amartya Sen speaks about missing women (Sen, 1990). Les women's non-governmental organizations (NGO) try to reduce these disparities by denouncing the desolation or the murder of the children girls and especially to educate the women and the girls to dike this phenomenon.

IV. PARTICIPATION OF THE WOMEN IN THE DEVELOPMENT OF SOCIETIES

The increase of the poverty in the world and the ecological imbalance led the economists to question the relation between the development and the growth. New surrounding areas of the wealth are listened. The human development becomes the preoccupation of the international programs. At the same time, analyses on ethics and economy, ethics and company develop and come along with a requirement of behavior by the canal the citizens' steps within the framework of the objectives of durable development. All these analyses suggest putting in the center of the development the human being and the ecology, to reduce the ascendancy of the economic values of the market. Surrounding areas of gender join this movement and send back to the approach of the development proposed by Amartya Sen. This one connects the prosperity and the function of agent, because it is important to recognize the capacities of initiative and responsibility of the individuals, notably as regards the women. If it exists a wide space of intersection enters the improvement of their good to be and the function of agents (capacity of initiatives), it is advisable to distinguish both. The relation women-men is a stake in development, the opening at the women and at the men to understand himself better and better understand the other one is an element to think of the development of a more human society. The notions current of human development and durable development lean on the concept of human resources (development of the individual capacities, notably by the access to the education) and social capital (social relations, participation in the democracy). The situations of the individuals degrade very quickly when the disparities are notably too important, relative those in sex. The care, the education, the participation in the public life, the employment of which are deprived the women hinder the development of countries.

Within the framework of the studies on the development, the constituent theoretical elements of the concept of gender concerns three roles (reproductive, economic and social), the practical or concrete needs (of material order) and the strategic needs (of political order), five approaches concerning the projects and the programs of development (the prosperity, the equality of opportunity, the fight against the poverty, the efficiency, the obtaining of the power) which determine or not a place to the gender (Jacquet, 1995). The consideration of these elements transforms the approach of the development and reports the important role of the women in the creation of wealth, even if this role is still very often darkened, recognized. In a world of wealthiest and disparities, the liberties play an essential role to fight the misery and the oppression. They are at the same moment the ultimate end of the development and its main means. Far from opposing, economic freedom and political freedom strengthen.

They favor the action of the individuals, in particular the women, whose emancipation is a decisive factor of change.

The approach women and the development arise from the historic approach of the integration of the women in the development. Boserup (2001) showed that for lack of integrating them completely into the process of development, the economic progress tends to be made at the price of the marginalization of the women. In this approach, the development of the contribution of the women is perceived as an element of the economic and social modernization. The accent is put on the high returns, in terms of prosperity and human resources, the investment in the education and the greater participation of the women, the account held notably by the delay accumulated in this domain.

Since Tunisian's independence, the improvement of the status of the women became a priority for the policy of human resources. In this the Personal Status Code, afforded women full and equal rights and remains one of the most progressive family laws in the today's Arab world. Since that time, forces marriage, polygamy and unilateral divorce (repudiation) have been abolished; they have been replaced by judiciary divorce and the rights of divorced women to the custody children have been reinforced. Tunisian Personal Status Code sought to develop a new phase of Islamic thinking distinct from the Islamic law in other Muslim countries. The last round of reforms brought Tunisian law in accordance with international human rights standards: these reforms are not an abandonment of Islamic values but an evolution for the modern period. Tunisia signed the Convention on the Elimination of all Forms of Discrimination against Women (CEDAW) on September 1985 with reservations as regards conflict with Islamic values. At the institutional level, the Ministry for Women and Family Affairs designs national policy for the promotion of women and families, and oversees that really respected and that laws in this field are improved. This ministry coordinates programs and activities for integrating women in different sectors. Women's governmental and non-governmental organisations effectively promote the status of women's rights within the family and the economic sphere. The 1990s witnessed increases both in the number of active women's organisations and women's rights. For instance, more than 20 women NGO's have been established since 1989, whereas, only one organisation existed in Tunisia before 1986 (the National Union of Tunisian Women founded in 1956). Women's progress is evident in their increased educational attainment at the tertiary level, access to labour market, and diversity in professional careers. The education of girls has been also among priorities of the government. In fact, the school enrolment of girls at the age of 6 reached 99.1 per cent in 2003-2004 and today more than 50 percent of university students are women: the percentage of young women in universities rose to 51.9 per cent in 2000-2001 to 57 today (compared to 25.8 in 1975).

In 1964, Tunisia adopted an ambitious family planning program. An important program of health and family planning education was also launched; family planning and maternal-child health services were combined in basic health care centres. These services were made more available to remote rural areas through mobile units. In the beginning of 1990s, the acceleration of the policy for integration of basic reproductive health, especially services related to fertility and family planning, has had a very noted effect on all women's health indicators. For example, in 1995, the rate of pregnant women presenting for prenatal consultations was 88 per cent in urban areas and 69 per cent in rural one. The fertility rate was 2.1 per woman, among the lowest in developing countries. Health-related social policies have included the legalization of import and sale of contraception, the limitation of family allowances to the first three children to encourage smaller families, the legalization of regulated abortion in 1973, the creation of an agency for the protection of mother and child.

The major victims of illiteracy are women, that way; a national plan has been set up to combat illiteracy entirely among women between the age of 15 and 45 by the year 2006. Some 66,690 young women aged 15 to 29 are enrolled in literacy centres. The rate of women literacy increased from 24 per cent 1966 to 77.1 in 2004. Tunisia's success in this field earned it the 1994 UNESCO prize for literacy, awarded to the National Union of Tunisian Women.

Tunisian labour legislation has developed in harmony with international legislation. The percentage of economically active women is currently 37.5 and the percentage of women in the working population has risen from 6 in 1966 to 25 in 2003. They have conquered all sectors and branches of activity. Women have an important representation particularly in the professions of pharmacology and dentistry, banking sector, civil services. However, the women's unemployment rates remain high (15.3 per cent in 2001). In large cases, this high rate of unemployment has involved many women to move toward informal sector and micro - enterprises. Indeed, it is estimated that about 1/5 of jobs in informal sector are held by women. For instance, they represent 32 per cent of people who active in farming and fishing activities.

A recent study on women's entrepreneurship showed the facts that in Tunisia, women have more difficulty to obtain loans and financing for news enterprises. In addition, women are less likely than men to request bank financing. Seventy per cent of women questioned in the study said that they drew on personal savings to begin their business, those at the level of micro-enterprises had often received credit from an NGO. Despite these difficulties, women – owned businesses appear to prosper; the survival rate after five years for women owned -businesses was almost twice as high as for businesses started and owned by men.

V. GENDER AND REGULATIONS OF THE CONFLICTS

The Human Development 2005 of UNDP shows that though the number of conflicts decreased since the 1990s, the last century remains very murderous. The victims of these new conflicts are not any more essentially soldiers or military staff, but civil populations, and in particular the most vulnerable such as the women and the children (the number of civil losses in the current conflicts borders the 90 per cent, for the greater part women and children, UNO source). Because of their social status and of their sex, the women are subjected to several types of violence, the rape, the sexual slavery, the forced pregnancy, the mutilation or still the forced sterilization. Besides, the cost due to the violent conflicts does not concern only the number of victims, it is also necessary to take into account the consequences on the human development, connected to the reduction of the growth because of the destruction of infrastructures, the dislocation of the food systems, the health, educational. In the situations of conflict, men and women have no same access to the resources, to the power and to the decision taking before, hanging and after the conflict. The women represent 80 per cent of the human losses at the world level and 80 per cent of the displaced persons and the refugees are women and children. The objective fixed by Kofi Annan about the number of women among the soldiers of the peace (50 per cent) is far from being realized, even in the political functions devolved to the UNO.

And nevertheless, all which revolves around the conflicts (war, prevention or regulation) was always seen as the privilege of the men. The national and international institutions in charge of these questions are generally formed by men. The specificity of the role of the women is not integrated nevertheless yet as well for the reintegration of the fighting women after the war, their participation in the processes of regulation and prevention of the conflicts or the reconstruction after the war. The feminist associations worked a lot at making listen the voice of the women and tempt to increase their representative in the various political authorities.

VI. MALE-FEMALE, THE LEARNING OF THE DIFFERENCE AND THE UNITY

Levinas (1982) translates his understanding of the ethics by the responsibility, which we have of the other one, the face of the other one. The ethics, it is the human being as human being, the only absolute value, it is the human possibility of giving onto one a priority to the other one, the responsibility is born in an instant when the other one affects me, and this affectation makes me responsible in spite of me. The condition of freedom becomes the responsibility, the responsibility of one and the others, responsibility of the consideration of the otherness. The imperative of ethics, formulated, by Kant resumes identical objectives: "act so that you consider the humanity as well in your person as in the person of quite other, always, at the same time as the end, and never simply as the means".

Christiane Singer, in the last book, which she signed before dying, writes: *"When we analyze quite scientifically, we have scientific results. The science engenders the science, Perfect tautology and closed system, which nothing threatens. We have results but no fruits for all that. For the fruit, the one has to burst are needed both. On the horizon of the knowledge has to join the vertical line of the stranger. It is only when the scientific horizon of lucidity and research joined the vertical line of the secret that the fruit can be born"* (Singer, 2007). This magnificent passage can already be a first answer on the contribution of the women to the public sphere. It is not a question of establishing a feminine power on the male; it is a question of recognizing both to allow the birth of the fruit, the opening of the other glances. This cooperation becomes necessary in front of the complexity and the multiplicity of the world in which we live. Go out exactly of the rational to suspect the other possible and give a place to the feminine, which detains every man. The approach of the gender, by the study of the situations, the roles and the social functions of the man and the woman, the relations between these two poles with for ambition to be in closer of the human being and to allow him to position in best in our world.

The feminine is often invisible, forgotten, depreciated and it disturbs. However, the depreciation of the women can have important consequences on the men. On one hand, the humiliation of the women spatters on their sons and it is more and more visible with the globalization and the development of the communications. Besides, these practices can exclude the men of the private sphere and the relation to the children and they impose them strong social representations of success, power, force that all do not want or are not to assume. This situation has the effect of forbidding the expression of their feminine part while both male and feminine aspects are present in each one. This means that in turn, they undergo a mutilation, which remains often unconscious but can express itself by a renewal of violence towards the women.

The society needs both male and feminine poles. For Randon (1998) the recognition of the role of the feminine is indispensable for the survival of the alive. The problem of the global survival asks for the consideration of a global reality based on the duality. If the male brain creates the complexity, *"the feminine is associated to the mystery of the alive, that is to the reality which is more than the matter, made of invisible where express themselves the order and the disorder, the unpredictable one quantum which is the tension of dynamic and contradictory aspects ... The feminine intelligence and the sensibility complete the male, but it is necessary to recognize the fundamental values because there is urgency to save the alive order and the human race; we can reach there only by a new global consciousness where the feminine will play a fundamental role"*.

In the same work, Serres (1998) speaks about both sexes of the spirit and the complementarities of the feminine and the male. The recognition of the necessary equality of the women and the men participle of the evolution of all the human beings, the participation in the male and in the feminine being the own of every human being. The sexual difference, the role different from sexes imposes an identical / different report which is the base of all the scientific thoughts and all the systems of representation. It does not foresee from the hierarchy of the sexes and however we can notice in all the societies "differential valency of the sexes", that is the power of a sex on the other one or the valuation of a (male) sex and the depreciation of the other one. She also allows us to make the learning of the democracy, of other, different from us by nature. The report man / woman is built on the report relative / child and more generally previous / later, the anteriority meaning the superiority.

During a conference in Amsterdam, Isabelle Rauber from Argentina, answers the question of why be interested in the gender in three words: *"To be happy!" The fights of the women were so marked by sufferings, tears and renunciation which you should not forget that our purpose is above all to be happy (and happy)"*.

This remark could connect with the approach of Viveret (2005) in its work *why that does not go more badly?* Speaking about current crises of the society, he explains us that *"the best service which we can return to the future generations it is to be happy and to pass on the taste of the happiness to our children. Because the happiness is not destructive: it signs the reconciliation with the nature by the beauty, the reconciliation with others by the friendship, the reconciliation with itself by the serenity"* (Viveret, 2005). That's why, it is important to be interested in the approaches by the gender. This approach by the knowledge of the difficulties living men and women allows us to build better one to live together.

Documentary evidence, if necessary, of the necessity of being interested in the gender is connected to the functioning of our brain. The scientific researches showed that we arrange two intellectual hemispheres, the more rational left hemisphere and more often used by the men, the right hemisphere more bound to the intuition and more connected to the feminine. Both are indeed on necessities to analyze at the same moment, feel and act.

REFERENCES

Boserup Esther (2001) : *La Femme face au développement économique* (avec Marie-Catherine Marache), coll. Sociologie d'aujourd'hui, Puf, (french translation of Woman's Role in Economic Development. 283 pp. London and New York, 1970).

Eisen, A. (1994): *Survey of Neighbourhood-based, Comprehensive Community Empowerment Initiatives*, Health Education Quaterly, 21 (2), 235-252.

Jacquet, I. (1995) : *Développement au masculin, féminin - le genre, outils d'un nouveau concept*, L'Harmattan, Paris.

Le Bossé, Y. and Lavalée, M., (1993) : Empowerment et psychologie communautaire Aperçu historique et perspectives d'avenir, *Les Cahiers Internationaux de Psychologie Sociale*, 18, 7-20.

Levinas, E. (1982) : Ethique et Infini, Fayard, Paris.

McWhirter, E. H. (1991): Empowerment in Counselling, *Journal of Counseling and Development*, 69 (3), 222-227

Meda, D. (2001) : *Le temps des femmes : pour un nouveau partage des rôles*, Flammarion, Paris, p.199.

Perrin, J. (2004) : Valeur et développement durable : questionnement sur la valeur économique, L'harmattan, Paris.

Randon, M. (1998) : Entretiens avec Michel Randon, le féminin au secours du vivant in *Le couple intérieur* (sous la direction de Paule Salomon), Albin Michel, Paris.

Sen, A., (1990): More Than 100 Million Women Are Missing, *New York Review of Books*, 37 (20), available at: http://www.nybooks.com/articles/3408

Sen, A. (2000a) : La liberté des femmes, atout du développement, Le Monde Diplomatique, septembre, p. 22.

Sen, A. (2000b): *Un nouveau modèle économique, développement, justice, liberté,* Editions Odile Jacob, Paris.

Serres, M. (1998) : Entretiens avec Michel Serres, le féminin au secours du vivant in *Le couple intérieur* (sous la direction de Paule Salomon), Albin Michel, Paris.

Sherraden, M., (1991): *Assets and the Poor: A New American Welfare Policy*, M.E. Sharpe Inc., Armonk, New York.

Sherwin, S. (1992): *No Longer Patient: Feminist Ethics and Health Care*, Temple University Press, Philadelphia, p.286.

Singer, C. (2007) : *Derniers fragments d'un long voyage*, éditions Albin Michel.

Viveret, P. (2005) : *Pourquoi ça ne va pas plus mal ?*, Éditions Fayard.

12

Recasting Human Development Indices: A Look into the State of Gender Empowerment in Karnataka

Sanjeev D Kenchaigol[1], [2]

I. INTRODUCTION

Ever since the launching planning in India, developmental interventions are generally gender neutral. The policies so framed keeping family in mind with the mistaken belief that the improvements in income and other social interventions would achieve equality between men and women by improving the quality of life within the family with equal measure.[3] Gradually it was discovered that the development strategies that targeted women's development overlooked patriarchal power relations, norms and traditions, hence failed to achieve the expected goals. Such development efforts did not contribute much to curb the gender bias in human development and emancipation of women.

---

[1] Center for Multi-disciplinary Development Research (CMDR), Dharwad, Karnataka, India, Email: sanjeevk_77@hotmail.com

[2] This paper constitutes a part of my PhD research work. My sincere thanks are due to my research guide Prof. Gopal K. Kadekodi for his valuable suggestions and guidance I obtained for this research. Thanks also due to Dr. Mihir Kumar Mahapatra and Dr. Rajesh Raj S N for their continued academic encouragement and support. I remain solely responsible for any errors in the text.

[3] For example see GoK, 1999; p.99.

Much of the gender literature has revealed that despite considerable achievements in terms of socio-economic and human development aspects, gender inequality, the emancipation and discrimination of women still continue to persist. This is true in developing countries as well as in most advanced countries of the world. The UNDP human development report, 1997 explicitly admits that no society treats its women on par with men (UNDP HDR, 1995 and 1997). The human development reports since 1990, more specifically the report that appeared in the year 1995, for the first time produced indicators of gender inequalities and gender empowerment in human development. A good number of studies have shown that there exist wide disparities in socio-economic, demographic and gender aspects of women's living conditions across the various states of India[4].

In the present paper, we analyse secondary data on the status of women in Karnataka in terms of their human and gender development perspectives. The existing literature reveals that women suffer from more inequalities in terms of their health, educational achievements, and their access to resources etc., as compared to their male counterparts. The existing data more explicitly reveal the persisting gender bias in important human capabilities in different districts of Karnataka. To take the discussion further, section 2 presents a brief profile of Karnataka, whereas section 3 overviews women's status with the human development perspective.

---

[4] For instance, see Agarwal, 1998 and Panda *et al*, 2005; for persisting gender inequalities in access to land holdings and property; see Batliwala, *et al* 1998; Vishwanathan, 2001; Rao, 2002; for gender inequalities and violence against women in case of rural Karnataka; consult UNDP HDR, 1995; Kamdar, 2007; Mitra *et al*, 2004; Rajivan, 1996; Jejeebhoy, 2000; GoK, 1999; 2005 among others for gender inequalities in human development; Sekher *et al*, 2004 and 2005; Kishore *et al*, 2004; for diverse demographic situations of women. For gender inequalities in human capabilities and functionings, see, Nussbaum, 2000; Alkire, 2003; Sen and Sengupta, 1983; Sen, 1985b; 1990c/2006; 1992; and 1999 among other contributions.

Section 4 discusses the methodological issues of the construction of district wise GEM index whereas the section 5 deals with different data sources. The analysis of the status of gender empowerment can be found in the sections 6 and 7, that respectively discuss the same both at disaggregate as well as aggregated levels. The final section provides some concluding remarks.

II. THE STATE OF KARNATAKA: A PROFILE

Karnataka state was formed on 1st November 1956 as a result of merger of five territories, inhabited by Kannada speaking people. These include four districts from erstwhile Bombay state; three districts of erstwhile princely state of Hyderbad; two districts and one sub district (taluka) from Madras state; the former part C state of Coorg (now, Kodagu) and the nine districts of the former princely state of Mysore. This (Kannada speaking) region was called as the Mysore state, and in the year 1973, Mysore state was rechristened as *Karnataka*. The state is divided into 27 districts [5] and 175 talukas (sub district units). The total geographical area of Karnataka is 192000 sq. km and is equal to 6.31 per cent of the nation's total geographic area[6].

III. STATUS OF WOMEN: A HUMAN DEVELOPMENT PERSPECTIVE

The human development perspective of gender well-being is well accepted universally and provides the backdrop for analysis in the present research. The Analysis of secondary data on prevailing gender status, hence, would serve more

---

[5] In the year 1997, the seven new districts were formed. These districts were Udupi (from Dakshina Kannada), Chamarajnagar (from Mysore), Koppal (from Raichur), Bagalkot (from Bijapur), Gadag and Haveri (from Dharwad), and Davanagere (from Chitradurga, Shimoga and Bellary). The Bangalore Urban district was created in 1986.

[6] See Karnataka Development Report, 2007, p. 43.

helpful for the understanding of macro-level picture of gender well being in Karnataka.

TABLE 1
HDI AND GDI FOR THE TOP 7 STATES, 2001

State	Value	HDI Rank	Value	GDI Rank
Kerala	0.746	1	0.724	1
Maharastra	0.706	2	0.693	2
Tamil Nadu	0.687	3	0.675	4
Punjab	0.679	4	0.676	3
Gujarat	0.655	5	0.642	5
Hryana	0.653	6	0.636	7
Karnataka	**0.650**	7	**0.637**	6
India	0.621		0.609	

Source: KHDR, 2005

Table 1 presents the list of top 7 states in terms of human development and gender well being for the year 2001. Among the Indian states, Karnataka represents the medium level performance with the 7th place in terms of human development and 6th place in terms of gender development.[7] The state portrays both the human development and gender development well above the national average. Kerala, the most developed state in India by social indicators, occupies the first place both in terms of human development as well as gender well-being. Maharastra acquired the second place in terms of both the indices, whereas Tamil Nadu stands third in terms of human development and fourth in terms of gender development. The northern state such as Punjab has a rank of third place for gender development, while the state of Gujarat occupies the fifth place in terms of both human development and gender advancement. Haryana overtook Karnataka in terms of human development with sixth rank and stood behind the former with the one point as far as gender development is concerned.

---

[7] For instance see, Karnataka Human Development Report 2005, p. 29.

TABLE 2
HDI FOR KARNATAKA, 2001 AND 1991

District	HDI 2001	HDI 1991	District	HDI 2001	HDI 1991
Bagalkot	0.591 (22)	0.505 (20)	Gulbarga	0.564 (26)	0.453 (25)
Bangalore Rural	0.653 (6)	0.539 (11)	Haveri	0.603 (20)	0.496 (22)
Bangalore Urban	0.753 (1)	0.623 (4)	Hassan	0.639 (11)	0.519 (16)
Belgaum	0.648 (8)	0.545 (9)	Kodagu	0.697 (4)	0.623 (3)
Bellary	0.617 (18)	0.512 (18)	Kolar	0.625 (17)	0.522 (15)
Bidar	0.599 (21)	0.496 (23)	Koppal	0.582 (24)	0.446 (26)
Bijapur	0.589 (23)	0.504 (21)	Mandya	0.609 (19)	0.511 (19)
Chamarajnagar	0.576 (25)	0.488 (24)	Mysore	0.631 (14)	0.524 (14)
Chitradurga	0.627 (16)	0.535 (13)	Raichur	0.547 (27)	0.443 (27)
Chikmagalur	0.647 (9)	0.559 (7)	Shimoga	0.673 (5)	0.584 (5)
Davanagere	0.635 (12)	0.548 (8)	Tumkur	0.63 (15)	0.539 (12)
Dakshina Kannada	0.722 (2)	0.661 (1)	Udupi	0.714 (3)	0.659 (2)
Dharwad	0.642 (10)	0.539 (10)	Uttara Kannada	0.653 (7)	0.567 (6)
Gadag	0.634 (13)	0.516 (17)	**State**	**0.650**	**0.541**

Note: Figures in parentheses indicate ranking of districts in terms of HDI and GDI performances

Source: KHDR, 2005, Appendix: Statistical Tables, p.330

Table 2 presents information on human development for all the districts of Karnataka for the two successive decadal years i.e., 2001 and 1991. Among the districts, it was the state capital Bangalore urban district that achieved the highest level of human development and ranked first in the year 2001. Dakshina Kannada district that possessed the first rank in terms of human development in 1991, stood at the second place for the year 2001 and Udupi occupied the third place. In the year 1991, Dakshina Kannada ranked the most developed district in terms human development while, Udupi and Kodugu respectively earned the second and third places in achieving human development. The districts that showed poor performances in human development belong to Hyderbad Karnataka region. Among these districts, Raichur ranked the lowest (27th rank) performing district for both the years, while Gulbarga, another backward district by socio-economic indicators possessed the 26th rank in the year 2001 and 25th in the year 1991. Koppal district, a part of erstwhile Raichur District, ranked 26th in the year 1991, whereas the southern district of Chamrajnagar, showed a poor performance in human development and ranked as 24th and 25th respectively for the years 1991 and 2001.

Overall, the Malenad and Coastal districts have shown an excellent attainment in terms of human development, particularly in 1990s, whereas the districts of Hyderabad Karnataka showed poor performance for the same year. In the successive decade, Bangalore urban showed the highest level of human development in Karnataka, while already well-performing districts showed a speedy pace in their performances for the year 2001.

IV. THE STATUS OF GENDER EMPOWERMENT IN KARNATAKA

With the advent of human development indices in development literature, the concepts of human development and gender development are well debated and universally accepted despite the persistence of some criticisms over them. As far as the concept of gender *empowerment* is concerned, the UNDP HDR, 1995 itself claimed that the GEM was not a prescriptive index at the local level since the indicators used in the index were supposed to reflect the extent of women's economic and political powers in the post industrialized societies. In this respect, the criticisms on the UNDP GEM were aimed at the proposition of empowerment indices that clearly reflect the local level social political and cultural settings and contexts. It is in this perspective with the backdrop of UNDP methodology; in this paper we construct a district level gender empowerment measure (GEM) for Karnataka using the micro–level indices to reflect the local level situations.

Methodology

The UNDP gender empowerment measure (GEM) is conceptually different from Gender-related Development Index (GDI). It examines whether women and men are able to actively participate in economic and political life and take part in decision making[8]. In other words, Instead of measuring gender inequality in human development, GEM measures the extent of gender equity in political and economic power and hence it measures not achievement in well-being but equity in *agency* (Bardhan and Klasen, 1999: 999). The computation of districtwise gender empowerment measure for Karnataka follows the methodology of UNDP HDR 1995 and the methodology of Karnataka human development report, 2005 for the computation of earned income for the different districts. Since the computation of GEM poses different data and methodological constraints for the local level, the essential

---

[8] As far as GDI is concerned, it focuses on the expansion of people's capabilities, while GEM concentrates on the use of those capabilities to achieve certain functionings. For the detailed look on GEM and GDI, see UNDP HDR, 1995, Chap. 3, pp. 72-86.

modifications in variable selection and computation have been made to reflect the micro level situations.

The UNDP HDR 1995 uses the following variables to compute the three important indices of GEM[9].

1. To reflect the economic participation and decision-making power, women's and men's percentage share of administrative and managerial positions and percentage shares of professional and technical jobs are used. Here the separate indices for each variable are calculated and then added them together.
2. The second variable chosen to reflect the political participation and decision-making power is women and men's percentage shares of parliamentary seats.
3. The third variable to reflect the power over economic resources is unadjusted real GDP per capita (PPP$).

It is claimed that UNDP GEM is not a prescriptive index since the existence of diverse geographical, social, cultural and political setting and norms around the world do not allow this index to fit a particular context (UNDP HDR, 1995; Mehta, 1996; and Bardhan and Klasen 1999 among others). According to the differing contexts, many studies have tried to construct the gender empowerment measure in India and elsewhere using the alternative indices but at the backdrop of UNDP methodology. Following the existing studies, using micro-level indices we propose to construct gender empowerment measure for Karnataka.

In case of Karnataka, to represent the UNDP GEM indices, the following variables have been chosen and indexed.

1. The Index of Political participation

Since the index is constructed at the district level, following Mehta (1996), the available indices such as Percentage of women's and men's share in Grama Panchayat (village level), Taluka Panchayat (block level) and Zilla

---

[9] For the methodological overview of the construction of GEM at the global level, see UNDP HDR, 1995, Technical note 2, pp. 132-33.

Panchayat (District level) were used to reflect women's political participation and decision-making in public life at the district level. In this perspective, UNDP index uses the share of professional, administrative, managerial and technical jobs. Due to data constraints we still rely on the former indices. To derive the equally distributed equivalent percentage (EDEP) [i.e., given society's aversion to gender inequality, the EDEP would be as socially valued as the actual unequal percentages of men and women] of both the females' and males' achievements, the parameter of social aversion to gender inequality [$1- \in$ (read as 1 minus epsilon)] is used and the value of $\in$ is set equal to 2. The UNDP methodology assumed that if there were gender equality, the EDEP would equal to 50%. The greater the disparity between female and male shares, the lower the EDEP will be relative to 50%. This is why the range of female and male achievements is kept between 0 (minimum) and 50% (maximum). After indexing, all three categories are added together, giving equal weight to each.

2. Knowledge and Decision making Index

As it is argued earlier, the present GEM index is constructed so as to reflect the local level context, the variables such as literacy to reflect the level of knowledge[10] and the percentage of female headed households to represent the decision making power of women in the households[11], have

---

[10] For instance, among others, Mehta (1996) uses the literacy variable to construct the GEM index at the national level, since it facilitates and enhances agency and empowerment.

[11] The studies such as Kabeer (1999), Karl (1995), among others showed that women's decision-making facilitates their empowerment and Bose, (2006) and Krishnan (2007) in their studies show the extent of female headed households in different districts of India. The Indian Population Census, 2001 defines *head of the household* (She or he) is generally the person who bears the chief responsibility for managing the affairs of the household and takes decision on behalf of the household. Thus, In female headed households females take all the decisions and responsibility of the household and hence claimed to be empowered on par with their male counterparts, for

been chosen to construct the knowledge and decision-making index. Since the available data indicates that in Karnataka, the Udupi district has a maximum of 35.00 percent female-headed households (Bose, 2006), it is assumed that 0 to be our minimum and 50.00 per cent to be the maximum value of male female shares in female headed households. This implies that if there exist higher-level gender inequality, the lesser will be this ratio relative 50.00 per cent. The same methodology has been used to derive the EDEP of female and male percentages with the same value of epsilon. According to the universal significance of literacy for its empowering capability, a 2/3 of weightage and 1/3 of weightage to the variable head of the households is given. At the final stage both the indices are added together to derive a combined knowledge and decision-making index.

3. Earned Income Index

The third and final variable that is used to reflect on power over economic resources is unadjusted real district GDP (PPP$) per capita. Unlike adjusted real GDP per capita that is used in UNDP HDI and GDI and ranges from $100 to $5,448, unadjusted real GDP per capita ranges from $100 to $40,000[12]. Since computation of earned income index for GEM follows the methodology of the GDI, the method to derive the per capita real district GDP for different districts in Karnataka is

---

instance, see Bose (2006) for how women heads of households in East Khasi Hills of Meghalaya with ancient matrilineal society are entitled with ownership of household property and Agarwal 1994/1998, for how women being heads of households empowered in different strata of life through having control over property in India as well as in South Asia.

[12] The UNDP HDI and GDI assume that the average world real GDP per capita $ 5,448 as the required amount of money needed to achieve one's human development or in other words, to afford the basic needs of life of a person and any income beyond this limit is assumed to have the diminishing marginal importance (utility) of additional income and hence is discounted downward. In case of GEM, the world average real GDP is left unadjusted since the latter index explains gender inequality in power over economic resources rather than in human development. For instance, see UNDP HDR, 1995.

adopted from Karnataka HDR, 2005. To arrive at the final index of earned income, we need to calculate female and male shares of earned income. To do this, the ratio of the average female wage to average male wage and the female and male percentage shares of economically active population aged 15 and above are calculated. In the context of Karnataka, the share of earned income is calculated by using the female and male agricultural wage rates since Karnataka's population is predominantly an agrarian (Mathew; 2003 and KHDR, 2005)[13]. The female and male work participation rate is taken as the percent of economically active population.

From the ratio of female to male wages, two ratios are derived[14]:
1. The ratio of the female wage to the overall average wage and
2. The ratio of the male wage to the overall average wage.

Second, multiplying the ratio of the average female wage to the overall average wage by the female share of economically active population derives an estimate of the female share of income. The male share is calculated in the same way or by subtracting the female share from 1.

In the third step, we estimate gender disparities in income by calculating the female and male shares of income as

---

[13] We follow the methodology of earned income index for GDI in Karnataka Human Development Report, 2005. For the methodology of GDI, see KHDR, 2005, pp 516-17.

[14] The following equations are drawn from UNDP HDR, 1995. These ratios are worked from the following definition of the total wage.

$$W = W_f L_f + W_m L_m,$$

Where W is the average wage and L is the total labour force, and the f subscript denotes female, the m subscript male. Dividing this equation through by $W_m L$, the ratio of average wage to male wage (W/W_m) is solved.

$$W/W_m = (W_f/W_m)(L_f/L) + (W_m/W_m)(L_m/L).$$

The reciprocal of this result is taken to solve for W_m/W

We can now solve for W_f/W : $\quad W_f/W = (W_f/W_m)/(W/W_m).$

proportion of female and male shares of population. The discounting for gender inequalities is done by forming two proportional income shares by dividing the female and male shares by the female and male shares of population. If there is gender equality, each proportional share is equal to 1. Then we derive the EDEP of earned income by applying the $(1-\in)$ averaging – with $\in$ equal to 2. The more gender inequality there is, the lower the ratio relative to 1. Next, we multiply the equally distributed proportional income share by the average unadjusted real district GDP per capita (PPP$) to derive a measure of GDP per capita, which would be discounted for gender inequality. We obtain the final income index by using the following formula.

$$Index = \frac{Actual\ Value - Minimum\ Value}{Maximum\ Value - Minimum\ Value}$$

In the final step we add all the three indices of earned income, political participation, and knowledge and decision-making and divide by 3. This gives the overall index of gender empowerment measure.

V. DATA SOURCES

The data sources for the construction of gender empowerment measure, basically sought from KHDR, 2005; Census 2001, PCA for Karnataka; HPCFRRI, final report, 2002; and Krishnan, (2007). The computation of gender empowerment index for all 27 districts possibly creates some constrains due to scarcity of required data. The needed data on different variables such as agricultural wage rates, female and male share of population, female and male work participation rates, share in Grama Panchayat, Taluka Panchayat and Zilla Panchayat, District GDP were available from the Karnataka human development report, 2005 for the year 2001. The data on literacy levels were availed from HPCFRRI, Final Report, 2002. The data on percent of female-headed households for the districts of Belgaum, Bangalore (Urban), Bidar, Kolar and Mandya were calculated using the data from Census 2001, and the data on rest of the districts were sourced from Krishnan (2007). The data on the district real GDP per capita (PPP$) were calculated by the author.

VI. ANALYSIS OF GENDER EMPOWERMENT AT THE DISAGGREGATE LEVEL

The indices used for the construction of gender empowerment measure include women's political participation, knowledge and household decision-making and economic participation. The gender empowerment status viewed in terms of these three indicators, and their respective ranks can be seen as follows.

Status of Women's Political Participation

In this section, the index of political participation follows the concept of women's political decision-making and participation in public life. This has been captured by using women's share in Grama Panchayat (Village level), Taluka Panchayat (Block level), and Zilla Panchayat (District level) so as to represent women's participation at the three levels. The combined index of political participation can be found in the Table 3. Among the districts that fared extremely well in terms of political decision-making are Dharwad, Chikmagalur, Gadag, Haveri and Bangalore urban districts that were respectively ranked as first, second, third, fourth and fifth. On the other hand, the districts that performed relatively poor include Bagalkot, Belgaum, Gulbarga, Udupi, Tumkur, Kodagu, Chamarajnagar and Chitradurga. Among these districts, Chamarajnagar and Chitradurga that are doing very poor and respectively ranked as 19th and 20th in terms of women's participation in political decision-making.

As the concept of empowerment bears the notion of power, political participation provides the greatest impetus for women for the possession of control over political power and decision-making in that arena. In this regard, women in the districts such as Dharwad are relatively enjoying more political powers and decision-making opportunities whereas women in the districts like Chitradurga lack these capabilities and opportunities. This can also be seen in the Figure 1.

TABLE 3
INDEX AND RANKING OF POLITICAL PARTICIPATION, 2001

District	Political Participation Index Value	Rank	District	Political Participation Index Value	Rank
Bagalkot	0.956	18	Gulbarga	0.960	17
Bangalore Rural	0.972	10	Haveri	0.981	4
Bangalore Urban	0.980	5	Hassan	0.965	14
Belgaum	0.956	18	Kodagu	0.956	18
Bellary	0.968	11	Kolar	0.974	9
Bidar	0.974	9	Koppal	0.966	13
Bijapur	0.974	9	Mandya	0.967	12
Chamarajnagar	0.933	19	Mysore	0.968	11
Chitradurga	0.922	20	Raichur	0.961	15
Chikmagalur	0.987	2	Shimoga	0.977	7
Davanagere	0.974	9	Tumkur	0.961	15
Dakshina Kannada	0.978	6	Udupi	0.961	15
Dharwad	0.995	1	Uttara Kannada	0.976	8
Gadag	0.984	3	**State**	**0.972**	

Source: Author's Calculation

Index of Knowledge and Decision-making

As it is quite evident from the literature that 'literacy' acts as an extreme source of empowerment. Even though the UNDP GEM index does not include this indicator, but gives way to use the micro-level indicators to measure the state of empowerment which women enjoy. Apart from the variable literacy, the variable percentage of female-headed households was used to measure the extent of women's household decision-making in the context of intra-household power relations. The combined index has been derived by giving a 1/3 weight for variable female-headed households and a 2/3 weight for the variable literacy.

Figure. 1. Political Participation Index

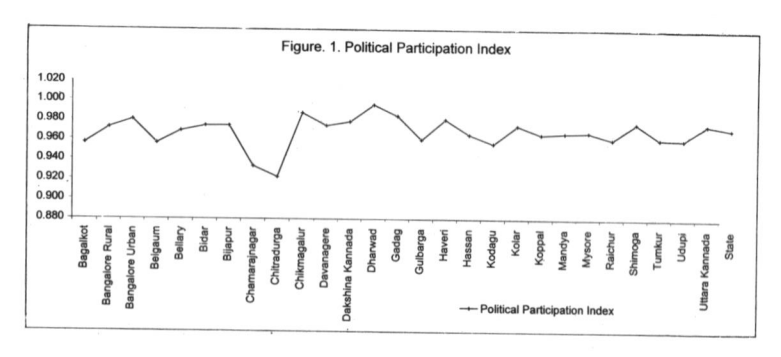

Table 4 presents the level of women's knowledge and decision-making. As far as this index is concerned, women show good performances in the regions where the human development indices are stronger. As studies show that the female-headed households in Karnataka are more centered in Udupi and Dakshina Kannada and the relative achievements in literacy rates can also be seen in highly developed districts by human development indicators. From Table 4, it is more evident that in terms of knowledge and decision-making index, the districts such as Udupi, Dakshina Kannada, and Uttara Kannada respectively with the index values of 0.828, 0.777 and 0.687 show the significant achievements, while Belgaum, Bidar and Mandya, among other districts observed poor status of knowledge and decision-making.

Figure 2 reveals the state of knowledge and decision-making in different districts of Karnataka. As it is mentioned earlier, the combined index particularly goes stronger with the high human development achievements. Women who are basically heads of the households tend to take the whole responsibility of the family and hence play an important role in managing the household matters. This gives way to women to exercise their choices and decision-making in the households.

TABLE 4
INDEX AND RANKING OF KNOWLEDGE AND DECISION-MAKING, 2001

District	Knowledge and Decision-making Index Value	Rank	District	Knowledge and Decision-making Index Value	Rank
Bagalkot	0.538	18	Gulbarga	0.466	23
Bangalore Rural	0.589	13	Haveri	0.597	10
Bangalore Urban	0.568	16	Hassan	0.594	11
Belgaum	0.426	24	Kodagu	0.684	4
Bellary	0.556	17	Kolar	0.425	25
Bidar	0.404	27	Koppal	0.523	19
Bijapur	0.517	20	Mandya	0.408	26
Chamarajnagar	0.509	21	Mysore	0.583	14
Chitradurga	0.571	15	Raichur	0.482	22
Chikmagalur	0.626	7	Shimoga	0.647	5
Davanagere	0.602	9	Tumkur	0.592	12
Dakshina Kannada	0.777	2	Udupi	0.828	1
Dharwad	0.639	6	Uttara Kannada	0.687	3
Gadag	0.607	8	**State**	**0.585**	

Source: Author's Calculation

Figure 2 Knowledge and Decision-making Index

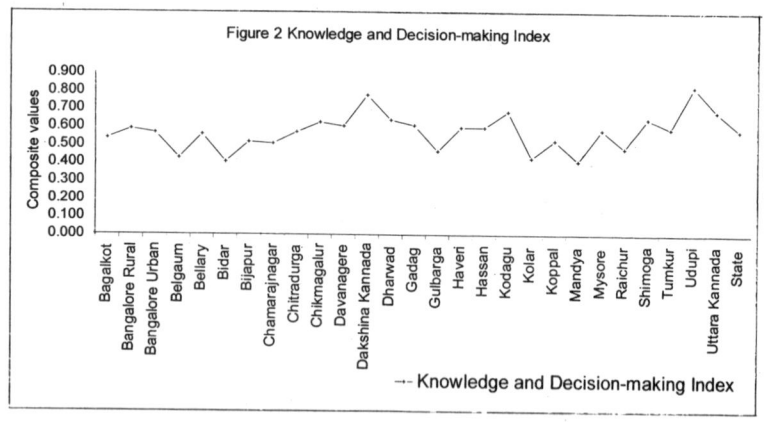

Bose (2007) presents the information of the Khasi women in Meghalaya who are entitled with the traditional headship of the households and they are equally empowered on par with men. In this respect, the combined index will show the better index of empowerment for the districts, which have relatively good status of gender equality in terms of decision-making.

This is quite visible in Figure 2. The districts that show the poor performance are relatively more patriarchal societies as well as low literate districts for women.

Index of Earned Income

For the construction of combined index of gender empowerment the variable of 'earned income' was considered as one of the components since it has the potentials of economic power for women to exercise their choices. Several studies pertaining to economic empowerment of women, endorse micro-credit as an empowering strategy.

In this perspective, male and female agricultural wage rates were used as the source of their incomes since the Karnataka economy is basically an agrarian. Table 5 provides the information on female share of earned income.

TABLE 5
INDEX AND RANKING OF EARNED INCOME, 2001

District	Earned Income Index Value	Rank	District	Earned Income Index Value	Rank
Bagalkot	0.046	12	Gulbarga	0.032	18
Bangalore Rural	0.071	4	Haveri	0.041	15
Bangalore Urban	0.089	2	Hassan	0.046	12
Belgaum	0.048	10	Kodagu	0.087	3
Bellary	0.056	7	Kolar	0.043	13
Bidar	0.025	19	Koppal	0.042	14
Bijapur	0.038	16	Mandya	0.038	16
Chamarajnagar	0.036	17	Mysore	0.043	13
Chitradurga	0.046	12	Raichur	0.032	18
Chikmagalur	0.057	6	Shimoga	0.051	8
Davanagere	0.042	14	Tumkur	0.041	15
Dakshina Kannada	0.097	1	Udupi	0.062	5
Dharwad	0.047	11	Uttara Kannada	0.050	9
Gadag	0.051	8	**State**	**0.051**	

Source: Author's Calculation

The scenario of women's economic empowerment in different regions in Karnataka is more or less equal to the human development situations. From Table 5 it would be clear that the districts like Dakshina Kannada, Bangalore urban, Kodagu and Bangalore rural have better levels of earned income resources and have been ranked respectively as first, second, third, and fourth among the 27 districts. These better performing districts show better economic situations for women as compared to the poor performing districts such as Bidar, Gulbarga and Raichur that belong to basically backward region of Hyderabad Karnataka. In the former regions, women are just marginal workers and the economy has not generated full employment for them, which relegates them relatively poorer category if we compare to either Bombay Karnataka region or south Karnataka.

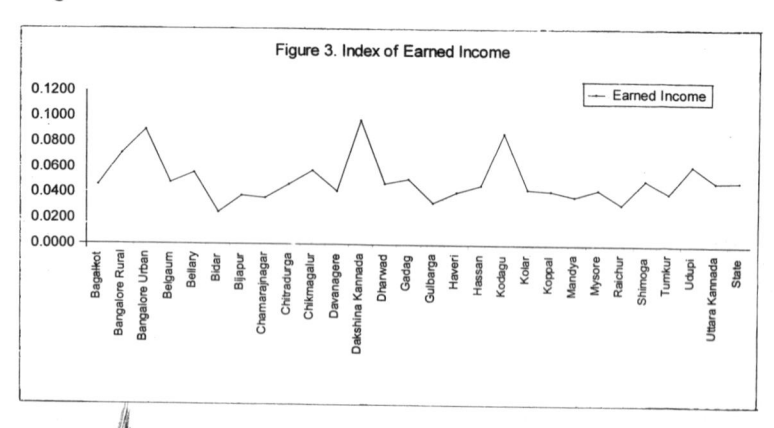

Figure 3. Index of Earned Income

The trends in women's economic situations can also be viewed from Figure 3. The presence of women in marginal work force and agricultural wage laborers render them unequal share in economic resources, and finally resulting in feminization of poverty (KHDR, 2005), whereas women in the household industries, show better economic situations and belong to the south and the coastal regions of Karnataka, which are predominantly well developed by social indicators.

Another important aspect that determines economic situations is the differential and trend in agricultural wage rates. We have already discussed that there always persist gender discrimination in division of labour and wage differentials. As Karnataka Human Development Report, 2005, concludes, in both absolute and relative terms, the gap in female and male wages increased sharply, providing one more reason to conclude that female workers have fared worse than their male counterparts during the decade (Ibid, p. 180). These differences were starker in Bidar, Gulbarga and Koppal, where male wage rates were two times more than that of females.

These trends determine the relative position of women in terms of their economic autonomy in the households as against their male counterparts and even render comparative insights over their female counterparts in different regions of Karnataka.

TABLE 6
COMBINED INDEX AND RANKING OF GENDER EMPOWERMENT MEASURE, 2001

District	Combined GEM Index Value	Rank	District	Combined GEM Index Value	Rank
Bagalkot	0.513	15	Gulbarga	0.486	20
Bangalore Rural	0.544	9	Haveri	0.540	10
Bangalore Urban	0.546	8	Hassan	0.535	12
Belgaum	0.477	22	Kodagu	0.576	2
Bellary	0.527	14	Kolar	0.481	21
Bidar	0.467	24	Koppal	0.510	16
Bijapur	0.509	17	Mandya	0.471	23
Chamarajnagar	0.493	18	Mysore	0.531	13
Chitradurga	0.513	15	Raichur	0.492	19
Chikmagalur	0.557	6	Shimoga	0.558	5
Davanagere	0.539	11	Tumkur	0.531	13
Dakshina Kannada	0.617	1	Udupi	0.617	1
Dharwad	0.561	4	Uttara Kannada	0.571	3
Gadag	0.547	7	State	0.536	

Source: Author's Calculation

VII. ANALYSIS OF GENDER EMPOWERMENT AT THE AGGREGATE LEVEL

Even though, the methodology used for the construction of gender empowerment measure (GEM) for

Karnataka has been adopted from the UNDP HDR, 1995, the micro-level indices included in the index provide useful insights on the overall picture of the extent of women's autonomy or state of empowerment relative to men. In the earlier discussion, we saw a disaggregated picture of women's empowerment in terms of their political participation, knowledge and decision-making status and their state of economic situations separately. In this index these three indicators are averaged to derive a combined GEM index at the district level.

The overall scenario of the gender empowerment, after getting an aggregated index, completely differs as Dharwad district that ranked 10th in terms of human development, achieves a gender empowerment rank of 4th. Obviously, women from the districts such as Dakshina Kannada, Udupi, Kodagu, Uttara Kannada, Shimoga, Chikmagalur, Gadag, Bangalore urban and Bangalore Rural are more empowered relative to their counterparts in Bidar, Mandya, Belguam, Gulbarga Raichur, Chamarajnagar, and Koppal among other districts, which showed relatively poor performances.

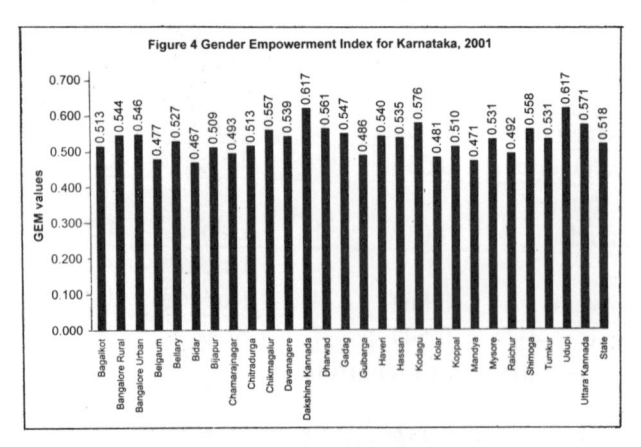

Figure 4 Gender Empowerment Index for Karnataka, 2001

District	GEM
Bagalkot	0.513
Bangalore Rural	0.544
Bangalore Urban	0.546
Belgaum	0.477
Bellary	0.527
Bidar	0.467
Bijapur	0.509
Chamarajnagar	0.493
Chitradurga	0.513
Chikmagalur	0.557
Davanagere	0.539
Dakshina Kannada	0.617
Dharwad	0.561
Gadag	0.547
Gulbarga	0.486
Haveri	0.540
Hassan	0.535
Kodagu	0.576
Kolar	0.481
Koppal	0.471
Mandya	0.510
Mysore	0.531
Raichur	0.492
Shimoga	0.558
Tumkur	0.531
Udupi	0.617
Uttara Kannada	0.571
State	0.518

Among the districts that showed the medium level performances include Haveri, Davanagere, Hassan, Mysore, Bellary, and Bagalkot. Figure 4 more clearly presents the status of gender empowerment among the districts. One important aspect of human development is that the persistence of inequalities in terms of gender empowerment. Traditionally high-developed districts by social indicators again fared excellent in this respect, whereas the districts from backward regions still lag behind. Belgaum district that fared well in terms of HDI and GDI has been included with districts that belong to Hyderabad Karnataka region due to its poorer performance in gender empowerment. Despite the high level of human development in certain districts, the status of gender empowerment is just poor. This can be observed in the districts such as Bangalore urban, Belgaum, Hassan and Bangalore rural, which reveal that the state of human development and gender empowerment never go hand in hand. Among the districts that achieved relatively high level of gender equality, such as Dakshina Kannada, Uttara Kannada and malenad region of Kodagu present relatively better status of gender empowerment. But the achievements are not evenly distributed, which infers that the concept of gender empowerment entirely differs from human development and registered high level of achievements in the regions, where women predominantly involve in political and economic decision-making.

VIII. CONCLUSIONS

In this chapter we analyzed the secondary data pertaining to women's status in Karnataka, with respect to the human development perspectives that included gender development and gender empowerment. The two human development reports that were prepared for Karnataka in the year 1999 and 2005 provided very indispensable insights on the human development as well as gender development aspects of population in Karnataka. Karnataka was second state in India after Madhya Pradesh, to initiate state level human development reports since 1999.

The two subsequent human development reports provided rich insights on micro-level information on human well-being and gender development at the district levels (but not on the state of gender empowerment).

These insights further contributed for the numerous micro-level studies on human development aspects as well as gender empowerment. Further Gender empowerment measure (GEM) index for districts of Karnataka were constructed and analysed, since the foremost purpose of this study is to understand the status of female empowerment in Karnataka.

As far as the human development, gender development and gender empowerment are concerned, women still are suffering with patriarchy and male dominance in exercising individual choices.

The second Human Development Report of Karnataka presents the clearer picture of persisting gender inequalities, particularly in Raichur, Gulbarga, Koppal and Chamrajnagar. Apart from this, regional disparities in gender development can also be found in the state.

The district wise gender empowerment measure (GEM) index provides an excellent idea of persisting disparities in gender empowerment. The persisting gender disparities in human development and gender empowerment create a context for the micro-level research for further understanding of the nature and trends in gender inequalities and the status of women's empowerment.

REFERENCES

Agarwal, Bina (1994/1998): *A Field of One's Own: Gender and Land Rights in South Asia,* Cambridge University Press, New York.

Alkire, Sabina (2002/3): Valuing Freedoms: Sen's Capability Approach and Poverty Reduction, Oxford University Press, Oxford (Indian Reprint 2003, OUP, Delhi).

Bardhan, Kaplana and Klasen, S. (1999): UNDP Gender-Related Indices: A Critical Review, *World Development*, 27 (6): 985-1010.

Batliwala, Srilatha, Anitha, B. K., Gurumurthy, A. and Wali, C. S. (1998): *Status of Rural Women in Karnataka*, National Institute of Advanced Studies (NIAS), Bangalore.

Bose Ashish (2006): Where Women Prevail, *Economic and Political Weekly*, 41(22): 2192-94.

Government of India (2001): Census of India 2001.

Government of Karnataka (GoK) (2005): *Karnataka Human Development Report 2005*, Bangalore.

GoK, (1999): *Human Development in Karnataka*, Bangalore.

Jejeebhoy, Shireen (2000): Women's Autonomy in Rural India: Its Dimensions, Determinants and the Influence of Context, in Harriet B Presser and Gita Sen (eds.), *Women's Empowerment and Demographic Processes: Moving Beyond Cairo*, Oxford University Press, New York, pp. 204-238.

Kabeer Naila (1999): Resources, Agency, Achievements: Reflections on the Measurement of Women's Empowerment, *Development and Change*, 30(3): 435-464.

Mitra, T.K. and Sinha, G. (2005): Women Empowerment and Human Development in India, *Indian Economic Review*, December, 47 (3): 351-366.

Karl Marilee (1995): *Women Empowerment: Participation and Decision-Making,* Zed Books Ltd., London.

Rajivan, A. K. (1996): Measurement of Gender Differences Using Anthropometry, *Economic and Political Weekly,* 31(43): WS-58-62.

Kishore, Sunita and Gupta, K. (2004): Women's Empowerment in India and Its States: Evidence from the NFHS, *Economic and Political Weekly,* 39(7): 694-712.

Krishan, Gopal (2007): Map Series 10—India: Female Headed Households - 2001, *Man and Development,* 29 (3): 161-172.

Mathew, Joseph (2003): Performance of Southern States: A Comparative Study, *Economic and Political Weekly,* 38(37): 3915 – 30.

Mehta, Asha Kapur (1996): Recasting Indices for Developing Countries: A Gender Empowerment Measure', *Economic and Political Weekly,* 21(43): 80-86.

Nussbaum, Martha C (2000): *Women and Human development: A Capabilities Approach,* Kali for Women, New Delhi.

Panda, Pradeep and Agarwal, Bina (2005): *Marital Violence, Human Development and Women's Property Status in India,* Working Paper Series No. E/256/2005, Institute of Economic Growth (IEG), New Delhi.

Planning Commission (2007): *Karnataka Development Report,* Govt. of India, New Delhi.

Rao, Vijayendra (1998/2002): Wife-Abuse, its causes, and its impact on Intra-Household Resource Allocation in Rural

Karnataka, in Krishnaraj Maithreyi, Ratna M Sudarshan and Abusaleh Shariff (Eds), *Gender, Population and Development*, Oxford India Paperbacks, New Delhi.

Sekher, T. V, and Raju, K.N.M. (2004): Fertility Transition in Karnataka, *Social and Economic Change Monograph Series*, No. 5. ISEC, Bangalore.

Sekher, T. V, Raju, K. N. V. and Sivakumar, M. N. (2005): Fertility Transition in Karnataka: Levels, Trends and Implications, in Guilmoto, C. Z and S. Irudaya Rajan (eds.), *Fertility Transition in South India*, Sage Publications, New Delhi. Pp. 137-166.

Sen, Amartya and Sengupta, Sunil (1983): 'Malnutrition of Rural Children and the Sex Bias', *Economic and Political Weekly*, 18(19-21): 885-864.

Sen, Amartya Kumar (1985b/1999): *Commodities and Capabilities*, Amsterdam: North Holland. Reprinted by Oxford University Press, New Delhi.

Sen, Amartya Kumar (1992): *Inequality Reexamined*, Oxford India Paperbacks, and New Delhi. Reprinted in 1999.

Sen, Amartya Kumar (1999): *Development as Freedom*, Oxford India Paperbacks, New Delhi.

United Nations Development Program (1995): *Human Development Report, 1995*, Oxford University Press, New Delhi, for UNDP.

United Nations Development Program (1997): *Human Development Report, 1997*, Oxford University Press, New Delhi, for UNDP.

Vishvanathan, Renuka (2001): Development, Empowerment and domestic Violence: Karnataka Experience, *Economic and Political Weekly,* 36(24): 2173-77.

13

Human Development in Orissa: An Inter-District Analysis from the Perspective of Infrastructure

Amar Kumar Mohanty[1], Narayan C Nayak[2], Bani Chatterjee[3]

I. INTRODUCTION

Over time, various alternative approaches have been developed as markers of development viz. growth approach, human resource development approach, welfare approach and basic needs approach. Economic growth models primarily emphasize on expanding the country's Gross National Product (GNP) rather than enhancing the quality of human lives. Human resource development approach, on the contrary, treats human beings as a means of production. Welfare approaches, however, consider human beings as beneficiaries and not as agents of change in the development process. The basic needs approach, which may be considered as an advancement over the welfare approach, focuses on providing material goods and

---

[1] Department of HSS, Indian Institute of Technology (IIT), Kharagpur, India, Email: amar@hss.iitkgp.ernet.in.
[2] Department of HSS, Indian Institute of Technology (IIT), Kharagpur, India, E-mail: ncnayak@hss.iitkgp.ernet.in.
[3] Department of HSS, Indian Institute of Technology (IIT), Kharagpur, India, Email: bani@hss.iitkgp.ernet.in.

services to the deprived rather than on enlarging human choices in all fields (UNDP, 1995).

Since the early 1990s, the human development approach has, however, occupied the centre stage. Encompassing the earlier concerns, human development goes beyond them. This approach analyses from people's perspective all issues that pertain to a society's development including employment, income, health, education, political freedom, culture and the like. Primarily, this approach focuses on enlarging people's choices and raising their living standards. The basic purpose of human development is to create an enabling environment for people to enjoy long, healthy and creative life (UNDP, 1995). It applies unequivocally to both developing and developed countries alike.

Since the inception of the concept of human development in 1990 by UNDP in its first Human Development Report (HDR) (UNDP, 1990), human development has emerged not only as a measure of development but also as a development paradigm (Hirway and Mahadevia, 2004). Further, it assumes importance for the basic reason that income alone is not always a satisfactory measure of welfare as there is no automatic relationship between rate of growth of GNP and improvement in quality of life (Morris and McAlpin, 1982; Mazumdar, 1990).

There are four major elements encompassed in the concept of human development namely productivity, equity, sustainability and empowerment. To illustrate further, people must be enabled to increase their productivity and participate fully in the process of income generation; they must have access to equal opportunities so as to garner maximum benefit; access to opportunities must be ensured not only for the present generation but also for future generations, and development process should be people-oriented and all-inclusive (UNDP, 1995). To be more specific, human development embraces two sides: formation of human capability on the one side and productive use of the acquired capability on the other. It is imperative that both the sides are closely balanced (UNDP, 1995).

The HDR ranks countries on the basis of composite index, popularly known as human development index (HDI). It also computes other indices such as Human Poverty Index (HPI), Gender Development Index (GDI), and Technology Advancement Index (TAI) for most of the countries in the world (UNDP, 2007). In line with the approaches as developed by UNDP on human development, India brought out its first National Human Development Report (NHDR) 2001 (GOI, 2002). Some states including Orissa have also published their respective HDRs by undertaking studies at the sub-aggregate levels[4]. Besides, several independent studies have attempted to construct HDIs (Kumar, 1991; Prabhu and Chatterjee, 1993; Malgavakar, 1994) at the country level taking states as the units of analysis.

Needless to say, although there are studies on human development in India, studies at the sub-aggregate level taking districts as the units of analysis are very few in number. Moreover, an analysis of the extent of human development at the district level in the state of Orissa and its possible implications is seldom found in development literature. Orissa Human Development Report, 2006 provides information about the state of human development in Orissa across its districts. However, it does not draw implications of the findings. Thus, the present study is an attempt to examine not only the level of human development in Orissa at the aggregate level but also the variations in its nature and magnitude across the districts of the state. It also attempts to ascertain the possible causes of such variations while analyzing from the perspective of the availability of socio-economic infrastructure. Three different periods, namely 1993-94, 1997-98 and 2003-04, are

---

[4] See Orissa Human Development Report, 2004, Government of Orissa.

considered to elicit the changes, if any, in the level of human development in the state and its constituent districts.

Accordingly, the paper is organized into five different sections. In section II, database and methodology of the study are outlined. Section III presents the level of human development in Orissa and its constituent districts. In section IV, possible reasons of low and unequal human development across regions of Orissa are ascertained from the perspective of infrastructure. Section V concludes the findings.

II. DATABASE AND METHODOLOGY

The study is based on secondary data as collected from various published sources. The major sources include Census of India (Orissa), National Sample Survey Organization (NSSO), National Family and Health Survey (I and II), HDRs, Sample Registration Systems and District Statistical Handbooks of Orissa.

As successive HDRs suggest, the HDI is a summary measure of human development (UNDP, 2007). It measures accurately the average achievements in a country or a state or at any other sub-aggregate level in three basic dimensions of human development. Those are (i) a long and healthy life as measured by life expectancy at birth; (ii) knowledge as measured by adult literacy rate (with 2/3 weight) and the enrollment ratio (with 1/3 weight); and (iii) a decent standard of living as measured by GDP per capita (PPP US$).

In line with the above approach, the present study computes the indices for health, education and income and accordingly, chooses minimum and maximum values as follows:

1. Health Index

In the present study, due to paucity of data at district level on life expectancy at birth, infant mortality rate is taken to compute the health index. Infant Mortality Rates with maximum and minimum values respectively for three different periods as chosen for the study are 166 and 22 for 1993-94,

170 and 14 for 1997-98, and 146 and 6 for 2003-04. The chosen values represent the maximum and minimum values as prevalent during the periods under study. The data on infant mortality rate are taken from Sample Registration System (SRS) and the estimates built up by the International Institute of Population Sciences (IIPS), Mumbai.

2. Educational Index

Adult literacy rate is taken from Census of India and NSSO; and enrolment ratio for children between 6-14 years of age is taken from National Family Health Survey I and II.

3. Income Index

The income index is calculated using adjusted Gross Domestic Product (GDP) per capita (PPP US$). Income index = log Xi – log (100) / log (40000) – log (100)

In order to construct the HDI, the first step is to compute the component indices. The indicators are made scale-free for this purpose by applying the following formula:

$$I_{ij} = X_{ij} - \min X_{ij} / \max X_{ij} - \min X_{ij}$$

where I_{ij} is the factor score for the jth district with respect to i^{th} variable. 'Min' and 'Max' are minimum and maximum goal posts selected for the indicator. Then, the overall HDI (I_j for j^{th} district) is worked out by aggregating the component indices and dividing it by total number of indices.

i.e. $$I_j = \sum_{i=1}^{n} I_{ij} / \sum_{i=1}^{n} i$$

To put it otherwise, HDI = 1/3 (Life expectancy Index +Educational Index +Income Index). On the basis of the above procedures, composite index of human development is constructed for all the 30 districts of Orissa to elicit the regional patterns of human development in the state. In order to construct the composite index, the data for 1993-94, 1997-98 and 2003-04 are taken into consideration.

Further, principal component analysis (PCA) is used to prepare the composite index of infrastructure. The principal component is based on the covariance matrix of the relevant variables and literally weighted average of underlying variables.

PCA is used because it gives mathematical weight in a purely objective manner and provides solution to the problem of multicollinearity. This method aims to construct a set of variables, X_J's ... (j = 1, 2, 3...k) of new variables (P_i) called 'principal components' which are linear combinations of the X's (Koutsoyiannis, 2001). The present study uses the first principal component only. The first principal component is that linear combination of weighted variables, which captures the highest proportion of the variance in the original variables. Thus,

$$P_i = \frac{\sum a_{ij} X_{ij}}{\sigma_{X_{ij}}} = \sum a_{ij} Z_{ij}$$, where i indicate the variables

$Z_{ij} = \frac{X_{ij}}{\sigma_{Xij}}$ is the standardized i^{th} variable for j^{th} district. $\sigma_{X_{ij}}$ is the standard deviation of X_{ij}. a_{ij} is the factor loading for j^{th} variables as included in constructing the first principal component for i^{th} variables.

Following indicators under economic and social infrastructure are chosen for analysis:

INDICATORS	UNIT OF MEASUREMENT
Transport:	Road length in the district per 100 sq km area
Communication	Number of telephones per lakh population; and Number of post offices per lakh population.
Power	Percentage of villages electrified
Irrigation	Irrigated area as a percentage of net sown area
Banking	Number of commercial bank branches per lakh population; and Number of cooperative societies per lakh population
Education	Number of schools per lakh population; and Teacher-student ratio in the schools
Health	Number of hospitals and dispensaries (Allopathic, Homeopathic and Ayurvedic) per lakh population; Number of doctors per lakh population; Number of hospital beds per lakh population; and Percentage of villages with drinking water facilities

III. HUMAN DEVELOPMENT IN ORISSA AND ITS CONSTITUENT DISTRICTS

Over the years, amongst the major states of the country, Orissa has remained not only one of the poorest states but also it has experienced abysmally low human development having consistently fallen amongst the lowest five states of the country. As per the NHDR, 2001 (GOI, 2002), although there was improvement in its HDI from a low of 0.267 in 1981 to a high of 0.404 in 2001, Orissa still maintained its position at 11th amongst 15 major states. During 2001, the only other four states which had remained below Orissa were Madhya Pradesh followed by Uttar Pradesh, Assam and Bihar (see Table 1). The present study, considering the period 1993-94 to 2003-04, also provides similar trend in the level of human development for Orissa. The value of HDI for the state as a whole was 0.3603 in 1993-94, which increased to 0.4382 in 1997-98 and further to 0.4732 in 2003-04 (see figure 1). Orissa, thus, still remains a least developed state in terms of its human development.

The scenario of the districts within the state is far more precarious. Considering the situation since 1993-94, it is found that while neither of the districts attained the level of medium human development in 1993-94, as many as 21 districts were still having low human development in 1997-98, which marginally fell to 18 in 2003-04. Amongst the districts that attained medium human development, most of them had just surpassed the previous levels. Kendrapara was the only district that attained a value of HDI little above 0.6. However, it could not maintain that status in 2003-04. During this period, Jharsuguda improved its position and became the only district with HDI little above 0.6, thanks to its rapid industrialization (see Tables 2, 3 and 4).

The inter-district relative disparity in terms of attainment of human development has remained unchanged over the entire study period as evident from the coefficients of variations[5].

TABLE 1
HUMAN DEVELOPMENT INDEX IN MAJOR STATES OF INDIA

States	1981	1991	2001
Andhra Pradesh	0.298(9)	0.377(9)	0.416(10)
Assam	0.272(10)	0.348(10)	0.386(14)
Bihar	0.237(15)	0.308(15)	0.367(15)
Gujarat	0.360(4)	0.431(6)	0.479(6)
Haryana	0.360(5)	0.443(5)	0.509(5)
Karnataka	0.346(6)	0.412(7)	0.478(7)
Kerala	0.500(1)	0.591(1)	0.638(1)
Madhya Pradesh	0.245(14)	0.328(13)	0.394(12)
Maharashtra	0.363(3)	0.452(4)	0.523(4)
Orissa	**0.267(11)**	**0.345(12)**	**0.404(11)**
Punjab	0.411(2)	0.475(2)	0.537(2)
Rajasthan	0.256(12)	0.347(11)	0.424(9)
Tamil Nadu	0.343(7)	0.466(3)	0.531(3)
Uttar Pradesh	0.255(13)	0.314(14)	0.388(13)
West Bengal	0.305(8)	0.404(8)	0.472(8)
All India	0.302	0.381	0.472

Note: Figures in Parentheses are HDI ranks in descending order.
Source: Government of India (2002)

This suffices the fact that no matter how insignificant the level of improvement that the districts have attained over the years, that has been by and large uniform. There persist inequalities across districts in any single period considered for study. This necessitates a further probe through clustering of

---

[5] The coefficient of variation has been computed for the three periods separately using HDI values of all the districts of Orissa. The computed value is 0.19 in each period.

the districts in terms of their relative status. The latter may help us understand the actual scenario in various regions and in turn, require differentiated intervention strategies (see Tables 2, 3 and 4).

TABLE 2
DISTRIBUTION OF DISTRICTS BY HDI VALUES FOR THE PERIOD 1993-94

Districts	HDI Value ≤ 0.5	Rank	Districts	HDI Value ≤ 0.5	Rank
Balasore	0.3725	17	Nuapada	0.2703	27
Bhadrak	0.3806	16	Puri	0.3302	20
Balangir	0.3822	15	Rayagada	0.3054	23
Boudh	0.3659	18	Sonepur	0.289	25
Gajapati	0.2937	24	Angul	0.435	3
Ganjam	0.3926	12	Bargarh	0.4064	9
Kalahandi	0.2678	28	Cuttack	0.4238	4
Kandhamal	0.2311	30	Deogarh	0.4002	11
Keonjhar	0.3914	13	Dhenkanal	0.4210	6
Khurda	0.3514	19	Jagatsinghpur	0.4372	2
Koraput	0.3156	21	Jajpur	0.4117	8

Source: Calculated by the authors

FIGURE 1

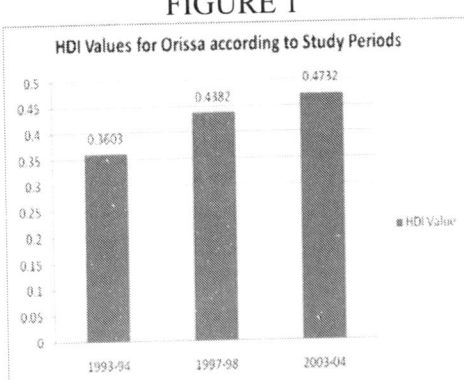

HDI Values for Orissa according to Study Periods

- 1993-94: 0.3603
- 1997-98: 0.4382
- 2003-04: 0.4732

Source: Calculated by the authors

TABLE 3
DISTRIBUTION OF DISTRICTS BY HDI VALUES FOR THE PERIOD 1997-98

Districts	HDI Value ≤ 0.5	Rank	Districts	HDI Value ≥ 0.5 < 0.8	Rank
Gajapati	0.2983	27	Angul	0.5084	9
Kandhamal	0.2526	29	Bhadrak	0.5253	8
Keonjhar	0.3965	24	Cuttack	0.5516	4
Koraput	0.2799	28	Deogarh	0.5402	6
Malkangiri	0.2446	30	Jharsuguda	0.5569	3
Nabarangpur	0.3111	25	Khurda	0.5711	2
Rayagada	0.3004	26	Puri	0.5284	7
Balasore	0.4509	14	Sundargarh	0.5428	5
Bargarh	0.4376	16	Kendrapara	0.6049	1
Balangir	0.4199	21			
Boudh	0.4054	22			
Dhenkanal	0.4352	18			
Ganjam	0.4030	23			
Jagatsinghpur	0.4256	19			
Jajpur	0.4371	17			
Kalahandi	0.4885	11			
Mayurbhanj	0.4989	10			
Nayagarh	0.4533	13			
Nuapada	0.4620	12			
Sambalpur	0.4494	15			
Sonepur	0.4251	20			

Source: Calculated by the authors

Considering the period 1993-94, it is found that Sundargarh topped the list followed by Jagatsinghpur, Angul, Cuttack and Sambalpur. On the other hand, Kandhamal followed by Nabarangpur, Kalahandi, Nuapada and Malkangiri were the five least developed districts in the same period whose HDI values were abysmally low that varied between 0.231 and 0.286. In 2003-04, Jharsuguda was ranked first in terms of human development followed by Angul, Jagatsinghpur, Khurda and Sundargarh. Kendrapara, which had been ranked first in 1997-98, was relegated to the 6th position in 2003-04, while Cuttack was relegated to 9th and Sambalpur was further down to 11th. At the other extreme, Malkangiri was the worst performer followed by Nabarangpur, Koraput, Rayagada and Kandhamal. Although Kalahandi and Malkangiri were found to have outperformed a few other districts, their levels of human development were still very low and thus, they occupied 24th and 23rd positions respectively.

TABLE 4
DISTRIBUTION OF DISTRICTS BY HDI VALUES FOR THE PERIOD 2003-04

Districts	HDI Value ≤ 0.5	Rank	Districts	HDI Value ≥ 0.5 < 0.8	Rank
Gajapati	0.3739	25	Angul	0.5675	2
Kalahandi	0.3879	24	Balasore	0.5063	12
Kandhamal	0.3724	26	Bargarh	0.5159	7
Koraput	0.3633	28	Cuttack	0.5115	9
Malkangiri	0.3482	30	Jagatsinghpur	0.5452	3
Nabarangpur	0.3548	29	Jajpur	0.5152	8
Bhadrak	0.4885	16	Kendrapara	0.5175	6
Balangir	0.4727	19	Khurda	0.5415	4
Boudh	0.4377	22	Sambalpur	0.5073	11
Deogarh	0.4543	21	Sonepur	0.5103	10
Dhenkanal	0.4920	14	Sundargarh	0.5292	5
Ganjam	0.4582	20	Jharsuguda	0.6175	1
Keonjhar	0.4764	18			
Mayurbhanj	0.4843	17			
Nayagarh	0.4903	15			
Nuapada	0.4221	23			
Puri	0.4994	13			
Rayagada	0.3665	27			

Source: Calculated by the author

Further probe into the individual indices provide some interesting findings (see Tables 5, 6 and 7). Ironically, no district recorded high development in any of the three dimensions. In education, Jagatsinghpur outperformed the rest in 1993-94 as well as in 2003-04. In 1997-98, Kendrapara district topped the list. In all three periods under study, top five districts which had better education index were belonging to coastal region only namely Jagatsinghpur, Kendrapara, Khurda, Cuttack and Puri. The districts at the lowest rung were Malkangiri, Gajapati, Rayagada, Nabarangpur, Nuapada and Koraput. None of them is found to have attained a satisfactory level of education. They have only changed their positions in various periods. In 2003-04, the education index for these districts varied between a low of 0.301 in Malkangiri and a high of 0.349 in Gajapati. These districts have highest concentration of scheduled tribe population. It appears that all the efforts of the government and non-government organizations towards their uplift have not made any headway in these districts.

During 1993-94, Mayurbhanj was the only district with a health index above 0.5 and continued to maintain the first position till 1997-98 with a very satisfactory level of 0.782. During the same period, as many as ten other districts including Deogarh, Kalahandi, Khurda and Sundargarh had surpassed the low level of development in health dimension. However, in 2003-04, surprisingly, the situation turned out to be worse again. Not only the health index deteriorated but also the number of districts that had attained education index equal to or above 0.5 fell to mere four only. Those districts were Mayurbhanj, Jharsuguda, Sonepur and Bargarh. Apparently, the districts that have larger tribal population were the worst performers in all the periods under study barring exceptions. Taking the case of 2003-04 only, it was found that Kandhamal, Gajapati, Rayagada, Kalahandi, Malkangiri and Nabarangpur fell at the lower end of the rank.

TABLE 5
INDEX VALUES OF INDIVIDUAL COMPONENTS OF HDI AMONGST THE DISTRICTS OF ORISSA IN 1993-94

Sl. No	Districts	Education Index	Education Rank	Health Index	Health Rank	Income Index	Income Rank	HDI Index	HDI Rank
1	Angul	0.4833	12	0.3750	14	0.4467	2	0.4350	4
2	Balasore	0.5290	8	0.2986	20	0.2898	26	0.3725	17
3	Bargarh	0.4497	15	0.4375	7	0.3321	10	0.4064	10
4	Bhadrak	0.5530	6	0.2986	19	0.2901	25	0.3806	16
5	Balangir	0.3822	22	0.4514	4	0.3131	16	0.3822	15
6	Boudh	0.3940	20	0.3958	9	0.3080	20	0.3659	18
7	Cuttack	0.5852	3	0.3750	13	0.3113	17	0.4238	5
8	Deogarh	0.4172	19	0.4375	6	0.3460	8	0.5275	1
9	Dhenkanal	0.5116	10	0.4236	8	0.3278	11	0.4210	7
10	Gajapati	0.2975	25	0.2292	23	0.3544	6	0.2937	24
11	Ganjam	0.4187	18	0.2292	22	0.5301	1	0.3926	12
12	Jagatsinghpur	0.6278	1	0.3750	12	0.3087	19	0.4372	3
13	Jajpur	0.5413	7	0.3750	11	0.3187	15	0.4117	9
14	Jharsuguda	0.4882	11	0.3125	18	0.4178	3	0.4062	11
15	Kalahandi	0.3161	24	0.2014	25	0.2860	28	0.2678	28

16	Kandhamal	0.3832	21	0.0208	30	0.2894	27	0.2311	30
17	Kendrapara	0.5808	5	0.3750	10	0.3069	21	0.4209	8
18	Keonjhar	0.4302	16	0.4653	2	0.2788	30	0.3914	13
19	Khurda	0.5941	2	0.1042	29	0.3558	5	0.3514	19
20	Koraput	0.2695	27	0.3333	17	0.3439	9	0.3156	21
21	Malkangiri	0.2217	29	0.3333	16	0.3039	23	0.2863	26
22	Mayurbhanj	0.3687	23	0.5208	1	0.2845	29	0.3913	14
23	Nabarangpur	0.2074	30	0.2292	21	0.3101	18	0.2489	29
24	Nayagarh	0.5197	9	0.1042	28	0.3009	24	0.3083	22
25	Nuapada	0.2902	26	0.2014	24	0.3194	14	0.2703	27
26	Puri	0.5820	4	0.1042	27	0.3046	22	0.3302	20
27	Rayagada	0.2596	28	0.3333	15	0.3233	12	0.3054	23
28	Sambalpur	0.4778	13	0.4375	5	0.3490	7	0.4214	6
29	Sonepur	0.4264	17	0.1181	26	0.3226	13	0.2890	25
30	Sundargarh	0.4765	14	0.4514	3	0.3938	4	0.4406	2
	ORISSA	0.4361		0.3125		0.3323		0.3603	

Source: Calculated by the authors

TABLE 6
INDEX VALUES OF INDIVIDUAL COMPONENTS OF HDI AMONGST THE DISTRICTS OF ORISSA IN 1997-98

Sl. No	Districts	Education Index	Education Rank	Health Index	Health Rank	Income Index	Income Rank	HDI Index	HDI Rank
1	Angul	0.5388	11	0.4808	12	0.5058	2	0.5084	9
2	Balasore	0.5830	8	0.4423	18	0.3275	27	0.4509	14
3	Bargarh	0.5036	14	0.4487	17	0.3605	12	0.4376	16
4	Bhadrak	0.5843	7	0.6731	8	0.3184	29	0.5253	8
5	Balangir	0.4414	20	0.4679	15	0.3503	18	0.4199	21
6	Boudh	0.4390	21	0.4231	20	0.3541	16	0.4054	22
7	Cuttack	0.6190	4	0.6859	7	0.3499	19	0.5516	4
8	Deogarh	0.4652	18	0.7756	2	0.3799	6	0.5402	6
9	Dhenkanal	0.4816	16	0.4679	14	0.3559	14	0.4352	18
10	Gajapati	0.3489	25	0.1731	28	0.3730	7	0.2983	27
11	Ganjam	0.4745	17	0.4038	21	0.3306	26	0.4030	23
12	Jagatsinghpur	0.6362	2	0.2885	25	0.3521	17	0.4256	19
13	Jajpur	0.6138	6	0.3333	24	0.3640	10	0.4371	17
14	Jharsuguda	0.5407	10	0.6346	9	0.4955	3	0.5569	3
15	Kalahandi	0.3700	24	0.7628	3	0.3328	23	0.4885	11
16	Kandhamal	0.4277	22	0.0064	30	0.3237	28	0.2526	29

17	Kendrapara	0.6451	1	0.5962	11	0.5734	1	0.6049	1
18	Keonjhar	0.4841	15	0.3397	23	0.3655	9	0.3965	24
19	Khurda	0.6164	5	0.7244	4	0.3726	8	0.5711	2
20	Koraput	0.2893	28	0.2179	27	0.3324	24	0.2799	28
21	Malkangiri	0.2670	29	0.1218	29	0.3450	20	0.2446	30
22	Mayurbhanj	0.4114	23	0.7821	1	0.3032	30	0.4989	10
23	Nabarangpur	0.2614	30	0.3397	22	0.3321	25	0.3111	25
24	Nayagarh	0.5635	9	0.4615	16	0.3348	22	0.4533	13
25	Nuapada	0.3319	26	0.6923	6	0.3618	11	0.4620	12
26	Puri	0.6268	3	0.6218	10	0.3366	21	0.5284	7
27	Rayagada	0.2938	27	0.2500	26	0.3574	13	0.3004	26
28	Sambalpur	0.5154	13	0.4359	19	0.3969	5	0.4494	15
29	Sonepur	0.4454	19	0.4744	13	0.3554	15	0.4251	20
30	Sundargarh	0.5306	12	0.6923	5	0.4056	4	0.5428	5
	ORISSA	0.4783		0.4679		0.3682		0.4382	

Source: Calculated by the authors

TABLE 7
INDEX VALUES OF INDIVIDUAL COMPONENTS OF HDI AMONGST THE DISTRICTS OF ORISSA IN 2003-04

Sl. No	Districts	Education Index	Education Rank	Health Index	Health Rank	Income Index	Income Rank	HDI Index	HDI Rank
1	Angul	0.5860	12	0.4571	9	0.6595	2	0.5675	2
2	Balasore	0.6076	9	0.4714	7	0.4398	23	0.5063	12
3	Bargarh	0.5691	14	0.5000	4	0.4785	11	0.5159	7
4	Bhadrak	0.6409	6	0.4143	18	0.4102	29	0.4885	16
5	Balangir	0.5060	19	0.4571	8	0.4550	17	0.4727	19
6	Boudh	0.4992	22	0.3643	22	0.4497	20	0.4377	22
7	Cuttack	0.6587	4	0.4214	15	0.4542	18	0.5115	9
8	Deogarh	0.5363	17	0.3429	23	0.4837	8	0.4543	21
9	Dhenkanal	0.6028	11	0.4143	17	0.4589	15	0.4920	14
10	Gajapati	0.3762	26	0.2786	29	0.4668	13	0.3739	25
11	Ganjam	0.5055	20	0.4286	13	0.4406	22	0.4582	20
12	Jagatsinghpur	0.6926	1	0.4500	10	0.4929	6	0.5452	3
13	Jajpur	0.6405	7	0.4357	12	0.4695	12	0.5152	8
14	Jharsuguda	0.6220	8	0.5571	2	0.6733	1	0.6175	1
15	Kalahandi	0.4265	24	0.3071	27	0.4301	27	0.3879	24
16	Kandhamal	0.5015	21	0.1929	30	0.4227	28	0.3724	26

17	Kendrapara	0.6737	2	0.4000	19	0.4788	10	0.5175	6
18	Keonjhar	0.5272	18	0.4214	14	0.4806	9	0.4764	18
19	Khurda	0.6528	5	0.4786	6	0.4932	5	0.5415	4
20	Koraput	0.3300	27	0.3214	24	0.4384	24	0.3633	28
21	Malkangiri	0.3014	30	0.3071	26	0.4360	25	0.3482	30
22	Mayurbhanj	0.4670	23	0.5786	1	0.4073	30	0.4843	17
23	Nabarangpur	0.3193	29	0.3143	25	0.4309	26	0.3548	29
24	Nayagarh	0.6056	10	0.4143	16	0.4510	19	0.4903	15
25	Nuapada	0.4157	25	0.3929	21	0.4577	16	0.4221	23
26	Puri	0.6592	3	0.3929	20	0.4462	21	0.4994	13
27	Rayagada	0.3281	28	0.2857	28	0.4857	7	0.3665	27
28	Sambalpur	0.5728	13	0.4429	11	0.5063	4	0.5073	11
29	Sonepur	0.5658	15	0.5000	3	0.4651	14	0.5103	10
30	Sundargarh	0.5606	16	0.4786	5	0.5484	3	0.5292	5
	ORISSA	0.5317		0.4143		0.4737		0.4732	

Source: Calculated by the authors

In income dimension, the scenario was worsening in the entire period under study. While in 1993-94, only one district (Ganjam) could attain the income index value little above 0.5, in 1997-98, only two districts (Kendrapara and Angul) attained that level. In 2003-04, the situation did not improve much as only four districts (Jharsuguda followed by Angul, Sundargarh and Sambalpur) had income indices little above 0.5. Even Khurda, which houses the capital Bhubaneswar, despite having occupied the fifth position, has attained an income index less than 0.5. At the lower end stand the districts like Mayurbhanj, Bhadrak, Balasore, Kalahandi, Malkangiri, Kandhamal, Keonjhar, Ganjam and Nabarangpur. This clearly indicates that in income front, Orissa has not made any significant progress. Thus, in terms of income poverty, Orissa remains as one of the poorest states. The districts that have made some progress in income front are the ones where rapid industrialization has just set in. Interestingly, some of the coastal districts, which have performed relatively well in two other dimensions of human development lag behind in income front. This is perhaps due to their overdependence on agriculture which is, if not stagnant, but underdeveloped and there has been no significant industrialization in these districts. These districts are also relatively densely populated.

It may, however, be mentioned here that the overall index does not suffice that all the people in a district are equally well off or worse off. A further probe into the inter-personal achievements across the districts may through some light on the actual scenario, which is beyond the scope of this study. Assuming that the achievements within the districts are uniform, the present study finds considerable variations amongst the districts both in individual dimensions as well as in the overall human development. Besides, it is also evident that the human development scenario in the entire state is not very encouraging.

IV. POSSIBLE REASONS

It is found that no single pattern of human development emerges from the performance of the districts. Balasore, which performs well in education index, performs miserably in health as well as income index. Mayurbhanj, which performs badly in income and education index, records good performance in health index. However, the study has given scope to identify the perennially lagging districts which need our urgent intervention. Primarily, the districts dominated by tribal population are the worst performers in almost all dimensions of human development. They may need special attention.

Given the inequalities that persist among the districts, differential treatment may be required in addressing the issues. It may be, in this context, imperative to find out the reasons for such a situation for Orissa as well as its constituent districts. This can be analyzed from various perspectives. Among all, the availability of quality infrastructure, both economic and social, may be considered as a key factor towards attaining a satisfactory level of human development. The infrastructure may consist of the factors like health, education, transport, communication, power, irrigation, banking, et cetera. While it is considered that development of quality infrastructure is a precondition to rapid industrialization, there are evidences to suggest that the former can also directly enable a state to attain high human development and low poverty (Sen and Pal, 2005; Ali and Pernia, 2003). The present study also establishes a direct relationship between infrastructure and human development taking the data for the state of Orissa (see Table 8). The composite index as computed here considers the factors like health, education, transport, communication, power, irrigation and banking. This reaffirms the role of infrastructure in the context of human development and thereby requires an examination of its availability in the state and its various districts.

TABLE 8
REGRESSION RESULTS BETWEEN COMPOSITE INDEX OF INFRASTRUCTURE AND HUMAN DEVELOPMENT

Year	DV	IV	UC β	UC Std. Error	SC β	t	R² (F)
1993-94	HDI	Constant	0.213	0.047	0.514	4.492	0.265
		Cinf	0.017	0.005		3.174*	(10.075*)
1997-98	HDI	Constant	0.146	0.066	0.652	2.203	0.425
		Cinf	0.029	0.006		4.551**	(20.710**)
2003-04	HDI	Constant	0.162	0.043	0.811	3.798	0.658
		Cinf	0.028	0.004		7.348**	(53.990**)

Note ** implies significant at 0.01 level; * implies significant at 0.05 level; Cinf: composite index of infrastructure; DV: Dependent variable; IV: Independent variable
Source: Calculated by the authors

Orissa's status in the development of infrastructure is not at all encouraging. The Centre for Monitoring Indian Economy (CMIE) in its estimation of the Composite Development Index (CDI) related to infrastructure development of 15 major states of India has ranked Orissa at 12th in the descending order (CMIE, 2000). The inter-district profile is, however, more disturbing. Analyzing the pattern of changes in composite index of infrastructure from 1993-94 to 2003-04, it is evident that the relative disparities in infrastructural facilities across districts have accentuated during this period. The coefficient of variation in 1993-94 was 11.17, which increased to 21.68 in 1997-98 and then declined to 18.24 in 2003-04 (see Table 9). Despite such decline, the relative disparities were reported to be still higher in 2003-04 as compared to 1993-94. The result as estimated between 1993-94 and 2003-04 is found to be statistically significant at 1 percent level.

TABLE 9
COMPOSITE INDEX OF INFRASTRUCTURE ACROSS DISTRICTS OF ORISSA

Sl. No.	Districts	1993-94 Index	Rank	1997-98 Index	Rank	2003-04 Index	Rank
1	Angul	7.8706	23	10.2033	16	11.0676	18
2	Balasore	9.6893	8	10.6113	12	11.8660	9
3	Baragarh	8.5279	17	9.9086	18	11.4236	14
4	Bhadrak	9.3414	11	10.2832	15	11.3019	15
5	Balangir	8.0851	22	9.4922	21	11.0623	19
6	Boudh	6.5278	26	9.7337	20	10.1238	22
7	Cuttack	10.8732	4	13.6035	3	12.8135	5
8	Deogarh	8.5012	18	15.3397	1	11.2795	16
9	Dhenkanal	11.4235	3	7.0611	27	11.6283	11
10	Gajapati	6.6814	25	8.6746	23	7.5710	28
11	Ganjam	8.9963	14	10.9919	7	9.6749	25
12	Jagatsinghpur	10.7893	5	10.8769	9	13.1138	3
13	Jajpur	9.0152	13	11.5642	5	12.1591	7
14	Jharsuguda	9.4745	9	10.3633	14	12.2167	6
15	Kalahandi	8.1935	21	9.8548	19	9.8854	24
16	Kandhamal	8.4561	19	8.7026	22	10.2764	21
17	Kendrapara	10.3722	6	10.3671	13	13.0175	4
18	Keonjhar	9.3588	10	10.6242	11	11.8572	10
19	Khurda	12.1015	2	14.6821	2	13.9909	2
20	Koraput	5.2673	29	7.4924	25	7.7679	26
21	Malkangiri	4.6183	30	6.9224	30	6.5379	30
22	Mayurbhanj	8.2310	20	7.3184	26	10.5746	20
23	Nabarangpur	5.6573	28	6.9635	28	7.0078	29
24	Nayagarh	8.5473	16	10.1952	17	10.0919	23
25	Nuapada	7.3327	24	8.3491	24	11.0736	17
26	Puri	12.3622	1	13.2944	4	14.6650	1
27	Rayagada	5.9545	27	6.9301	29	7.7072	27
28	Sambalpur	9.7140	7	10.9448	8	11.5890	12
29	Sonepur	8.8835	15	11.4738	6	11.9085	8
30	Sundargarh	9.2399	12	10.7651	10	11.4309	13
Orissa		17.8247		10.1196		10.8895	
Coefficient of Variation		11.17		21.68		18.24	

Source: Calculated by the authors

The study makes clusters of the districts on the basis of their relative position in infrastructure development. The factor scores of the districts from zero to the maximum positive and negative limits fall within +SD and –SD respectively. The districts falling on the extreme positive side of the distribution (i.e. within +1SD and +3SD) are designated as developed. Those falling on the extreme negative side of the continuum (i.e. within -1SD and -3SD are treated as less-developed. The districts falling in between (i.e. within +1SD to –1SD) are considered as moderately developed (Suar, 1984).

The cluster approach to the infrastructure development (see Table 10) indicates that in all the three periods under study, Puri, Khurda, Cuttack and Jagatsinghpur, all from the coastal regions of the state and only Sambalpur from the rest have continued to remain at the top, while districts like Gajapati, Boudh, Nabarangpur, Rayagada, Koraput, and Malkangiri have remained least developed. While the number of developed districts in terms of infrastructure increased from 8 in 1993-94 to 15 in 2003-04, the number of districts with least availability of infrastructure also increased from 7 in 1993-94 to 11 in 2003-04. In course of time, some districts have changed their relative positions towards both the directions. While the relative positions of Kalahandi, Kandhamal, Mayurbhanj and Nayagarh worsened between 1993-94 and 2003-04 from moderate to less developed ones, moderately developed districts for 1993-94 like Bhadrak, Balasore, Jajpur, Deogarh, Baragarh, Sonepur and Keonjhar registered steady progress in infrastructure and were considered developed in 2003-04. Kendrapara, Jharsuguda and Dhenkanal regained their developed status in 2003-04 as against a fall in the middle period. However, Ganjam and Sundargarh respectively were relegated to the least developed and moderately developed positions in 2003-04 having, however, made an entry into the developed ones in 1997-98. Kalahandi and Nayagarh became relatively less developed in 2003-04 after having maintained a moderate status in 1997-98.

TABLE 10
COMPOSITE INDEX OF INFRASTRUCTURE
ACCORDING TO CLUSTERS OF DISTRICTS

Year	Developed	Moderately Developed	Less Developed
1993-94	Puri Khurda Cuttack Jagatsinghpur Kendrapara Jharsuguda Dhenkanal Sambalpur	Ganjam Jajpur Sundargarh Balangir Balasore Kalahandi Bhadrak Mayurbhanj Sonepur Angul Keonjhar Deogarh Baragarh Kandhamal Nayagarh	Nuapada Gajapati Boudh Nabarangpur Rayagada Koraput Malkangiri
1997-98	Deogarh Sonepur Khurda Ganjam Cuttack Sambalpur Puri Sundargarh Jajpur Jagatsinghpur	Jharsuguda Angul Balasore Kendrapara Keonjhar Nayagarh Bhadrak Baragarh Kalahandi	Boudh Koraput Bolangir Mayurbhanj Kandhamal Nabarangpur Gajapati Dhenkanal Nuapada Rayagada Malkangiri
2003-04	Puri Balasore Khurda Keonjhar Jagatsinghpur Dhenkanal Kendrapara Sambalpur Cuttack Deogarh Jharsuguda Baragarh Jajpur Bhadrak Sonepur	Sundargarh Nuapada Balangir Angul	Mayurbhanj Gajapati Nayagarh Koraput Kandhamal Rayagada Boudh Nabarangpur Kalahandi Malkangiri Ganjam

Source: Calculated by the authors

It is found that the districts which have poor infrastructure base are the ones that have shown low human development, barring exceptions. Districts like Malkangiri, Kandhamal, Kalahandi, Nabarangpur, Koraput, Gajapati, Rayagada have performed very badly in human development in the entire period under study. These are also the districts that are least endowed with infrastructure. To develop the above-mentioned districts' human developments score, they need special attention by the non-government organizations, national and international governments and agencies.

V. CONCLUSION

Orissa, which is poised for rapid industrialization, may be seriously handicapped to achieve that unless it attains a high level of human development across its entire region. This may necessitate inter alia adequate availability of quality infrastructure, both economic and social, in all its districts. In recent years, the state has made attempts to build its infrastructure base to address twin objectives namely rapid industrialization and high human development. Given the plight of the scenario the state is faced with particularly in human development, perhaps it is pertinent to increase the quantity and quality of infrastructure significantly. While doing so, the state has to provide a favourable treatment to the lagging districts.

REFERENCES

Ali, I. and Pernia, E. M. (2003): Infrastructure and Poverty Reduction: What is the Connection? *ERD Policy Brief Series No. 13*, Asian Development Bank, 1-13.

CMIE (2000): *Profiles of Districts*, Mumbai.

Government of India (2002): *National Human Development Report 2001*, Planning Commission of India, New Delhi.

Government of Orissa (GoO) (various Years): *District Domestic Product at a Glance Orissa (1993-94 to 2001-02)*, Directorate of Economics and Statistics, Orissa, Bhubaneswar.

GoO (Various Years): *Statistical Abstracts of Orissa for 1993, 1997 and 2000*, Directorate of Economics and Statistics, Bhubaneswar.

GoO (2004): *Orissa Human Development Report, 2004*, Bhubaneswar.

Hirway, I and Mahadevia, D (2004): *Gujarat Human Development Report: 2004*, Mahatma Gandhi Labour Institute, Ahmedabad.

International Institute for Population Sciences (IIPS) (1992-93): *National Family Health Survey, India, 1992-1993 (NFHS-1)*, Mumbai.

IIPS (1998-99): *National Family Health Survey, India, 1998-1999 (NFHS-2)*, Centre for Operations Research and Training, Vadodara and International Institute for Population Sciences, Mumbai.

Kumar, A. K. Shiva (1991): Human Development Index for Indian States, *Economic and Political Weekly*, 26 (41): 2343-2345.

Koutsoyiannis, A. (2001): *Theory of Econometrics*, Palgrave MacMillan, New York.

Mazumdar, D. (1990): *Poverty in Asia: an Overview*, A paper presented at Policy Dialogue and Pacific Development Centre, Hanvi.

Morris, D. M. and McAlpin, M.B. (1982): *Measuring the Condition of India's Poor: The Physical Quality of Life Index*, Promia and Co., New Delhi.

Malgavkar, P. D. (1994): *Human Development in Indian States*, Centre for Policy Research, New Delhi.

National Sample Survey Organisation (Various Rounds): Adult Literacy Rates, Ministry of Statistics and Program Implementation, Government of India, New Delhi.

Prabhu, K. S. and Chatterjee, S. (1993): *Social Sector Expenditures and Human Development: A Study of Indian States*, Department of Economic Analysis and Policy, Reserve Bank of India, Mumbai.

Registrar General of India (1991): *Census of India (Orissa): 1991*, Government of India, New Delhi.

Registrar General of India (2001): *Census of India (Orissa): 2001*, Government of India, New Delhi.

Registrar General of India (2000): SRS Analytical Studies Report-1, 2000, Government of India, New Delhi,

Sen, J. and Pal, D. P. (2005): On Infrastructure and Economic Development, *Artha Vijnana*, 47 (1 and 2): 87-98.

Suar, D. (1984): Development Indicator Identification and Regional Disparity in Orissa: A Factor Analytic Study, *Indian Journal of Regional Sciences*, 16 (2): 108-120.

United Nations Development Program (UNDP) (1990): *Human Development Report: 1990*, Oxford University Press, New York.

UNDP (1995): *Human Development Report: 1995*, Oxford University Press, New York

UNDP (2007): *Human Development Report: 2007-08*, Palgrave Macmillan, New York.

14

Human Development, Economic Development and Income Earning Capacities of the Common Man: The Case of North East India

Keya Sengupta[1]

I. INTRODUCTION

Economic growth and well being of the common man as measured by Human Development are not contradictory, as some economists wrongly tend to opine. In fact, they are complimentary and no economic growth can be initiated and sustained at low level of human development just as high-level of human development can only be sustained, with resources obtained through high rate of economic growth. Growth does not automatically transform itself into human development. All depends on the nature and extent to which policies and programs of an economy are geared to harmonize economic growth with human development. Achieving these two goals simultaneously should form part of every development goal and effort. It is here that the role of the state assumes importance and the study of human development assumes significance from the point of view of policy perspective. The widespread criticism of trickle down theory, which has proved ineffective in the Indian context, and least of all for the north-

---

[1] Keya Sengupta, Department of Economics, Assam University, Silchar, Assam, India, E-mail: kysengupta@yahoo.co.in

eastern region, can be made a meaningful exercise through changing the entire perspective of policy formulation. It is, therefore, essential to draw attention to the crucial fact that efforts at raising human development does not end only with attempts at providing better education and better health conditions. It is extremely crucial that people are to be provided the opportunities of using up the capabilities that they develop. This is possible only when they are provided with adequate opportunities for employment in the market. This is also important because individual income not only raises the rank on Human Development Index (HDI), but no state can continuously provide education and health facilities to all the common man. After attaining a certain degree of development the people themselves have to make these provisions for themselves and their children. Therefore economic investment can directly provide job opportunities for the people and therefore economic development and human development can never be contradictory experience in during development process.

Policies focusing human development should also make people equal partners in development. Encouragement should therefore be provided to people to participate in development process. At the same time, it is also crucial to focus attention to the fact that too much emphasis on either economic growth or only human development may result in unbalanced growth of the economy, which may once again jeopardize the very process of long-term sustainable development (Sengupta, 2002). Sustaining the process of development is the pivotal issue of Human Development paradigm. If the states of north east have to survive on aid from the center on a permanent basis, sustainability of developmental efforts in the region will be seriously impaired. Making the growth process sustainable by emphasizing on human development implies that not only enough of the resources created at present should be invested in education and health of today's generation, but people should also be provided with income earning opportunities so that such social opportunities may also become self-sustaining. These people in turn may sustain the process of economic development of the future generations also, so that the future generation need not pay the debts of today's generation.

The main tenets of the paradigm of human development are therefore the people. Every aspect of economic development is also assessed from the point of view of the people. The objective of growth is the betterment of people's lives and not merely expansion of production processes. This paradigm further necessitates that people should not only build capabilities, by building their health, education and skills, but must also be provided with all the opportunities to use up these capabilities through adequate employment opportunities. Full expansion of the GDP and the macro-economic variables, which are considered as means of economic development, are as important as the end, which are the people.

In the 1950's and 1960's many nations had experienced economic development, yet the living conditions of the masses remained extremely deplorable. It was only in the seventies that realization dawned upon the planners that something must have gone wrong somewhere. The fact that development was purely an economic phenomenon in which the GNP growth would trickle down to the masses, for the wider distribution of economic and social benefits of growth, did not seem to work. This resulted in discarding GNP as the only true indicator of growth. Direct attack on poverty, low level of living, inequitable income distribution and rising unemployment, were the pivotal issues which were incorporated in the new concept of human development, and were gradually forming part of development policies. Similar was the view of the World Bank, which during the eighties championed economic growth as the goal of development and had taken a much broader view of development. This is evident from 1991 World Development Report, in which it maintained, "The challenge of development is to improve the quality of life. Especially in the world's poor countries, a better quality of life generally calls for higher incomes – but it involves much more. It encompasses as ends in themselves better education, higher standards of health and nutrition, less poverty, a cleaner environment, more equality of opportunity, greater individual freedom and a richer cultural life".

The fact that it has still not been possible to solve the problems of hunger, illiteracy, malnutrition and poverty of the states of the north eastern region where the condition of quality of life in most places is much lower than the all India level, only reveals the choice of wrong strategy of development for the north east. The assumption of the Trickle Down Theory has totally failed in the region like the rest of India. Western paradigms are therefore no longer accepted blindly with the same degree of fervor. Voices of disagreement have characterized the nations of the Third World countries, who in turn slowly and gradually started adopting their own development paradigm. Development experience of China can be cited as a wonderful example. The developmentalists of the western paradigm are now considered "as false prophets whose faulty paradigm led to massive misdirection of effort" (Dube, 1988).

The result of all the futile efforts over the years, at developing the economy, particularly that of the North East reveals that we have once again to rediscover the basic truth of all development strategy – that people should occupy the center-stage of all development. Even in India itself, different states have developed at different rates, in spite of similar physical investment. States with rich natural resources or heavy capital investment, have not displayed any satisfactory record in terms of economic development. In contrast, some states with insufficient resources, both natural as well as financial, have performed much better, when the people of those states have greater capability and are therefore much harder working.

II. HUMAN DEVELOPMENT AND ECONOMIC DEVELOPMENT

Development strategy may be growth led, by creating an initial favourable condition for people's participation, as was the case in China. It may be growth led with unfavourable initial condition, and corrective public policies at a later stage as have happened in Malaysia. The other strategy may be strong emphasis on public policy to provide social services but with low growth. Such a strategy however is unsustainable over the long period. Such a strategy was adopted in Jamaica and Srilanka and Kerala in India. The Kerala model, with high level of human development but a stagnant economy has become a matter of great controversy in development context. In developed economics where growth models are launched with an already satisfactory achievement in social indicator, further spending on these items, enables the economy to reach the take-off stage. Consequently, when people reach a high level of human development, they are able to look after and spend for their own socio-economic needs provided they are engaged in remunerative employments and earn sufficient income by using up the capabilities that the state has helped them to acquire. This enables the government to concentrate on economic growth, leaving the people to spend for themselves. Consequently expenditure on social sector declines after a certain point. However, in a less developed economy with a low level of per capita income, people tend to have a dependency syndrome, and they expect the government to continuously spend for them. This is one of the factors responsible for the paradox of the Kerala model.

A school of thought has therefore developed which erroneously opines that spending scarce resources for raising human development would only be at the cost of economic development, particularly for a less developed nation. However, it needs to be realized by economists as well as social workers that economic development and human development are not contradictory; in fact they are both complimentary. It is therefore extremely essential to understand the meaning of this concept. Human Development does not confine itself merely in pushing up the statistical figures on health, education and other socio-economic indicators. Such a narrow view of human development would make all efforts at raising human development totally meaningless, with an extremely short-run connotation. The concept of human development is much wider. Human Development is a process of enlarging people's choices (UNDP, 1995). Enlarging people's choices therefore, is not confined to any specific period, but spills over several generations. The main purpose of human development is to prepare the people, to have access to resources needed to lead a decent standard of living. This preparation takes the form of acquiring knowledge and good health. They should also have political, economic, social and cultural freedom. The Human Development Report (HRD) 1995, therefore, maintains that Human Development has two sides. Hence, much of the misunderstanding between economic and human development has arisen in the past. The concept of Human Development is much broader than the traditional theories of economic development. Even the welfare theories of economic development fail to capture the essence of Human Development. Welfare approaches of economic theories consider people as the beneficiaries of economic development. It attempts to provide material goods and services to deprived population, rather than in enlarging human choices in all fields.

The concept of human development is much broader since it brings together production and distribution of commodities along with the expansion and use of human capabilities. Therefore, all aspects of the economy, including economic growth, trade, employment, political freedom or cultural values are viewed from the perspective of the people. Economic growth and human development are, therefore, not contradictory and cannot be viewed in isolation. The achievement of one is impossible without the achievement of the other. Attainment of Human Development is impossible without economic growth, since resources required for raising Human Development can be acquired only through a high rate of economic growth. An impoverished nation, with insufficient resources, has to make extra efforts to acquire resources for raising Human Development. Though this is not to suggest, that economic development and human development are highly correlated.

It also needs to be highlighted that economic growth by itself is meaningless without Human Development. If the fruits of development are concentrated only in a few hands, by depriving the majority from the growth benefits, economic development would be meaningless. Experience has revealed that nations, which do not concentrate on Human Development, have witnessed growing concentration of income in a few hands. Economic growth by itself cannot automatically transform itself into higher levels of Human Development. All depends on how the policies can be geared to achieve such objectives. At the same time, it is also crucial to focus attention to the fact that too much emphasis on either economic growth or Human Development alone might result in unbalanced growth of the economy, which may jeopardize the very process of long-term.

III. ECONOMIC STATUS AND HUMAN DEVELOPMENT

Capabilities acquired by the people through investment for building up human development leads to variations in "Social opportunities" of the type described by Amartya Sen, which in turn influence economic performance. To a large extent, achievement on these fronts is determined not only by the economic status of the respective groups, in a spatial context, but is also governed by the facilities relating to physical amenities offered by both the state as well as the market. On the other hand, such facilities offered also influence the ability to acquire the required capabilities. In other words, various types of amenities and facilities offered, not only indicate a good quality of life, but are also connected with capabilities of the people in a very crucial way.

We will, therefore, examine the economic status of the population of the region, in the spatial context as well as across various socio economic groups. Economic status is the composite effect of several factors, like the work participation rate of both males and females, sources of income, as well as per capita income. Behavioural pattern relating to these aspects of economic status will be analyzed with the help of empirical findings, in the subsequent sections in sixteen districts of the states on north east India. Such findings, which may perhaps be a maiden effort in this line of study, may highlight the interconnection between economic achievement and the indicators of quality of life, both in terms of infrastructure amenities, as well as capabilities in terms of education and health. The need of the time, and the urgency in social policies relating to public action, may be highlighted through such discussion. It is already a well-known fact of the Indian economy that inadequate attention to any major change in social policies along with economic reform initiated recently is a major failure. This had serious negative implications for the possibilities of improving the living condition of the common man. The north eastern region too, cannot be isolated from the experience of the rest of India. Though some of the indicators relating to education and gender gap in some of the states and for certain groups is far better than the Indian average, yet the lack of economic opportunities may make such achievements in social sector totally meaningless and may fail to contribute in any substantial manner to the overall development of the region. Therefore, once again, we would like to focus attention to the fact that human development can, not only be attained with simultaneous economic development, but both the types of development are highly interrelated and complimentary.

The growth of real income per head, which is the outcome of work participation and structure of occupation, is recognized even in the new development economics. The central feature of the process of economic development is expansion of human capability. Economic poverty, results in deprivation with respect to the opportunities that enables people to lead a healthy life. Poverty is, thus, ultimately a question of "capability deprivation". Therefore analysis of economic status will be relevant in this study from the point of view of 'capability deprivation', which in turn restricts "social opportunities". The importance of per capita income in influencing individual life was emphasized right from the days of classical economists of Smith and Mill to modern development economics. In spite of rejecting the role of per capita GNP, as an indicator of growth, it has never totally rejected its contribution and role in improving the quality of life of an individual.

In view of the important role played by the income and occupation of the individual, in the following section, we shall make a detailed examination of the various indicators of economic well being of the people of this region. We shall firstly examine the work participation rate in the various districts of the different states of the region. For the purpose of the study we have collected data from the states of Assam, Meghalaya, Mizoram, Nagaland, Tripura and Arunachal Pradesh. The data has been collected through multistage stage stratified sampling method, selecting twenty percent of the population from the state, district blocks, and villages. Total sample size is 350.

Analysis of Table 1 reveal that 38.5 percent of the work participation rate (WPR) which is the highest in the region, is reported in Kamrup district of Assam, followed by 37.8 percent in Aizwal district, and 35.35 percent in Kohima. North Cachar Hill district records the lowest work participation of only 23.25 percent Twelve out of sixteen districts of the region has WPR of less than 35.0 percent. The

WPR is a reflection of the economic opportunities of the respective places, which again is a reflection of the level of economic development of the respective places. Apart from this feature, another clear pattern that can be discerned in the WPR is that it is much better in all those districts, which has the state capital and decreases as one moves to the peripheral regions. This is mainly due to greater economic opportunities in core areas of every state because of greater concentration of economic activities in such places. It needs to be noted that Aizwal district of Mizoram recording the best performance with respect to the various indicators of health and education has a high WPR in the region. On the other hand, poor performing districts like Barpeta and N.C. Hills also record the worst performance in terms of indicators of human development. On the other hand, WPR of districts like Jorhat, Kamrup, Cachar and the two districts of Arunachal Pradesh do not match their performance in human development. Cachar district of Assam, Itanagar and Tirap districts of Arunachal Pradesh witnessing extremely poor performance in human development (Sengupta, 2006), record higher level of WPR. It is quite possible that though WPR is high, yet it is quite possible that per capita income may be on the lower side, and WPR is higher may be due to greater concentration of jobs in the informal sector. All these issues are expected to be classified when we make a detailed examination of per capita income and other such related issues. Kamrup district, which do not have an impressive record as far as the indicators of quality of life, is concerned, has a higher WPR whereas Jorhat district with satisfactory performance in such indicators do not have high WPR. On the whole, we may conclude that no clear-cut relationship can be observed, between record on human development and WPR. We may, therefore, concede that indicators of quality of life are not a direct function of WPR, though Human Development Index is influenced directly by the level of income.

A perusal of the Table 1 reveals that female work participation rate is lower in all the districts of the region, but the gender gap in WPR is the highest in N.C. Hills, followed by Barpeta and Karimganj districts of Assam. These are also the districts with poor performance with respect to human development, which may, therefore, be an indication of the fact that WPR of women may play an important role, in human development. Women who are economically independent often have a greater decision making power, in matters relating to education and health of their family members. Districts performing better in human development have also a lower gap in WPR. Both the districts in Arunachal Pradesh are the only exceptions, where in spite of unsatisfactory record on human development, gender gap in WPR is quite narrow.

TABLE 1
WORK PARTICIPATION RATE BY SEX
(IN PERCENT)

State	Districts	Male	Female	Female/Male Ratio
Assam	Cachar	49.5	16.86	0.32
	Karimganj	43.52	22.02	0.24
	Kamrup	38.05	20.7	0.37
	Barpeta	43.62	16.58	0.23
	Jorhat	48.64	15.66	0.29
	N.C. Hills	37.82	10.62	0.22
Mizoram	Aizawl	50.7	23.74	0.46
	Chintuipui	49.18	21.6	0.44
Nagaland	Kohima	49.4	21.04	0.42
	Wokha	47.62	13.56	0.26
Tripura	North Tripura	46.14	14.74	0.25
	West Tripura	50.5	21.02	0.31
Arunachal Pradesh	Itanagar	45.28	22.5	0.46
	Tirap	44.44	23.84	0.49

Source: Estimated from primary data

To have in-depth knowledge of the WPR and its nature, we have also divided the work according to the nature of the jobs. The sources of income have broadly been divided into the following groups such as agriculture and allied activities, trade and business and services. It is interesting to note that out of the sixteen districts examined by us in eleven or in almost 69 percent of the districts, concentration of occupation is in business and trade. Only in three districts agricultural activities occupy the main occupation. Nature of occupation may not have much to do with human development because both the best performing districts as well as the poor performing districts have majority of its population in business and trade.

Though WPR and the sources of income, depending upon the nature of occupation, can convey some idea relating to the economic status, nevertheless idea about the quality of life may remain concealed in the absence of any information about the proportion of the population belonging to various income groups or per capita income in various states. In Table 2, we present the percentage of households by income groups in the various districts of the region. The entire populations have divided into rural and urban sector. Number of households within the income group of below INR 20,000 per annum has been categorized as low-income group (LIG); between INR 20,000 - INR 40,000 as lower middle income group (LMIG); between INR 40,000 – INR 62,000 as middle income group (MIG); in the range of INR 62,000 – INR 80,000 as upper middle income group (UMIG); and above INR 86,000 as high income group (HIG).

Analysis of the Table 2 reveals that in the rural area, 71 percent of the household, which is the highest in terms of our survey belongs to Tirap district of Arunachal Pradesh. A possible explanatory factor for lower level of human development may be that a major section of the population of this district belongs to LIG. In other words high degree of economic poverty implies lower level of human development,

Human Development, Economic Development and Income... 367

TABLE 2
HOUSEHOLDS BY INCOME GROUPS

(IN PERCENT)

STATE	DISTRICTS	RURAL					URBAN				
		LIG	LMIG	MIG	UMIG	HIG	LIG	LMIG	MIG	UMIG	HIG
Assam	a) Cachar	62.2	21.6	7.3	4.5	4.4	33.2	35.7	20.3	6.5	4.3
	b) Karimganj	63.1	19.2	6.5	5.9	5.3	60.2	18.1	7.8	8.5	5.4
	c) Kamrup	59.2	18.2	6.1	7.3	9.2	58.1	19.2	6.2	7.0	9.5
	d) Barpeta	58.3	17.1	6.4	8.1	10.1	57.2	11.1	9.1	9.4	13.2
	e) Jorhat	6.15	19.1	8.2	6.1	5.1	58.6	17.2	9.1	8.1	7.0
	f) N.C. Hills	64.2	20.5	7.4	3.8	4.1	62.3	19.2	7.2	6.1	5.2
Mizoram	a) Aizawl	53.2	15.8	7.1	10.7	13.2	51.3	13.2	9.2	11.2	15.1
	b) Chintuipui	58.1	17.2	10.3	3.3	11.1	56.3	16.1	9.2	9.3	9.1
Nagaland	a) Kohima	59.8	18.5	7.4	6.1	8.2	58.3	17.4	8.1	7.0	9.2
	b) Wokha	60.3	19.4	6.1	7.0	7.2	59.2	18.3	8.0	6.1	8.4
Tripura	a) North Tripura	60.2	19.3	8.2	7.1	5.2	59.7	17.4	8.3	8.5	6.1
	b) West Tripura	62.1	20.4	7.5	5.2	4.8	59.7	17.5	8.1	8.0	5.9
Arunachal Pradesh	a) Itanagar	68.3	19.1	5.2	4.1	3.3	68.3	20.7	6.1	5.3	4.3
	b) Tirap	71.2	22.3	4.2	2.1	0.8	69.3	23.2	4.3	2.6	0.6

Source: Estimated from primary data

implying that economic status is an important determinant of human development. Similar is the situation, even in the urban area of the same district, which records 69 percent of households in low-income bracket. The per capita income in the LIG in the district is INR 867, which is not only the lowest in the whole of north east India, but is also one of the lowest in India as well. It may, therefore, be contended that poverty is an important factor governing human development. The subsidies and other efforts made by the state to alleviate poverty can only marginally improve the level of living and are only short-term measures. In other words, efforts at economic development expand the scope of economic engagements of the population. Once the economic status of the people is raised, efforts at human development by the state can be sustainable. Efforts to raise human development, only on the basis of government aid is only short term and may not be sustainable, and economic development, therefore, is the long term and correct strategy to raise human development which can than be self sustaining.

Our findings are further supported by the fact that Itanagar district, which records performance with respect to indicators of human development, only marginally better than Tirap district of the same state. The analysis reveals that Tirap district has only 0.8 percent of the households belonging to the HIG, preceded by Itanagar district with 3.3 percent. In the whole region, these two districts of Arunachal Pradesh record the least number of households in the highest income bracket. The state has the highest number of people, who are economically poor and are subject to the maximum extent of deprivation, resulting in poor quality of life. This has also resulted in lowering the level of "capability formation". For exactly the reverse reasons, it is observed that Aizwal district of Mizoram which has been identified as the district with the best record with regards to the indicators of human development, followed by Chintuipui district of the same state have both the lowest percentage of households in the LIG, both in the rural as well as urban areas. Aizwal district has the maximum proportion of households of 13.2 percent and 15.1 percent in rural and urban areas respectively in the HIG. This clearly indicates that places where we come across people who are economically well off, the quality of life is much better and capabilities are much higher, raising the human development of the people of the state. Economic status of the individuals, which is determined by the economic opportunities available in the place, which in turn is governed by the level of economic development, is thus a necessary means for human development. Consequently, it is reiterated that economic development and human development are not contradictory but complimentary.

The other districts of the region, such as the Barpeta district and N.C. Hills of Assam which record lower level of performance with respect to human development, also record a very high proportion of households in the LIG and the lowest number in the HIG. This is more relevant for the rural sector, though the situation improves marginally as one moves to the urban sector. In other districts of the state, like Karimganj and Cachar, which record relatively poor performance with respect to human development, though not the worst, also record the maximum number of households in the LMIG and MIG, both in the rural as well as urban areas. Similar, is the case in both the districts of Nagaland. In both the districts of the state, like Kohima and Wokha, performance with respect to human development is quite satisfactory even if not the best. In these two districts, it is observed that the highest number of households belong to the UMIG, and not the HIG.

The overall analysis, therefore, clearly reveals that a definite relationship exists between economic well-being and human development. This is not surprising and only goes to reveal that in the absence of adequate support by the state with respect to social infrastructure, economic status of the individual, has a crucial role to play in determining human development. This is evident from the experience of countries like Sri Lanka, who in spite of belonging to LMIG, records impressive performance in human development, because of the strong support provided by the state in this respect. A holistic idea of development, is to the advantage of everyone in the society. It is about the accumulation of both physical and human capital, synchronization of ideas and skills, various ways in which the produced and non-produced factors of production are combined and managed to initiate and sustain growth. In fact, the new development economics aims not only in raising per capita income alone as in the case of neo-classical economics, but more importantly in distributing it more equitably by an overall transformation of the structure of demand, trade, production and employment (Chenery, 1981). Such an approach necessitates pragmatism in the formulation of policies, to transform the benefits of economic growth to human development.

In this context, "business as usual" which the mainstream economists have created cannot be the sole index of rationality in thinking about such issues. Ethical considerations focus our attention to crucial development and global concerns – such as poverty, distributional inequities and unemployment – which neo-classical economists lack. In a region like the north east, where many states and districts within a state are "located in far flung areas to make economic growth sustainable, it should be equalizing and poverty reducing. At the same time, policies need to be geared so that the wide gap that marks income level between different income groups may be reduced. Such an achievement, in turn will also help economic growth. Such planning strategies is especially relevant for the backward north eastern region because social justice has to be in the forefront, for many sensitive reasons and this has to be properly balanced with high rates of economic growth for political, economic and moral reasons. Such concerns have been the very basic text of UNDP's human development strategy". Released from the artificial confines of the basic neo-classical assumptions, development economics explicitly focuses on the problem of reconciling economic growth with improving the distribution of income and eradication of the worst form of poverty in a manner that is socially and politically acceptable (Naqvi, 2002).

The remote corners of this region have never received adequate attention in policy formulations. Added efforts with special packages of development both human and economic is urgently called for, particularly in the remote areas, which still lag behind in terms of all forms of development criteria, resulting in extremely poor quality of life.

REFERENCES

Banerjee, Sarmial and Roy, Samik (1998): On Construction of District Development Index in west Bengal, *Economic and Political Weekly*, 33 (47 and 48): 3019.

Bhattacharya, B. (1998): Urbanization and Human Development in West Bengal: A District Level Study and Comparison with Inter-State Variation, *Economic and Political Weekly*, 33 (47 and 48): 3027.

Chakraborty, A. (2002): Issues in Social Indicators, Composite Indices and Inequality, *Economic and Political Weekly*, 37 (13): 1199.

Chakraborty, A. (2005): Kerala's Changing Development Narratives, *Economic and Political Weekly*, 40 (6): 541.

Chenery, H. B. (1983): Interaction between Theory and Observation in Development, *World Development*, 11 (10): 853-861.

Chopra, Kanchan (2002): Social Capital and Development Processes: Role of Formal and Informal Institutions, *Economic and Political Weekly*, 37 (28): 2911.

Dube, S. C. (1988): *Modernization and Development: the Search for Alternative Paradigms*, Vistaar Publication, New Delhi.

Government of India (2002): *National Human Development Report 2001*, Planning Commission, New Delhi.

Haq, Mahbub ul (1996): *Reflections on Human Development*, Oxford University Press, New Delhi.

Kannan, K.P. (2005): Kerala's Turnaround in Growth: Role of Social Development, Remittances and Reform, *Economic and Political Weekly*, 40 (6): 548.

Kunda, A., Pradhan, B. K. and Subramanian, A. (2002): Dichotomy or Continuum: Analysis of Impact of Urban Centers on their Periphery, *Economic and Political Weekly*, 37 (50): 5039.

Naqvi, S. H. N (2002): *Development Economics: Nature and Significance*, Sage Publications, New Delhi.

Putman, R. (1993): *Making Democracy Work : Civic Traders in Modern Italy*, Princeton University Press, Princeton, New York.

Rath, N. (2004): Twelfth Finance Commission and Minimum Needs, *Economic and Political Weekly*, 39 (26): 2668.

Reddy, V.R. (2001): Declining Social Consumption in India, *Economic and Political Weekly*, 34 (29): 2750.

Rostagi, Anupam (2004): Restructuring Public Finances, *Economic and Political Weekly*, 39 (26): 2756.

Sengupta, K. (2002): Indian Economy: Economic Growth and Human Development, *Man and Development*, 24 (1): 37.

Sengupta, K. (2006): *Status of Human Development in North East India*, Unpublished Report under UGC Major Research Project, Assam University, Silchar.

Serra, R (2001): Social Capital: Meaningful and Measurable at the State Level, *Economic and Political Weekly*, 36 (8): 693.

Todaro, Michael P. and Smith, Stephen C. (2006): *Economic Development*, Pearson Education, New Delhi.

UNDP (2007): *Human Development Report 2007/2008*, Palgrave Macmillan, New York.

World Bank (1991): *World Development Report 1991*, Oxford University Press, New York.

15

Disparities in Human Development and Economic Development: The Case of Assam

Sumanash Dutta[1]

I. INTRODUCTION

The theme of regional disparities has been well researched both theoretically and empirically. Guner Myrdal (1957) explained regional disparities at national and international plain with the help of Backwash Effect and Spread Effect. The term region in his analysis refers to units of geographical areas exhibiting more or less same level of economic, social and cultural development both at national and international level. Therefore, regional disparities mean the disparities that exist among different regions. The regions may be as small as administrative units such as districts with in a state. On the basis of the level of development achieved, the districts can, however, be lumped together to identify regions showing high, medium and low growth rates as per objectives laid down (Ryngynga, 2003). The size of region may vary depending on what type of disparity the study attempts to focus on.

The term regional disparity is wide in scope and application. It may explain disparities prevailing in different

---

[1] Department of Economics, Assam University, Silchar, Assam, India, E-mail: duttasu2003@yahoo.com

fronts such as political, social, cultural and economic. Among these, political and cultural disparities are not very popular terminology in the literature of regional disparities. These are rather termed as diversities and very often construed as strength rather than weakness. Coexistence of different political and cultural systems in regions and countries make the world a more attractive place to live in. However, political and cultural diversities have significant influences on human development, which are often explained in terms of inequalities in political freedom, opportunities and predicaments. Questions such as "How will the new constitution of Iraq satisfy demands for fair representation for Shiites and Kurds?" and "Will the French legislature approve the proposal to ban headscarves and other religious and cultural symbols in public school?" ought to have strong bearings on human development. A study on understanding human welfare under Chinese political system of governance and that of India's will definitely focus on political disparities prevailing in these regions. Similarly, a study on *Ahoms* of Assam and *Tripuries* of Tripura cannot afford to ignore the cultural disparities that exist between the two communities.

There is no denying fact that the existing literature on regional disparities broadly refers to disparities in economic development. There is plethora of studies on regional disparities in economic development, which took in to consideration different indicators of economic development. Selecting eight agricultural indicators, twelve industrial indicators and six indicators of service sector, Kantawala and Rao (1992) analyzed the inter-state disparities in sectoral development in India. The study found that over the period from 1970-71 to 1985-86, the relative position of states in India have not changed significantly, considering the over all development. Rangacharyulu (1993) examined the rural development of major 17 states in India by selecting five core indicators of rural development. The study observed that there was no significant change in the position of majority of the states in rural development over the period from 1971 to 1987. Subramanian (1995) examined the inter-state differences in the level of family health of all the states of India except Tripura. On the basis of composite index of family health, he classified all states in to three categories – high, low and medium ranked. Studying the inter-state disparities on the basis of large number of social, economic and infrastructure factors, Rana (1997) found that the pattern of development of Indian economy was not in unison with respect to all the indicators rather it was of mixed nature. Bhatia (1999) highlighted inter-state variations in rural infrastructure development and emphasized the need for increased investment in rural infrastructure from the point of view of increasing agricultural growth and productivity. Gulati (1999) in his study included 17 major states of India to examine regional disparities in economic development. The findings indicated that the inter-state disparities had widened during the study period of 1960-1991. In his study of regional disparities in north-east region, Dutta (2003) observed that the states of north-east region are suffering from paucity of funds and the states are far behind the other states of India so far as the basic amenities of life are concerned.

Since economic welfare does not merely depend upon the level of development but also on its distributive aspect, disparities in economic development have always remained as a matter of great concern for the social scientists. Different studies conducted at different point of time in India not only have indicated the existence of strong economic disparities among the regions, a good number of studies have also found that the degree of disparities have been widening over time making poor regions poorer in relative term. As identification of poorer regions is an important part of development planning, the present paper attempts to find poorer regions in terms of some selected indicators within the state of Assam. In section II a brief discussion on the over all economic condition of Assam is carried out. Section III describes the methodology of the study. Section IV analyses the results. Finally, section V concludes the paper.

II. ECONOMIC CONDITION OF ASSAM

The economy of the state of Assam exhibits some direct symptoms of illness, which no one can even pretend to ignore. The Assam Human Development Report 2003 confirms the common perception that from 1980 to 2001 that the state's GDP grew at a rate of only 3.3 percent (GoA, 2003). From 1951 to 1979, Assam's GDP grew more or less at the same rate as the rate of India. But since then Assam has been continuously slipping in the process of economic growth compared to the other states. As per Planning Commission's estimates, 36.09 percent of the state population is below the poverty line (BPL), compared to the all India average of 26.1 percent in 1999-2001 (GoA, 2005). GoA (2003) has stressed that poverty in Assam has been primarily a rural phenomenon as 40 percent of the rural people are in the BPL category where as in urban areas; it is low at 6.29 percent. The district wise poverty statistics quoted in the report reveal that the western plains are flood prone and the thickly populated south-east Plains and Tribal areas of the state are the poorest. The density of population has been increasing over time with galloping strides. More importantly, there are some alarming zones such as Nagaon, Dhurbi, Kamrup where density of population is as high as near about 600 as in 2001.

The East India Human Development Report prepared by NCAER 2004 presents a dismal picture of the socio-economic condition of Assam. According to this report, Assam is distinctly a laggard in terms of important indicators of socio-economic well being even among the states of north-east India. In urban areas of the north-east India, the monthly per capita consumption expenditure is lowest in Assam at Rs.169.93 only. In rural areas also, it is lowest in Assam at Rs.153.6 only. Although in case of effective literacy, the state Assam is ahead of the national average, the gender disparity in literacy rate in

Assam is as high as 15.9 percent. The rural-urban disparity in respect of literacy is also quite pronounced in Assam. Among the north-east states the drop out rate is also higher in Arunachal Pradesh, Assam, Tripura and Manipur. The expectation of life at birth in Assam of males and females based on the 1980 mortality rate, as revealed by the Sample Registration System (SRS) are 58.7 years and 58.5 years respectively. This is worse than that of India for both males and females. Men live longer than women in Assam though for the country as a whole, women live longer than men. In regard to health care services, the condition of Assam is worse-off as compared to other north-east states. As against the all India figure of 0.73 hospital beds for every 1000 persons, Assam has only 0.06 hospital beds per thousand people. The population served per doctor is the highest in Assam among north-east states. The state has one hospital for 107,000 persons. Assam has also the lowest number of Family Welfare Center per lakh population at 0.6. Data relating to the total dependent population reveal that the size of dependent population is the second highest in Assam (84.2 percent) among the north-east states. The work participation rate is also lowest (36.5 percent) in Assam.

Among the fifteen major states of India, the rank of Assam as per life expectancy index is 14 (GoI, 1998). In terms of educational index, the rank of Assam is six with educational attainment index value of 0.4187 (GoI, 1996). The per capita real State Domestic Product (SDP) index of Assam is 0.28 and its rank is eight out of fifteen major states (GoI, 1995). As per urbanization index, the rank of Assam is in the last in the 15 major states, with Urbanization Index value of 0.11 (CMIE, 1996). The above figures together point towards the fact that the state of Assam is poverty afflicted and is an economically and socially back ward state of India.

III. METHODOLOGY AND DATABASE

In order to understand the inter-regional disparities of economic development of Assam, the present study considered the Districts of Assam as units of study. Several variables are taken in to consideration as indicators of economic development. The selected variables are:

i. Per Capita Gross Domestic District Product in Rupees (X_1)
ii. Literacy Rate in percentage (X_2)
iii. Percentage of Villages Electrified (X_3)
iv. Percentage of Habitations having drinking water facilities (X_4)
v. Number of Medical Centers [Hospitals, PHC, Dispensaries] (X_5)
vi. PWD Road length in Km per one 100 Sq.Km (X_6)
vii. Sex ratio (X_7)
viii. Percentage of Main Workers to total workers (X_8).

Data pertaining to the selected variables are collected for each district of Assam with reference year mainly of 2001. However, data of couple of variables are of 2004-05, as data of 2001 were not readily available. Variables have been selected under guiding principle that higher values of these would mean higher economic development.

The Standardized values of each variable corresponding to all the Districts are found out by using the formula:

Standardized Value = (X – Mean) / SD

Where X is the Unit Observation of Concerned Variable
Mean is the Arithmetic Mean of the Variable
SD is the Standard Deviation of the Variable.

The aggregate value of the standardized values of all the variables pertaining to a particular district will be the Composite Development Score (CDS) of that district. The CDS of the district would be a strong indicator of disparities of economic development (defined by the selected indicators) of the districts of Assam.

As the Assam Human Development Report 2003 is published and all the districts of Assam are ranked according to Human Development Index (HDI) with district-wise values of HDI, a comparative analysis of HDI and the CDS of the district is attempted by converting the CDS into values ranging from zero to one, as like HDI, by using Dimension Index of Development (DID) where,

$$DID = \frac{(ActulaCDS - MinimumValuesofCDS)}{(MaximumValuesofCDS - MinimumValuesofCDS)}$$

Applying tools such as Coefficient of Correlation and Coefficient of Variation would also find out the relative disparities in the two sets of data. The selected indicators (X_1, X_2, X_3, X_4, X_5, X_6, X_7 and X_8) of economic development have different units of measurement. The possible effects of different units of measurement are wiped out by finding out the standardized values of the variables. Therefore, the aggregate score of the standardized values can be considered as Composite Development Score (CDS).

IV. ANALYSIS OF RESULT

Table 1 shows the district wise CDS and DID values. The degree of association between HDI and DID values is estimated by correlation coefficient (r). In addition to that, rank correlation coefficient (R) is also estimated to through light on the degree of association between the ranking of HDI and DID. Disparities of HDI values and DID values are estimated by coefficient of variation which is a simple relative measure of dispersion.

The estimated values of correlation coefficient HDI and DID values [r (HDI, DID)], the rank correlation coefficient of HDI and DID ranks [R (HDI, DID)], the coefficient of variation of HDI values [CV (HDI)] and DID values [CV (DID)] are shown in Table 2.

The values of correlation coefficient and rank correlation coefficient indicate that the degrees of association between HDI values are very low. HDI measures the average achievements in only three basic dimensions of human development namely, a long and healthy life, knowledge and a decent standard of living as measured by income per capita.

TABLE 1
DISTRICT-WISE CDS AND HDI

Districts	HDI Value	HDI Rank	CDS Value	DID	DID Rank
Jorhat	0.65	1	1.809	0.759	7
Kamrup	0.574	2	3.881	0.922	3
Golaghat	0.54	3	1.029	0.697	9
Karbianglong	0.494	4	-2.077	0.452	18
Morigaon	0.494	4	2.094	0.781	5
Dibrugarh	0.483	6	2.037	0.777	6
Sibsagar	0.469	7	4.867	1	1
Cachar	0.402	8	0.329	0.642	12
Borpeta	0.396	9	0.351	0.644	11
Tinsukia	0.377	10	-3.225	0.362	22
NC Hills	0.363	11	-7.814	0	23
Hailakandi	0.363	11	-2.229	0.44	20
Sunitpur	0.357	13	-1.929	0.464	17
Nagaon	0.356	14	4.666	0.984	2
Kokrajhar	0.354	15	-2.199	0.443	19
Nalbari	0.343	16	3.439	0.887	4
Lakhimpur	0.337	17	-1.867	0.469	16
Goalpara	0.308	18	-1.141	0.526	15
Karimgang	0.301	19	-0.299	0.593	14
Dhemaji	0.277	20	-3.017	0.378	21
Bongaigoan	0.263	21	1.098	0.703	8
Darrang	0.259	22	0.394	0.647	10
Dhubri	0.214	23	-0.198	0.601	13

Source: Calculated by the author

However, HDI is not a very comprehensive measure of human development. A high HDI value need not necessarily guarantee access of human beings to other basic amenities of life such as drinking water, electricity, sanitation, health care et cetera, which are essential components of economic development. DID, which included many variables is addition to income per capita and literacy, is more reflective of economic development of a district than HDI which measured achievements of a district in three basic dimensions only. The low values of correlation coefficient indicate that not all the districts of Assam, which have high HDI values (Jorhat, Golaghat, Karbianglong), are good performers in other areas of basic amenities of life. The values of standard deviation and coefficient of variation suggest that there exist disparities of human development, as measured by HDI, among the districts of Assam. The degree of disparity among the districts of Assam has increased in the case of DID which included eight variables as indicators of economic development.

TABLE 2
ESTIMATED VALUES OF CORRELATION AND DISPERSION

MEASURES	VALUES
Standard Deviation (HDI)	0.109
Standard Deviation (DID)	0.232
r (HDI, DID)	0.348
R (HDI, DID)	0.277
CV (HDI)	27.99
CV (DID)	37.62

Source: Calculated by the author

V. CONCLUSION

The disparities of economic development are much higher among the districts of Assam in comparison to human development, as is evident from the values of CV (HDI) and CV (DID). In the case of human development, the Assam Human Development Report 2003 has ranked all the districts of Assam according to the values of HDI. The district Jorhat tops the list with HDI value of 0.65 and Dhubri district is at the bottom of the list with HDI value of 0.214. It is interesting to note here that in between HDI values of 0.65 and 0.273, there are as many as 58 countries in the world, which are ranked according to HDI values, in HDR 2004 prepared by UNDP. The country which has lowest rank (177th) in HDR 2004, is Sierra Leone, a very small Sub-Saharan African country having a population of size 4.5 million only. Near about 50 percent of the population of Sierra Leone are undernourished and have no sustainable access to improved sanitation and water source. This country has HDI value 0.273 which is higher than the HDI value of Dhubri district of Assam, the lowest rank holder in AHDR 2003. Although the procedures followed for calculating State level HDR in India is quite different from that in HDR prepared by UNDP and therefore no comparison between the two can be meaningful, the above discussion, nevertheless, focuses on the width that accommodates 58 countries of the world in between HDI values of 0.65 and 0.273 and only 23 districts in between HDI values of 0.65 and 0.214 in Assam. This is clearly an indication of greater disparities of human development in the districts of Assam.

The DID values are calculated with reference to the goalpost of values set by Sibsagar district which has highest composite development Score value of 4.867 and N.C. Hills which has lowest CDS value of (-7.814). However, the DID values within the range of zero to one, are good indicators of the status of economic development of different districts of Assam. The DID values indicate that the districts of Assam have relatively high degree of disparities of economic development. The Districts are less consistent as is evident from the higher value of CV (DID). Furthermore, Assam is divided into three principal geographical regions: the Brahmaputra Valley in the north; the Barak Valley in the south; and the Mikir (Karbianglong) and Cachar (N.C.Hills)

hills that divide the two regions. The average HDI and DID values of the districts in Brahmaputra Valley are 0.3917 and 0.6691 respectively. The corresponding figures for Barak Valley are 0.3553 and 0.5583 and for Karbianglong - N.C.Hills 0.4285 and 0.226 respectively. The figures show that in terms of the indicators of economic development, Karbianglong and N.C.Hills region is the poorest region of the state. The regional disparities of economic development are glaring and there is need to address the problem through purposive planning and compassionate outlook.

REFERENCES

Bhatia, M. S. (1999): Rural Infrastructure and Growth in Agriculture, *Economic and Political Weekly*, 34 (13): A43-A48.

Center for Monitoring Indian Economy (CMIE) (1996): *Indian Social Sector 1996*, Mumbai.

Dutta, P. C. (2003): Regional Disparities and Its Consequences in North Eastern Region of India, In *Economic Liberalization and Rural Disparities in India*, A. C. Mahapatra, C. R Pathak (Ed.), Star Publishing House, Shillong.

Government of Assam (GoA) (2003): *Assam Human Development Report 2003*, Planning and Development Department, Guwahati, Assam.

GoA (2005): *Statistical Handbook of Assam 2005*, Directorate of Economics and Statistics, Guwahati, Assam.

Government of India (GoI) (1995): Indian Public Finance Statistics, 1995, Ministry of Finance, New Delhi.

GoI (1996): Economic Survey of India, 1995-96, Ministry of Finance, New Delhi

GoI (1998): Economic Survey of India, 1997-98, Ministry of Finance, New Delhi.

Gulati, R. K. (1999): *Regional Disparities in Economic Development*, Deep and Deep Publications Pvt. Ltd, New Delhi.

Kantawala and Rao (1992): Sectoral Development in India - An Inter-state Analysis, *Indian Journal of Regional Science*, 24(1): 27-35.

Myrdal, Gunner (1957): *Economic Theory and Underdeveloped Regions*, Vora and Co. Publishers Pvt. Ltd., Delhi.

Rangacharyulu, S. V. (1993): Composite Development Index of Rural Areas, *Journal of Rural Development*, 12(1): 35-56.

Rana, R. K. (1997): A Study of Inter-state Disparities and Pattern of Development in India, *Indian Economic Association Conference Volume*, Hyderabad, pp. 493-500.

Ryngynga, Kamtibon (2003): Levels of Development in the Hills of North-East India, In *Economic Liberalization and Rural Disparities in India*, A. C. Mahapatra, C. R Pathak (Ed.), Star Publishing House, Shillong.

Subramaniam, M. S. (1995): Inter-state Variation in the Development of Family Health in India -A Taxonomic Approach, *Indian Journal of Regional Science*, 27 (1 and 2): 57-61.

16

Livelihood Diversification: Pathway Out of Rural Poverty

P.S. Sujithkumar[1], [2]

I. INTRODUCTION

The contribution made by livelihood diversification to rural livelihoods and to rural development has often been unnoticed by policy makers. Diverse livelihood systems are less vulnerable to natural calamities, market fluctuations, risk, and poverty than non-diversified livelihoods (Evans and Ngau., 1991; Reardon, Christopher, and Peter, 1992; Hart, 1994). The concept of economic diversification has to be distinguished from the diversification of livelihoods. The former refers to the process by which economies become more diversified and the latter refers to the same process at the individual or household levels. Even though economic reforms initiated since 1991 provide greater incentive to rural economy, government intervention will still be required if the rural economy is to expand in a productive manner.

This paper highlights the importance of livelihood diversification. It attempts to check the level of occupational

---

[1] Department of Economics, Bharathidasan Government College for Women, Puducherry, India, E-mail: sujithkodanad@yahoo.com.
[2] The author is grateful to Dr. P. Govindarajan, formerly Professor and Head of the Department of Economics, Presidency College, Chennai for his valuable comments and suggestions. However, the author is solely responsible for all errors and inadequacies, if any.

diversification in rural India by using census data. Some policy measures have been identified for government intervention which can diversify rural economy. The paper proceeds as follows: section II introduces the concept of livelihood diversification; section III discusses diversification in a macro perspective; section IV deals with the effect of diversification on rural livelihoods particularly in livelihood security and poverty; section V discusses various policy measures; and section VI concludes it.

II. CONCEPT OF LIVELIHOOD DIVERSIFICATION

Livelihood diversification is the process by which households construct a diverse portfolio of activities and social support capabilities for survival and in order to improve their standard of living. It is an infinitely heterogeneous process differentiated in its causes and effects (Ellis, 1998). Livelihood diversification includes both on-farm and off-farm activities. It includes production of commercial crops and livestock, non-farm wage employment, non-farm rural self employment, and other income including property income in terms of rent, remittances et cetera. The literature identifies a range of different motives and pressures that contribute to explaining why diversification occurs and the patterns of diversity that are observed. Some main determinants of diversification are seasonality, differential labour markets, risk strategies, coping behaviour, credit market imperfections, and inter temporal savings and investment strategies. Motivating causes for keeping a diversified income source may differ among households. Poorer households in times of a stress arising out of crop failure decide to diversify into non-agricultural activities some times. It can also occur from a position of strength as prosperous cultivating households diversify into non-agricultural activities for achieving higher standard of living. Share of non-agricultural income in the total income and the factors influencing the amount of non-agriculture income may differ in different regions. Each household has its' own strategy of decision-making on allocation of resources among different income-generation activities. Different members of the household engage in different activities to generate income. Some time a member finds multiple sources of income at a particular time or at different times of the year. Place of activity may be within the village or beyond the village.

III. DIVERSIFICATION IN A MACRO PERSPECTIVE

The traditional view of processes of economic change is that the process involves transition between states of economic structure. There is an inverse relationship that exists between economic progress and the extent of dependence of the workforce on the primary sector (Kuznets, 1974). The shift in occupational pattern from primary sector to secondary sector and tertiary sector or shift in the origination of income from agriculture to industry and tertiary sectors is considered to be a natural process of economic development. Thus, diversification is considered to be a movement to a better one. Evidence across the world has shown that rural households are increasingly engaging a diverse set of activities to generate income. Reardon et al (1998) find an average share of 42 per cent of non – farm income in total rural household income in Africa, 40 per cent in Latin America and 32 per cent in Asia.

Economic diversification involved both crop diversification and non-agricultural diversification. Crop diversification is the process in which cultivators spread their cropping pattern and non-agricultural diversification deals with the shift from agricultural activities to non-agricultural activities. Time has come to Indian agriculture to have a drastic change due to its inherent characters and trade liberalization. The average size of land holding in India is small and most of the holders do not have an economic holding, which ensure a minimum satisfactory standard of living to a family. These farm groups are focused in the production of cereals only, which make them more vulnerable to risks related to agriculture. India's productivity levels in cereal production are nowhere near to those of the best producer in the world, which leave enough room for betterment. An improvement in the productivity of cereals can release more land for non-cereal crops that make a crop diversification without challenging the food security of the country. The world trade environment holds out many opportunities for Indian agriculture in the form of crop diversification. India is richly endowed with its innate comparative advantage in several products. We can export fruits, vegetables and cut flowers in a big way because Indian prices are comparatively lower than the prices in the developed countries. For tackling the emerging opportunities in the context of the General Agreement of Tariffs and Trade (GATT), crop diversification and value addition should be the key words of Indian agriculture in the coming days. Creation of essential infrastructure for preservation, cold storage, refrigerated transportation, rapid and cheap transit, grading, processing, packaging and quality control would be the key areas for such a strategy

To analyze economic diversification, last three census data have been used. Work force have been classified into four industrial categories (1) cultivator (2) agricultural labourers (3) household industry (4) other workers. Cultivator is a person who is engaged either as employer, single worker or family worker in cultivation of land owned or held from government or held from private persons or institutions for payment in money, kind or share. Cultivation includes supervision or direction of cultivation. A person is considered as agricultural labourer if he /she work in another person's land for wage in money, kind or share. Under household industry manufacturing, processing, service and repairs in household industry have considered. Other workers include livestock, forestry, fishing, hunting and plantations, orchards and allied activities, mining and quarrying, manufacturing, processing, servicing and repairs in other than household industry, construction, trade and commerce, transport, storage, communications, and other services.

TABLE 1
INDUSTRIAL DISTRIBUTION OF RURAL WORKFORCE

(in Percentage)

Workforce	1981	1991	2001	Change (91-81)	Change (2001-91)	Change (2001-81)
Cultivators	51.10	48.39	40.14	- 2.71	- 8.25	- 10.96
Agricultural Labourers	29.88	31.64	33.20	1.76	1.56	3.32
Total agriculture	80.98	80.03	73.34	- 0.95	- 6.69	- 7.64
Household Industry	3.08	2.16	3.77	- 0.92	1.61	0.69
Other Workers	15.94	17.80	22.90	1.86	5.1	6.96
Total non-agricultural	19.02	19.96	26.67	0.94	6.71	7.65

Source: Census 1981, 1991, 2001, Government of India

According to Census 2001, 26.67 per cent of the rural population was engaged in non-agricultural activities. Share of non-agriculture workers in the total rural workforce has increased by 7.65 per cent during 1981-2001. During 1981-91, increase in the share of non-agricultural workforce is negligible and only with in 1991-2001 there has been a considerable increase in the share of non-agriculture workforce. Thanks to the reform efforts which rejuvenate industry as well as service sector.

Table 2 shows that during 1981- 2001 percentage of rural male workforce engaged in non-agricultural activities has increased by 9.48 per cent and it is higher than the percentage increase in the share of rural female workforce (7.41 per cent) for the same period. There is a sharp decline in the percentage of male cultivators (12.97 per cent) where as it is negligible (0.61) in the case of female cultivators, where as in the case of agricultural labours, rural male have increased its share by 3.48 per cent same time rural female agricultural labours has decreased its share by 6.79 per cent. Table 1 and 2 point out the fact that levels of diversification in the rural area is low.

TABLE 2
SEX WISE DISTRIBUTION OF WORKFORCE
(in Percentage)

Workforce	Male				Female			
	1981	1991	2001	Change (01-81)	1981	1991	2001	Change (01-81)
Cultivators	55.16	51.58	42.19	- 12.97	37.07	38.93	36.46	- 0.61
Agricultural Labourers	24.00	25.97	27.48	3.48	50.19	48.49	43.40	- 6.79
Agricultural workforce	79.16	77.55	69.67	- 9.49	87.26	87.42	79.86	- 7.4
Household Industry	2.87	1.91	2.83	- 0.04	3.79	2.91	5.44	1.65
Other Workers	17.97	20.54	27.49	9.52	8.94	9.68	14.70	5.76
Non-agricultural workforce	20.84	22.45	30.32	9.48	12.73	12.59	20.14	7.41

Source: Census 1981, 1991, 2001, Government of India

IV. DIVERSIFICATION AND POVERTY

Rural livelihood diversification has far reaching effects. A number of studies have reached a conclusion that diversification helps the household to have a higher income profile and improve livelihood security (Saleth, 1997; Hart, 1994; Sujithkumar, 2007) by making better use of available resources and skills. Diversification in income generation helps the rural households to reduce the adverse effects of food insecurity due to the mismatch between uneven farm income streams and continuous consumption requirements. Different activities have different risk profiles. The factors that create risk for one source should not be the same as those that create risk for another. Diversified income source reduce the risk of income failure overall, by diluting the impact of failure in any single income source. Income generated from diversification may be used to better the quality of physical and human capital and that can be used to enhance future income generating opportunities. It is possible for diversification to improve the independent income-generating capabilities of women and in doing so influence the gender relations in the household. There are studies that supports that higher the income in the hands of women higher the spending on family welfare (Hoddinott and Haddad, 1995). The relationship between diversification and rural inequality is not uniform in all the regions that made generalization difficult. On the one hand, studies by Chinn (1979); Haggblade and Hazell (1989); and Adams Jr. (1994) inferred that diversification has an equalizing effect on rural income. On the other hand, studies by Evans and Nagu (1991) and Reardon, Delgado and Matlon (1992) inferred that diversification has an un-equalizing effect on rural income because the better off are able to diversify in more advantageous labour markets than the poor. Both the case diversified income will act as a safety value for rural poor and it is the way out of poverty.

V. POLICY MEASURES

Economic policies of the governments, relating to internal prices and external prices, taxes and subsidies, agriculture, industry and service sectors, trade and budgetary priorities, have a direct impact on the profitability of agriculture and rural enterprise and hence on diversification. Most important role of the governments in fostering a successful rural diversification process is in creating an overall appropriate policy environment. For accelerating the process of diversification, governments' active roles in the following areas are required. Improved rural infrastructure has a potential impact on rural diversification by way of improving the working of markets, fastening the flow of information, reducing the cost of production and increasing the mobility of people, resources and outputs. Illiteracy has been identified as a critical constraint inhibiting diversification. Government has to take special attention in the delivery and quality of rural education, training and skill acquisition. A major problem experienced by the rural economy is the shortage of capital. Improved rural financial markets can broaden participations in the formal credit market that can finance short-term investments by farmers in new crops and entrepreneurs to start small-scale industries. Growth of agro-based industries will provide an excellent nexus in promoting integrated development of agriculture and industry. Rural Service sector can play a better role in employment and income generation in the rural areas. Governments' active participation in these areas would transform a stagnant rural economy into a dynamic and buoyant economy.

VI. CONCLUSION

The process of livelihood diversification in rural areas has to be strengthened to minimize the risk and uncertainty in the income earning capacity of rural people and to smoothen the income flow so that the rural poverty can be brought down and the levels of living can be enhanced. As a result of growing recognition of this, increased attention has begun to be paid in recent years to the development of policies and programs for diversifying the rural economy with a view to create employment opportunities in rural non-farm activities. However, not much progress has yet been made towards the development of purposeful and viable strategies for the purpose. Governments will need to give more attention to planning for rural livelihood diversification. The process of diversification may turn the tiny and marginal farmers to 'part-time' agriculturists then only can rural poverty be brought down and rural development can be achieved.

REFERENCES

Adams Jr., R, H. (1994): Non-Farm Income and Inequality in Rural Pakistan: A Decomposition Analysis, *Journal of Development Studies*, 31 (1): 110-133.

Chinn, D. L. (1979): Rural Poverty and the Structure of Farm Household Income in Developing Countries: Evidence from Taiwan, *Economic Development and Cultural Change*, 27 (2): 283-302.

Ellis, Frank (1998): Household Strategies and Rural Livelihood Diversification, *Journal of Development Studies*, 35 (1): 1-38.

Evans, H. E. and Ngau, P. (1991): Rural - Urban Relations, Households Income Diversification and Agricultural Productivity, *Development and Change*, 22 (3): 519-545.

Haggblade, S. and Hazell, P. (1989): Agricultural Technology and Farm-Non-Farm Growth Linkages, *Agricultural Economics*, 3 (4): 345-364.

Hart, Gillian (1994): The Dynamics of Diversification in an Asian Rice Region", In *Development or Deterioration? Work in Rural Asia,* Bruce Koppel, John Hawkins, William James (eds.), Lynne Rienner Publishers Inc, Boulder, pp. 47-71.

Hoddinott, J. and Haddad, L. (1995): Does Female Income Share Influence Household Expenditure Pattern? Evidence from cote d'Ivoire, *Oxford Bulletin of Economics and Statistics,* 57 (1): 77-96.

Kuznets, Simon (1974): *Modern Economic Growth: Findings and Reflections, In Population, Capital and Growth: Selected Essays,* Heinemann, London.

Saleth R. Maria (1997): Diversification Strategy for Small Farmers and Landless: Some Evidence from Tamil Nadu, India, *Journal of Agricultural Economics*, 52 (1).

Reardon, T., Christopher, D. and Peter, M. (1992): Determinants and Effects of Income Diversification amongst Farm Households in Burkina Faso, *Journal of Development Studies*, 28 (2): 264-296.

Reardon, T., Stamoulis, K., Balisacan, A., Cruz. M. E., Berdegue, J. and Banks, B. (1998): *Rural Non – farm income in Developing Countries: Importance and policy implications in the state of food and agriculture*, Food and Agricultural Organization, Rome.

Sujithkumar, P. S. (2007): Livelihood Diversification: A Case Study in Rural Tamilnadu, *Indian Journal of Labour Economics*, 50 (4): 715-722.

Index

A
Adam Smith (1723-1790), 4
Adjusted Intensity of Formal Education (AIFE), 244
Age-structured human capital, 132
All India Educational Survey (AIES), 248
Analysis of Gender Empowerment at the Aggregate Level, 319
Analysis of Gender Empowerment at the Disaggregate Level, 312
Anand and Sen (2000), 8
Applied Systems Analysis and Vienna Institute of Demography's (IIASA-VID), 154
Axiomatic characterization of group differential, 55

C
Centre for Monitoring Indian Economy (CMIE), 347
Chen and Conley (2001), 148
Chronic Poverty Report 2004-05, 220
Chronic Poverty Research Centre (CPRC), 220
Collective agencies of social action, 17
Composite Development Score (CDS), 380
Concept of Livelihood Diversification, 389
Convention on the Elimination of all Forms of Discrimination against Women (CEDAW), 291

D
Depletion and Degradation of Forest Resources, 242
Depletion and Degradation of Land Resources, 242
Depletion and Degradation of Water Resources, 242
Determining Factors of Healthcare Scenario, 192
Development of the Concept of HD, 4
Dimension Index of

Development (DID), 32
Dimensions and Magnitude of Social Insecurity, 220
Diversification in a Macro Perspective, 390

E
East India Human Development Report, 378
Economic Condition of Assam, 378
Economic Performance and Human Development in India, 212
Economic Status and Human Development, 362
Economic sustainability and HD, 8
Efficient and Full Utilization of Human Potentials, 17
Enhanced Economic Growth (EG), 232
Environment, Human Development and Economic Growth of Indian States after Liberalization, 29
Environmental Degradation Index (EDI), 238
Environmental Kuznets Curve (EKC), 261
Environmental Performance Index (EPI), 236
Environmental Quality Index (EQI), 239, 242
Equally Distributed Equivalent Percentage (EDEP), 308

F
Fifth Pay Commission Recommendations, 205
Fighting Climate Change, 18
Five Year Plans (FYPs), 227

G
Gender and Human Development, 30
Gender and Regulations of the Conflicts, 294
Gender Development Index (GDI), 329
Gender Empowerment Measure (GEM), 30, 306
Gender Empowerment Measure (GEM), and the Human Poverty Index (HPI), 63
General Agreement on

Tariffs and Trade
(GATT), 391
General scenario in North
Eastern Region, 74
Green House Gases
Emissions (GHGS),
242
Gross Domestic Product
(GDP), 2, 204
Gross State Domestic
Product (GSDP), 214
Gunnar Myrdal (1957),
375

H
Health Care Scenario in
India, 195
Health Infrastructure in the
Public Sector, 207
High Income States (HIS),
215
Human Development and
Economic
Development, 359
Human Development and
Healthcare Scenario,
189
Human Development in
India and North
Eastern Region, 74
Human Development in
India vis-à-vis Selected
Countries, 186
Human Development in
India: Issues and
Challenges, 28

Human Development in
Major States of India,
187
Human Development in
Orissa and its
Constituent Districts,
333
Human Development
Index (HDI), 27, 32,
212, 239, 243,
Human Development
Report (HDR), 1, 241,
87
Human Development
Report (UNDP, 2007),
74
Human Poverty Index
(HPI), 329

I
Index of Earned Income,
316
Indicator of Human
Development (ISDH),
282
Indicator of Human
Poverty (IPH), 282
Indoor Air Pollution
Potential, 242
Infant Mortality Rate
(IMR), 197
Integral Human
Development (IHD),
19
International Institute for

Applied Systems Analysis (IIASA), 155
International Labour Organization (ILO), 12

J
Janani Suraksha Yojana (JSY), 227
Joint Forest Management (JFM), 234
Journal of Human Development, 6
Journal of Political Economy, 133

K
Key Demographic Indicators, 195
Key Determining Factors of Health Scenario, 202
Knowledge and Decision-making Index, 308

L
Latent Variable Approach, 241
Livelihood Diversification, 32
Low Income States (LIS), 215

M
MacGillivray (1991), 22
Maternal Mortality Ratio, 201
Means and Ends Debate, 9
Measurement of Human Development, 65
Measures of Group Differential, 57
Middle Income States (MIS), 215
Millennium Development Goals (MDGs), 288

N
National Family and Health Survey, 330
National Human Development Report (2001), 214, 329
National Rural Health Mission, 201
National Sample Survey Organization (NSSO), 330
National Social Assistance Program (NSAP), 227
Natural Growth Rate (NGR), 196
Nayak and Thomas (2007), 71
Net State Domestic Product (NSDP), 217
Non-point Source Pollution Potential (NPSP), 242

O
Orissa Human

Development Report, 2006, 329

P
Participation of the Women in the Development of Societies, 289
People-centered Strategies, 18
Pollution from Energy Generation and Consumption, 242
Principal Component Analysis (PCA), 331
Principal Components based Human Development Index (PCHDI), 88
Public Expenditure on Health, 204

R
Regional Planning, National Development and Conflict Resolution, 27
Relationship between Economic Growth and Human Development, 241
Relationship between Environment and Human Well-being, 239
Relationship between HDI Score and Individual Environmental Groups, 258
Relationships between Environmental Quality and Economic Growth, 237
Report of the Working Group on Social Protection Policy – NSAP, 227
Robert Malthus, 4

S
Sample Registration System (SRS), 379
State Domestic Product (SDP) Index of Assam, 379
Status and Trend of Human Development in North East Region of India, 26
Status of Women's Political Participation, 312
Structure of Conditional Covariance, 151

T
T. W. Schultz, 5
Technology Advancement Index (TAI), 329
Testing the Existence of

the Environmental
    Kuznets Curve (EKC),
    256
The Index of Political
    Participation, 307
The Status of Gender
    Empowerment in
    Karnataka, 305
Two Alternative
    Conceptions of Human
    Well-Being, 41

U

United Arab Emirates
    (UAE), 185
United Nations
    Development Program
    (UNDP), 281

V

Vienna Institute of
    Demography (VID),
    155
Voices of the Poor (2000),
    222

W

Work Participation Rate
    (WPR), 31, 363
World Development
    Report, 357

DOWNTOWN CAMPUS LRC

HD 4904.7 .H85857 2009

Human development